READING JOYCE'S *ULYSSES*

By the same author

DISRAELI'S FICTION

CONRAD: 'ALMAYER'S FOLLY' TO 'UNDER WESTERN EYES'

CONRAD: THE LATER FICTION

THE HUMANISTIC HERITAGE: CRITICAL THEORIES OF THE ENGLISH NOVEL FROM JAMES TO HILLIS MILLER

READING JOYCE'S
ULYSSES

Daniel R. Schwarz

Professor of English
Cornell University

St. Martin's Press   New York

First published in the United States of America in 1987

Printed in Great Britain

ISBN 0–312–66458–3
ISBN 0–312–00086–3 (pbk)

Library of Congress Cataloging-in-Publication Data
Schwarz, Daniel R.
Reading Joyce's Ulysses.
Bibliography: p.
Includes index.
1. Joyce, James, 1882–1941. Ulysses. I. Title.
PR6019.09U692   1987   823′.912   86–6680
ISBN 0–312–66458–3
ISBN 0–312–00086–3 (pbk)

For Ian Gregor and for my students with whom I have made the odyssean journey through Ulysses

Contents

Acknowledgements   viii

Introduction: "O, Rocks. . . . Tell Us in Plain Words"   1

1 Joyce as "Lord and Giver" of Language: Form and
   Metaphor in *Ulysses*   7

2 Joyce's Concept of a Hero   37

3 The Odyssey of Reading *Ulysses*   58

4 The Movement from Lyrical to Epical and Dramatic
   Form: the Opening of *Ulysses*   71

5 Joyce's Irish Jew: Bloom   103

6 The Concept of Artistic Paternity in "Scylla and
   Charybdis"   138

7 The Adventure of Reading: the Styles of the Odyssey
   and the Odyssey of Styles   153

8 "Circe" as the Climax of Joyce's Humanistic Vision   207

9 Metaphoricity in "Eumaeus" and "Ithaca"   231

10 "Penelope": Molly as Metaphor   258

Appendix   277

Selected Bibliography   281

Index   286

Acknowledgements

Since this book results from my experience not only as a reader, but as a teacher of *Ulysses*, my greatest debt is to my students at Cornell where I have been teaching *Ulysses* regularly for the past eighteen years.

My Cornell colleagues, especially Phillip Marcus, have been generous and helpful in dialogues about *Ulysses*, but I want also to acknowledge the ubiquitous influence on my work of M. H. Abrams, and the friendship and collegiality of Tom Hill and Michael Colacurcio.

As my student and my graduate assistant in two summer session courses on *Ulysses*, Beth Newman has provided stimulating and challenging conversation on *Ulysses*. I have also learned from the work of my graduate student William Thickstun. For more than twenty years, since I was his student at Edinburgh in 1961–2, I have had the benefit of Ian Gregor's advice and friendship. I am grateful to the participants in my 1985 National Endowment for the Humanities Summer Seminar for high-school teachers for helping clarify some points in my argument. I appreciate the splendid and loyal secretarial support of Phillis Molock, the proofreading assistance of Diane McPherson and Mary Ann Naples, and the encouragement of my wife and sons.

I would like to thank Random House and The Bodley Head for permission to quote from James Joyce's *Ulysses*, and for the Society of Authors for permission to reprint Joyce's schema as it appeared in C. H. Peake's *James Joyce: the Citizen and Artist* (Stanford University Press, 1977).

Cornell University   DANIEL R. SCHWARZ
Ithaca, New York

Introduction: "O, Rocks. . . . Tell Us in Plain Words"

This study is for readers of *Ulysses*. It attempts to comment on the major issues confronting a reader as he tries to make sense of the novel. In the title of my Introduction, I playfully use Molly's response to Bloom's explanation of metempsychosis ("O, rocks! . . . Tell us in plain words") to indicate that *Ulysses* is a readable novel – rather than an elaborate puzzle or a Rosetta Stone or a hieroglyph. For *Ulysses*, while presenting unique challenges, depends upon readers who have a good deal of reading experience in more traditional narratives.

Ulysses is first and foremost a novel about three individuals – Stephen Dedalus, Leopold Bloom, and Molly Bloom – who live in turn-of-the-century Dublin. But it should also be read as a social, political, and historical novel. *Ulysses* is Joyce's inquiry into the question of what values are viable in the twentieth century urban world where, according to Joyce's view, God does not exist and traditional notions of heroism are obsolete. Among other things, *Ulysses* is an effort to redefine the concept of the hero. Joyce uses the marginal Jew Bloom to redefine heroism in secular humanistic terms. As he examines recent Irish history and culture, Joyce proposes Bloom as an alternative to the xenophobia and fantasies of the Celtic Renaissance as well as a successor to Parnell.

There is a danger that the study of *Ulysses* has become like ground that has been farmed for so long that it now only supports exotic crops like persimmons. While we have a vast array of critical apparatus, we have neglected the questions of how and what the novel means. In terms of the vast critical landscape of *Ulysses*, I shall attempt to provide a bridge between those who stress *Ulysses* as a novel that reveals the psyche and

1

motives of characters and those who stress *Ulysses* as an elaborate rhetorical experiment. While taking account of essential
arguments of prior critics and acknowledging their contribution
in the appropriate places, I shall try to focus on the novel rather
than on the tradition of commentary produced by the thriving
cottage industry of Joyce scholarship. While discussing *Ulysses* in
terms of the relationships among the three basic units of formal
criticism – author, text, and audience, I shall use contextual
information when necessary.

Joyce transforms the nominalistic events of one day in the lives
of his three characters – events based often on details of his own
life – into significant events. We shall explore how Joyce creates
the metaphorical and allusive relationships on which meaning
depends, and we shall examine how Joyce gives significance to
events in the lives of the major figures on one single day, 16 June
1904. We shall not only examine how Joyce makes use of his
major sources – *The Odyssey*, the Old and New Testaments, and
Shakespeare, but how he uses in important ways *The Iliad*, as
well as the works of Wilde, Yeats, Dante, Milton, Tennyson,
Swift, and Blake.

Ulysses teaches us how to read itself. Put another way, we
should think of our experience of reading it as the reader's
odyssey. We shall stress what the novel does to us as we read it
and how the ventriloquy of its various styles establishes an
unusually complex relationship between text and reader. Unlike
some recent critics who believe that Joyce's interest in style
deflects the reader from his characters, I believe that the focus in
every chapter returns to the subjects of Stephen, Bloom, Molly,
and the Dublin world they inhabit. To be sure, in the chapters
from "Sirens" through "Oxen of the Sun", we are aware of a
tension in Joyce's imagination between interest in style and
interest in character, but in the climax of every chapter his focus
returns to his major figures and their significance. As odyssean
readers turning the pages of the novel and progressing through
the one crystallizing day in the lives of the major figures, we
must overcome the difficulties of style and the opacity of content
– just as the modern Ulysses must resist temptations which
threaten to deflect him from his journey home.

In my view the principle interest of Joyce's stylistic exper-
imentations should be how they shape a reading of the novel. For
the odyssean reader is invited to see that Bloom and Stephen

survive and transcend what Karen Lawrence in her *The Odyssey of Style in "Ulysses"* calls "the wealth of detail and . . . the protean transformations of style".[1] I think Lawrence's title privileges style over character, in part because it sees style as something that is embodied in the text separate and distinct from the effects it creates. By contrast, I find style inseparable from what it *does* to the events and characters it describes and what it *does* to the reader as he negotiates his journey through the novel to his final destination, the novel's end. Since Joyce's focus – notwithstanding frequent rhetorical flourishes and word-play for its own sake – always returns to the characters and their meaning, we should assume that the effects of his language upon the reader were never far from his mind.

As odyssean readers, we must wend our way through a variety of experiences, but these experiences can best be understood in terms of the novel's two major and contradictory formal principles: its insistence on integration and its refusal to allow every word to signify in terms of coherent thematic or structural patterns. The first formal principle urges the reader to see *Ulysses* as a completely organic and integrated novel in which one can conceive in every part some aspect of the grace and harmony of the whole. In his book *Godel, Escher, Bach*, Douglas Hofstadter describes the graph of a mathematical function INT (x), every section of which is a replica of the whole; since every individual part of each section is also a replica of the whole, the graph consists of an infinite number of copies of itself.[2] INT (x) becomes an apt expression for reading *Ulysses*, because it expresses the Viconian idea that history repeats itself and that the whole can be perceived within the component of one aspect of a culture. Another model for organic unity is the genetic code which determines the macrostructure of an organism, but which is contained in every separate part of the organism.

But opposed to the totalizing perspective is the second formal principle which insists that, as Geoffrey H. Hartman puts it, "literary language displays a polysemy, or an excess of the signifier over the signified".[3] Resisting the odyssean reader's efforts to understand *Ulysses* in terms of organic unity are a plethora of catalogues, barely relevant details, marginalia, false clues, linguistic games, and playful attempts to undermine the reader's quest for unity. On the one hand, *Ulysses* insists that its readers interpret every detail in terms of larger patterns, and thus urges the book's own argument that even the most particular details of the individual lives of Bloom and Stephen are important because Bloom and Stephen iterate major historical and mythical figures in western civilization. But, on the other hand, by focusing on the quirky and idiosyncratic aspects in human behaviour, *Ulysses* immerses the reader in the nominalistic world of the lives of a few characters during one day.

Does not Joyce's insistence on exploring the eccentricities of language for its own sake – its local wit, word games, ventriloquism, and typography – urge the reader to pause and enjoy (without imposing interpretive patterns or judgments upon) the peculiarities and oddities of human behaviour? For *Ulysses* is full of moments which immerse the reader in the local pleasures of the text and resist interpretation. At times, the novel's interest in moments of life and linguistic pyrotechnics for their own sake temporarily deflects the reader from allegories of reading that propose organic unity. For the sake of intellectual housekeeping, it would be neater either to give the two modes of reading – the one that insists on moving from immersion to interpretive reflection, the other that stresses immersion in the text for its own sake – equal importance or to claim that the latter deconstructs the former. But it is more accurate to say that at most points the novel invites the first mode of reading *Ulysses*, the traditional humanistic mode of reading that stresses unity of form and content, rather than the latter, deconstructionist mode of reading which questions meaning, coherence, and significance. Yet the dialectic between the two modes of reading – a dialectic which enacts more vividly than any other literary work I know the contending claims of the two dominant ideologies of reading on today's critical mindscape – is crucial to the experience of reading *Ulysses*.

My study of *Ulysses* is based on some fundamental assumptions about reading novels. Let me briefly summarize them. I assume that the author has created an imagined world, an ontology separate and distinct from the real one, and that the created world of a good novel is organized according to orderly principles and is apprehensible by orderly principles, although the reader's concepts of order may be different from those of the author. The structure of a novel is an evolving process in which the reader participates with the author. After all, the author embodies in his work a structure of effects that arouses expectations and subsequently fulfils, modifies, transforms, postpones, or deflates them. Since each novel generates its own aesthetic, we need to inquire into how a particular novel signifies. We must define the voice of the novel by continually asking who is speaking to what implied audience and with what intended effects.

Finally, the language of a novel presents a concatenation of events or episodes that comprise a narrative; this narrative – notwithstanding the kind of stylistic eccentricities and deliberate efforts to subvert the expectations of traditional narrative that we find in a novel like *Ulysses* – makes a coherent statement about the way life is lived in the imagined world within the text. Moreover, our interest in imagined worlds depends upon their relation to real ones; although that relation may be oblique, we do look for kinds of representation in our fictions, and we do understand events in fiction in terms of signification beyond as well as within the imagined world of the novel.

Thus it is not only appropriate but necessary to inquire into the relationship between the presence embodied in the form of the novel and the real author. Reading is a mode of perception, and reading about characters within an imagined world appeals to us because such reading is an extension of how we perceive and understand the events in our lives. Of course, we must understand that characters in fiction are functions of the formal properties of a novel's imagined world. But, despite some recent attacks on the "metaphysics of presence", we should not be apologetic for or embarrassed by thinking of characters in literature as if they were humans within the "hypothesis" of their imagined worlds, or as reflections, distortions, or parodies of their creators.

The aforementioned concerns define a rather more humanistic canon of modern British literature than the one defined by the New Critical emphasis on "Exit Author" or the tendency of recent theories to view the author as a kind of historical accident whose vision and style are dialectically shaped by the *Zeitgeist* in which he wrote. Readers of my prior work, including *The Humanistic Heritage*, my recent study of Anglo-American novel theory, will recognize a kinship between my approach to *Ulysses* and the substantive claims I have been making for the pluralistic Anglo-American tradition of reading novels. For lack of a better term, I have called this tradition humanistic formalism. I conceive this tradition as progressive, evolving, and open to entering into a fruitful dialogue with structuralism, deconstruction, and semiotics about how and why novels signify, *Reading Joyce's "Ulysses"* is, among other things, an effort to demonstrate that this tradition of reading – because of its resourcefulness, flexibility, energy, and potential for assimilating other modes of inquiry – provides the best means of coming to terms with complex literary works.

*   *   *

Quotations refer to *Ulysses: A Critical and Synoptic Edition*, edited by Hans Walter Gabler with Wolfhard Steppe and Claus Melchior (London and New York: Garland, 1984). Within the text I refer to this monumental work of scholarship as the Gabler edition. While I have my misgivings about some of its corrections, and am aware that some of its findings have been called into question and will be challenged by subsequent textual scholarship, this edition must be regarded as authoritative. In addition to the episode and line number in the Gabler edition, I have included page references to the 1961 Random House edition. Where there is a change in the Gabler edition from the Random House edition, I have underlined the episode and line number. The appendix provides Joyce's schema for *Ulysses*.[4]

NOTES

1. Karen Lawrence, *The Odyssey of Style in 'Ulysses'* (Princeton University Press) p. 6.
2. Douglas Hofstadter, *Godel, Escher, Bach: an Eternal Golden Braid* (New York: Basic Books, 1979).
3. Geoffrey H. Hartman, "The Culture of Criticism", *PMLA*, 99:3 (May 1984) p. 386.
4. My scheme follows C. H. Peake's in *James Joyce: the Citizen and the Artist* (Stanford University Press, 1977) pp. 120–1. Peake combines Stuart Gilbert's scheme in his *James Joyce's 'Ulysses': a Study* (1930; rev. New York: Random House, 1952) p. 41, with the "Correspondences" column which Hugh Kenner published in his *Dublin's Joyce* (London: Chatto & Windus, 1955) pp. 226–7.

1 Joyce as "Lord and Giver" of Language: Form and Metaphor in *Ulysses*

I begin from the premise that literary criticism must first pose the necessary questions about a work and that each work generates its own line of inquiry. The major questions to ask when teaching or writing about *Ulysses* are what does it signify and how does it signify? Can we reconcile its symbolic implications and its vast historical and literary scope with its nominalistic texture of experience – experience that often has its origin in the life of Joyce? How can a novel that takes its significance from the author's biography be discussed? Does it have aesthetic autonomy? Can we discover something about its form that tells us what kind of novel we are reading and helps us define its approach to representation? Is the naturalistic novel of the experience of Leopold Bloom and Stephen Dedalus on one ordinary if possibly important day at odds both with the novel's pretensions as the modern epic and its insistence that the experiences of Stephen and Bloom reiterate those of major figures of the past? How does Joyce's obsession with the scheme of the novel – with each chapter's organs, colours, techniques, symbols, and correspondences to mythic and historical figures – reinforce, but also at times undermine both the metaphorical implications and the basic story and characterization? Can we locate within the language principles of signification that might elude our focus on plot, character, and even narrative form? As we answer these questions, we shall see that *Ulysses* teaches us how to read itself, or, put another way, that it creates its own readers.

Reading *Ulysses* depends on understanding Joyce's concept of metaphor and how it defines the fundamental relationship between words and reality. The significant form of *Ulysses* depends upon the kinds of metaphorical substitutions Joyce makes when he lets Bloom and Stephen signify and be signified by historical figures. Reading the novel establishes how Stephen and Bloom become metaphors or signifiers for one another as well as, in their potential fusion, a metaphor for the creative presence who narrates the novel. It is not too much to say that much of the originality and power of *Ulysses* depends upon its examination of the possibilities of metaphor.

I THE GENRE OF *ULYSSES*

Ralph Rader has written, "[*Ulysses*] is to be understood as deriving its significance from, and a continuation of, [Joyce's] own experience which requires the reader to understand the relation between Joyce and Stephen and Bloom as quite definite and unambiguous".[1] Rader continues, "The separation of the book from life is the direct manifestation of its connection with it, since the goal of fictional recreation requires, as autobiography does not, that the artist break the explicit premise of connection and with it the emotional bond to his represented experience. He is to recreate his life as if he were not part of it. But this apartness, or detachment, was nevertheless meant to be understood as a fully implicit relation."[2] We are indebted to Rader for focusing on the unique formal relationship between author and novel, and for proposing an aesthetic which includes the principle that a book's significance may depend in part on knowing something of what happened to the author between the time of the action and the time the book was written. Recognizing the validity of such a principle is obviously crucial to a book in which the relationship between author and major character is often autobiographical: "Joyce's shifts of style from episode to episode are intended as a continuous manifestation of the presence which everywhere translates the random real to the order of art."[3]

However, we must ask whether we can read *Ulysses* as if Joyce's "fictional recreation" enabled him to "break the explicit premise of connection and with it the emotional bond to his represented experience". Or is the explicit relationship between *Ulysses* and Joyce's life – particularly as presented in Richard

Ellmann's canonical biography – inevitably part of our reading experience? I shall argue that we must see the fictional presence as a character within the imagined world whose full significance depends on a dynamic and varying relationship with the creator. Just as the explanatory Talmud has become part of the Torah for observant Jews, and just as for believing Christians biblical interpretation is as much a part of God's message as the New Testament, the biographical and critical apparatus has become part of the process of reading *Ulysses*. By distributing his schemata for the novel, and by helping Budgen write his early biography and Gilbert write his critical study, Joyce deliberately and willfully shaped the interpretation of *Ulysses*. It is as if God had given both the Holy Word and the subsequent exegeses.

Perhaps we should first turn to Joyce's own discussion of genre in *Portrait*:

> [A]rt necessarily divides itself into three forms progressing from one to the next. These forms are: the lyrical form, the form wherein the artist presents his image in immediate relation to himself; the epical form, the form wherein he presents his image in mediate relation to himself and to others; the dramatic form, the form wherein he presents his image in immediate relation to others. . . . The lyrical form is in fact the simplest verbal vesture of an instant of emotion. . . . He who utters it is more conscious of the instant of emotion than of himself as feeling emotion. The simplest epical form is seen emerging out of lyrical literature when the artist prolongs and broods upon himself as the centre of an epical event and this form progresses till the centre of emotional gravity is equidistant from the artist himself and from others. The narrative is no longer purely personal. The personality of the artist passes into the narrative itself, flowing round and round the persons and the action like a vital sea. . . . The dramatic form is reached when the vitality which has flowed and eddied round each person fills every person with such vital force that he or she assumes a proper and intangible esthetic life. The personality of the artist, at first a cry or a cadence or a mood and then a fluid and lambent narrative, finally refines itself out of existence, impersonalises itself, so to speak. The esthetic image in the dramatic form is life purified in and reprojected from the human imagination. (P. 214–5)[4]

In applying Joyce's aesthetic to his own works, we should think of literary works not as purely lyrical, epical, or dramatic, but as mixed modes that contain aspects of more than one genre. A *Portrait of the Artist as a Young Man* begins in the lyrical mode, but, to the degree to which it is ironic, approaches the epical mode. If we understand the relationship in *Ulysses* between the three genres as a dynamic process – as a trialogue among them – we can better understand the novel's form and meaning. Thus in *Ulysses* Joyce progresses from the lyrical to the epical and finally to the dramatic. The first three chapters oscillate between the lyrical perspective of Stephen and the epical perspective of Joyce's omniscient but not entirely distanced narrator, a narrator who is never far from Stephen's consciousness and who does not enter into the consciousness of any other characters. By using the lyrical mode, Joyce establishes the continuity with *Portrait* of both Stephen and of the narrative presence, and calls attention to the process of fictionally re-examining and recreating his own life. By allowing the lyrical mode to dominate over the epical mode with which *Portrait* had concluded, he shows that Stephen has taken a step backward in his artistic development, for the mature artist needs the objectivity Stephen lacks.

Gradually, as we shall see, Joyce distances himself from Stephen and establishes him as a potential character in an epic – the character of the young artist trying to find himself amidst personal and historical confusion so that he might develop into the writer of a novel like *Ulysses*. Presenting Bloom is the means by which the Joyce-presence places his characters – not only Bloom, but Stephen, too – at a distance from himself. Joyce conceived Bloom as a character that would enable him to achieve the epical mode ("prolong[ing] and brood[ing] upon himself as the centre of an epical event").

Joyce's desire to objectify part of himself in a character that seems to be the diametric opposite of Stephen, the artist based on his younger self, was probably influenced by Wilde's theory of masques; Wilde believed that we must assume a masque in order to liberate ourselves from our customary conventional daytime selves. Yet for the very reason that Bloom is still enough of the mature Joyce who is living in Europe and writing *Ulysses*, Joyce had to struggle to achieve the objectivity and distance that are the prerequisites of the dramatic mode. Perhaps we can say that beginning with "Circe" and climaxing with "Penelope," the artistic personality becomes – to use Joyce's terms from the passage from *Portrait* I quoted above – "impersonalized" and "reprojected from [*Joyce's*] human imagination". Indeed, it is Molly, based on the physicality and ingenuousness of Nora, that allows him to achieve the necessary objectivity and impersonality to use comfortably the dramatic mode. Molly Bloom displaces the narrative presence or, to say the same thing, the ventriloquy of the voice is so complete that we almost – but not quite – forget that the narrative presence contains all the varied voices, including some, such as the snarling ally of the Citizen in "Cyclops" and the speaker of sentimental pulp in "Nausicaa", that he assumes only to discredit.

Perhaps the most notable aspect of the dramatic mode is the protean speaker whose virtuosity enables him to assume various and conflicting voices. For the unique styles of each chapter can be equated with the voices of characters in drama. This ventriloquy calls attention to the presence of an objective artist impersonalizing himself and looking at the personae of the plot as well as at the various tellers from a detached, ironical perspective. Does not the recurrence of Stephen Dedalus, the major figure of *Portrait*, make particularly striking the contrast between the diverse voices of *Ulysses* and the third person omniscient narrator of *Portrait*, who renders Stephen's perspective almost exclusively?

The reader understands that the possibility of discovering an appropriate fictional form for the modern epic novel is itself one subject of *Ulysses*, a subject that self-consciously hovers over the entire novel. Since, for Joyce, inclusiveness is itself an essential prerequisite and a value for the modern epic, he wished to include within *Ulysses* not only the epic mode, but also the lyrical and dramatic. (It is worth noting that Joyce's own definitions of form focus on narrative distance, insist on the relation of work to author, and assume the imitation of an a priori world.) Central to his inquiry into the putative form for the modern epic were what voice to assume, what style to employ, and what kind of characters could possibly imply the universality he required.

Since, at the end of *Portrait*, Stephen, as Ellmann nicely puts it, "could no longer communicate with anyone in Ireland but himself", Joyce could not rely on Stephen's consciousness.[5] In *Ulysses*, Joyce decided to make the creation of the *mature* artist the subject. But how? Why not dramatize how the warmth and generosity of an obscure middle-class Jew – a man as marginal as the egotistical but self-doubting young artist who has not fulfilled his potential – open doors and windows of experience to the latter? Why not demonstrate that on one particular crucial day Stephen began the journey from an immature artist to the mature epic artist who was now writing *Ulysses*. Why not show that Shakespeare, the artist that Joyce regarded as his major precursor in the English language, also used his own life as his subject?

Indeed, Joyce's creative imagination works, as we shall see, the way that in the ninth episode Stephen defines Shakespeare's. For the purpose of defining the form of the novel, the ninth section is as much what Joyce called the "clou of the book" as the last episode.[6] Stephen praises Shakespeare for qualities that are essential to the artistic conception of *Ulysses* and the narrative presence he creates to tell it. Despite the hyperbole, despite Stephen's doubt about his own argument, this chapter educates his reader to read his novel in terms of the aesthetic principles with which he interprets Shakespeare; these principles argue that for the creative genius the personal past is as important as the historical past because such a figure can universalize his own idiosyncratic and nominalistic experience. From his 1922 vantage point, Joyce has Stephen predict the relationship between his 1904 self and his retrospective fictionalized self: "In the intense instant of imagination, when the mind, Shelley says, is a fading coal, that which I was is that which I am and that which in possibility I may come to be. So in the future, the sister of the past, I may see myself as I sit here now but by reflection from that which then I shall be" (U.194; IX.381–5). By defining the relationship between the creative imagination of Shakespeare and the biographical Shakespeare whose actual experience is the crucial source for the activity of the imagination, this passage educates the reader to understand the relationship between Stephen and Joyce.

We should not think that the fictionalized presence is simply a more mature version of Stephen. Rather, the retrospective "future" self is Joyce fictionalized, within the imagined world of the novel, as a mature omniscient presence whose experience is more inclusive and whose knowledge of life is more profound than we have any reason to believe that Stephen's could ever become. For the creative imagination of this presence not only embodies

Stephen's creativity and artistic values, Bloom's experience and humanity, and Molly's female perspective and acceptance of the body, but also is an artistic crucible for discovering universal and epic implications within the nominalistic lives of his three characters.

As we read the novel and feel the presence of Joyce trying to transform his fictionalized reminiscence into significant form and to define a voice and values that transcend the perspectives of Bloom, Stephen, and Molly, we understand that, like the reader, Joyce had to struggle between the pleasures of immersion in story and the demands of interpretation. In other words, the reader's odyssey recapitulates in important ways the author's odyssey. Do we not experience an active fictionalized presence not merely trying to transform fact into fiction, but trying to transform the bread and wine of ordinary daily experience into an imagined world with its own teleological significance? Joyce undertakes these projects by establishing both metaphorical parallels between different historical eras and metonymical relationships between such radically different characters as Bloom and Stephen.

II METAPHORICITY IN *ULYSSES*

Joyce's concept of metaphor defines the fundamental relationship between words and reality in *Ulysses*. I understand metaphor as the use of words to suggest a resemblance between something that is part of the teller's focus of attention – part of his real or imagined world – with something that is not literally or actually a part of the phenomenon that is engaging his mind. We can, I think, apply the concepts of recent criticism to discussions of traditional humanistic questions of meaning and significance, and, in particular, to questions about the relationship between, on the one hand, form or technique or *how* a novel says and, on the other hand, meaning or *what* it says and signifies. Since the unique aesthetic form of each major literary work creates its critical inquiry, *Ulysses*, with its emphasis upon linguistic patterns and its de-emphasis of traditional plot, requires serious discussion in terms of its language and internal verbal relationships. From our vantage point we can see that

Ulysses is Joyce's inquiry into how language signifies; it is about the creation of metaphors and their importance as a means of understanding ourselves and the world we live in.

Joyce would have been skeptical about much of Deconstruction, but he would have understood why Derrida quotes Nietzsche on metaphor: "Logic is only slavery within the bounds of language. Language has within it, however, an illogical element, the metaphor. Its principle force brings about an identification of the nonidentical; it is thus an operation of the imagination. It is on this that the existence of concepts, forms, etc. rests."[7] Joyce is interested in the process or "operation" of the imagination where something absent and nonidentical is summoned into the present to both enrich and be enriched by that present.

We might think of metaphor as a radical version of the copula "to be". For metaphor brings into existence something that is absent simply by declaring its presence. Both seek to transform, in Derrida's words, "a 'subjective excitation' into an objective judgment, into a pretension of truth".[8] Certainly, metaphor depends on the ability of the verb "to be" to declare the presence of something absent from the immediate field of vision that the author is presenting to the reader. Metaphor is by definition synchronic and knows no temporal boundaries. Joyce's title *Ulysses* announces the metaphoricity of the novel; it announces "This man is Ulysses" in a novel in which Bloom, not Odysseus, is the major figure. By its implied use of the present tense of the verb "to be", metaphor summons what is absent from the literal world and by doing so implies what that world lacks. In the case of *Ulysses*, what is summoned are the historical figures and literary characters of the past; they in turn summon the cultural milieu and values of the historical era to which they properly belong. For the reader, the relationship between past and present is a continuing variable in the adventure of reading; as Booth notes, "What any metaphor *says* or *means* or *does* will always be to some degree alterable by altering its context."[9] And of course every chapter – indeed, every passage – provides different mixtures of historical and literary allusions and places its stress on different resemblances between contemporary and prior eras.

The significant form of *Ulysses* depends upon the kinds of metaphorical substitutions Joyce makes when he lets Bloom and Stephen be signified by literary and historical figures as well as by real and imagined cosmological events. Reading the novel establishes how Stephen and Bloom become metaphors or signifiers for one another as well as, in their potential fusion, a metaphor for the creative presence who narrates the novel. But Joyce's concept of metaphor includes both historical allusions that evoke the values and personalities of past eras and the styles he parodies to evoke a variety of perspectives, past and present. By showing his power to make whatever metaphoric and metonymic substitutions he wishes, Joyce shows that he is, as Stephen puts it in "Oxen of the Sun", the "lord and giver" of language, the God in his imagined world (U.415; XIV.1116). By creating an original world within his imagination, Joyce shows that the aspiring artist need not replicate the art of his artistic fathers, including Shakespeare, and can thus himself be the "father of all his race" and the "father of his own grandfather" (U.208; IX.868–9).

Ulysses depends upon a continuing dynamic relationship between two members of a comparison. The comparison may be drawn between someone within the imagined world (Bloom) and someone whose identity derives from literary or historical sources (Odysseus); it may be drawn between two characters (Stephen and Bloom) who are part of the present imagined world of the novel's action; it may be drawn between, on the one hand, the characters (Stephen and Bloom) and, on the other, the fictionalized author (the narrative presence) for whom the characters are dramatized metaphors; or, it may be drawn between the fictionalized presence and the biographical author (Joyce). Metaphor in *Ulysses* depends, to adopt a distinction of Paul De Man's, not merely on "words substituting for each other", but on the "syntagmatic relationship" or "the contiguity of words to each another".[10] Thus Joyce is erasing the traditional distinction between metaphor and metonymy, a distinction that differentiates between metaphor, which depends on the necessary substitution of the figurative for the literal, and metonymy, which depends on the contiguity of two elements in a represented sequence.

For metaphoricity – the making of comparisons – is a way of bringing together apparently dissimiliar entities for the purpose of revealing resemblances and differences. It is a resource of the individual imagination – developed more intensely and subtly in the artist – by which we extend our experience. It can be a means by which we draw upon the experiences of others to supplement our own and to show the convergence between our experience and those of prior eras. Joyce's search for recurring cultural experiences and for the language to describe those experiences is characteristic of the search in the later nineteenth and twentieth centuries for a common reservoir of cultural and human experience. One thinks of the work of Fraser (*The Golden Bough*), Nietzsche, and the Cambridge ethnologists, Freud, and, later, Jung as they seek to locate a shared pattern of mythic and personal experience and to define a collective unconscious. The search for a common thread of universal experience was, as shared orthodox beliefs lost their hold after Darwin, a central theme in the work of British moderns from Yeats and Eliot to Lawrence and Forster.[11]

In the concepts of metempsychosis and parallax, Joyce believed he had discovered, respectively, mythical and scientific precedents for the kind of metaphoricity that depends not on substitution of one thing for another but upon simultaneous presence. Even if Joyce did not literally believe in the reincarnation of souls, the concept of metempsychosis provided Joyce with a paradigm for his idea that people do not change. In *Ulysses*, where the principal metaphors are the representation of one person by prior ones, metaphoricity is a linguistic version of metempsychosis because it keeps alive someone that is absent by comparing him to someone who is present. Thus metempsychosis gave Joyce conceptual grounding for the metaphorical systems of *Ulysses* – most notably, the pattern of Homeric allusions – that derive from extended literary and historical correspondence.

One might argue that when one character stands for another in a contiguous relationship, we have metonymy rather than metaphor. But, I would argue, metonymy is simply a kind of metaphor where the signified is explicit or implicit in the world represented. One could say that metonymy, the substitution of a part for the whole or the whole for a part, is a metaphor depending on contiguity, that is, a metaphor that depends upon the reader's perception of the substitutions among elements *within the imagined world*. This horizontal concept of metaphor, depending upon combinations of words and concepts within a text, enables Stephen and Bloom to represent one another. The concept of parallax – the phenomenon that the same object appears different from different points of observation or from different perspectives – appeals to Joyce precisely because, like metonymical correspondences, it depends upon the perceiver's resolving apparent differences within the same temporal plane. Just as parallax depends on the apparent difference of an object when viewed from different perspectives, so historical, literary, or personal figures look different even while they actually are, in crucial ways, counterparts.

In *Ulysses*, the figure of Leopold Bloom substitutes for the absent Odysseus or Elijah or Shakespeare, the way in the line, "my love is a red red rose", "red red rose" substitutes for "my love". But, in Joyce's mythic method, the pervasive metaphorical systems – *The Odyssey*, the life and works of Shakespeare, the Passover story and its rituals, the Christ story – become a supplement to what is already complete within itself, namely the story of Stephen and Bloom. Rhetorically, these metaphorical systems urge readers to understand that they must read not only literary texts but like the modern artist, they must "read" day-to-day life in the contemporary world within the context of an interpretive framework. In other words, the metaphoricity of the novel not only reveals that what is present requires something more, but that whatever might be present in the contemporary world – a world which seems to lack purpose and meaning – would necessarily require the something more of metaphors.

Writing to his brother Stanislaus, Joyce remarked: "Don't you think there is a certain resemblance between the mystery of the Mass and what I am trying to do? I mean that I am trying . . . to give people some kind of intellectual pleasure or spiritual enjoyment by converting the bread of everyday life into something that has a permanent artistic life of its own . . . for their mental, moral, and spiritual uplift."[12] Metaphors are the means by which he achieves this process of conversion. Thus he saw Dublin as a metaphor for the modern city. He once remarked: "[If] I can get to the heart of Dublin I can get to the heart of all the cities of the world."[13] Joyce believed in "the significance of trivial things", and wanted to show that significance to the reader.[14] He also believed that language had the potential to discover the value of trivial things, and the energy, variety, experimentation, sounds, discrimination, and ingenuity of the language in *Ulysses* demonstrate the validity of that belief.

Cumulatively, the various styles make a very compelling statement about the possibilities of language in the twentieth century, and Joyce's successors from Woolf to Faulkner and Pynchon have understood this.

In "Scylla and Charybdis" Christ signifies Shakespeare and Shakespeare signifies Christ; Stephen's epiphanic fusion brings them together in "Christfox in leather trews" (U.193; IX.337). "He Who Himself begot" is both God who begets his son and the artist who begets the son of his imagination – including Stephen who is recreating Shakespeare in this chapter (U.197; IX.493). The novel depends upon this kind of interchangeable metaphoricity where each member of a comparison is both signified and signifier and thus is at the same time different from and consubstantial with the other member or members. This kind of metaphorical structure in which both terms of the metaphor become simultaneously the image and the thing imaged is basic to the extended allusive comparison of Bloom to Ulysses and Elijah, Stephen to Telemachus and Hamlet, and both Stephen and Bloom, as well as of the narrative presence to Shakespeare. Finally, it is the basis of the parallel between Stephen and Bloom, between the narrative presence of fictionalized Joyce and Stephen, Bloom, and Molly, and between the fictionalized Joyce and the actual Joyce.

One aspect of Joyce's metaphorical process depends upon our seeing Stephen as a metaphor for Joyce or, put another way, proceeding from the fictional *towards the real*. Thus Stephen is a metaphor for the younger Joyce who must mature before *Ulysses* can be written, and Bloom is a metaphor for that part of Joyce which in 1904 still had to be discovered and developed. That the book progresses from Stephen to Bloom and Molly – from Stephen's inexperience to Bloom's wordly and practical experience and Molly's sexual experience – illustrates the maturity that must occur before Stephen can become someone who might hope to write *Ulysses*. Even without the knowledge that reading Ellmann's *James Joyce* gives us of the historical Joyce, we understand that the three major figures signify the fictionalized Joyce who is now speaking and that, in this crucial sense, "One life is all" (U.202, 280; IX.653, XI.907–8).

But even if our sense of the biographical Joyce and the Joyce we import from his other works and letters signifies and is signified by the fictionalized presence, we can only say that we as readers define the character and values of the speaking voice we hear from within the novel as the "real" Joyce. For as readers we cannot journey from the fictional to the real, only from the seemingly more fictional to the seemingly less fictional. In a literary version of Zeno's paradox, the real is always outside the imagined world and thus, finally, unreachable to readers. One can approach but never reach the "real" Joyce and Joyce knew this without reading about the metaphysics of presence. Our sense of the "real" voice is based on our own selecting and ordering principles of the words we read. Paradoxically, the more real the voice within the imagined world, the more fictive – in the sense of distorting the biographical or historical reality that precedes the novel – the voice may actually be. Thus while we might speculate about the "real" Joyce in 1922, the novel is calling attention to the values of the fictional teller and his relationship to the characters and action he describes. Does not the novel teach us that, just as Shakespeare can be recreated as a metaphor for Stephen's aesthetic ideology, and just as the artistic presence recreates Ulysses and Elijah to make sense of his world, we readers can and should recreate whatever image of the Joyce artist figure helps us to make sense of our lives? More than for any other major novel except *Finnegans Wake*, reading *Ulysses* depends upon our actively creating our own narrative form – our own coherent interpretive "discourse" – to shape the piecemeal data.

If for no other reason than the radical nature of his metaphors and the dazzling variety of his styles, we become aware of the speaker as a very special and distinct voice. As Booth notes, "every speaker who uses any figure with the intent that it be recognized as a figure, instead of using it as an art that disguises art, calls attention to himself in ways that the user of 'ordinary, usual,' untwisted language does not".[15] Thus we are aware of the narrative presence who is making the crucial comparisons on which *Ulysses* depends. These include not only both the metonymical interchange of Stephen and Bloom, but also the metaphorical substitutions of Odysseus and Telemachus for Bloom and Stephen and the reverse substitutions of Bloom and Stephen for Odysseus and Telemachus. We are aware of a narrative presence who is proposing, by means of his historical and literary metaphors, a radical way of seeing the details of everyday life.

To reach into the pattern of collective and recurring experience, Joyce uses historical and literary allusions which erase the distinctions between different eras and make the past a vital part of the present. We might say that these allusions are metaphors that carry the responsibility of historical signification. In "Scylla and Charybdis", Stephen uses allusions to Shakespeare's life and works to propose Shakespeare as a paradigm for understanding major literary figures and, ultimately, himself. That he does so shows that he is beginning to develop into the kind of author who might write *Ulysses*.

III   JOYCE'S METAPHORS AND HIS HISTORICAL PERSPECTIVE

Joyce's metaphoricity or, to use a pun Joyce might have approved of, *metaferocity*, illustrates Joyce's belief that examining the events of 16 June 1904 enables him to define what has been significant in human history and what can be significant in the future. Allusions for Joyce are kinds of metaphors that depend on the process of bringing the past into proximity with the present, with trying to spatialize the temporal or historical dimension. Because Joyce was skeptical about the supremacy of past eras or prior authors, his historical and literary allusions are not in the nostalgic mode of T. S. Eliot. For Joyce, Bloom's dignity, quiet courage, sense of self, humanity, and integrity are equivalent, if not superior, to the values glorified by Homer or even the Bible; for Joyce, the Bible is not a source of God's revelation but a humanistic narrative – and thus a model for *Ulysses* – that reveals man's hopes and aspirations.

When Eliot wrote of "the immense panorama of futility and anarchy which is contemporary history", in his famous *Dial* review of *Ulysses*, he is more accurately describing his own work than Joyce's.[16] Joyce writes less in the nostalgic mode than Eliot and perhaps even than his major contemporaries, Hardy, Conrad, Yeats, Lawrence, Forster, and Woolf. What is unique about *Ulysses* is that prior literary and historical figures are not merely extrinsic to the text but are summoned into the world of the text. Let me overstate a distinction: In *The Rainbow* and even for the most part in *The Waste Land*, the author no sooner brings together two distinct worlds than he satirically compares the modern world disfavourably to a previous one; by doing so, Lawrence and Eliot imply devolution from past to present and thus implicitly re-establish a diachronic perspective as an argument for the superiority of the past to the present. By contrast, *Ulysses* examines the modern world and prior ones by the same synchronic standards.

Joyce is not content merely to refer to his major predecessors; rather, he insists on critically examining them. He not only establishes himself as their successor, but becomes more inclusive than they were. Put another way, he identifies with his literary antecedents even as he cannibalizes them – in the sense of scavenging among his reading and devouring what he reads when the needs of his own perspective require it. *Ulysses* is in part a literary parody, if one understands that parody may be a strong respectful reading of literary antecedents. Parody depends on evoking the tradition against which the originality of the parody is measured. (Since the use of the Homeric material has been discussed exhaustively by a succession of critics, the most useful of which is still Stuart Gilbert in his *James Joyce's Ulysses*,[17] I shall only refer to Joyce's transformation of Homer in the context of my arguments.) Particularly in the early chapters, Joyce is committed to evoking the Homeric parallel; thus he begins, like Homer, with Telemachus at home preparing to start his journey in quest of his father. While the details of the parallel become less important than the central allusion to Bloom as the modern Ulysses, the second chapter, closely modelled in plot and texture on the Nestor episode (Book III) of the *Odyssey*, depends for its meaning upon the Homeric parallel. Just as Nestor's city is the first stop for Telemachus, so Stephen goes to Deasy's school. The school not only recalls Nestor's populous city of Pylos, but the entrance to both places requires passing through an imposing gate.

Deasy is a debased version of Nestor, the somewhat pompous but well-meaning old warrior who enjoys dispensing wisdom based on his practical experience. While Nestor is a benign false father figure for Telemachus, Deasy is a malicious one for Stephen. Deasy, notwithstanding his veneer of civilization and concern for the public welfare as instanced by his campaign against foot and mouth disease, lives in a world of abstractions in which experience is no longer a mentor and personal relations are defunct. Deasy is hilariously insensitive and stupid, responding with such jewels of interpersonal dialogue as his non sequitur announcement to Stephen, "I am happier than you" (U.34; II.389). Joyce turns Nestor's somewhat rambling tale of Clytemnestra's treachery into Deasy's misogynous diatribe, beginning "A woman brought sin into the world" (U.34; II.390). Unlike Telemachus who listens respectfully to the advice of his elder, Stephen is barely polite to Deasy and even more disdainful in his private responses.

Like his Homeric prototype, who is described by such epithets as "horse-driving" and "breaker of horses", Deasy is associated with horses and cattle; Stephen perceives him approaching on "gaitered feet" (U.29; II.186). Deasy's association with horses evokes the spirit of Swift, who like Deasy, was a member of the Protestant Anglo-Irish establishment; but unlike Deasy, Swift had a creative imagination and sympathy for the Irish. Deasy, despite his association with horses is not a Houyhnhnm but a brutish Yahoo; by contrast to Deasy, Stephen becomes for the moment the patriot and the creature of reason who is forced to serve the Yahoo schoolmaster. As an Orangeman who recalls the toast – "Glorious, pious and immortal memory" – to William of Orange, the man responsible for the conquest of Ireland, Deasy is part of the English–Irish establishment that Stephen sees himself unwillingly serving (U.31; II.273). By contrast, in the persona of M. B. Drapier, Swift wrote pamphlets in support of Irish independence.

Ironically, Deasy, the bigoted anti-Semitic schoolmaster whose wisdom consists of clichés rather than experience, is not even of sufficient stature to be a Polonius figure. Indeed, Joyce would have expected the reader to recall that the Shakespeare figure that Deasy quotes is the vicious Iago who is trying to gull Roderigo whom he repeatedly advises: "Put but money in thy purse" (U.30; II.239).

Joyce mocks the view proposed by Deasy that history moves toward one great goal; combining social Darwinism with traditional Protestant theology, this view that history is an upwardly evolving force dominated late nineteenth century thought. But Joyce does not embrace the historical despair of Eliot's Gerontion: "Think now/ History has many cunning passages, contrived corridors and issues, deceives with whispering ambitions/ Guides us by vanities." Joyce believed that history is cyclical and repetitious, and that the most important aspects of life and motivation for behaviour derive from such traditional family relationships as father and son and husband and wife. The motives, values, and problems of Odysseus and Shakespeare are not very different from those of Shakespeare and Bloom. As Ellmann puts it, "The characters pass through sequences of situations and thoughts bound by coincidence with the situations and thoughts of other living and dead men and of fictional, mythical men."[18]

Joyce found confirmation of his cyclical theory in Vico's *Scienza Nuova*, a book even more crucial to *Finnegans Wake*. *Ulysses* is based on Joyce's view that at any random point in time, one can evoke through allusions what has been significant in human history. His elaborate patterns of allusions to Homeric, biblical, and Elizabethan antecedents become extended metaphors in which contemporary events take some of their signification from the evocation of absent literary and historical figures, even as they in turn lend some of their own significance to the figures to whom they are being compared. Since history, he believed, repeats itself in crucial ways, literature is a central resource for discovering how people lived in past eras.

Within the novel history is a series of concentric circles proceeding outward from the centerpoint of 16 June 1904. For Joyce *any* one day could be defined as the centre of a series of concentric circles proceeding outward. We might examine history, Joyce believed, the way we examine the rings of a redwood tree. The closer circles at any one moment are those which can be shown to most resemble the events which are being dramatized, while the more distant ones are those which provide less important parallels. Thus, in "Lestrygonians", with the exception of the opening evocation of Elijah, the Homeric parallel is the closest circle; but in "Aeolus", the Homeric parallel is gradually superceded by the Passover story and in "Scylla and Charybdis", the Shakespeare era displaces the Homeric one as the closest circle.

The reader needs to realize, then, that literary and historical figures are present in the fabric of life on 16 June 1904. Odysseus, Shakespeare, and Elijah walk the streets of Dublin, and their presence in a contiguous relation with Bloom reveals something about them as well as about Bloom. Within *Ulysses*, the image or thing absent, once evoked, in turn becomes imaged by the person to whom the character is being compared. Derrida has noted, "all the concepts which have played a part in the delimitation of metaphor always have an origin and a force which are themselves 'metaphorical'".[19] Certainly this is true of metaphor in *Ulysses* where Joyce is erasing the boundaries between the literal and the figurative. For Joyce, everything in contemporary life signifies something else. Or, as Culler puts it: "a literal expression is also a metaphor whose figurality has been forgotten".[20] Of course the converse is true, and everything in the past represents something in contemporary life. Thus Bloom's presence evokes that of Odysseus, who becomes an image for the wily twentieth-century man who values home and lives by his wits. But Bloom also becomes an image for Odysseus, and Bloom's pacificism, reason, and self-consciousness comment on the life and times of Homer's Odysseus. The comparisons thus not only expand the significance of Bloom, but call into question the supposed superiority of heroic figures of the past. After all, does not the presence of Ulysses, Shakespeare, and Elijah in comic roles imply that they also had their all too human moments of foolishness?

IV   EPIPHANY AS METAPHOR

Let us examine epiphany in terms of our discussion of metaphor. We recall that in *Stephen Hero* Joyce defines epiphany as "a sudden spiritual manifestation, whether in the vulgarity of speech or of gesture or in a memorable phase of the mind itself. He believed that it was for the man of letters to record these epiphanies with extreme care, seeing that they themselves are the most delicate and evanescent of moments".[21] Epiphanies are moments of revelation when the meaning of events becomes completely clear to the subjective consciousness; it follows that epiphanies are also moments of artistic vision as well as the reader's perception of that vision after it has been transformed by the artist from life into art. In other words, Joyce's epiphanies are part of the novel's action and rhetoric. They include, then, both the artist's creation and the reader's understanding of crystallizing metaphors that reveal or signify something of import. Thus in *Ulysses* they are not only moments when characters have an exceptional insight, as when Bloom affirms the value of

life at the end of "Hades" or rejects physical and moral cannibalism in "Lestrygonians". But they are also moments when the
reader has an illumination about the significance of relationships
among the episodes, historical and literal correspondences, patterns of language, or the implications of characters' behaviour.

In the same passage from *Stephen Hero* Joyce defines epiphany
in terms of Aquinas's three prerequisites for beauty: "integrity, a
wholeness, symmetry and radiance". The first quality of beauty
is "wholeness", a quality which Joyce defines in a way that is
suggestive of how to respond to the major metaphors of *Ulysses*:
"Consider the performance of your own mind when confronted
with any object, hypothetically beautiful. Your mind to apprehend that object divides the entire universe into two parts,
the object, and the void which is not the object. To apprehend it
you must lift it away from everything else: and then you perceive
that it is one integral thing, that is *a* thing." And perceiving the
major metaphors of *Ulysses* also fulfils the second criterion,
"symmetry": "The mind considers the object in whole and part,
in relation to itself and to other objects, examines the balance of
its parts, contemplates the form of the object, traverses every
cranny of the structure. So the mind receives the impression of
the symmetry of the object. The mind recognizes that the object
is in the strict sense of the word, a *thing*, a definitely constituted
entity."

Finally, in *Stephen Hero* Joyce speaks of epiphany synony-
mously with radiance, or *claritas*: "After the analysis which discovers the second quality the mind makes the only logically possible
synthesis and discovers the third quality. This is the moment
which I call epiphany. . . . [W]hen the relation of the parts is
exquisite, when the parts are adjusted to the special point, when
we recognise that it is *that* thing which it is. Its soul, its whatness,
leaps to us from the vestment of its appearance. The soul of the
commonest object, the structure of which is so adjusted, seems to
us radiant. The object achieves its epiphany . . .". In a sense,
Ulysses – both as a whole and in the structure of its individual
chapters – fulfils the criteria of "integrity" or "wholeness",
"symmetry", and "radiance", and the novel depends for its
efficacy on creating a reader who reiterates the tripartite movement of the mind described in the definitions of these qualities.
The reader's perception of metaphorical relations in *Ulysses*

follows the pattern of the mind's movement that Joyce defines.
Are not the reader's epiphanies the moments when he perceives
the metaphorical relationships in their complexity and irony?
In practice, epiphanies can be a series of small insights build-
ing towards the promise of a grand moment of vision. Take, for
example, the conclusion of "The Dead", when Gabriel Conroy
gradually discovers his inadequacy prior to the last sentence:
"His soul swooned slowly as he heard the snow falling faintly
through the universe and faintly falling, like the descent of their
last end, upon all the living and the dead." His growing awareness is subsumed in the narrator's performance of a lyrical
feeling beyond consciousness. By his use of language that does
not signify beyond itself, the narrator dramatizes Gabriel in the
process of experiencing a moment when he feels rather than
intellectualizes. The reversal of "falling faintly", the bizarre
notion of Gabriel's hearing snow fall, and the indefinite antecedent for the final "they" all enact his final swoon out of
consciousness and show the suspension of his ego and self-
consciousness. But the promise of complete epiphany, a vision
out of time when the reader suspends his consciousness of
reading and his thoughts about his reading experience, can
never occur. Thus the reader's participation in Gabriel's loss of
ego and emotional awakening is qualified by his twin realization
that (1) no words can quite render Gabriel's feelings when, to
quote Yeats's *Sailing to Byzantium*, his "soul clap[s] its hands and
sing[s]" and (2) that, whatever transformation Gabriel experiences
individually, "The Dead", as the concluding story of *Dubliners*,
punctuates a concatenation of stories about the spiritual and
moral atrophy of Dublin.
Epiphany, then, is another version of metaphoricity, for it
substitutes a perception of significance for the fragmentation and
pedestrian quality of ordinary chronological time. In terms of
our inquiry into how *Ulysses* means, what does the process of
discovering epiphanies signify? Does epiphany represent a quest
for objectivity and for the spiritual unity that transcends intellectual understanding? Given the novel's cyclical nature of history
and its denial of a universe ordered by God, perhaps we should
say that epiphany is a quest both to compensate for the lack of
teleology in the universe, and to alleviate – by positing a way
of seeing and knowing in literature – the spiritual condition
dramatized in Dublin. Perhaps we should say that the experi-

ence of epiphany becomes a metaphor for the wholeness of soul
that spiritual enlightenment once afforded. It becomes a representation of the integrity, symmetry, and radiance which
Joyce's speaker is seeking, and for which his characters long.
Neo-Platonic in concept, epiphany is something that can only
be approached but never fulfilled. The moment of epiphanic
insight can never approach the purity of the relationship with
God that is open to the passionate believer. Nor can its transformation into words ever quite reach the moment of original
epiphanic perception. On one hand, the characters' epiphanic
moments must always elude the odyssean reader. Yet, on the
other, in his role of guide, Joyce enables the reader to approach
the order and meaning, the illumination and intensity, of epiphany – which is both a moment of enlightenment within the
narrative and the promise of revelation offered the reader if he
were to acquire (as, of course, no reader can completely) the
global, totalistic perspective transcending sequential narrative
that reading *Ulysses* requires.

V BATHOS AND METAPHOR

One cannot discuss metaphoricity in *Ulysses* without discussing
bathos, for Joyce rarely proposes a metaphorical pattern without
undermining it with laughter. Bathos, the descent from the
sublime to the ridiculous, is an essential part of the experience of
reading *Ulysses*. If form is conceived of as the arousing and
fulfilling of readers' expectations, we might think of bathos –
which depends on arousing and deflating our expectations as
readers – as an ironic inversion of the work's normative form.
Joyce uses bathos to question his metaphors, to raise doubts
about significance, to undermine ironically the possibility that
everything means. Bathos subverts the relationship between
signifier and signified by introducing the shadow of irony or
doubt into the reader's quest for meaning. The catalogues in
"Cyclops", the headlines in "Aeolus", the degeneration of language implied by the gibberish at the end of "Oxen of the Sun",
the associations of Rudy with Oscar Wilde and Bloom with
Fergus at the climax of "Circe", are all bathetic aspects of the
novel.

Bathos intrudes between the signifier and the signified and deflects the reader from an orderly humanistic response. By frequently placing metaphorical propositions in the context of doubt about their applicability and seriousness, bathos introduces puzzle, enigma, and cacophony into Joyce's imagined world. Thus, even as he is establishing Bloom's stature in "Ithaca", Joyce trivializes him by having the narrator think about the senseless enigma, "Where was Moses when the candle went out?" (U.729; XVII.2070). Or, in "Circe" when Bloom imagines himself as the New Messiah, his fantasy of a secular utopia where differences of religion and nationality are irrelevant rapidly degenerates into a crude denunciation by a chorus of obscene and hysterical voices.

Is not another example of bathos the inclusion of hints and traces of homosexuality in the presentation of the relationship between Stephen and Bloom? The relationship develops in the sixteenth chapter, a number which has homosexual connotations; sixteen is their difference in their ages and the date (16 June) of the novel. Yet Joyce expects his readers to reject homosexuality as the explanation for the friendship between Stephen and Bloom and to understand that we need terms other than those provided by our cultural conventions to define the male camaraderie between unrelated males of different generations that Stephen and Bloom share. In "Cyclops", the malefactor is hanged and then stands trial. That Gerty sees not only a Roman candle but what may be a shooting star – a phenomenon associated with the cosmological resonance of Bloom's and Stephen's mutual epiphany in "Ithaca" – is a bathetic response to the climax of Bloom's masturbation: "[S]he saw a long Roman candle going up over the trees, up, up . . . high, high, almost out of sight" (U.366; XIII.719–22). One could cite infinite examples, but one of the most effective occurs at the climax of "Eumaeus", when the horse drops three turds prior to the fictionalized Joyce's subsuming the fatigued voice of his semi-literate narrator and establishing the union between Stephen and Bloom.

That, given its length and the difficulty in reading it, relatively little happens in *Ulysses* is part of its bathos. To be sure, Stephen makes progress towards his goal of becoming a mature artist and, by asserting himself in "Circe", begins to exorcise the ghost of his mother. And Bloom courageously stands up to the Citizen in "Cyclops". But Bloom and Molly are not reunited, and Bloom is no closer to the son he so desperately wants than

Stephen is to the father he so desperately needs. Stephen has not begun the passionate relationship that he requires; nor has he started the national epic of Ireland, or, indeed any major artistic endeavour. Furthermore, each perspective, each voice, qualifies the others and undermines the possibility of authority. Finally, if each person can signify and be signified by whomever the speaker chooses, if metempsychosis and parallax are infinite resources, then meaning depends on the arbitrary imagination of the artist "weaving and unweaving" at will. Metaferocity becomes the action of writing on a page, an action that could be done differently and no more or less arbitrarily.

Perhaps interpretation is no more than, to paraphrase Eliot, fragments that we each create to shore against our fears that our reading, like our lives, may end in ruins. Indeed, in "Ithaca", Joyce's objective scientific voice takes an ironical tone to Bloom's acts of interpretation and, by implication, the kinds of reading that *Ulysses* requires. For Joyce understands that these interpretations are often subjective moves posing as objective facts: "The difficulties of interpretation since the significance of any event followed its occurrence as variably as the acoustic report followed the electrical discharge and of counterestimating against an actual loss by failure to interpret the total sum of possible losses proceeding originally from a successful interpretation" (U.676; XVII.343–7). Yet if every event has resonance, does not the passage argue for the significance of the relatively trivial events of 16 June 1904? Do we not achieve a kind of immortality in the endless sequence of events that derive, in a kind of ripple effect, from our actions and words? *Ulysses* urges the reader to see that if Bloom's deeds and Stephen's words touch only one person, they have an effect because that one person's behaviour and words in turn effect another and so on in an endless sequence. Indeed, that is why the Greek and Hebraic cultures have survived. It is because these cultures – their myths and values – survive as a living tradition that Joyce's metaphors can summon them from across Lethe and become "lord and giver of their life" (U.415; XIV.1116). When prior myths are abused or misused – as, for example, in "Aeolus", when Taylor uses ritualistic hyperbole to compare the bondage of the contemporary Irish with that of the Jews in Egypt – they refuse to answer the call and remain dead.

Throughout *Ulysses*, Joyce is aware that the possibility of

meaninglessness is inseparable from the probability of significance. Put another way: Joyce depends upon the reader's expectations of coherence and unity – what Wallace Stevens in "The
Idea of Order at Key West" calls our "rage for order" – even as
he challenges and ironically undermines our desire for order
with discrete details, catalogues, neologisms, and nonsense.
Joyce wants us to read the book as a sacred text in which
everything signifies and in which the words of the page become a
metonym for unity and wholeness in the modern world. Yet at
the same time he wants us to read profanely and see the book not
merely as inconclusive, but as skeptical about the possibility of
discovering significance from the plethora of details within his
novel and, by implication, skeptical of any effort to come to
terms with even one day in one's own life. By constantly proposing, testing, and discarding multiple identities for Bloom and
Stephen, Joyce urges us toward such a complex response. In
"Circe", no sooner does Bloom imagine himself as the Messiah
of the New Jerusalem than he has to be crucified. Moreover, the
crucifixion, like its parallel in "Cyclops", is really a verbal one –
a stylistic event – created by Joyce at the expense of his
character and performed for the reader.

The novel does not resolve whether Bloom is, finally, no more
important than the man in the mackintosh or whether he can
represent – in his ties to Sinn Fein, Free Masonry, his Jewish
heritage; his commitment to his family roles as husband, son,
and father; and his essential *Menschlichkeit* – a tradition on which
modern Ireland can establish itself. Our efforts to understand
the man in the mackintosh become a metaphor for our efforts to
read the novel. On one hand, we can say he is a metonym for
Bloom, the perpetual outsider, or for the inevitably anonymous
modern man who depends upon the perceptions of others to
authenticate him. On the other hand, he is a signifier without a
signified, an orthographic mark in the form of words that have
no meaning, a sign of the incoherence of text. Thus, in carrying
the supplement of metaphoricity and the trace of anonymity, the
man in the mackintosh becomes a signifier for the process of
reading the novel.

VI FALSE SIGNIFIERS

Like bathos, false signifiers invert the reader's expectations and impede his quest for meaning. By a false signifier, I mean a comparison which Joyce introduces only to show its inappropriateness in the context of the novel; in other words, the signifier's claims to signify are called into question. By deliberately proposing, testing, and discarding false signifiers, *Ulysses* calls attention to the arbitrariness of metaphor. For example, Joyce thought of D. B. Murphy, the wandering English sailor that Bloom and Stephen meet in "Eumaeus", as "Ulysses Pseudoangelos"; although Murphy's adventurous way of life superficially resembles that of the original Ulysses more than the life style of the urban advertising solicitor Bloom, he really makes no major claims to significance.[22] Wearing the number sixteen on his chest, he has arrived aboard the three-masted ship, but he is a nominalistic figure who brings no insight to Dublin or substantive meaning to the reader.

Another false signifier is the Reverend Dowie, the self-conceived "restorer of the church in Zion"; he is an ersatz Elijah figure who will offer nothing to Ireland's spiritual wasteland (U.151; VIII.13–14). If the old sailor in "Eumaeus" is a Ulysses Pseudoangelos, Dowie is an Elijah Pseudoangelos. He has predicted in his handout or throwaway that "Elijah is coming" in the form of Christ's return; indeed, Bloom has mistakenly thought when first glancing at the throwaway that the word "blood" in the phrase "Blood of the Lamb" was "Bloom" (U.151; VIII. 8–9).

The major false signifier is Mulligan. Stephen thinks of Malachi Mulligan as "pseudo Malachi" because he realizes that the mocking Malachi Mulligan is not going to prophesy anything that will be of value to the transformation of Stephen into the putative artist figure who will save Ireland (U.197; IX.492). Moreover, as we shall see, Mulligan is "pseudo Malachi" because he represents the aestheticism and frivolity of Wilde's art and the decadence of his personal values. When, in "Wandering Rocks", the appropriately named Artifoni offers in Italian to give Stephen singing lessons in order that he presumably might – following Artifoni's example – teach singing for a living, he is speaking not in the idealistic tradition of Dante, one of Stephen's frequently evoked literary ancestors, but in the debased commercial spirit of the modern world.

While Bloom notices in "Hades" that Martin Cunningham has a physical resemblance to Shakespeare ("Sympathetic human man he is. Intelligent. Like Shakespeare's face"), it is Bloom and Stephen who are signified by and in turn signify Shakespeare (U.96; VI.344–5). In fact, Martin Cunningham is rather patronizing to Bloom, although less unkind than Bloom's other companions in the funeral carriage. That the first two syllables of his name, "Cunning", suggest fox, while Shakespeare is given the epithet "fox" and "Christfox" ("Christfox in leather trews, hiding, a runaway in blighted treeforks, from hue and cry. Knowing no vixen, walking lonely in the chase. Women he won to him, tender people, a whore of Babylon, ladies of justices, bully tapsters' wives. Fox and geese") links him to Shakespeare (U.193; IX.337–40). Another link is that, like Shakespeare, Martin has trouble with a disloyal wife – in his case a drunken woman who sells his furniture behind his back and is, as Bloom puts it, "Leading him the life of the damned" (U.96; VI.351). The phrase "whore of Babylon" suggests the link between Mrs Cunningham and Ann Hathaway. When within Bloom's and Stephen's shared hallucination in "Circe", Shakespeare dissolves into a "paralytic rage" of sexual jealousy. "The face of Martin Cunningham, bearded, refeatures Shakespeare's beardless face" (U.568; XV.3853–5). Neither an artist nor a man with a vast soul, Martin is Shakespeare pseudoangelos.

In "Aeolus", Red Murray proposes a resemblance between William Brayden and Christ. That Bloom's analogistic mind considers and rejects this proposed resemblance demonstrates for the odyssean reader engaged in his quest for meaning that he must not accept every proposed comparison: "Our Saviour: beardframed oval face: talking in the dusk. Mary, Martha. Steered by an umbrella sword to the footlights: Mario the tenor" (U.117; VII.52–3). Finally, when told by Red Murray that Mario resembles Jesus, Bloom bathetically thinks of "Jesus Mario" singing from *Martha*, the comic opera that signifies for Bloom both the possibility of love with Martha Clifford and the restoration of love and therefore rebirth. (When Lionel apparently loses his beloved "Martha" – really Lady Harriet in disguise – he goes mad from grief; but he meets her again, and he not only is restored to full health, but marries her and presumably lives happily ever after.)

VII "PATERNITY MAY BE A LEGAL FICTION": PATERNITY AS METAPHOR

In "Scylla and Charybdis", Stephen, very anxious to separate himself from his own father, Simon Dedalus, contends that "Fatherhood, in the sense of conscious begetting, is unknown to man. It is a mystical estate, an apostolic succession, from only begetter to only begotten. . . . Paternity may be a legal fiction" (U.207; IX.837–9, 845). In the above passage, Joyce has in mind not merely Stephen's or even his own artistic paternity, but the whole issue of how literary and cultural paternity works. In my sixth chapter, I shall discuss the paternity theme in relation to Stephen's artistic quest. But here I want to emphasize that Stephen's argument is central to the aesthetic of *Ulysses* because it enables us to see characters as offspring of prior literary and historical characters with whom they are associated by allusion. Isn't the technique of allusion itself a kind of fatherhood where a predecessor gives meaning to a subsequent person or phenomenon? Joyce is arguing for a kind of metaphorical metempsychosis whereby he becomes the apostolic successor to Homer, Dante, and Shakespeare.

Joyce is using metaphors to make present the prior literary figures – his cultural fathers – in his work. In terms introduced by Harold Bloom, Joyce is not only a strong misreader of the literary tradition but also of the ways that tradition has been read. Among other things, *Ulysses* is a parody both of epics and of traditional novels. As a parody it acknowledges the paternity of traditions and pays tribute to them even as it insists on striking out on its own. Parody is literary patricide from which, phoenix-like, the literary son emerges; parody enacts one of Stephen's aphorisms and one of Joyce's basic tenets: "Where there is a reconciliation . . . .there must have been first a sundering" (U.193; IX.334–5).

Let us discuss the relationship of metaphor to the plot's basic theme of paternity. Joyce's major characters, Stephen and Bloom, are, respectively, signifiers of his younger iconoclastic artistic self and the middle-aged sensual bourgeois man who, he knew, was a part of himself – an objectification of qualities that his younger self, the self who wrote *Portrait*, would have despised. Like the continuous dynamic process of metaphoricity in *Ulysses*, Joyce's creation of Bloom illustrates the concept that the artist "[finds] in the world without as actual what was in his world within as possible" (U.213; IX.1041–2). Constantly seeking metaphors to endow their own lives with significance, Stephen and Bloom are engaged in the same activity within the imagined world as Joyce is in the act of creating that world. For are not Bloom's search for a son and Stephen's for a father both searches for someone who will give them a sense of wholeness by signifying for them what they require in order to feel more whole?

The concept of "the supplement" helps differentiate between what they believe they are seeking and what the reader understands that they are really looking for: "The supplement", as Culler puts it, "is an inessential extra, added to something complete in itself, but the supplement is added in order to complete, to compensate for a lack in what was supposed to be complete in itself."[23] Because Stephen and Bloom are incomplete within themselves, they seek a supplement – not as an inessential extra, a "something more", but as the putative completion of their essential meaning. Put another way, Stephen and Bloom are signifiers in quest of a signified which will complete them as signs, and within the novel they do make substantial progress on their quests. And it is precisely their partially successful quests which rhetorically urge the odyssean reader towards a traditional humanistic reading that believes in unity, signification, and anterior reality. Because *Ulysses* finally converts us to privilege this kind of reading, we subordinate to a secondary position a reading of the novel as an elaborate linguistic game in which the characters are less important as people than as images, marks, and sounds – such as the homophones for their names, "Blephen" and "Stoom" – that take whatever meaning they have from phonic, visual, and other intratextual relationships within the warp and woof of contiguous words.

It may be objected that what I am saying can be put in traditional terms and that I should simply contend that, even as Joyce delights in confronting the reader with the discrepancy between pattern – stylistic experiments shaped by literary parallels – and the story of Bloom and Stephen, he continually resolves the discrepancy by returning to his focus on his characters' quests. But I would argue that once we overcome our prejudices against new terminology and the desire to call it "jargon", we can see how Deconstruction does at times lead us to new perspectives and greater precision.

At the end of "Circe", do not Stephen and Bloom acknowledge one another in terms of the very kind of metaphors that Joyce uses to define their relationship to literary and historical figures? Stephen acknowledges Bloom as a surrogate or metaphorical father, and Bloom discovers Stephen as a substitute or metaphorical son. (Bloom temporarily accepts a number of surrogates or metaphors for Molly – Martha Clifford, Gerty MacDowell, Bella Cohen, but finally rejects them as inadequate to his needs.)

Indeed, one can define the major action of the novel as the expansion within the imagination of Stephen and Bloom of the possibilities of metaphoricity. Their mutual use of metaphoricity to create the meaning of their lives, as much as anything else, anticipates and signifies their union in the figure who is writing the novel based on metaphor. That their imaginations simultaneously work to perceive metaphorically in "Circe" shows their mutual growth toward the figure who will create *Ulysses*. Perceiving Shakespeare in the mirror prefigures the climax of "Circe", which in turn signifies the relationship that evolves in "Eumaeus" and "Ithaca". Does not such a linear series where one event signifies the subsequent one itself become a structural endorsement of the contiguous metaphoricity by which characters, events, and words signify and are signified by one another until the book becomes coterminous with recorded history and spatially equivalent to the whole world?

NOTES

1. Ralph Rader, "Exodus and Return: Joyce's *Ulysses* and the Fiction of the Actual", *The University of Toronto Quarterly*, 48:2 (Winter 1978/9) 149–71; see, p. 152.
2. Rader, p. 154.
3. Rader, p. 156.
4. Page references are to the Viking Critical Edition of *A Portrait of the Artist as a Young Man*, ed. Chester G. Anderson (New York: Viking, 1968). A capital P indicates references to *Portait*.
5. Richard Ellmann, *James Joyce* (New York: Oxford University Press, 1982; orig. ed. 1959) pp. 358.
6. *Letters*, I, p. 170.
7. Jacques Derrida, "The Supplement of Copula: Philosophy *Before* Linguistics", in Josue Harari, *Textual Strategies* (Ithaca, New York: Cornell University Press, 1979) p. 83.

8. Harari, p. 82.
9. Wayne Booth, "Ten Literal 'Theses'", in Sheldon Sacks, ed. *On Metaphor*, p. 173.
10. Paul de Man, "Semiology and Rhetoric", in Harari, p. 125.
11. See my, "'I Was the World in Which I Walked'": the Transformation of the British Novel", *The University of Toronto Quarterly* (Spring 1982) 51:3, pp. 279–97.
12. Quoted in Richard Ellmann, *James Joyce*, p. 163; from *My Brother's Keeper*, ed. Richard Ellmann (New York: The Viking Press, 1958) pp. 103–4.
13. Quoted in Richard Ellmann, *James Joyce*, p. 505.
14. Quoted in Richard Ellmann, *James Joyce*, p. 163.
15. Booth, "Metaphor as Rhetoric: the Problem of Evaluation", in Sacks, ed., *On Metaphor*, p. 55.
16. T. S. Eliot, "*Ulysses*, Order, and Myth", *The Dial* 35 (1923) 480–3; reprinted as "Myth and Literary Classicism" in *The Modern Tradition*, eds Richard Ellmann and Charles Fiedelson, Jr. (New York: Oxford University Press) pp. 679–81; see p. 681.
17. Stuart Gilbert in *James Joyce's 'Ulysses': a Study*.
18. Ellmann, *James Joyce*, p. 551.
19. This passage is quoted in Jonathan Culler, *On Deconstruction* (Ithaca, New York: Cornell University Press, 1982), from Derrida, *Marges*, p. 301.
20. Culler, *On Deconstruction*, p. 148.
21. Quoted from The Viking Critical Edition of *A Portrait of the Artist as a Young Man*, p. 288. In this section, all my quotes from *Stephen Hero* are from pp. 288–9 of this edition.
22. See Ellmann, *Ulysses on the Liffey* (New York: Oxford University Press, 1972) p. 154–5.
23. Culler, *On Deconstruction*, p. 103.

2 Joyce's Concept of a Hero

I THE TRANSFORMATION OF THE ULYSSES MYTH

Like Vico, Joyce believed that history is cyclical rather than progressive, and like Vico, he believed that the essential values of cultures could be discovered by examining their language, myths, and literature. He chose literary and historical sources that present what he believes to be the central recurring issues that appear within each cycle and that illustrate the universal values on which man's survival depends. Joyce chose the *Odyssey* as his primary epic model because it was the one major European epic that depends on the centrality of family and personal relationships – parent and child, particularly father and son; male friendship and rivalry; and heterosexual lovers, especially the complex ties between a long married husband and wife. Indeed, it begins with the son's quest for a missing father and soon turns to the hero's quest to displace a rival for his wife's affections and resume his proper place in his home.

But he also chose the *Odyssey* because it was the epic that stresses how an individual man uses his intelligence, judgment, and inner strength to overcome obstacles and, finally, to accomplish his goal. By announcing in his very title of *Ulysses* that his subject is a retelling of the Greek prototype, Joyce is consciously substituting what he regarded as this more civilized European tradition for the emphasis of Yeats and the Celtic Renaissance on the folk legends and the myths of the Irish gods. Joyce is interested far less in physical prowess than in moral courage. Unlike Cuchulain who physically expands and contracts at will when he is challenged, Ulysses is a hero who lives by his wits. Of course, one might object that his reading of the classical tradition is idiosyncratic, for had he chosen the *Iliad* or the Greek tragedies, he would have found models for bellicose behaviour. Joyce's focus on *Hamlet*, the Shakespearean tragedy that is most concerned with family relations and the mental and emotional

37

life of the individual, is consistent with his focus on private lives and interior space. His version of Hamlet hardly attends to its revenge tragedy aspects.

The novel redefines the traditional concept of a hero to emphasize not only pacifism, but commitment to family ties, concern for the human needs of others, sense of self, tolerance, and decency. Heroism for Joyce is a set of personal values that makes it possible to improve the quality of life ever so slightly for others – as Bloom does for the Dignam family, Mrs Purefoy, and, most of all, for Stephen and Molly. In creating Bloom as a modern Odysseus, Joyce has turned his back on the violent world of *The Iliad*. I am reminded of the opening of Joseph Brodsky's "Odysseus to Telemachus":

> My dear Telemachus
> The Trojan War
> Is over now; I don't recall who won
> it.

Joyce modifies the nineteenth century concept of Ulysses, epitomized by Tennyson's rejection of family values in favour of personal adventure. In his 1842 dramatic monologue "Ulyssess", the title character combines a commendable Victorian zeal for knowledge and new experience with aspects of discontent and even Byronic self-indulgence. But Tennyson's hero feels tinges of love and regret in leaving his home and justifies his departure by referring to Telemachus's maturation. Overcome by despair at Hallam's death, Tennyson's Ulysses is a metaphor for moral courage and psychological coherence. Tennyson had implied that Ulysses's goal of self-development was more important than his social responsibility to the people to whom he has finally returned. Yet it is worth noting that while Tennyson's Ulysses owes a good deal to Dante's hubristic hero, Joyce's Ulysses is not only without arrogance or iconoclasm, but is a domestic figure concerned with restoring his home and family. Tennyson derived his Ulysses less from the Homeric source that stressed his return to country and family than from Dante who condemned Ulysses for intellectual hubris. For Dante, Ulysses belongs in the Inferno as an evil counsellor who, because of his zeal for adventure when he should have been satisifed with life in

Ithaca, led his comrades to destruction. Tennyson turns this zeal into an unsatisfied desire for knowledge.

In stressing Bloom's commitment to home and family, Joyce believed he was returning to the original spirit of the Homeric source. Yet he retains something of Tennyson's stress on the need for courageously facing the struggles of life. Joyce continues the tendency in the later nineteenth century English novel – Dobbin, Alan Woodcourt, Clym Yeobright – to make the hero into a domestic figure committed to family values. In the Victorian world which believed that an upwardly evolving pattern could be discovered in history, we often find an implication that in some vague way the domesticated hero can do some good for the community. After all, Woodcourt is a physician and Clym is preaching his views to the rustic folk.

But one aspect of Bloom's heroism to Joyce is that he is a character whose adventures have metaphorical value. As C. H. Peake remarks,

> The parallel between Bloom and Ulysses extends to the actions and situations in which they are involved in a manner implicit in the common figurative use of the term 'odyssey' to mean the journey of a soul through the perils and temptations of this life – that is to say, by the treatment of the epic myth as, in part, allegorical. Insofar as the episodes are regarded as representative of universal human experiences, any specific location will modify only their accidental particulars, not their essences; and whether in the Mediterranean region or in Dublin, whether presented in the heroic or the realistic mode, they will compose a kind of spiritual geography of the hazards that lie in wait for the 'complete' man in his voyage through life, menacing or undermining his will to travel on.[1]

While Odysseus has to attend to the will of the Gods, the God whom Bloom must please is Joyce's narrative presence who confers and revokes value.

For the most part, Joyce's interest in the correspondences of his major characters to Homeric prototypes and, in particular, of Bloom to Odysseus, depends on showing the parallels in human behaviour. But there are moments when Joyce is less interested in what the correspondences signify than in his own ingenious performance of imagining the parallels. The reader's odyssey through the text not only oscillates from nominalistic details of 16 June 1904 to the significance of the larger patterns of meaning, but also oscillates between local enjoyment in the *tour de force* of parodying the *Odyssey* and understanding the larger impact of the parody. Thus our reading experience enacts the division in Joyce's imagination between, on the one hand, his compelling urge for unity and significance and, on the other hand, his delight in momentary glimpses of Dublin life and in displays of linguistic ingenuity.

While Joyce is aware of important differences between classical Greek and Jewish values, he stresses parallels between Odysseus's leading his followers homeward and Moses's leading his people to the Promised Land. While Moses and his people are escaping the enslavement of the Egyptians, Odysseus is enslaved a number of times, most notably by "Circe" and "Calypso". Both are engaged in prolonged arduous journeys, fraught with frustrating setbacks, towards a goal. Both these journeys are "returns" to a world defined by idealized fantasies of what the goal offers – in Odysseus's case, fantasies fed by personal memory but distorted by a need to create a utopian alternative while experiencing frustrating setbacks; in Moses's case, dreams of freedom, justice, and national fulfillment based on the Word of God. In a sense, both Odysseus and Moses anticipate Bloom in their being spurred on not so much by a physical place, but by a state of mind which offers the dream of a life ordered and perfected beyond the possibility of mortal life. That in "Proteus" Stephen thinks of the Homeric "winedark sea" in association with a blood-red sea immediately after he has alluded to the Red Sea ("That man led me, spoke. . . . Come. Red carpet spread. . . . Shouldering their bags they trudged, the red Egyptians. . . . Tides, myriadislanded, within her, blood not mine, *oinopa ponton*, a winedark sea") establishes verbally a link between the two myths which inform Bloom's odyssey – the Greek myth of personal redemption and the Jewish myth of national renewal (U.47; III.367–70, 393–4). Later in "Cyclops", an episode, as we shall see, filled with allusions to the Passover Seder, the anonymous denizen of the bar comically inverts the Passover story when he speaks of the possibility that God would punish Bloom for not standing him to a drink by throwing him into "the bloody sea" (U.338; XII.1662). The bloody sea combines the

Red Sea with the drowning of the Egyptians; the waters closed over them after God had parted the sea so that the Jews could escape.

Although *Ulysses* demonstrates the strong kinship between differing cultures, and the possibility of reconciling apparent cultural differences in personal and historical terms, *Ulysses* is informed by Joyce's distinctions between Greek and Jewish civilizations, distinctions derived from his classical education but generally supported by modern scholarship.[2] For the Greeks, mankind becomes important only when he achieves an heroic aspect. This occurs when an individual is a leader or major figure in great events – such as war or rebellion – that change history or when his deeds or words challenge the gods. Memories of legends of gods and prior heroes shape the decision-making and behavioral patterns of the classical Greek protagonists and their successors. In his obsession with the Christ story and the life of Shakespeare, isn't Stephen Dedalus in this Greek tradition? For the Jews, by contrast, human beings are the supreme beings on earth; they do not share space or focus with Gods or mythical heroes. Human life itself is not only sacred, but the way humans live and behave is an important subject for study. It follows that personal experiences and memories give shape to the lives of individual Jews. Thus Bloom's thoughts, feelings, and motives are shaped by memories of his own and his family's past.

Perhaps the best model for how Joyce regards Bloom can be found in the Jewish legend of the Lamed Vov. According to Schwarz-Bart in *The Last of the Just*, a novel based on this legend:

> The world reposes on thirty-six just men, the Lamed Vov, indistinguishable from simple mortals; often they are unaware of their station. But if just one of them were lacking, the suffering of mankind would poison even the souls of the newborn, and humanity would suffocate with a single cry. For the Lamed Vov are the hearts of the world multiplied, and into them, as into one receptacle, pour all our griefs.[3]

In the legend of the Just Men, God manifests himself through individual deeds of human kindness and justice. Those who, like Alexander J. Dowie, look for God's manifestation in apocalyptic terms are looking for the wrong clues, particularly if they await the condemnation of the Jews as sinners against the light:

"Sinned against the light and even now that day is at hand when he shall come to judge the world by fire" (U.428; XIV.1576–7). The legend of the Just Men depends upon the Jewish concept that all men are equal before God and that divinity can be found within any man; a member of the Lamed Vov can as easily be a humble simple shepherd or a seller of advertisements as a king or prophet. The legend appears in some older texts of the Haggadah, the book of ritual prayer used on the Passover which reiterates the Zionist hope, "next year in Jerusalem", that Bloom is thinking of all day; as we learn in "Ithaca", he possesses an "ancient haggadah book" which he has been reading (U.723; XVII. 1877–8). If one recalls Moses's words in *Deuteronomy* 10:18, one sees a crucial link not only between the legend of the Just Men and Moses, but also between Christ and Moses: "He doth execute justice for the fatherless and widow, and loveth the stranger, in giving him food and raiment. Love ye therefore the stranger; for ye were strangers in the land of Egypt." These words of Moses also remind the reader that the Jewish dream of a restored national destiny includes the dream of the family paradigm. When Bloom is annointed as leader of the "new Bloomusalem" in "Circe", he is at once Moses, Judas Maccabee, and the Messiah returned to rebuild the Temple (U.484; XV.1544).

Wouldn't Joyce have seen the parallels between the legend of the Just Men and the Christ story? Joyce wanted to use the Christ story as a prototype for the divinely human impulse in Bloom. Joyce focused on the humanity of the Christ story; he was interested in what happened to Christ while living as a man after the incarnation that turned the son of God into a man. Antecedents for a human Christ figure would have been found in the realistic depictions of Renaissance paintings. These paintings sometimes go so far as to include evidence of Christ's sexuality; he may possess a penis that has not only been circumcised but is capable of erection.[4] Within Joyce's concept of metaphor, where Bloom is as much a figure for Christ as Christ is for Bloom, the odyssean reader is urged to see Christ as man whose divinity derives from his consummate humanity on earth. We might note that such a humanizing of the Christ story was a persistent theme in early modern British literature, including Hardy's *Jude the Obscure* and Lawrence's *The Man who Died*, as well as in poems by Hardy ("The Oxen", "Near Lanivet") Yeats ("The Magi"), and Eliot ("The Journey of the Magi").

The novel confirms Bloom as "the new Messiah for Ireland" because it confirms him as a Lamed Vov (U.337; XII.1642). Within Bloom's secular, humanistic universe, Bloom is the Just Man who, although unappreciated by his fellows, cares about them and feels for them, even as he thinks of how to improve their lot with his utopian plans. Gradually Bloom emerges as a vessel of humanistic values within the novel. Persecuted by his anti-Semitic audience, Bloom speaks eloquently against the use of force and for his credo of love, tolerance, respect, and justice: "Force, hatred, history, all that. That's not life for men and women, insult and hatred. And everybody knows that it's the very opposite of that that is really life" (U.333; XII.1481–3). When Alf rather stupidly asks "What?", Bloom responds, "Love. . . I mean the opposite of hatred" (U.333; XII.1484–5). For Joyce, Bloom's values represent possible redemption for man in a post-Christian world. To evoke other Jewish traditions, Bloom is for the most part less in the Jewish tradition of *schlemiel*, the kindly buffoon who is his own worst enemy, than of the gentle, well-meaning folk hero who can turn self-acceptance of his lot and even ostensible self-denigration into triumph.

Bloom, as the successor to Moses and Parnell, represents the humane values that will lead Ireland out of its twin bondage to Catholicism and Britain. Bloom thinks of the Haggadah on several other occasions, most notably in "Aeolus" when he thinks of the Passover story in the very same chapter in which Stephen adopts a version of it for his "Parable of the Plums". When in "Nausicaa" Bloom thinks of the house of bondage in more personal terms we realize that despite his metaphorical expansion, he has not solved his personal problems: "Smelling the tail end of ports. . . . And the tephilim no what's this they call it poor papa's father had on his door to touch. That brought us out of the land of Egypt and into the house of bondage" (U.378; XIII.1155–9; in his house of bondage, as we shall see, he is consigned to smelling the tail end.). That Bloom is confused about the traditions he evokes puts the odyssean reader on guard that he should not suspend his own critical judgment of Bloom's claims to heroism. For "tephilim" is a phylactery containing four parts of the Pentateuch. But Bloom has confused "tephilim" with "mezuzah", which is hung over the door and contains twenty-two lines from *Deuteronomy*.

Even as *Ulysses* makes claims for Bloom's heroic stature, it introduces elements of doubt about him. In "Circe", Bloom's program no sooner arouses our expectations that he has the imaginative and intellectual energy to sustain a serious if vague utopian vision, than he bathetically degenerates into a hedonistic and mildly pornographic fantasy that undermines his pretensions to leadership: "Union of all, jew, moslem and gentile. Three acres and a cow for all children of nature. . . . General amnesty, weekly carnival with masked license. . . . Free money, free rent, free love and a free lay church in a free lay state" (U.489–90; XV.1686–7; 1690–93). Within his fantasy, Bloom becomes a buffoon and a sexual athlete prior to his imagining his denunciation. Must we not acknowledge in our account of how *Ulysses* means that at the level of story Bloom at times is inadequate to his intent, as perhaps the most well-meaning of us must be, even while Joyce, at the level of metaphor, is establishing his stature by showing us that he is denounced by discredited and irrelevant figures, including Theodore Purefoy, Alexander J. Dowie, and Dr Mulligan?

Of course, in *Ulysses* the artist is also a potential hero. Joyce shows that words can take the sting out of man's violent impulses. While Bloom's words do not convert the Citizen and his colleagues to pacifism, they have a notable effect on Stephen. Moreover, does not the reader understand that, in place of the violence of prior eras evoked by his allusions, Joyce is proposing that we funnel our passion and energy into making fictions just as Bloom, Stephen, and his voice have done? Does not Joyce's aggression take the form of overturning the vessels of what were the once accepted conventions of literature and of historiography? Joyce wants the reader to understand that imaginative violence, whether it be Joyce's energetic satires or Bloom's eloquent and forceful response to the Yahoos in "Cyclops", leaves no dead and no wounded. His radical metaphors depend on a cyclical view of history that *violently* rejects traditional ways of reading history.

II DANTE'S ULYSSES AND DANTE AS METAPHOR IN JOYCE'S *ULYSSES*

Homer's Ulysses is a domestic figure who longs for home. Dante's Ulysses is confined to Hell because of spiritual pride and intellectual hubris. He has been an evil counsellor who persuaded his comrades to follow him to destruction. He is something of a Faust-like hero seeking knowledge and experience in undiscovered worlds. After returning to their home, Ulysses and his followers sailed westward until they reached a mysterious mountain, the Mount of Purgatory, before suddenly drowning. As he is being led through the *Inferno* by Virgil – the poet of the fall of Troy, the flight of Aeneas, and the founding of Rome, Dante would hardly have been predisposed to admire the man whose intellect had devised the stratagem that led to the Greeks conquering Troy.

For Dante, Ulysses represented the potential of the analytic intelligence for wiliness, deception, and, ultimately, evil. Ulysses explains to Dante and Virgil why he was compelled to resume his travels and turn his back on his family responsibilities: "[N]either fondness for my son, nor reverence for my aged father, nor the due love which would have made Penelope glad, could conquer in me the longing that I had to gain experience of the world, and of human vice and worth."[5] The odyssean reader of *Ulysses* – on whom Joyce often places great demands – is called upon to differentiate between the priorities of Dante's Ulysses and those of Moses in the passage I quoted above from *Deuteronomy*.

In Joyce's novel it is Stephen who is guilty of spiritual pride and who recalls Dante's Ulysses figure. (Is he not also the ill-tempered Achilles of Homer's *Iliad* in contrast to Bloom as Homer's Ulysses?) Stephen inhabits his self-created Inferno. Like Achilles and Hamlet, Dante's Ulysses speaks disdainfully of inaction. W. B. Stanford in *The Ulysses Theme* writes:

> In general Dedalus-Telemachus represents the centrifugal, rebellious, destructive, home-abandoning element in the homo uluxcanus. . . . Like Dante's Ulysses, he will be deterred by no love of family or home from travelling into the unknown world to find new knowledge and experience. Bloom, on the other hand, like the Ulysses of Homer, Shakespeare, and Giraudoux, represents the centripetal, conservative, and constructive element in society. Dedalus rejects and struggles to overthrow; Bloom accepts and tries to improve. Dedalus denies; Bloom affirms. . . . In this way Dedalus marks the

negative pole of the Ulyssean character, Bloom the positive. Between them they encompass the whole cosmos of the tradition.[6]

Dante is a more complex literary father for Joyce than critics have realized. While Joyce self-ironically saw himself as a secular writer saturated with the very Catholicism he would reject, Joyce read Dante as a Catholic writer, who for all his Christian allegorizing, was drawn to human events for their own sake and fascinated by human idiosyncracies. Although Joyce would not have used the same terminology, Joyce would have recognized the validity of Auerbach's argument that Dante, "within the figural pattern brings to life the whole historical world, and, within that, every single human being who crosses his path!"[7] For he is trying to do the same thing in *Ulysses*.

In the section of the *Inferno* in which Ulysses appears, we certainly see the division within Dante's imagination between orthodox Catholicism and what medieval Catholicism would regard as worldliness. Joyce understood that Dante the Catholic poet, the poet whose every word is informed by spiritual values and by a vertical perspective ascending to God in heaven, was nevertheless also drawn to interest in this life and in depicting the all-too-human – as Dante's erotic love poetry shows.

Joyce saw that Dante enacts in his own work something of a struggle between the vertical and horizontal, between interest in the life lived by man and its place in a larger pattern. Joyce's own work has a similar division between the demands of unity and ideology and the claims of local matters – whether of the details of life or the pleasure of stylistic experiment. If Dante is deflected from his focus on larger spiritual issues by his sympathy for human frailty, and perhaps by curiosity about sexuality, to relax the stress on the relation of every human event to the eternality of God, Joyce is deflected from his focus on his larger thematic and formal concerns by the pleasures of both catching a moment of life in Dublin and playing with language; on these occasions, he abandons for a moment his effort to relate every detail to the teleology of the young artist in the process of becoming a creative genius.

The first allusion to Dante is when Stephen – who has paid the rent and knows that Mulligan is about to ask him for the key – angrily invokes the prediction of Dante's exile and bitterness by his great-great grandfather: "I eat his salt bread" (U.20; I.631). It is interesting that the first passage Stephen recalls from the *Inferno* is taken from Dante's description of Aristotle in Canto four: *"maestro di color che sanno"* or "master of all them that know." (*Inf.* 4:131; U.38; III.6–7).[8] The passage seems to endorse an Aristotelian focus on the empirical world: "Ineluctable modality of the visible. . . . Signatures of all things I am here to read" (U.37: III.1–2), and by implication to focus the reader's attention on the linear world of Homer. But *"che sanno"* also carries the implication of analytic learning and "logic-chopping" at the expense of experience. Moreover, as we shall see in "Aeolus", Dante is invoked as a spiritual and allegorical reader of experience; the reader is educated to understand that "Signatures of all things I am here to read" includes a lesson for the reader on how to read the metaphoric possibilities of literary allusions.

Dante functions as a metaphor in Stephen's mind for the poet who captured the essence of the civilization in which he lived. Stephen would have Dante play the same role for him as Virgil did for Dante. The headline in the passage of "Aeolus", in which Stephen quotes Dante is entitled "RHYMES AND REASONS" to suggest that Dante is the artist who masters his form and his subjects (U.138; VII.713). His mastery includes the subject of human sexuality which Stephen – who sees art and sex as metaphors for one another – needs to understand before he can create major work. Thinking of the rhymes of the poem he is writing ("mouth, south" [U.138; VII.714]), Stephen quotes phrases from the fifth canto of the *Inferno* which illustrate Dante's terza rima:

. . . la tua pace
. . . che parlar ti piace
mentrechè il vento, come fa, si tace. (U.138; VII.717–8)

. . . thy peace
. . . if thee to speak it please,
while the wind, as now, for us doth cease. (Stephen is quoting from *Inferno*: 5: 92, 94, 96. While the above phrases are Reynolds' translation, Singleton translates the full passage as follows: "Of that which it pleases you to hear and to speak, we will hear and speak with you, while the wind, as now, is silent for us.")[9]

Stephen quotes from the *Inferno* because, until he can make progress in fulfilling his ambition to assume Dante's mantle of the epic poet, he will continue to inhabit the hell of his own mind. Stephen is recalling an early passage from Francesca da Rimini's tale of her adulterous love with her husband's brother, Paolo. Since her husband murders the pair *in flagrante delicto* and cuts them off in their moment of adulterous passion from the possibility of repentance, they must suffer eternal damnation. Just as the winds of Hell – an appropriate image for "Aeolus", Homer's Cave of Winds – must cease for Francesca to deliver her parable about sexual excess, so Stephen must still the windy historical babble and the internal winds of guilt and self-doubt, before he can deliver his political "Parable of the Plums".

According to Francesca, it was *reading* the Lancelot story that inflamed her and her lover's passions. Thus Joyce uses Francesca's tale to imply the importance of reading in the very passage of which Stephen's powerful reading of Dante is the focus. Dante is addressing the very subject of adulterous sexuality which is the subject of *Ulysses*, the epic that the mature Joyce is telling. Just as the Lancelot story is a powerful text for Francesca and Paolo, and as Dante's *Inferno* is a strong text for Stephen, so, too, *Ulysses* is meant to be such an overwhelming text for its readers. And, indeed, to the rereader of *Ulysses* the violence of Francesca's husband looks far more culpable; for it strikingly contrasts with the "equanimity" and "abnegation" which control Bloom's "envy" and "jealousy" in response to Molly's adultery with Blazes (U.732; XVIII.2155). As Reynolds has noted, the contrast is stressed by a suggestion of the above passage in "Sirens", the chapter in which Bloom is most aware of his position as a cuckold because it takes place as Blazes leaves for Molly's house: "Through the hush of air a voice sang to them, low, not rain, not leaves in murmur, like no voice of strings or reeds or whatdoyoucallthem dulcimers touching their still ears with words, still hearts of their each his remembered lives" (U.273; XI.674–7).[10] Thus Joyce is not merely shaping how we read *Ulysses*, but how we read Dante.

Stephen thinks of the terza rima as three brightly dressed girls: "He saw them three by three, approaching girls, in green, in rose, in russet, entwining" (U.138: VII.720–1). Stephen's innocent vision is an unconscious attempt to wrench the subject of sexuality from Francesca's perverse tale of incestuous adultery. Thus he shifts his focus within the very next paragraph from Francesca's story of adultery and the brutal murder of her lover and herself by her husband to a recollection of Dante's vision of the Virgin Mary: *"quella pacifica oriafiamma, gold of oriflammme, di rimirar fè più ardenti"* (U.138; VII.721–2). This shift also implies that Stephen is progressing towards understanding, like Dante and his creator, both the inextricable relation and the inherent discrepancy between story – or the "reason" of art – and "rhyme" or the significant pattern of art. The mixture of the divine and the all-too-human also anticipates Molly who combines aspects of both Francesca and the Virgin Mary in herself. Doesn't Bloom worship Molly the way that Dante worships Beatrice, his Virgin Mary figure? (Molly recalls "his mad crazy letters my Precious one everything connected with your glorious Body everything underlined that comes from it is a thing of beauty and of joy for ever" [U.771; XVIII.1176–8]).

The vision of Rudy, the reward for Bloom's love, is a necessary preparation for his return to Molly, his eternal Beatrice figure. Ultimately, Molly's affirmation is the reward for his humanistic faith. Her "Yes" is the eternal "yes" of passionate, sexual love – the love that for Joyce was the highest form of love. Thus *Ulysses* is Joyce's response to *The Divine Comedy*, and his stress is on the comedy of human life – on the comedy of all of us who fruitlessly seek some form of permanence in religion or art or spiritualized love, but whose lives consist mostly of drab reality that is offered by the day to day events of passing time. In response to Dante's grand eternal scheme, Joyce demonstrates how life is lived by the denizens of Dublin on the one single day of 16 June 1904.

Joyce, then, invokes Dante as a model for the figurative reading that his novel requires. Unlike Homer and Shakespeare, Dante's world view is shaped by the Roman Catholic epistemology – and, more precisely, the philosophy of Aquinas – in which Joyce was educated, and in which most of his Irish audience was immersed. Thus it was important that Joyce's humanistic testament come to terms with Dante's example and create an alternative to his values. Isn't Joyce's three part structure a way of paying homage to Dante's influence? Indeed, one could argue that the first six chapters climaxing in Bloom's escape from Hell correspond to *Inferno*, that the middle chapters climaxing in Stephen's and Bloom's purgative visions of "Circe" correspond to *Purgatorio*, and that the last three chapters focusing on the union of Stephen and Bloom, of Bloom and Molly, and ultimately of all three major figures, correspond to *Paradiso*.

III   PARNELL AS METAPHOR

Joyce proposes Bloom as a substitute for Charles Stewart Parnell, the Irish nationalist and the political leader of the Irish Parliamentary party, who became known as "The Uncrowned King of Ireland". When Parnell's affair with Katherine O'Shea was revealed in O'Shea's divorce suit, he was deserted by many of his followers and he was deposed as leader of the Irish Parliamentary delegation. After Parnell died prematurely at the age of forty-five, rumours abounded that he was not really dead and would return. Joyce identified with Parnell as a figure of exceptional brilliance and ability whose merit was finally unappreciated by the Irish people. In a short piece (written originally in Italian) entitled "The Shade of Parnell" (1912), he wrote:

> The ghost of the "uncrowned king" will weigh on the hearts of those who remember him when the new Ireland in the near future enters into the palace . . . but it will not be a vindictive ghost . . .
> In his final desperate appeal to his countrymen, he begged them not to throw him as a sop to the English wolves. . . . They did not throw him to the English wolves; they tore him to pieces themselves.[11]

In "Ireland, Island of Saints and Sages" (1907), Joyce wrote: "[T]o deny the name of patriot to all those who are not of Irish stock would be to deny it almost to all the heroes of the modern movement – Lord Edward Fitzgerald, Robert Emmet,. Theobald Wolfe Tone . . . and, finally, Charles Steward Parnell, who was perhaps the most formidable man that ever led the Irish, but in whose veins there was not even a drop of Celtic blood."[12] By referring frequently to Parnell, by hinting at Bloom's involvement in political affairs, and, most of all, by having Bloom think of Parnell quite often, Joyce arouses our expectations that Parnell is a prefiguration of Bloom. Like Bloom, Parnell did not have Irish blood. But we feel that these expectations are only partly fulfilled and that a gap remains between Parnell as metaphorical vehicle or signifier and Bloom as metaphorical tenor or signified. An important part of reading *Ulysses* is our perceiving and experiencing these gaps between signifier and signified; they often take the form of proposals of potential relationships that are tested and either discarded or only partially confirmed.

The presence of Parnell hovers over the text. Among other things the obscure answer to the riddle in "Nestor", containing an allusion to Parnell's alias "Mr Fox", is a comic version of a biblical parable which can be interpreted any way one chooses. In the same chapter Deasy recalls, "A woman too brought Parnell low" (U.35; II.394). In "Hades", the funeral procession not only follows the approximate route of Parnell's funeral procession, but it brings Bloom to Parnell's grave: "Foundation stone for Parnell. Breakdown. Heart" (U.95; VI.320).[13] In a sense, when Bloom descends to Hell, he sees the ghost of his predecessor.

As Raleigh notes, in the hallucination at Bella Cohen's, "Bloom reenacts Parnell's career in a political fantasy, climbing to the top amidst cries of ecstatic admiration from his constituency only to fall with that same constituency heaping execrations upon him."[14] In that hallucination, when Bloom imagines himself as the leader of "the new Bloomusalem", John Howard Parnell, Parnell's very much less distinguished brother who still lived in Dublin in 1904, introduces Bloom as "Illustrious Bloom! Successor to my famous brother!" (U.483; XV.1513–14). At first he is applauded by onlookers, but very soon, like Parnell, he is denounced as a threat to Catholicism; according to Father Farley, Bloom "is an episcopalian, an agnostic, an anything-arian seeking to overthrow our holy faith" (U.490; XV.1712–13). The Mob cries: "Lynch him! Roast him! He's as bad as Parnell was. Mr Fox" (U.492; XV.1762). When the crowd of observers divides into Bloomites and anti-Bloomites and enters into a hyperbolic partisan debate on his merits, Joyce has in mind the division between Parnellites and anti-Parnellites. The leader of anti-Bloomites is Alexander J. Dowie, whom the reader recognizes as the Fundamentalist Christian leader whom Bloom is replacing as the Elijah figure: "Fellowchristians and antiBloomites, the man called Bloom is from the roots of hell, a disgrace to christian men" (U.492; XV.1753–4).

Joyce's serious point is that Bloom's secular humanism – with its sense of decency, emphasis on family relationships, toleration, bravery, and its vague socialism and even vaguer international- ism – represents a real alternative for Dublin, if only the Irish were perceptive enough to notice. The snarling Thersites figure in "Cyclops" reports the view of John Wyse that "it was Bloom gave the ideas for Sinn Fein to Griffith to put in his paper all kinds of jerrymandering, packed juries and swindling the taxes off of the government and appointing consuls all over the world to walk about selling Irish industries" (U.335–6; XII.1574–7). Molly recalls that Bloom "was going about with some of them Sinner Fein lately or whatever they call themselves talking his usual trash and nonsense he says that little man he showed me without the neck is very intelligent the coming man Griffiths" (U.748; XVIII.383–6). It should be recalled that Griffith's prog- ram for *Sinn Fein,* which means "Ourselves Alone" in Gaelic, emphasized not violence but the kind of passive resistance that is identified with Bloom in "Cyclops", (Specifically, Griffith pro- posed that the Irish refuse to pay taxes ad advocated that the Irish delegation refuse to attend Parliament; as Gifford and Seidman put it, "The *Sinn Fein* policy advocated that the Irish should refuse economic and political support to English institu- tions and should create their own political and economic institu- tions, whether or not the English were willing to recognize them as constitutional."[15]

When Joyce linked Parnell and Moses in "The Shade of Parnell", he spoke of Parnell as "another Moses, [who] led a turbulent and unstable people from the house of shame to the verge of the Promised Land".[16] It was common to associate the plight of the Irish under the English with the Israelites in bondage in Egypt. Like Moses, Parnell saw the promised land – Ireland as an independent nation – but was not permitted to enter it. Indeed, the metaphor in which the lost tribes of Israel are a figure for Ireland is the source of much of the windy rhetoric in "Aeolus", rhetoric for which Stephen's succinct and pointed "Parable of the Plums" is a response. Just as Moses is a prefiguration of Christ, Parnell is a fulfillment of the pattern of betrayal of the heroic figure typified by Christ. But in Joyce's mind the betrayal of Parnell also prefigured what he regarded as the continuing Irish betrayal of himself. In *My Brother's Keeper,* Stanislaus Joyce wrote: "One of the tragedies that obsessed my brother's imagination, beginning from the time when he first understood the Mass as drama, was the tragedy of dedication and betrayal. In later life, the story of Parnell became for him another aspect of the tragedy."[17]

Comically playing upon the biblical typology in which the Old Testament is read as an anticipation of the New, Joyce predicts the arrival of a putative replacement for Parnell. Indeed, on the very page when Bloom crosses the path of Parnell's brother, Joyce playfully teases the reader with Bloom's oracular: "Coming events cast their shadows before" (U.165; VIII.526). But also an important part of the novel's serious political theme is the chronological relation between the pacifist Bloom, representing the possibilities of the future, and the militant Parnell, representing the lost opportunities of the past. Within Irish history, Parnell, representing the Old Dispensation in the form of a somewhat parochial Irish nationalism which sees the need for confrontation, stands to the Old Testament as Bloom, representing internationalism, compromise, and ultimately love, stands to the New Testament. In "Oxen of the Sun", the ventriloquistic voice adopts the style of the King James Bible to speak of the betrayal of Bloom, the potential Moses figure, by an adulterous wife in terms that suggest echoes of Moses's reproach to the people of Israel before he ascends to the top of Pisgah: "Remember, Erin, thy generations and thy days of old, how thou settedst little by me and by my word and broughtedst in a stranger to my gates to commit fornification in my sight and to wax fat and kick like Jeshurum. Therefore hast thou sinned against my light and hast made me, thy lord, to be the slave of servants" (U.393; XIV.367–71). But the jeremiad also recalls the accusations brought against Parnell and anticipates those to be brought in "Circe" against Bloom during his fantasies of leadership and subsequent denunciation.

Within the novel Bloom combines the best of Parnell and Griffith. Although Bloom admires the charismatic and impulsive Parnell's techniques, his own personality and values seem closer to Arthur Griffith's: "[N]o go in him for the mob" (U.1641; VIII.462–3). Like Griffith, Bloom eschews violence and espouses reason. Indeed, when he meets Parnell's brother in "Lestrygonians", he is critical of Parnell's manipulative and intolerant personality: "His brother used men as pawns. Let them all go to pot. Afraid to pass a remark on him. Freeze them up with that eye of his" (U.165; VIII.511–13).

When, in "Cyclops", the romance-epic voice presents the crucifixion and subsequent trial of the malefactor, he not only anticipates how Bloom is treated and the hallucinations that derive from that treatment, but he has in mind, his Irish audience would have realized, the treatment Parnell had received. The speaker alludes to the fact that, before Parnell was buried, his body lay at night in St. Michan's Church: "There sleep the mighty dead as in life they slept, warriors and princes of high renown" (U.293; XII.69–70). That the Citizen and the speaker refer to Parnell focuses our attention on the political implications of Bloom's behaviour and his possibilities as the New Messiah of Ireland.

Joyce is very much aware of the historical irony that the paper, *The Irish Daily Independent* – the paper that Parnell planned on founding after the *Freeman's Journal* but which did not begin publication until he was mortally ill – soon passed into the hands of those opposing Parnell and eventually was owned by William Martin Murphy; Murphy broke a newspaper strike by locking out employees and thereby enshrined himself as the villain of Yeats's poem "September 1913". Because of the central role that newspapers played in Irish political history, the most public chapter in the book's first half takes place in a newspaper office. Griffith founded the weekly *United Irishman* which later became *Sinn Fein*. That the "Aeolus" chapter with its windy and ineffectual rhetoric takes place at the *Freeman's Journal*, the newspaper that for a long time did vigorously support Parnell is, of course, ironic.[18]

In the section of "Eumaeus" where Bloom is being proposed as a metaphoric version of Parnell, Joyce introduces the concept of metaphoricity into Bloom's delicious memory of his triumph in "Cyclops":

[Bloom], though often considerably misunderstood and the least pugnacious of mortals, be it repeated, departed from his customary habit to give him (metaphorically) one in the gizzard though, so far as politics themselves were concerned, he was only too conscious of the casualties invariably resulting from propaganda and displays of mutual animosity and the misery and suffering it entailed as a foregone conclusion on fine young fellows, chiefly, destruction of the fittest, in a word, (U.657; XVI.1595–602)

Joyce endorses Bloom's use of reason and eloquence as the tools of his pugnacity; in "The Shade of Parnell", he has praised Parnell for these very same qualities, although he also admired Parnell's willingness to move to more forceful forms of protest.[19]

The garrulous proprietor of the cabmen's shelter may be Skin-the-Goat Fitzharris who was a member of the Invincibles, a violent splinter group of the Fenians; the Invincibles were dedicated to assassinating members of the British government and were responsible in 1882 for the Phoenix Park murders. Fitzharris, or as is more likely, the person posing as him, invokes the spirit of Parnell with what may be a bogus quotation to support his own prophecy of England's decline: "His advice to every Irishman was: stay in the land of your birth and work for Ireland and live for Ireland. Ireland, Parnell said, could not spare a single one of her sons" (U.640; XVI.1006–9). By having different people quote Parnell to their own purposes, just as people appropriate Christ's teachings to support their views, isn't Joyce showing how Parnell has become a historical messianic figure? The apocryphal Skin-the-Goat's prophecy is a comic version of prefiguration: "One morning you would open the paper, the cabman [Skin-the-Goat] affirmed, and read: *Return of Parnell.* . . . Dead he wasn't" (U.648; <u>XVI.1297–8</u>, 1304). That Bloom is more expert on Parnell than one of the Invincibles helps establish his credentials as a patriot: "Highly unlikely of course there was even a shadow of truth in the stones and, even supposing, he thought a return highly inadvisable, all things considered" (U.649; <u>XVI.1310–2</u>; Gabler's change from "stories to "stones" is an example of textual editing at the expense of critical sensitivity).

The circumlocutious and clichéd style of "Eumaeus" undermines not only the authority of Fitzharris, but also that of Bloom. The style intrudes between Bloom as signified and Parnell as signifier. But so does the story, for how can Bloom be a successor to Parnell if he has no political program? Even if Bloom does have a vision of agrarian socialism, he presents his ideas in terms of waffling qualifications and hesitations that undermine the thrust of his views: "For instance when the evicted tenants question, then at its first inception, bulked largely in people's mind though, it goes without saying, not contributing a copper or pinning his faith absolutely to its dictums, some of which wouldn't exactly hold water, he at the outset in principle at all events was in thorough sympathy with peasant possession . . . (a partiality, however, which, realising his mistake, he was subsequently partially cured of)" (U.656–57; XVI.1585–91).

Bloom felt a human affinity with Parnell on the one occasion when he had met him: "He saw him once on the auspicious occasion when they broke up the type in the *Insuppressible* or was it *United Ireland*, a privilege he keenly appreciated, and, in point of fact, handed him his silk hat when it was knocked off and he said *Thank you*" (U.649–50; XVI.1333–6). Bloom's experience of Parnell's flesh – "He, B, enjoyed the distinction of being close to Erin's uncrowned king in the flesh" [U.654; XVI.1495–6] – anticipates Stephen's experiencing Bloom as "a strange kind of flesh of a different man" [U.660; XVI.1723–4]). He recalls John Henry Menton's quite different "thank you" for a similar favour at the end of "Hades": "[Parnell] thanked him with perfect *aplomb*, saying: *Thank you, sir*, though in a very different tone of voice from the ornament of the legal profession whose headgear Bloom also set to rights earlier in the course of the day, history repeating itself with a difference" (U.655; XVI.1522–6). Notice how the second reminiscence embroiders the original one as if to call attention to history repeating itself with a difference. That Bloom thinks of historical repetition in relation to Parnell calls attention to Bloom's role as Parnell's putative successor. But that he acknowledges the "difference" in similar events calls attention to the gap between himself as historically determined signified and Parnell – as well as Odysseus, Shakespeare, and Elijah – as historically determining signifiers.

NOTES

1. C. C. Peake, *James Joyce: the Citizen and the Artist*, p. 125.
2. Joyce knew perfectly well that his effort to reconcile the classical and Hebraic cultures flouted Arnold's distinctions in *Culture and Anarchy* between Hebraism and Hellenism.
3. Schwarz-Bart, André *The Last of the Just*, trans. Stephen Becker (New York: Atheneum, 1961).
4. See Leo Steinberg, *The Sexuality of Christ in Renaissance Art and Modern Oblivion* (New York: Pantheon, 1984).
5. *Inferno*, 26:91–7; quoted by Mary T. Reynolds, *Joyce and Dante: the*

Shaping Imagination (Princeton University Press, 1981) p. 186. I am indebted to Reynolds' work on Dante and Joyce; I follow her in using the Singleton translation.

6. W. B. Stanford, *The Ulysses Theme* (Oxford: Blackwell, 1954) p. 215; this passage is also quoted by Reynolds, p. 186.

7. Erich Auerbach, *Mimesis: the Representation of Reality in Western Literature*, trans. Willard Trask (Princeton University Press, 1953) p. 176.

8. See Gifford and Seidman, p. 33.

9. See Reynolds, p. 87; the Singleton translation is quoted in Reynolds, p. 104.

10. See Reynolds, p. 104.

11. *The Critical Writings of James Joyce*, ed. Ellsworth Mason and Richard Ellmann (New York: Viking, 1959) p. 228.

12. *The Critical Writings of James Joyce*, p. 162.

13. John Henry Raleigh, *A Chronicle of Leopold and Molly Bloom* (University of California Press, 1971) p. 119.

14. See Raleigh, p. 119.

15. Gifford and Seidman, p. 136.

16. *The Critical Writings of James Joyce*, p. 225.

17. Stanislaus Joyce, *My Brother's Keeper: James Joyce's 'Early Years'*, ed. Richard Ellmann (London & New York, 1958).

18. I am indebted to Gifford and Seidman for much of the historical material in this paragraph.

19. See *The Critical Writings of James Joyce*, p. 226.

3 The Odyssey of Reading *Ulysses*

I THE NARRATOR'S ODYSSEY

In his quest for meaning, the fictionalized Joyce – the speaker and writer of the events within the imagined world – becomes an Odysseus figure within the novel. While Odysseus goes from place to place, Joyce goes from style to style. By temporarily assigning characters to a position of marginality, Joyce is calling attention to himself as creative presence and showing how the imagined world is dependent upon his language. Moreover, he is implying that, because the modern, urban post-Christian world lacks order and coherence, his modern epic must not only be somewhat incomplete and inconclusive, but must present indeterminate and ambiguous passages to the reader.

For Joyce, no one perspective could represent or do justice to the diversity of plausible views of reality. Thus he required multiple perspectives to create what he calls – borrowing a term from mathematics to describe how the same object can look different if perceived from different places – parallax. Ellmann has pointed out the importance to Joyce of Bruno, who emphasized the kinship of opposites.[1] Bruno also believed that because our perception of the world is a function of our spatial–temporal locus, we cannot postulate absolute truth. (Joyce also would have identified with Bruno as a brilliant man who was burned at the stake for heresy.) As Wolfgang Iser has remarked, "Joyce wanted to bring out, if not actually overcome, the inadequacy of style as regards the presentation of reality, by constant changes of style. For only by showing up the relativity of each form could he expose the intangibility and expansibility of observable reality."[2]

Because Joyce did subscribe to the possibility of an authoritative view of reality, he was wary of the traditional omniscient narrator. Yet he does not completely abandon the traditional omniscient voice until he establishes, in the first nine chapters, the importance of his major characters, Bloom and Stephen. At that point he begins to create styles that mock and undermine Bloom, only to show that Bloom's humanity triumphs over the parodic style, just as Bloom triumphs over the belligerence and abuse of the Dubliners he encounters throughout the day, most notably in "Cyclops".

I am taking issue with Karen Lawrence who has recently contended in *The Odyssey of Style in 'Ulysses'*: "[*Ulysses*] ceases to be primarily a psychological novel and becomes an encyclopedia of narrative possibilities".[3] I shall argue that Joyce always returns from his fascination with stylistic innovation to focus on his characters. The effect of the centripetal role of character and action is to dramatize within his teller the triumph of his interest in man's morals and psyche over his interest in rhetorical and stylistic *tours de force*. Certainly, his interest in verisimilitude is implicit in his desire to create an imagined world which is a facsimile of the real one: "I want . . . to give a picture of Dublin so complete that if the city one day suddenly disappeared from the earth it could be reconstructed out of my book."[4] At times the very interest in the details of the Dublin landscape and in the quirks of his characters' local perceptions deflect him from the novel's evolving patterns of significance.

Indeed, even in the chapters with the most interest in style, the form – what is now being called "discourse" as opposed to content or "story" – increasingly focuses upon the significance of the action. The novel enacts in its choices of themes, subject matter, and climaxes to chapters the fundamental anthropocentricism and humanism of its protagonist, Bloom. With its multiplicity of facts, Joyce tests the alternative that the modern world will produce a novel that will resist our capacity for order. But he shows us that we need not assimilate all facts into one pattern to make sense of human actions. With its parody of styles, *Ulysses* questions the very potential of language and narrative to render motives, values, and external reality. If, as Lawrence maintains, "The play of the text begins to exceed the form of the novel it contains", and if "the text opens up to include other formal and stylistic possibilities besides those traditionally used in the novel, as well as details that deliberately flout the idea of coherent plot", nonetheless the novel's principles of order and significance continually reassert control in a dialectical process that itself becomes part of reading the novel.[5]

Finally, Joyce's own narrativity triumphs over the possibility of disorder, fragmentation, and incoherence. But when Lawrence asserts in her fine discussion of "Sirens" that "the deliberately oblique treatment of the action functions as a strategy for capturing the pain being repressed", isn't she acknowledging that it is unlikely that the novel's reader will allow, as she would have it, "the drama of the writing *to usurp* the dramatic action?"[6]

Lawrence has defined the normative style as a "literate, formal, poetic language" that not only in the first three chapters presents the external reality through "Stephen's poetic and melancholy perceptions of things", but that "exists independently in subsequent chapters": "In the first eleven chapters of *Ulysses*, this narrative style establishes the empirical world of the novel; it provides stability and continuity. . . . It is a style that orients the reader and offers him a certain security by establishing the sense of the solidity of external reality."[7] In support of this position, she cites such sentences as the following from "Wandering Rocks": "The young woman with slow care detached from her light skirt a clinging twig" (U.231; X.440–1). But this style also struggles with what might be called the significant style which insists on weaving a pattern to show that "Coming events cast their shadows before" and that "Every word is so deep" (U.165, 76; VIII.526; V.206.)

Lawrence believes that this normative style "[with] its seeming fidelity to the details of both the thoughts and actions of the characters . . . *its* precision and fastidiousness", persists as a factor until 'Cyclops'".[8] But what Lawrence fails to see is the relationship of this style to the constantly evolving voice. It is closer to the truth to say that what *Ulysses* has is not a normative style, but something that approximates a normative presence. Yet the very term "normative" is misleading in reference to *Ulysses* because it implies a stability within the imagined world that belies the speaker's continuing quest for an appropriate style. Part of our experience in reading the novel is perceiving the varying ironic distance between, on one hand, his moral and spiritual values and the characters's attitudes and, on the other, between his aesthetic values and the various styles and forms he assumes. The ironic distance between voice and character is the fundamental formal relationship of the traditional novel, but an ironic relationship between voice and style is more unusual.

While such an ironic relationship is occasionally used by Thackeray and Dickens, it usually depends on a clearly established normative style. By contrast, what Lawrence thinks of as a normative style is itself often viewed ironically by Joyce as the poetic language of a precocious but somewhat pretentious artist who has not found his subject.

If we ground our approach in the narrative presence rather than the chameleonic and elusive concept of style, we can better account for the protean quality of the reading experience. Thus, in contrast to Lawrence's vague remark that in "Aeolus", the headlines "seem to rise unbidden . . . from an unknown source", we have the more empirically reasonable explanation that the source of the headlines is Joyce's speaker, the Janus figure who lives within the imagined world, whose reports are directed to an implied audience of readers who exist in a world beyond the novel.[9] Surely it makes more sense to say that it is the speaker's written ventriloquy that is providing comic comments – or ironic headlines – in the form of newspaper headlines on the action.

II THE READER'S ODYSSEY

Stephen must grow into the artist who will write the national epic of Ireland, an epic which will draw upon the European tradition of *The Odyssey*, and be shaped, as *Ulysses* is, by "The moral idea . . . the sense of destiny" that according to Haines – who, in this case, offers views which although oversimplified echo Joyce's – is lacking in Irish myth (U.249; X.1083).

But Joyce must create readers for that epic. If the result of the action of *Ulysses* is to enable a more mature and gifted Stephen-Joyce to write *Ulysses*, the result of reading *Ulysses* is to enable us to become consubstantial with the plenitude of Joycean voices. The variety, inventiveness, and energy of each chapter illustrate the delight of the dramatized presence in the fabric of life and his joy in the possibilities of language. The infinite variety of his language combines with his historical and literary range to sustain our interest, despite the rather paltry and inconsequential action. For that voice reveals the portrait of the artist as the father of the human race, containing within himself "all in all in

all of us" (U.213; IX.1049–50). To Joyce, not only the Irish but
all of us have lost our way. The reader is the object of Joyce's
artistry, the figure who must be restored to his imagination and
to humanistic values.

If, as Stephen proposes, "Paternity may be a legal fiction",
perhaps we as readers can become the sons of the artist, "the son
consubstantial with the father" (U.207,197; IX.844,481). Put
another way, the reader is the Holy Ghost who must complete
the Trinity of Bloom as Father and Stephen as Son. The reader
participates in the expansion of Bloom's significance as well as in
his occasional deflation. Thus Joyce momentarily opens the
imagined world of his book to include us, as when he concludes
the "Hades" section with "How grand we are this morning!"
(U.115; VI.1033; the exclamation point in the Gabler Edition
emphasizes the exhilaration of both Bloom and his creator.) The
"we" includes the narrative presence – the portrait of the artist
as an epical voice – who is enjoying his *tour de force* of equating
Bloom's moods with the traditional epic descent into hell as he
progresses through the cemetery while at Paddy Dignam's funeral. But the "we" also includes the reader who has accompan-
ied Bloom on his depressing journey, and learned to share
Bloom's kindly, humane way of reading life in contrast to
Stephen's. The reader may even have seen parallels between the
frustrations and anxieties of Bloom's life as a lonely man in the
modern city and his own. This sharing makes all the more
effective and moving Bloom's ebullient affirmation of life, an
affirmation that is informed by his devotion to Molly: "Plenty to
see and hear and feel yet. Feel live warm beings near
you. . . . Warm beds: warm fullblooded life" (U.115; VI.1003–5).
(In "Calypso", does not his memory of her warmth in bed help
him overcome depression: "Be near her ample bedwarned flesh.
Yes, yes" [U.61; IV.238–91])?

We must read *Ulysses*, as we read other novels, in a linear or
chronologically progressive way, as we make our way though the
eighteen discrete yet tightly interrelated episodes. Yet *Ulysses*
must also be perceived in spatial terms. For one thing, the
eighteen episodes are held together, as if they were eighteen stars
in a constellation, in a spatial configuration by what we may call
the magnetism of significance. These episodes cohere into an
epic of one day in Ireland whose theme is the repetitious and
cyclical nature of human experience as well as a fictionalized

version of Joyce's life. For another, each episode – indeed, each scene – needs to be understood as the centerpoint of a series of concentric circles that move outward from the radial center of 16 June, 1904 to the several historical and literary contexts. Usually the most immediate circles surrounding a scene are the Homeric, biblical (the New Testament and, most prominently from the Old Testament, the stories of Elijah and Moses), and Shakespearean parallels; the middle circles are often from Dante, Yeats, and Irish political history and mythology; and the outer, less crucial circles, are from Milton, Blake, Swift, and Wilde. But, at any given point, the closest circles might be from any of the above sources, and indeed, on occasion, from some not mentioned above.

The reader of *Ulysses* must be willing to abandon his reliance on, to borrow terms from Stephen Jay Gould, "logical and sequential thinking" and depend instead upon "a kind of global, intuitive" or "integrative" insight.[10] *Ulysses* educates us to avoid reading in a reductionist sequential way and invites us to see the totality of the situation in Dublin and the evolving relationship between Bloom and Stephen, even when they are not together physically in the same place or present in the same chapter.

Ulysses also educates us to realize that passages need not signify something about empirical reality but can, like movements in a ballet or ingredients of a collage, signify in terms of their own radical juxtaposition. The odyssean reader can neither abandon plot or chronology, nor depend upon it as an ordering principle. Nor can he always depend upon myth or prior literary works to order his perceptions. Sometimes, he must negotiate a passage without penetrating beyond its surface level and must experience the inability to understand the mysterious and the unknown. But the compensation is our experience of a dazzling display of linguistic inventiveness and enjoyment of an imagined world where language itself becomes, like musical notes or brush strokes, the focus of interest. Yet the striking effects of Joyce's non-mimetic language depends on our expectations that the language will be imitative of a prior reality. Finally, our reading depends on defining the originality of experience in response to the traditional reading skills we bring to it. By invoking and parodying prior texts, Joyce's art continually turns our attention to our prior reading.

In a sense each major work includes its own ideology of

reading which the reader inculcates as he moves from page to page and episode to episode. That Joyce from the outset resolves the seemingly disparate elements of his imagination – including his characters' sometimes disjointed perceptual experience and the stylistic fragments with which he renders that experience – into unified chapters and patterns educates the reader to expect that Stephen and Bloom, seemingly on disparate paths, will serendipitously meet and that their meeting will have significance. Just as Bloom overcomes the patronizing styles in "Cyclops" and "Nausicaa", so the reader overcomes the digressions and indeterminate moments in the text to establish patterns of meaning.

III   THE HEROIC READER

The role of the reader in making sense of the novel is crucial to the form of *Ulysses*. For the possibility of meaning in the modern world is one of Joyce's major subjects. In the modern world there are no epic heroes; nor are there omniscient narrators who consistently and reliably provide translucent summaries of the characters' thoughts for the readers. Imperfect readers, like imperfect heroes, try as best they can to make sense of what they experience.

Given the difficulty of the novel and its allusive and elusive texture, can we not say that the novel depends upon an heroic reader who boldly insists that the text be a dialogue between himself and the speaker rather than a monologue? Joyce's dialogue with his reader is very much part of the form. Haines's dream in "Telemachus", Stephen's riddle in "Nestor", and the "Parable of the Plums" in "Aeolus" call attention to the activity of interpreting and structurally stress the continuity between perceiving and reading. At times, Joyce will use a phrase both to describe the action or to characterize the person in whose mind the phrase appears and to self-consciously address the reader. Take, for example, Bloom's memory of his father's reading the Bible – "Every word is so deep, Leopold" or his thought when seeing AE a second time: "Coming events cast their shadow before" (U.76, 165; V.206, VIII.526). The narrative code of Joyce's art depends upon a perspicacious reader whose retentive mind moves backwards and forwards, weaving the connections he discovers into the pattern of his narrative.

Figuring out the mysteries of the text becomes a kind of heroism. Like the narrative presence who is rewriting Stephen from the retrospective vantage point, like the characters who rewrite their lives everyday (but particularly on this crucial day of 16 June, 1904), the reader is weaving and unweaving only to reweave his or her own image of both the novel and – to the extent that the novel is a significant event in his or her life – of himself or herself. As readers of *Ulysses*, are we not often in the position of the baffled students who hear Stephen's virtually insoluble riddle and the bizarre answer in "Nestor"? But gradually, as we become more sympathetic with Stephen's character and more savvy about reading and rereading *Ulysses*, we become more responsive than those who hear his "Parable of the Plums" in "Aeolus" and than Stephen's listeners to his theory of Shakespeare and the artist in "Scylla and Charybdis".

What Guiseppe Mazzatto has written about *The Divine Comedy*, one of Joyce's important literary sources, is also true of *Ulysses*: "*The Divine Comedy* dramatizes in a fundamental way the activity of interpretation; it recounts the efforts of the poet–exegete to read the book of the world."[11] The role of pilgrim-spectator – the role of the man who will read the "Signatures of all things" – that Dante assigns to himself as he accompanies his guide Virgil is divided in *Ulysses* among Stephen, Bloom, and the narrator. But, in another sense, the reader, guided by the narrator-guide who shows him the mindscape of Dublin and the modern city as well as the possibilities for renewal, and faced with the nearly insuperable task of interpreting the fragments of experience and the experiments and the eccentricities of the language with which the narrator–guide renders those signatures, is both pilgrim and spectator.

To be sure, reading *Ulysses* is easier for an experienced and adventurous reader who has negotiated the perils of difficult modern texts before beginning this most challenging of reading journeys. But what the novel *requires* is a mature, open-minded, wily reader who can face challenges with humour, seriousness, humanity, and integrity; in other words, the book requires a reader who has many of Bloom's virtues. Like Odysseus and Bloom, the reader of *Ulysses* must combine innocence and experience as well as reason and imagination. The reader must maintain his sense of humour and capacity for wonder as well as a sense of openness to adventure, while retaining his patience, tolerance, and mature judgment. The heroic reader is, like all of Joyce's heroes, the butt of his irony. He is a Ulyssean figure, a wanderer wending his way through the shoals of the text and trying to organize the material into meaningful patterns, even while often being baffled by the plethora of details and the abstruse nature of some of the references. The possibility of being caught in the entangled web of half-sense and nonsense constantly faces him; his capacity to read and understand is continually challenged. Threatened with entanglement in Joyce's web of confusion, a web that recalls Mino's confinement of Daedalus and Icarus in the very labyrinth that Daedalus had built, the reader is also invited to see himself as a Daedalean figure. Daedalus built man-made wings to escape; to successfully escape Joyce's labyrinth, the reader must follow the example of Daedalus in using his or her creativity and intelligence. But the reader is also faced with an example of unsuccessful escape from the labyrinth in the form of Icarus's flying too high – metaphorically, of overreaching and the homophonic overreading.

Expecting from his prior reading of major literary works that every detail will be part of an organic unity, the first reader inevitably tries to relate every fragment in the "overture" in "Sirens" to what follows or to show how each of the nineteen sections of "Wandering Rocks" relates to the seventeen other chapters of the novel. But *Ulysses*, the book that Joyce pointedly describes in "Oxen of the Sun" as "this chaffering allincluding most farraginous chronicle", includes many discrete, nominalistic details that resist coalescing into a unified pattern and thus presents a first reader with a seemingly insoluble puzzle (U.423; XIV.1412). Yet, in his quest for meaning the experienced reader establishes hierarchies; while some details such as the catalogues in "Cyclops" and "Ithaca" resist meaning, and others insist upon interpretation even while not providing sufficient data (the man in the macintosh), the vast majority of details yield meaning in terms of their relationship to major characters. (Thus, for example, the Elijah throwaway is not a gratuitous "throwaway" but a mock annunciation of Bloom's significance and potential transformation into humanistic hero.)

The odyssean reader has to make sense of the novel's process of establishing significance. In particular, he must understand how Joyce is using Odysseus as a metaphor for Bloom and vice versa. Metaphor depends on the cognition of the reader, but that cognition depends on entering into a hermeneutical circle in which the reader participates with the audience. As Ted Cohen has written, "There is a unique way in which the maker and the appreciator of a metaphor are drawn closer to one another. Three aspects are involved: (1) the speaker issues a kind of concealed invitation; (2) the hearer expends a special effort to accept the invitation; and (3) this transaction constitutes the acknowledgement of a community. All three are involved in any communication, but in ordinary literal discourse their involvement is so pervasive and routine that they go unremarked."[12] When interpreting metaphors, we cannot separate the image from what it represents; nor can we separate ourselves as perceivers from what we perceive. Indeed the relationship between the creator of the metaphor and the reader is an intimate one, dependent on the reader's sharing with a speaker an imagined world from which, during the act of reading, everyone else is excluded.

Joyce is trying to challenge our prior expectations of narrative order, expectations that make us believe that each passage is equally privileged as part of an organic whole. We not only want to know who the man in the macintosh is, but we also want to know about Bloom's ties to the Fenians, the identity of both the proprietor of the coffeeshop in "Eumaeus" and the mysterious sailor whom Bloom and Stephen meet there; we want to know what happens to Stephen after he leaves Bloom's house. But Joyce's novel often raises questions rather than provides answers. Just as Bloom and Stephen must try to make sense of the world they encounter, the reader must organize disparate details into a coherent narrative of the experience he encounters. Like them, he is often baffled by data which refuse to yield to the mind's desire to impose order.

Before Stephen can write the text of the world, he must first learn to read the text of the world, and reading the text of the world is one subject of "Proteus": "Ineluctable modality of the visible: at least that if no more, thought through my eyes" (U.37; III.2). The reader shares Stephen's problem, but the phenomena the reader must perceive are not those of the visible world, but the artist's words: "Signatures of all things I am here to read" (U.37; III.2). The reader must make his way in a verbal world where meaning is often only partially accessible. The reader must eschew Stephen's spiritual and intellectual solipsism when reading the text and enter into the worlds of the characters. When, in the first three sections of *Ulysses*, Stephen reads the world in terms of his own problems and cannot get beyond himself, we recall that in *Portrait* Stephen "retain[ed] nothing of all he read save that which seemed to him an echo or a prophecy of his own state" (P.155). Unlike the characters, but very much like the narrative presence, the reader as *rereader* can return again and again to the signatures of all things in the world of the novel, and read the earlier experience in the context of what follows. Unlike Odysseus, Stephen, or Bloom, but very much like the Joyce presence who is his guide, he can repeat and repeat his journey.

Bloom's humanistic response to Dignam, Mrs Purefoy, and finally Stephen creates for the reader a paradigm of how to read. The reader is necessarily an intruder into the privacy of the characters who share their anxieties and disappointments. That reading Stephen's interior monologues and responding to his thoughts and words gradually becomes comprehensible as we become interested in his plight and make a greater effort to respond to him is very much Joyce's point; for, shaped by the lesson of Bloom, who cares about and makes an effort to understand virtually everyone except Blazes, the reader is becoming more humane and sympathetic.

Recently, much has been made of how reader's responses and hence critical strategies parallel those of the characters within a book. But isn't that exactly what is supposed to happen? That successful novels create their readers testifies to their authors' ability to build a structure of effects into the process of reading their novels. Inevitably, the history of the criticisms of a text re-enacts the tensions within that text. If *Ulysses* is about the quest for meaning in a confused world lacking moral certainties and the quest for an appropriate style for that world, and if the text is about resonances of other works and periods, should not the reader and critic produce criticism, or, in current terms, "stories of reading" that address those issues? Deconstruction congratulates itself on discovering that, "Quarrels between critics about the story are in fact an uncanny transferential repetition of the drama of the story, so that the most powerful structures of the work emerge not in what the critics say about the work but in their repetition of or implication in the story."[13] Given that traditional criticism has tried to recreate the process of reading as much as possible, and given that traditional criticism believes that stories of reading should approach stories of writing because the reader responds to the rhetorical structures created by the author, does not this discovery fault traditional criticism for accomplishing its very purposes? Our reading necessarily iterates the agon of Joyce's struggle to discover the appropriate form for the material he narrates and the necessary values for Ireland. Our reading also iterates the efforts of the characters to make sense of the world they encounter. Finally, our reading participates in Joyce's centrifugal experiments in style and narrativity, even as it watches him centripetally return to focus on Bloom, Stephen, and the mindscape of Dublin.

NOTES

1. Ellmann, *Ulysses on the Liffey*; see pp. 53–6.
2. Wolfgang Iser, *The Implied Reader: Patterns of Communication in Prose Fiction from Bunyan to Beckett* (Baltimore: Johns Hopkins University Press, 1974) p. 192.
3. Karen Lawrence, *The Odyssey of Style in 'Ulysses'* (Princeton University Press, 1981) p. 14. In the next several paragraphs, I quote Lawrence frequently because her position is representative of views I wish to refute.
4. Quoted in Lawrence p. 11; originally quoted in Frank Budgen, *James Joyce and the Making of 'Ulysses'* (1934), repr. Indiana University Press, 1960, pp. 67–8.
5. Lawrence, p. 79.
6. Lawrence, pp. 93, 100. Thus I am refuting Lawrence's view that, beginning with "Aeolus", Joyce abandons the traditional novel of character: "A hermeneutic shift occurs: whereas the stream-of-consciousness technique of the early chapters is designed to reveal the process of the characters trying to interpret their worlds, in 'Aeolus,' the narrative strategy illuminates the process of interpretation on the part of the reader and writer" (Lawrence, p. 59). But when Lawrence asserts in her fine discussion of "Sirens" that "the deliberately oblique treatment of the action functions as a strategy for capturing the pain being repressed", isn't she acknowledging that it is unlikely that the novel's reader will allow, as she would

have it, "the drama of the writing to usurp the dramatic action"? (Lawrence, pp. 93, 100).

7. Lawrence, pp. 42–3.
8. Lawrence, p. 43.
9. Lawrence, p. 62.
10. Stephen Jay Gould, review essay of Evelyn Fox Feller, "A Feeling for Organism: The Life and Work of Barbara McClintock", *New York Review of Books*, 31:5, 20 March 1984, pp. 3–6.
11. Quoted by Mary Reynolds, *Dante and Joyce*, Princeton University Press, 1981, pp. 220.
12. Ted Cohen, "Metaphor and the Cultivation of Intimacy", in *On Metaphor*, ed. Sheldon Sacks (University of Chicago Press, 1978) p. 6.
13. Johnathan Culler, *On Deconstruction: Theory and Criticism after Structuralism* (Ithaca, New York: Cornell University Press, 1982) p. 270.

4 The Movement from Lyrical to Epical and Dramatic Form: the Opening of *Ulysses*

I ENTER STEPHEN

As soon as we enter into the imagined world of *Ulysses*, we realize that Stephen is a man in trouble. He is living with a man he dislikes and who patronizes him, in a Martello tower which was intended to be a British fortress against a French invasion during the Napoleonic era. Although it is early morning in late spring, a time of hope and promise, the artistic expectations aroused by the ending of *Portrait* are unfulfilled. By providing a traditional omniscient narrator whose voice is separate and distinct from Stephen's, Joyce uses the opening of *Ulysses* to provide a critique of the lyricism and subjectivity of *Portrait*: "Stately, plump Buck Mulligan came from the stairhead, bearing a bowl of lather on which a mirror and a razor lay crossed" (U.2–3; I.1–2).

In *Portrait* Joyce oscillates between objectifying Stephen and using him as a thinly disguised autobiographical figure in a fictionalized reminiscence – a reminiscence that contains a quirky combination of Joyce's moral and spiritual autobiography, confession, and artistic credo even as it provides an occasion for his stylistic experimentation. From the outset of *Ulysses*, Stephen is clearly the result of Joyce's conscious effort to dramatize, with some detachment and objectivity, a character within the imagined world of the novel. Put another way, in the opening chapters of *Ulysses*, Stephen has become, in terms of Joyce's genres, less of a lyrical figure and more of an epic figure; as Telemachus setting out on his journey in search of his father and ultimately his mature identity, Stephen must be a distinct

71

objectified character rather than a lyrical figure whose thoughts and emotions reflect the author's. Thus, although Stephen's stature within the imagined world is sharply reduced, Joyce's narrator – as opposed to Stephen – has made vast progress towards achieving the artistic goals, defined in *Portrait*, of impersonality, detachment, and stasis.

Reading the first three chapters of *Ulysses*, we inevitably refer to *Portrait*. Put another way, *Portrait* is a special case of Joyce's use of the literary and historical past. That is, we not only measure Stephen against Telemachus and Hamlet, but we hold him up against the younger version of himself who had first left Ireland in spring, 1902 and who had returned in August, 1903 to see his dying mother. The richness of these first three chapters depends in part on our responding to echoes of prior language and incidents. It is as if for the reader the past were accompanying Stephen as, to recall what George Eliot wrote about Bulstrode in *Middlemarch*, a "still quivering part of himself".[1] Or, as Stephen puts it in the closing pages of *Portrait*, "The past is consumed in the present and the present is living only because it brings forth the future" (P.251). In a process not unlike pentimento where images of an earlier and supposedly painted over version peek through the painting that we are examining, Stephen's past, as we know it from *Portrait*, insists on intruding its shadows upon our perception of Stephen. At times Stephen is aware of how he is partially reiterating and reliving the past. But he is not aware, as we are, that Joyce is rewriting it.

What is essential here is that the meaning Joyce imposed upon Stephen's experience in *Portrait* is undone by subsequent events which cause Stephen to lose hold of some of his imaginative gains and to slip back into artistic and moral confusion. This meaning was earned not only at a very expensive cost to Stephen's psyche, but its order and form were imposed at a great expense of Joyce's imagination and energy. Let us leave aside the personal cost to Joyce the creator as he unweaves the pattern of meaning he has imposed on his surrogate self, and consider the formal implications of rewriting Stephen's story. The echoes in *Ulysses* of prior passages and incidents in *Portrait* are very much part of our reading experience. Do not our minds read with the prior novel always at the forefront of our memories?

Because *Portrait* had moved teleologically towards Stephen's escape from Ireland and his self-definition as an artist, the opening chapters of *Ulysses* are all the more poignant and bathetic. We refer back continuously to what in the context of these first chapters is a searingly ironic conclusion to the former novel. Do we not at times feel that Joyce is rewriting what we have already read, opening up experience that we thought was behind us? Does not this process raise questions about whether we can consign any experience to the past or even whether we can impose order on past experience? When *Ulysses* dramatizes a movement to maturity as a man and an artist, does not the reader remember the process by which such gains were radically modified and indeed, in large part, erased? In other words, the modification of the teleology of *Portrait* calls into question the reliability of the teleology of *Ulysses*.

If, in *Portrait*, the narrator had viewed with gentle irony both Stephen's concluding dialogue with Cranly and his subsequent diary entries, now Stephen regards himself with bitter self-conscious irony. In place of the ebullient brilliance and confidence in his role as an artist, which we saw in his dialogue with Cranly in the last section that precedes the diary entries in *Portrait*, Stephen reveals, in his opening dialogue with Mulligan, self-hatred, loneliness, and cynicism: "You behold in me, Stephen said with grim displeasure, a horrible example of free thought" (U.20; I.625–6). Not completely undeserving of Mulligan's diagnosis "General paralysis of the insane", he is paralytically self-conscious; looking in the mirror he thinks. "As he and others see me. Who chose this face for me? This dogsbody to rid of vermin" (U.6; I.128–9, 136–7). In a sense, Stephen is back where he was at the beginning of the last section of *Portrait* when, partly in response to the devolution in the family fortunes, "his heart [was] already bitten by an ache of loathing and bitterness" (P.175). Now, living on his own with Mulligan, a deeply resented surrogate father, he is in the same mood; it is as if the liberation of the concluding pages of *Portrait*, in which he defined himself as a priest of the imagination who would discover the conscience of his race, had not occurred.

When we recall the euphoric expectations of the penultimate diary entry in *Portrait*, we realize that Stephen's artistic career has become stalled: "Welcome, O life! I go to encounter for the millionth time the reality of experience and to forge in the smithy of my soul the uncreated conscience of my race" (P. 252–3). Because the reality of experience in the form of passionate feelings and empirical knowledge of life is what he lacks, he is not yet ready to be the writer of the epic that Ireland requires. For Joyce, Stephen's apostasy is his inability – one could say a refusal based on immaturity – to transform his personal and cultural experience into epical and dramatic art. Before Stephen can write an epic of modern Ireland, he must turn his back on various forms of aestheticism that preached "art for art's sake" and glorified a separation between life and art. In his 1922 *Ulysses* Joyce is rejecting the aestheticism and solipsism of Stephen's credo in the 1916 *Portrait*: "I will try to express myself in some mode of life or art as freely as I can and as wholly as I can, using for my defence the only arms I allow myself to use – silence, exile, and cunning" (P.247).

Unlike his mythical namesake Daedalus, who has adapted the arts to the reality of experience, Stephen is lost in the world of his own dreams. Like Daedalus and his son, who were imprisoned by Mino in their own labyrinth, Stephen is imprisoned in a labyrinth of his own making. He is an Icarus figure who has flown too near the sun rather than, like his namesake, a man who has flown successfully. Stephen had wanted to adopt Daedalus as his mythic father without taking on the inevitable identity of the drowning Icarus: "Old father, old artificer, stand me now and ever in good stead" (P.253). The emphasis on drowning images in "Telemachus" underlines Stephen's position as an Icarus figure rather than the Daedalus figure that he would like to be: "He would create proudly out of the freedom and power of his soul, as the great artificer whose name he bore, a living thing, new and soaring and beautiful, impalable, imperishable" (P.170). In "Scylla and Charybdis", Stephen, the man who desperately wants to be his own father, acknowledges his identity as the poignant son who did not heed his father's advice: "Fabulous artificer. The hawklike man. You flew. Whereto? Newhaven-Dieppe, steerage passenger. Paris and back. Lapwing. Icarus. *Pater, ait.* Seabedabbled, fallen, weltering. Lapwing you are. Lapwing be" (U.210; IX.952–4; see I.453). Although Daedalus successfully escaped into exile in Sicily and lived a creative life, Joyce would have also expected the reader to remember that the jealous Daedalus had murdered his nephew Talus whose inventiveness threatened to rival his own.[2] Perhaps the ironic parallel to the murder is Stephen's need to demean his artistic rivals; just as Bloom does not murder the modern Polyphemus, the Citizen, but rather uses words, so Stephen slays his ✓ rivals with the lancet of his art.

For some time Stephen seems to have acceded to Mulligan's patronizing dominance. He had returned from his exile in Paris for his mother's death, but it is not clear why he remains in Dublin. Morbidly savoring his own misery, he has been wearing black since his mother's death ten months ago and is still locked in bitterness, self-pity, and melancholy. Like Hamlet with whom he identifies, Stephen realizes that he is paralyzed but he does not know what to do about it. Like Claudius, Mulligan is a false father who would usurp his affections, were Stephen, like Hamlet, not intent on rejecting him. The awkward relationship with Mulligan, in which Stephen is displeased with himself and always on guard, helps us to understand his need for an alter ego to help him overcome loneliness and a sense of isolation, a need which explains his later responsiveness to the kindly, sympathetic Bloom.

Stephen, of course, needs to achieve intellectual and emotional self-sufficiency and complete the movement to self-possession initiated in *A Portrait*. But to do so, at this point he desperately needs an empathetic other, someone who will provide the responsive consciousness that prior generations found in a prayerful relation with God. Should we not see the parallel between Stephen's need for a double, a secret sharer, with whom he might communicate in an amoral indifferent cosmos, and the needs of Conrad's Captain in "The Secret Sharer" and both Jim and Marlow in *Lord Jim*, Hardy's Sue and Jude in *Jude the Obscure* and Lawrence's Paul and Miriam in *Sons and Lovers*?[3]

Our response to the morbid, humorless Stephen would be different and less sympathetic had we not read *Portrait*. But because we had responded to the development of his creative imagination, we do not so readily abandon him and, at least in part, we see him as a victim of an indifferent father, insensitive and at times predatory friends, and a mediocre, narrow-minded, and repressive culture. And by the second half of "Nestor", he does become more sympathetic in the conversation with the bigoted and myopic Deasy, an Orangeman who represents the mediocre and materialistic English culture that is infesting Ireland.

Ulysses, among other things, defines in its first sections Stephen's problems and dramatizes what Stephen requires. Thus, to emphasize Stephen's hyperintellectuality and his failure to have a mature physical relationship, the first three chapters are the only ones without characteristic organs. It remains for the last section of the triad, dominated increasingly by Molly even before "Penelope", to provide the essential physical organs – nerves, skeleton, and, finally, flesh – to complete the epic of the body. Before dramatizing by its form, scope, and especially by the characterization of Bloom, what kind of art is necessary to create the "conscience of [the Irish] race", the first chapters of *Ulysses* propose and test various kinds of Irish art, including Mulligan's song, Stephen's riddle, Celtic legends endorsed and disseminated by Yeats, and the iconoclastic wit of Oscar Wilde.

The first three chapters in which Joyce searches for an artistic father are also *his* Telemachiad. Joyce finally rejects as artistic pseudoangelos – as false fathers which Stephen must turn aside just as Joyce had to – the alternatives offered by Yeats and Wilde. If Stephen is to become the epic artist of Ireland, if he is to write epical and dramatic art, he must reject the examples of Wilde and Yeats.

With his completely open yellow dressing gown, "Stately, plump", flamboyant, and licentious Buck Mulligan not only resembles Wilde in physical appearance and life style, but quotes from Wilde's Preface to *The Picture of Dorian Gray* (1891), and, at least teasingly offers the alternative of homosexuality: "Make room in the bed" (U.22; I.713). For Joyce homosexuality is an alternative to the fruitful intercourse with the world that Stephen requires, intercourse for which a passionate heterosexual relationship is a prerequisite. Even without blatant homoeroticism, the banter and bluster of the male camaraderie of the tower have narcissistic overtones that deflect Stephen from serious relationships. Stephen associates Mulligan with Cranly, whose offer of affection in *Portrait* Stephen – in his willed isolation – had found disturbing: "Cranly's arm. His arm" (U.7; I.159). Wearing Buck's castoff boots, he thinks with bitter irony of what he believes is Mulligan's agenda in exchange for his generosity: "Staunch friend, a brother soul: Wilde's love that dare not speak its name. His arm: Cranly's arm. He now will leave me. And the blame?" (U.49; III.450–2; in the new edition, the restoration of the previously omitted phrase, "His arm: Cranley's arm," inverting the prior "Cranly's arm. His arm" in "Telemachus", brings the unwanted male affection offered by Mulligan into sharper focus.)

When Buck speaks of the need to "Hellenise" Ireland, isn't he suggesting among other things the Greek penchant for homosexuality? When at his trial Wilde defended the phrase "the love that dare not speak its name", he invoked the example of Plato: " 'The love that dare not speak its name' in this century is such a great affection of an elder for a younger man as there is between David and Jonathan, such as Plato made the very basis of his philosophy. . ..".[4] Given that the influence of Lord Alfred Douglas led Wilde astray, and that Wilde had died only four years before the novel takes place, it is not surprising that Stephen is very self-conscious about the putative influence of Mulligan. It is ironic that Mulligan warns Stephen that Bloom represents the very threat that Mulligan himself presents: "He knows you. He knows your old fellow. . . . [H]e is Greeker than the Greeks" (U.201; IX.614–5); later in the chapter Mulligan returns to this theme: "The wandering Jew, Buck Mulligan whispered with clown's awe. Did you see his eye? He looked upon you to lust after you" (U.217; IX.1209–21).

Joyce spoke of Wilde as one of the Irish writers who became a "court jester to the English".[5] Joyce has Stephen think of Mulligan not only as a clown, as in the above passage, but specifically as a jester performing for Haines: "A jester at the court of his master, indulged and disesteemed, winning a clement master's praise" (U.25; II.43–5). In "Circe", Mulligan appears "in particoloured jester's dress of puce and yellow and clown's cap with curling bell" (U.580; XV.4166–7). That Stephen's definition of Irish art as "The cracked lookingglass of a servant" is partially indebted to the Preface to *The Decay of Lying* (1889) shows that he is in danger of becoming inculcated with Wilde's cynicism. (Wilde had written: "I can quite understand your objection to art being treated as a mirror. You think it would reduce genius to the position of a cracked looking glass.")[6] We should not forget the links between Stephen's aestheticism in *Portrait* and Wilde's theories and behaviour; as Darcy O'Brien has noted, "Indeed, resemblances between Stephen's aestheticism and the art for art's sake movement of the eighties and the nineties are obvious enough in the search for the beautiful; in the scorn of bourgeois society; in the love of the languorous, the self-conscious, the elegantly eccentric, even in Stephen's (and Joyce's) walking stick."[7]

To Joyce, Yeats's idealization of Irish culture represents a kind of neo-Platonism that interferes with the artist's intercourse with the real world. Stephen mocks the folk literature being published at the turn of the century by Yeats's sisters in projects under Yeats's auspices: "Five lines of text and ten pages of notes about the folk and the fishgods of Dundrum. Printed by the weird sisters in the year of the big wind" (U.12–3; I.365–7). But, notwithstanding this irony, Stephen is tempted by the escapism to faeryland – and by implication to an artistic realm divorced from the real world – that is implied in the poem "Who Goes with Fergus?"

It is paradox of *Ulysses* that it is the most temporally and spatially ambitious of epic novels as it ranges far and wide through man's experience, even as it is the most nigglingly nominalistic and compulsively naturalistic novel in its focus on the pedestrian details of life in Dublin on one day. Convincing his readers that Stephen and Bloom are universal figures embodying significant cultural values is an artistic problem that Joyce must solve if he is to write his national epic. Joyce manages to have the characters think in terms which are appropriate to their characters in a realistic Dublin novel that takes place in 1904 and which simultaneously resonate with historical and cultural implications. Thus the allusions play the role of metaphors in evoking past eras and historical contexts into the very texture of our reading experience.

Let us consider how in one crucial passage in "Telemachus", Joyce transforms the nominalistic into the representative and thus begins the process of educating his reader to see the significance of this one day in the lives of his major characters. Thinking of Mulligan's patronizing attitude to him and his own dependence on Mulligan, as well as of the obsequious relationship that Mulligan has with the English visitor Haines, Stephen chastizes himself for being "A server of a servant" (U.11; I.312). But Stephen, as a potential artist – indeed, as the self-elected artist required by Ireland – identifies with Ireland and sees himself as a "servant of two masters . . . an English and Italian:" "The imperial British state" and "holy Roman catholic and apostolic church" (U.20; I.638, 643–4). When he speaks of a "third . . . who wants me for odd jobs", he may have in mind both Ireland and art. As we noted above, he had defined "The cracked lookingglass of a servant" as the symbol of Irish art (U.6; I.146). Like his mother demanding that Stephen pray for her soul, Ireland demands his service in the form of undesirable tasks, such as teaching school for Mr Deasy.

We should now look at what the passage tells us about Stephen's evolution as an artist. We recall that in *Portrait* he had first said in the climactic dialogue with Cranly: "I will not serve", because he perceived his mother as a surrogate – indeed, a metaphor, a substitution – for the traditional values that he had to reject (P.239). And he expands on that refusal later in the same dialogue: 'I will not serve that in which I no longer believe whether it call itself my home, my fatherland or my church" (P.246–7). That refusal echoes the words attributed to Lucifer in the sermon at the retreat, words that are the essence of the rebellious Satan's consummate spiritual pride: "*no serviam: I will not serve*" (P.117). In his mind, he fuses his mother with the old milkwoman to create the traditional allegorical image of Ireland as an old woman: "A crazy queen, old and jealous. Kneel down before me" (U.20; I.640). (According to legend, Ireland looks like a poor old woman to all but true patriots to whom she looks like a young girl).[8]

As we shall see, the novel finally proposes Molly – passionate, vibrant, sexual, and fecund – as a metaphor for the Old Woman of Ireland, and specifically as an alternative for Stephen's allegorized version of Ireland: "Silk of the kine and poor old woman, names given her in old times" (U.14; I.403–4). That he abandons this kind of talk – talk which is derived from the Celtic Renaissance and which is, in Stephen's mind, identified with Yeats – in his "Parable of the Plums" and substitutes his ironic image of the old midwives whom he sees on the strand shows that Stephen is progressing from the romanticism and subjectivity of *Portrait*.

The odyssean reader journeys from the twin images of the milkwoman and Stephen's dreams of ghostly visitations of his dead mother to the fecund sexuality of Molly. Like Stephen, both the implied Irish reader that Joyce originally addressed, and the modern reader that Joyce's novel now addresses, must overcome debilitating images of the historical and personal past if he is to renew himself. In *Portrait*, Joyce is ambivalent about the Irish propensity for living in the past. On one hand, he mocked Simon Dedalus's alcoholic nostalgia and rejected the Celtic revival: "Do you know what Ireland is? asked Stephen [of Davin] with cold violence. Ireland is the old sow that eats her farrow" (P.203). Yet, on the other hand, Stephen's quest to write the Irish epic answers Davin's question, "What with your name and your ideas. . . . Are you Irish at all?" (P.202). "To discover the mode of life or of art whereby [his] spirit could express itself in unfettered freedom", he must turn to the subject that he once thought had imprisoned him (P.246). One might say that it is because he cannot completely fly through the nets of his culture that he is able to write *Ulysses*. He must serve the culture that produced him and which is responsible for his themes and values. *Ulysses* shows that there is really no freedom in "silence, exile, and cunning" (P.247).

In a sense Joyce demystifies the metaphor of the Old Woman of Ireland by substituting a physical figure for an allegorical one. But the very focus on her physical nature becomes paradoxically a metaphor for the very values that are essential for Ireland, as well as for Bloom, Stephen, and the reader. Finally, then, Bloom, who will also think and dream of himself in universal terms, becomes the true patriot when he turns to Molly, Joyce's version of Ireland. By learning that the hypersexual, bawdy, and profane Molly who is obsessed with thoughts of fucking can signify an accepted cultural symbol, such as the Old Woman of Ireland, the odyssesn reader discovers something about metaphor – something that is an essential tool for reading the novel – namely, that the meaning of a metaphor depends upon its context within an imagined world rather than upon something inherent in language.

Reading *Ulysses* often depends upon recognising the submerged metaphor in the stream of consciousness of the major characters. This is especially true of Stephen whose mind works in metaphorical terms. For example, Stephen's association of the sea with the "bowl of white china . . . holding [his mother's] green sluggish bile which she had torn up from her rotting liver by fits of loud groaning vomitting" depends upon his responding to Mulligan's shaving bowl as a transitive but submerged metaphor signified by the present members of the metaphorical series – the sea and the bowl of bile – and in turn signifying them (U.5; I.108–10). Stephen is a hydrophobe whose neurosis depends upon metaphors taking precedence over logic. He has imaginatively created a metonymical series which aligns water with his refusal to pray for his mother's soul, and in turn aligns his mother's subsequent suffering with his refusal to pray; in his tortured conscience, the green sea and green bile cannot be separated from his apostasy.

Stephen's metaphoricity illustrates how the mind's energetic association of parallels from diverse areas of experience can create striking relationships that defy the logic of cause and effect. But it also warns us of the disruptions to our sense of temporal continuity, cause and effect, and traditional order that such imaginative activity creates. That Stephen's imagination obsessively creates metaphors within the novel from his personal experience, in much the same way that Joyce creates metaphors to create the novel, formally shows the kinship between the two.

Yet it is ironic that when we meet Stephen, the man who as an artist would control words to create an imagined world, he is the captive of the words of others – in this case, Mulligan's quoting Swinburne's epithet for the sea "a grey sweet mother" – and a reluctant participant in their skits and plays (U.5; I.77). Moments later, it is Mulligan whose quoting of "Who Goes with Fergus" ("And no more turn aside and brood/Upon love's bitter mystery/For Fergus rules the brazen cars") returns him to his morbid memories, via a line that Stephen provides, "White breast of the dim sea":

A cloud began to cover the sun slowly, wholly, shadowing the bay in deeper green. It lay beneath him, a bowl of bitter waters. Fergus' song: I sang it alone in the house, holding down the long dark chords. Her door was open: she wanted to hear my music. Silent with awe and pity I went to her bedside. She was crying in her wretched bed. For those words, Stephen: love's bitter mystery. (U.9; I.239–41, 244–5, 248–53; The Gabler edition restores "wholly", and more importantly, changes "behind" to "beneath" which sharpens the sense of the isolated poet in the ivory tower torn between reluctant engagement in life and the iconoclastic view that he would like to assume.)

It may be that the "bowl of bitter waters" refers to the bowl of salt water signifying the tears of the oppressed Jews in the land of bondage and hence is part of the typology that predicts Bloom as a Moses and Elijah figure.[9] That Bloom in "Calypso", also his first chapter, sees the same cloud and becomes depressed as he thinks, like Stephen, regretfully of his past, but more of his racial

– his Jewish – past than his personal past, establishes a parallel with a difference. While Stephen would if he could reject aspects of his Irish heritage, Bloom is trying to come to terms with his Jewishness.

By showing us how the stream of consciousness within an interior monologue extends the possibilities of understanding the consciousness of characters, Joyce is eschewing the possibility that language cannot signify or that the concept of character is dead. Indeed, one could argue that for the odyssean reader the most important parallel between Stephen and Bloom is the similarity in the way that their patterns of association self-dramatize their distinct selves. The narrator, while occasionally smiling at their hyperbole and distortion, takes their thoughts and feelings very seriously. While their reading of the world is often radically different, both read their worlds in terms of their experience and psychic needs. Both characters are desperately trying to make sense of their lives. Their process of making sense is the major structural and thematic principle of the novel, and teaches us how to come to terms with the experience that the novel presents – in other words, to read the novel.

Even when later chapters raise questions about the possibility of establishing a normative narrative technique or about whether language reveals a world prior to the telling, we need to refer back to the epistemology of these first six chapters which stand as a judgment on the experiments in technique and voice that follow. Just as the ominiscient voice in *Lord Jim* establishes standards by which Jim must be judged as Marlow becomes increasingly involved and apologetic, the efficacy of the first six chapters of *Ulysses* becomes a standard by which we judge the novel's later ventriloquism and temporary interest in modes of writing for their own sake. These chapters establish their efficient and unobtrusive technique as a value by which we measure the artistic peregrinations of the later chapters.

Joyce wants us to understand Stephen as an artistic genius in search of a subject and to see how the poignant eccentricities of Stephen's metaphors reflect his sexual confusion, his guilty conscience, and his artistic quest. Stephen's love of language temporarily suspends his self-pity and wins our affection: "A hand plucking the harpstrings, merging their twining chords. Wavewhite wedded words shimmering on the dim tide" (U.9;

I.245–7). As a young artist Stephen's first perception of Mulligan is in metaphoric terms; he "looked coldly at the shaking gurgling face that blessed him, equine in its length, and at the light untonsured hair, grained and hued like pale oak" (U.3; I.14–6). Again, at the chapter's end, Mulligan is the occasion for Stephen's artistic sensibility when he perceives Mulligan, whom he resents for displacing his mother in his imagination, as "A sleek brown head, a seal's, far out on the water, round" (U.23; I.742–3). Thus Mulligan, the man who mocks and patronizes him, becomes the occasion for his artistic perception. Put another way, Stephen's imagination triumphs over the rational, positivistic, cynical Mulligan even if Stephen's morbid humorlessness makes him unattractive. In a sense, Stephen's imagination as an artist enables him to usurp the usurper, and Stephen recognizes the potential force of his art in terms which compare it to Mulligan's surgical tools: "He fears the lancet of my art as I fear that of his. The cold steel pen" (U.7; I.152–3; the corrupt "steelpen" of prior editions took some of the force out of the parallel between the surgeon's and writer's tools.) We hear the echo of Stephen's ironic appropriation of the medical student's equipment in Deasy's comment at the school: "I like to break a lance with you, old as I am" (U.35; II.424–5).

Indeed, Deasy's stress on battles, and particularly the Trojan War, makes us realize that Stephen is being depicted more as an ironic Achilles pouting ineffectually on the strand and dreaming of fleeing from a claustrophobic situation than as a questing Telemachus looking for his father. In another literary pentimento, we see vestiges of the bellicose *Iliad* in the early chapters of *Ulysses* as if to remind us that Bloom, the hero who lives by his wits, has to displace the more primitive heroes who lived by brute force. Among other things, Stephen has to shed the identity of the rigid and intransigent Achilles and adopt that of the questing, educable Telemachus before he can discover what he needs. Odysseus is the antithesis of the bellicose Achilles; yet as the heir to the Pelian armour, he is also the heir of Achilles. To Joyce, he represents a more civilized hero who is oriented to the future and receptive to experience.[10]

Like Gabriel Conroy, Stephen oscillates wildly between two poles; while one pole is marked by a combination of extreme egotism, an exaggerated sense of importance, narcissism, and self-aggrandizement, the other pole is defined by self-doubt, guilt, purposelessness, and self-diminution. These later qualities are responsible in part for his "reading" the world in terms of hyperbolic and immature metaphors which interfere with his fulfilling his artistic potential. In a weird image based on the image in *Revelation* where Christ descends to take the redeemed soul as his bride, Stephen imagines his mother having sexual intercourse with the Irish saint Columbanus: "His mother's prostrate body the fiery Columbanus in holy zeal bestrode" (U.27; II.143–3). Because Columbanus left his mother against her will, he becomes an apt metaphor in Stephen's mind for his own disobedient refusal to kneel in prayer at his mother's bedside. But if Stephen perceives Columbanus as a substitution for himself, do we not have the spectre of Stephen imagining or rather, accusing himself, of incest?[11]

Of course, Joyce is making fun of Stephen's hyberbolic and immature imagination. Isn't this the kind of excessive and jejune metaphor that Joyce would have wanted his reader to associate with aestheticism and decadence, with Wilde and Beardsley? Such a passage emphasizes the distance that Stephen has to journey towards artistic maturity and personal self-confidence and towards integrating his art and his experience. Put in other terms, his hyperbolic metaphors must be replaced by the more sustained and controlled historical and literary parallels of the teller.

II   THE ROLE OF MULLIGAN

"Stately plump" Mulligan is a Falstaff figure for Stephen, a man who must cast off his irresponsible life and assume his proper mission of becoming the writer of the Irish epic. But, unlike Prince Hal, Stephen is very grudging about participating in his humour and prefers an inconoclastic stance. Mulligan is, among other things, Joyce's satire of the stage Irishman – boisterous, insensitive, living for the moment, and hostile to serious art. But he also demystifies the pretentions of religion and art and brings Stephen down to earth. That Mulligan speaks of Stephen as a "dreadful bard" anticipates Stephen's putative assumption of the role of Shakespeare's successor (U.6;I.134).

Mulligan is also a Mephistophelean figure; While, as Ellmann has pointed out, "Mephistopheles is the spirit of denial within the universe . . . [and] within Faust's mind", Mulligan is the spirit of denial only within the interior space of Stephen's mind.[12] Mulligan is a man who mocks the very metaphorical process that the novel affirms. The novel opens with Mulligan's performing a mock mass: "For this, O dearly beloved, is the genuine christine: body and soul and blood and ouns. Slow music, please. Shut your eyes, gents. One moment. A little trouble about those white corpuscles. Silence, all" (U.3; I.21–3). If we understand that Joyce perceived the Eucharist as a metaphor for the transformation of the Word into flesh, then we can see how Mulligan's positivism makes him an apostate figure who is proposing a false premise. Just as in the Mass the wine becomes the blood of Christ and the mystery of Christ is present and alive again, the artist recaptures the actuality of past life through his words. And one could say that, as in the Eucharist, the artist's recreated world is more real than the actual day to day one because it has significance. The Eucharist – representing the replacement of one reality by another – is also a figure for the very process of metaphoricity in the novel. According to the *Layman's Missal*: "The Mass is an act in which the mystery of Christ is not just commemorated, but made present, living over again. God makes use of it afresh to give Himself to man; and man can use it to give glory to God through the one single sacrifice of Christ."[13] Just as Christ's mystery is made living and present, Joyce recreates on 16 June 1904 the worlds of Homer and Shakespeare and, indeed, Christ.

We recall how Stephen in *Portrait* had seen himself as "a priest of eternal imagination" (P.221). While creating his villanelle, he had thought of the creative process in terms which suggest the Incarnation: "In the virgin womb of the imagination the word was made flesh" (P.217). The homophonic relation of word and world throughout *Portrait* suggests the relationship between artistic creativity and the Eucharistic moment when the word is made flesh. It is based on biblical tradition ("In the beginning was the Word") and anticipates the same relation in *Ulysses*. Even as a young adolescent, Stephen depends on the word to make his imaginative world flesh: "Words which he did not understand he said over and over to himself till he had learned them by heart: and through them he had glimpses of the real world about him" (P.62). That he perceives the young girl in terms of a bird at the end of the third section shows how he uses the images of his imagination to create reality: "Her image had passed into his soul for ever and no word had broken the holy silence of his ecstasy. Her eyes had called him and his soul had leaped at the call. To live, to err, to fall, to triumph, to recreate life out of life!" (P.172).

Stephen cannot escape the Catholic epistemology in which he has been educated. Stephen disbelieves as only a former believer can. For Stephen is deeply offended by Mulligan's sacrilegious behaviour – his mocking the Eucharist while his gown is open and his exposing himself. Thus, on the opening page, when Mulligan chants the prayer from the early part of the Mass before the priest or Celebrant ascends to the altar, Stephen feels himself placed in the position of acolyte or altar boy or, in terms of the Catholic liturgy, Servant or Minister, to the Celebrant. He is tortured by the accusation he attributes to his mother: "Ghoul! Chewer of corpses!" (U.10; I.278). He is deeply offended by Mulligan's undergraduate wit, and cannot forget Mulligan's insensitivity. Indeed, Mulligan does not even remember saying, "*O, it only Dedalus whose mother is beastly dead*", in part because as a medical student he has come to accept death as an inevitable part of the life cycle: "I see them pop off every day in the Mater and Richmond and cut up into tripes in the dissectingroom. It's a beastly thing and nothing else. It simply doesn't matter. . . . To me it's all a mockery and beastly" (U.8; I.198–9, 205–7, 210). Mulligan's cynical pleasure in man's mortality, like his narcissism and ersatz artistry, offers a challenge to the significance of human life that the rest of the novel answers. Mulligan's heretical song, "The Ballad of Joking Jesus", mocks the story of the Incarnation, a legend which prefigures the way the artist transforms the word into flesh, as well as the legend of Daedalus, the man who invented wings to escape the bondage of Mino's labyrinth;

Goodbye, now, goodbye! Write down all I said
And tell Tom, Dick, and Harry I rose from the dead.
What's bred in the bone cannot fail me to fly
And Olivet's breezy–Goodbye, now, goodbye! (U.19; I.596–9)

Indeed, by flapping his arms as if to fly, Mulligan himself suggests Icarus who flew too close to the sun and fell into the sea.

III JOYCE'S NEW NEW TESTAMENT

Ulysses is Joyce's version of a secular humanistic New New Testament. By providing hints and prefigurations of what is to come, the first three chapters of the novel comically stand in the same relationship to the subsequent chapters as the Old Testament does to the New. Joyce chose the name Malachi for Mulligan because it is in the book of Malachi, the last of the prophets of the Old Testament, that Elijah's return or Second Coming as the Messiah is announced; "Malachi" is Hebrew for "my messenger". That Mulligan in his "Ballad of Joking Jesus" also announces Christ establishes a relationship between Bloom as an Elijah figure and Bloom as a Christ figure. Malachi is the only prophet whose name corresponds to an actual Irish king and to an Irish prelate, Saint Malachy, who, according to Gifford and Seidman, "was traditionally believed to have had the gift of prophecy".[14]

But Stephen wants to displace Malachi as messenger. Later in the day after his personal and artistic growth has progressed, he recognizes Mulligan as one of the "Brood of mockers", and "pseudomalachi", and he replaces Mulligan as his mentor and prophet with Bloom (U.197; IX.492). Stephen thinks that the old milkwoman, who is associated with morning, is "maybe a messenger" (U.13; I.399–400); the reader realizes that she is something of a Malachi figure who heralds a very special day. Bloom is an apt successor to Malachi, the mysterious and anonymous figure whose prophecy stresses human brotherhood and religious tolerance, even to heathens.[15] And Joyce, writing especially for his Irish audience but also for western civilization, undoubtedly saw himself as the successor to Malachi; for Malachi spoke when "doubt paralyzed the souls of men" and "Sordidness, callousness and moral disintegration" were rife.[16]

Let us look at how this prophetic tradition shapes our reading, even while understanding that Joyce deliberately leaves his typological passages vague and laconic in order to stress that this kind of biblical reading has an arbitrary aspect. Haines's dream of shooting a "black panther" is a comic prefiguration of Bloom, whose name suggests leopard and who is dressed in black all day. Rereading, we think of the novel's indentification of Bloom with Parnell, not only because Parnell is related to fox as Bloom is to leopard, but because Bloom himself is given the metaphorical identity of fox when he acknowledges the common Jewish heritage he shares with Dlugacz, the butcher whose wares include pork: "A speck of eager fire from foxeyes [Bloom] thanked him. He withdrew his gaze after an instant. No: better not: another time" (U.60; IV.186–7). That the annunciation of Bloom is one and the same with the dream of shooting Bloom implies that betrayal or crucifixion is a necessary part of the story of any especially gifted or heroic figure that Ireland might discover. It also shows how the Englishman Haines, who has insinuated himself into Stephen's house, will be an inevitable part of the demise of the Irish hero.

Bloom's arrival is predicted in terms which echo the kinds of language with which Christ's presence and effect are described in the New Testament as well as in scholastic commentaries and traditional sermons: "a darkness shining in brightness which brightness could not comprehend" (U.28; II.160). In "Wandering Rocks", Stephen, perhaps thinking of the incongruity of Christ's message and the present materialistic age as he looks into a jeweller's window, cynically thinks of the darkness of Mammon threatening God's light: "Born all in the dark wormy earth, cold specks of fire, evil, lights shining in the darkness" (U.241; X.805–6; the restoration in the new edition of the comma after "evil" clarifies how jewelry, created by tradition in hell, and associated by Stephen with man's quest for wealth as opposed to values, represents an alternative kind of light shining in darkness to the metaphorical light of God's Word which the novel associates with Bloom). If we think of the specks of fire in Bloom's eyes in terms of Joyce's comic but significant typology, we see that Bloom offers a challenge to contemporary materialism.

Stephen is also recalling the jeweled Jews of Paris whom he thought of in "Nestor" with some sympathy as fellow exiles and wanderers who were misunderstood by others; this occurred when Deasy had spoken of the "darkness" in the Jews' eyes because they had "sinned against the light": "Their eyes knew their years of wandering and, patient, knew the dishonours of their flesh" (U.34; II.361; 371–2). That his gratuitous annunciation of Bloom anticipates the narrator's use of the Elijah references to expand Bloom's significance may be a sign of the putative convergence of Stephen and the narrator. Sometimes the typology has a comical aspect as in Mulligan's "Ballad of Joking Jesus" ("If anyone thinks that I amn't divine/He'll get no free drinks when I'm making the wine/But have to drink water and wish it were plain/That I make when the wine becomes water again" [U.19; I.589–92]), or when Stephen dreams of being led by a man with a melon in "Proteus" pages before Bloom thinks of the putative melonfields in Jaffa (U.47,60; III.367–8, IV.194).

As he writes his New New Testament, Joyce is poking fun at the scholastic tradition of the biblical exegesis where every detail of the Old Testament is taken as a typological foreshadowing of Christ. Stephen's imagination creates his own secular typology; while writing his derivative poem on the strand in "Proteus", he thinks: "He comes, pale vampire, through storm his eyes, his bat sails bloodying the sea, mouth to her mouth's kiss" (U.48; III.397–8). His poem is really a pastiche of a Douglas Hyde translation of an Irish song from his 1895 *Love Songs of Connaught*: "On swift sail flaming/From storm and south/He comes, pale vampire,/Mouth to my mouth" (U.132; VII.522–5). The poem not only anticipates his acknowledgement of Bloom, at the end of Circe, as "Black panther vampire", but his identification of Bloom with Christ and bat in "Scylla and Charybdis"; the crucified Christ, according to Stephen, "was nailed like bat to barndoor, starved on crosstree" (U.197; IX.495). Joyce contrasts bats and vampires – mysterious night creatures – with the doves and lambs usually associated with Messianic figures. Since before he can write *Ulysses*, Stephen must learn to think metaphorically, his subsequent substitutions at the climax of "Circe" of Bloom for bat and vampire should be taken as progress.

The symbolic importance of the bat depends on recalling *Portrait*. Despite Stephen's skepticism about Irish nationalism, he found himself drawn to the primitive energy he identified with Davin; he is particularly fascinated with Davin's experience of being invited to bed by a lonely married country woman whom he thinks of "as a type of her race and his own, a batlike soul waking to the consciousness of itself in darkness and secrecy and loneliness and, through the eyes and voice and gesture of a woman without guile, calling the stranger to her bed" (P. 183). The bat is an image for the sexuality and passion that Stephen seeks as well as for the mysterious possibilities of life that lure him to explore nighttown in the vain hope that he will find them there; these possibilities are linked to the potential discovery of a passionate dimly acknowledged nighttime self. (That we are supposed to recall this passage – a passage that is twice repeated with little variation in *Portrait* – is underlined by Bloom's seeing a bat flying overhead at the end of "Nausicaa" after Gerty offers her rather explicit sexual invitation to Bloom.)

Seeing the dead dog on the strand, Stephen, recalling Mulligan's specific epithet for Stephen ("poor dogsbody") and Mulligan's cynical acceptance of mortality, transforms Deasy's Victorian view of an upwardly evolving historical pattern shaped by a teleology into thoughts of the inevitable movement toward the death of mankind and most particularly himself: "moves to one great goal. Ah, poor dogsbody! Here lies poor dogsbody's body" (U.6,46; I.112; III.351–2).

"Dogsbody" is part of the novel's ironic typology; it anticipates the novel's frequent references to dog as an inversion of God. This inversion – crystallized by Elijah's question to Bloom in "Circe", "Are you a god or a doggone clod?" – stresses Joyce's insistence on the inextricable relationship, in the life that mankind lives right here and now, between what we think of as animal or physical and what we think of as the divine or spiritual (U.507; XV.2194). That Stephen picks his nose and urinates – possibly after sexually arousing himself but not consummating the act of masturbation – shows that he is discovering the body that he often would deny. But these all too human excremental actions also, I think, comment on the quality of the poem that he writes. Do not his thoughts of Dante's lines a few moments later in the section of "Aeolus" headlined "Rhymes and Reasons" provide an ironic reminder for us, and the odyssean readers, of how far Stephen has to progress as an artist?

It is a characteristic of Stephen's imagination that both his quest for a coherent identity and his search for a subject for his art take the form of a search for the appropriate metaphors. (As we shall see, according to Stephen's aesthetic theory, this is true of all artistic geniuses, and most notably of Shakespeare.) The metaphors an author chooses and the way he presents those metaphors reveal the author's character and values. And a character is no different, particularly if the character is in the process of becoming an author. In "Nestor" when Stephen thinks of *Lycidas* where the intervention of Christ saves the drowned man, we recall that in "Telemachus" Stephen identifies with the drowned man: "The man that was drowned. . . .

Here I am" (U.21; I.675–7). That Stephen identifies more with the drowned Edward King than with Milton shows how far he has strayed from his art: "Sunk though he be beneath the watery floor" (U.50; III.474). He also identifies more with the drowned Alonso in *The Tempest* than with Ariel who sings of him: "full fathom five thy father lies" (U.50; III.470).

Yet we know that Alonso has been rescued and that for Lycidas death is the birth of the eternal soul. Recalling Christ's words on the cross, "I thirst", Stephen knows that water represents the rebirth that he requires (U.50; III.485). Stephen's thoughts of a possible thunderstorm not only suggest the heavenly disturbance that took place at the crucifixion, but the putative beginning of a new historical and personal cycle for Stephen. Stephen's mind begins to turn away from Christ to Lucifer's rebellion, a rebellion with which he self-flagellatingly identifies: "Allbright he falls, proud lightning of the intellect, *Lucifer, dico, qui nescit occasum.* No" (U.50; III.486–7). Translated as "Lucifer, I say, who knows no fall", the aforementioned Latin is from the Catholic service for Holy Saturday which precedes Easter Sunday; it occurs, according to Gifford and Seidman, "near the end of the Exultet, a chant in praise of the paschal candle, 'acclaiming the light of the risen Christ'" and calls attention to the possibility of renewal.[17] Furthermore, Stephen concludes his thoughts of Lucifer with the negative "No". Thus, at the end of Joyce's Telemachiad, Stephen has begun to turn away from his identification with Lucifer's spiritual pride. Excepting the nightmares and hallucinations in "Circe", he will no longer identify with Satan.

IV STEPHEN'S RIDDLE

The riddle that Stephen asks of his students in "Nestor" shows how far Stephen has to go to communicate with his audience:

The cock crew,
The sky was blue:
The bells in heaven
Were striking eleven.
'Tis time for this poor soul
To go to heaven. (U.26; *II.102–7*)

The narcissistic riddle shows us that Stephen is still locked into the "lyrical" mode of *Portrait* and that his imagination cannot reach beyond himself. Given the impenetrable verse query provided by the morbid and self-indulgent Stephen, nobody could have figured out the answer: "The fox burying his grandmother under a holly bush" has no relation to the riddle (U.27; II.115). But the bathetic disjunction between riddle and solution does engage the reader in a quest to discover what is going on in Stephen's abstruse mind. Stephen's riddle calls attention to the difficulty of reading incomplete and partial texts that do not provide sufficient information for understanding them. Stephen's answer is a thinly veiled reference to himself. The grandmother is not only his own mother, but his Irish heritage, indeed, the Old Woman of Ireland for whom to Stephen the milklady in "Telemachus" is a symbol. Holly, the traditional evergreen of the Christmas season, represents renewal, but renewal – with its implications of restoring to a prior state – has an ironic aspect since Stephen is trying to put his past behind him. Perhaps Stephen realizes that the artist must not only be an idealistic romantic but also a wily and shrewd man – not unlike, the rereader understands, the foxy Odysseus and his twentieth century counterpart, Bloom.

Stephen also identifies with Parnell, who took the alias of Mr. Fox; Stephen sees himself as a fellow victim of Ireland because he feels that he, too, had been betrayed by Irishmen. But he also sees himself as a sly fox, a wily beast, trying to bury his prey before he is discovered: "on a heath beneath winking stars a fox, red reek of rapine in his fur, with merciless bright eyes scraped in the earth, listened, scraped up the earth, listened, scraped and scraped" (U.28; II.148–50). The reader understands that foxy Stephen sees himself as an heir to Parnell who, in his role as artist, will liberate Ireland. The very act of assuming another identity binds him to Parnell, since as an artist Stephen will necessarily assume a variety of roles as he imagines how others think and feel. Since early in "Calypso", the next chapter, Bloom is identified with Parnell and given the epithet "foxeyes" – "A speck of eager fire from foxeyes thanked [Dlugacz]" – in conjunction with brightness, the rereader sees that Stephen is both linked to Bloom and unwittingly prophesying Bloom's appearance and significance (U.60; IV.186).

In "Scylla and Charybdis" Stephen thinks of Shakespeare as

"Christfox", an image which combines three figures – Shakespeare, Christ, and Parnell – whom he regards as precursors and spiritual fathers because they were victims of misunderstanding: "Christfox in leather trews, hiding, a runaway in blighted treeforks from hue and cry" (U.193: IX.337–8). Stephen proposes through the rich metaphor of the fox an apostolic succession from God to Christ to Shakespeare to Parnell to himself. Foxy Stephen who is trying to bury his past – who is living on the margin of society because he conceives himself as an outcast – identifies with the mysterious figure who is trying to avoid capture. But we should note that no sooner does Stephen propose himself, the putative artist, as "Christfox", a potential saviour for Ireland, than he imagines the persecution and demise of that figure.

Isn't Stephen speaking, like Christ, in parables? And, we recall, Christ spoke in parables only to those who did not know the significance of his words and deeds, namely, the outsiders; in *Matthew*, 13:34–5 Jesus says: "I will open my mouth in parables, I will utter what has been hidden since the foundation of the world."[18] But does Stephen have command of his riddle? That Stephen has not solved the riddle of his arts may be indicated by his very first words: "Tell me, Mulligan" (U.4; I.47). For Joyce, too, speaks in riddles and parables which are not completely comprehensible to a first reader; do we have sufficient evidence to know how many lovers Molly really has or who the man in the macintosh is or, indeed, what is the effect upon Stephen of this crucial day? To the reader of *Ulysses*, as T. S. Eliot (adopting the words of Lancelot Andrewes) puts it in "Gerontion", "Signs are taken for Wonders."

V STEPHEN'S PATERNITY

Stephen is obsessed with the actual act of intercourse that conceived him: "Wombed in sin darkness I was too, made not begotten. By them, the man with my voice and my eyes and a ghostwoman with ashes on her breath. They clasped and sundered, did the coupler's will" (U.38; III.45–7). That in the preceding passage he cannot speak of the participants as his father and mother indicates his estrangement from his father and his guilty feelings about refusing to obey his mother's wishes, feelings that have an oedipal component. Reflecting his problem with his mother's sexuality which we saw in the image of his mother having intercourse with the Irish saint Columbanus, Stephen defines conception in terms of the one model – the Christ story – in which the woman plays less than a full role; and even within this story he virtually ignores the role of Mary.

Stephen's Jesuitical training shapes the form and substance of his arguments about the relation of father to son. Stephen thinks of the concept of paternity in terms of the scholastic debate of the relation between God the father and Christ the son. Thus Stephen draws upon his ecclesiastical training for metaphors about the relationship between father and son. But, ironically, for authority figures to support his apostasy, he often looks to the very medieval scholastics who have been branded as heretical by the Church. He evokes Arius who denied the consubstantiality of the Father and Son. By denying that God the father and Christ the son were the same substance, Arius provides Joyce with a precedent for establishing that paternity is a legal fiction and for choosing his own father. Since Christ cannot be thought of as having the same substance [*homoousios*] but rather as having a like substance [*homoiousis*], he is not equal to God. Arius was condemned as an heretic in 325 when the Nicene Creed repudiated his position.[19] Joyce wants us to see that Stephen is something of an Arian, and wants us to smile at how Stephen rather brilliantly adopts Arianism to suit his definitions both of the artist and paternity. For Stephen who sees the artist as the Creator, who sees writing as a metaphor for Genesis and vice versa, it is important to deny the consubstantiality not only of his own father but of anyone or anything. For the artist to be conceived as a Creator who makes an imagined world in his own image, the artist must be different not merely in degree but in kind.

Stephen is also attracted to what Father Noon calls "the other principle Trinitarian heresy, Sabellianism".[20] Sabellius, a rationalist and a Platonist, denied the distinction between the three figures in the Trinity; Sabellius thought of the three entities as merely manifestations of God in the outer world, as kinds of replicas of the real Divine Essence. His heresy is his claim that "Father", "Son", and "Spirit" – or "Holy Ghost" – are names that man used for the same Divine Being.[21] Again Stephen finds this heresy attractive because, within his metaphorical system in which God the Father is a figure for the creative artist, it establishes the preeminence of the artist as different not merely in degree but in kind. More subtly, this heresy abolishes the possibility of speaking of paternity by denying as illusory the notion of relationships between God the Father and his Son – and, by extension, within Stephen's metaferocious imagination, between Simon and Stephen.

One might ask why Stephen, son of Simon Dedalus but not himself a father, is so obsessed with denying the Godhood of the Son. But the point is that Christ's identity as God derives finally from God's stature and Stephen wants to provide an alternative metaphor in which the son can derive his identity from another source – that is, provide a metaphor in which the son can choose his own father. At the same time he wants to establish the supremacy of the Creator, his metaphor for the artist. Stephen knows that Aquinas proposes elaborate arguments for establishing the relationship and sequence between God the Father and Son: "The Son is He Who proceeds from the Father, the Father is He from Whom the Son proceeds."[22] (We recall that in *Portrait* Stephen spoke of his aesthetic theory in Chapter 5 as "applied Aquinas".)

Yet later in the library Joyce has Stephen emphasize that God the Father creates his own Son, as he as artist has created Stephen Dedalus, the son of his imagination:

> He Who Himself begot middler the Holy Ghost and Himself sent Himself, Agenbuyer, between Himself and others, Who, put upon by His fiends, stripped and whipped, was nailed like bat to barndoor, starved on crosstree, Who let Him bury, stood up, harrowed hell, fared into heaven and there these nineteen hundred years sitteth on the right hand of His Own Self but yet shall come in the latter day to doom the quick and dead when all the quick shall be dead already. (U.197–8; <u>IX. 493–9</u>)

Note that in the above passage Stephen not only does not use the word Son, but that he proposes that God send someone quite different from the traditional figure in the Trinity. That the figure "Agenbuyer" sent by God the father contains the first two syllables of Stephen's "Agenbite of Inwit" and of Bloom's "Agendath Netaim" suggests how these two different men are moving on parallel courses and at least raises the possibility for the reader of a potential relationship. For Stephen and for Joyce, God whose Word created the world is a metaphor for the author. That God sends a fusion of Bloom and Stephen emphasizes that in Joyce's imagined world the author controls everything, creating order from apparent disorder, and unity from bits and snips of experience. Indeed, isn't the entire sequence in the above passage derived from God, even including the fiends who torture the figure he sends? Doesn't this parallel the way that the artist's imagination generates the entire sequence of a narrative from beginning to end?

Is not the above parable of God sending himself an ironic version of Stephen's insistence that – given the awkwardness and, indeed, unnaturalness, of the relation of fathers and sons – the best that can be hoped for is reconciliation after sundering?

> Who is the father of any son that any son should love him or he any son? . . . They are sundered by a bodily shame so steadfast that the criminal annals of the world, stained with all other incests and bestialities, hardly record its breach . . . . The son unborn mars beauty: born, he brings pain, divides affection, increases care. He is a new male: his growth is his father's decline, his youth his father's envy, his friend his father's enemy. (U.207–8; IX. 844–5; 850–2; 854–6; Gabler's restoration of "new" stresses more sharply the relation between the son's development and the father's decline.)

Apparently only when God and His Son are the same can the son please the father and vice versa. Otherwise the appropriate metaphor for Stephen's relationship with his father, as we have seen, is Lucifer's rebellion and the permanent sundering implied by that rebellion. That Stephen holds this conception of paternity makes it necessary for him to seek an unlikely or disguised father figure on the very periphery of Stephen's attention – namely Bloom who, recalling Odysseus's disguise as a shepherd when he returns home, wears the masque of a marginal middle-class Jew.

Does not Stephen's idea of reconciliation following sundering describe the way that Joyce makes interchangeable the signifier and signified in the novel's extended metaphors? The artist's way of sending himself to redeem the world is to weave the details of his past into unifying patterns and imaginative analogies. Because each era is distinct and yet part of a cyclical pattern, because paradigmatic relationships are at the heart of every civilization, the novel proposes metaphors that can reconcile the characters from each period on one spatial plane even while maintaining, from another perspective, their separation. The concepts of metempsychosis and parallax propose kinds of reconciliation that follow sundering. Yet the separate temporal periods inevitably dissolve back into different planes and ironize Joyce's metaphoricity.

VI THE OPENING OF "PROTEUS"

Ulysses is Joyce's inquiry into how modern fiction can reconcile the demands of both a synchronic or spatial perspective, which assumes the coterminous existence of all events, and a diachronic perspective, which assumes that events are sequential. The historical and literary metaphors meet the demands of synchronicity; the hour by hour chronicle and the careful attention to Stephen's and Bloom's biography meet the demands of traditional diachronic narrative Since *Ulysses* is, among other things, about the writing of itself, about Stephen's solving the intellectual and artistic problems that make the book possible, it behooves Stephen to reconcile the demands of space and time. That *Ulysses* must be read both spatially and temporally is emphasized by Stephen's effort to include in his perceptions *nacheinander*, one thing after another, and *nebeneinander*, one thing next to another.(U.37; III.10ff.). These ways of reading correspond to the novel's efforts to present both diachronic and synchronic historical perspectives. (In *Portrait*, Stephen had argued: "An esthetic image is presented to us either in space or in time. What is audible is presented in time, what is visible is presented in space." [P.212].) Stephen's "reading" of experience calls attention to ways of reading the text. Yet, at times, such as the aforementioned riddle in "Nestor", Stephen's modes of perception may place the reader in a labyrinth; the odyssean reader may confront passages that, while expressing Stephen's problems in sense-making, actually interfere with the reader's quest to understand the text and to achieve the intimacy with Joyce that successful reading requires. In other words, because Joyce cannot separate himself from Stephen – cannot move, to use Joyce's terms, from the lyrical mode to the epical and dramatic ones – he commits the fallacy of imitative form; the process of imitating a character's confusion causes the reader's confusion.

The opening of "Proteus" calls attention to the artist's creative mission. Just as Menelaus had to wrestle with the continually changing Proteus, Stephen must wrestle with the protean nature of his experience. Under the tutelage of Aristotle, who went as far as possible in exploring the visible world, he is turning away from the Platonism of the Church Fathers and the Celtic Twilight and towards the world of experience which must be the subject of his art: "Ineluctable modality of the visible: at least that if no more, thought through my eyes. Signatures of all things I am here to read . . ." (U.37; III.1–2). Yet Stephen also seeks to go beyond knowing the visible, factual world and to explore the possibilities of his imagination. For he thinks of both the poet of passionate Christian visions. Dante, and, while walking with his eyes closed, the Romantic prophet Blake – invoked by "*Los Demiurgos*," which combines Los, the creative imagination, with "Demiurgos", in Gnostic theory, the creator of the world.[23] For Stephen at this point, Dante's epithet for Aristotle, "*maestro di color che sanno*" or "master of those that know", may have something of a condescending aspect because it implies a privileging of inspired visionary *seeing* and *feeling* over rational *knowing*.

Later, in the "Scylla and Charybdis" chapter, prior to his argument that Shakespeare used his life as the essential ingredient of his art, he redefines "Ineluctable modality of the visible" to "Space: what you damn well have to see" (U.186; IX.86). In that chapter which takes place in the library, an appropriate place to discuss how books should be read and written, Joyce has Stephen show how Shakespeare, by recreating reality in terms of his imaginative needs, met the opposing demands of time and timelessness; of nominalistic facts and representative values; and of rendering experience that fulfilled his psychological needs and presenting for the reader universal interests. More importantly, Joyce shows how Stephen is progressing towards reconciling these demands.

VII   STEPHEN'S QUEST FOR THE "WORD"

Readers have been puzzled by Stephen's query, "What is that word known to all men?" a query which is part of a rather narcissistic passage in which Stephen poignantly dwells on his own loneliness and imagines himself being sexually fondled: "Touch me. Soft eyes. Soft soft soft hand. I am lonely here. O, touch me soon, now. What is that word known to all men? I am quite here alone. Sad too. Touch, touch me" (U.49; III.434–6). In the nightmare world of "Circe", he "eagerly" requests of his mother's ghost: "Tell me the word, mother, if you know now. The word known to all men" (U.581; XV.4192–3). The Gabler edition makes clear that the "word known to all men" is love; for in "Scylla and Charybdis", while *performing* his aesthetic theory in the library, Stephen thinks to himself: "Do you know what you are talking about? Love, yes. Word known to all men. *Amor ver aliquid alicui bonum vult unde et ea quae concupiscimus . . .*" ("Love indeed wishes some good to another and therefore we all desire it"); IX.429–31).[21] Stephen requires love of every kind – parental love, heterosexual love, the asexual love of his fellows – but he also must learn how to love generously and passionately, something Bloom knows. In fact, the prior passage links Stephen's personal needs with his artistic needs, for love is the precondition of Shakespeare's artistic creativity. What Stephen has to do is make the journey from the ironic detachment of *Portrait* to the active emotional involvement in life exemplified by Shakespeare and Bloom.

Stephen is speaking of the biographical basis of Shakespeare's plays and, in particular, of the young women of the later plays: "Marina . . . a child of storm, Miranda, a wonder, Perdita, that which was lost. What was lost is given back to him: his daughter's child. *My dearest wife*, Pericles says, *was like this maid*. Will any man love the daughter if he has not loved the mother?" (U.195; IX.420–4). These women are idealized versions of what Stephen desperately needs, namely a woman who might love him, but they are also examples of how the artist as father figure incestuously creates versions of his own past experience: "Will he not see reborn in her, with the memory of his own youth added, another image?" (IX.427–8; the Gabler edition restores this passage). In other words, Shakespeare has done just what Stephen had predicted that he himself might do in his own work

– and what Joyce has done in *Ulysses*: "As we, or mother Dana, weave and unweave our bodies . . . from day to day, their molecules shuttled to and fro, so does the artist weave and unweave his image . . . . So in the future, the sister of the past, I may see myself as I sit here now but by reflection from that which then I shall be" (U.194; IX.376–8; 383–5).

VIII   THE CLOSING OF "PROTEUS"

Since our interest is in the way *Ulysses* signifies, let us examine the closing lines of the Telemachiad in terms of its relationship to what precedes and follows in *Ulysses*, in terms of its modification of a prior passage in *Portrait*, and in terms of what it indicates about the ethos of the narrative presence who is telling the tale to us. In each case, we are speaking of a process by which the reader sees a passage in terms of its signification; he substitutes a metaphorical reading for the actual one or, at the very least, provides a strong supplement to the literal reading.

The quiet, restful conclusion to "Proteus" contrasts with the rapid movement of Stephen's thoughts and his depression. Stephen's perception of the arriving ship reflects the tendency of his imagination to conceive in symbolic terms – terms that combine his preoccupation with scholastic debate about the Trinity – his self-pitying identification with the crucified Christ, and his inability to escape his Catholic training: "Moving through the air high spars of a threemaster, her sails brailed upon the crosstrees, homing, upstream, silently moving, a silent ship" (U.51; III.503–5). But does not the omniscient narrator – the fictionalized Joyce – reassert his presence by suggesting a trace of his original presence at the beginning of the first chapter and thus reminding us that he has been there all along? The last word of the passage with which the Telemachiad ends, "ship", begins and ends with the letters of the first two words, "Stately plump", of "Proteus". It is almost as if the "threemaster" ship becomes the artistic womb from which Stephen as artist will emerge. The "threemaster ship" prefigures the novel's union of the three characters and the union of the human aspects that each character signifies: Stephen (mind), Bloom (both soul and experience), and Molly (body); it also is a metaphor for the tripartite novel which is divided into sections that begin with the letters "S",

"M", and "P" – letters which indicate the focus of the central characters' quests. Stephen is focused on himself; but Bloom's section begins with "M" because "Molly" is the object of his quest, and Molly's begins with "P" because "Poldy" is still, as her monologue indicates, the focus of her concern.

This closing passage of "Proteus" takes some of its meaning from the passage in *Portrait* in which Stephen dreamed that Brother Michael arrived to announce Parnell's death and that the crowd, who had lost their leader, responded with sorrow; the dream had been based on the ship *Ireland's* bringing the body of Parnell to Kingston. Thus the mysterious ship which seems to be moving *upstream*, calls attention to the ghostly presence of the artist – the fictionalized Joyce – who can reinvent his world as he wishes: "Creation from nothing" (U.37; III.35). To the rereader, the passage implies that Parnell's successor will be the creative artist which results from the merging of the three major figures. In a sense, the ship announces the answer to Stephen's query: "Who ever anywhere will read these written words?" (U.48; III.414–5). The obvious answer is the mature artist figure who will write the book. But another answer is we, the readers, who will read not only the fragments of the jejune poem that Stephen is writing on the strand, but the book that transforms those and other fragments into significance. When Bloom finally comes to rest at the end of "Ithaca," the first response to the question "With?" is "Sinbad the Sailor;" containing echoes of this last sentence from "Proteus;" it and the subsequent variations suggest Stephen's perception of the sailing ship and by synecdoche Stephen himself (U.737; XVII.2322ff).

NOTES

1. George Eliot, *Middlemarch: a Study of Provincial Life*, ed. Quentin Anderson (New York: Collier Books, 1962) p. 569.
2. See Gifford and Seidman, p. 7.
3. See my "'I Was the World in Which I Walked': the Transformation of the British Novel", *University of Toronto Quarterly*, 51:3 (Spring 1982) 279–97.
4. H. Montgomery Hyde, *The Trials of Oscar Wilde* (New York: Dover Publications, 1962) p. 201.
5. *Critical Writings of James Joyce*, p. 202.
6. See Gifford and Seidman, p. 8.

7. Darcy O'Brien, *The Conscience of James Joyce* (Princeton University Press, 1968) p. 11.
8. See Gifford and Seidman, p. 12.
9. For this view, see Daniel Mark Fogel, "Symbol and Context in *Ulysses*: Joyce's 'Bowl of Bitter Waters' and Passover", *ELH* 46 (1979) 710–21.
10. See George DeF. Lord, "The Heroes of *Ulysses* and Their Homeric Prototypes", *Yale Review*, 62:1 (October 1972) 43–58.
11. See Gifford and Seidman, p. 22; they quote from Butler's *Lives of the Saints* (London, 1938).
12. Richard Ellmann, *The Consciousness of Joyce* (Toronto and New York: Oxford University Press, 1977) p. 20.
13. Gifford and Seidman, p. 6, quote from the *Layman's Missel* (Baltimore, Md., 1962).
14. Gifford and Seidman, p. 7.
15. *Pentateuch and Haftorahs*, ed. J. H. Hertz (London: Soncino Press, 1980) pp. 102–3, 759.
16. Hertz, p. 1005.
17. See Gifford and Seidman, pp. 46–7; their source is *Layman's Missel*.
18. See Frank Kermode, *The Genesis of Secrecy* (Cambridge, Mass.: Harvard University Press, 1980).
19. See Father William Noon, S.J., *Joyce and Aquinas* (New Haven, Conn.: Yale University Press, 1957); my discussion takes issue with Father Noon's argument that Stephen rejects the Arian position.
20. Father Noon, p. 110.
21. See Gifford and Seidman, p. 15.
22. Father Noon, p. 111.
23. See Gifford and Seidman, p. 33.
24. I am accepting Richard Ellmann's translation; see his "The Big Word in 'Ulysses'", *The New York Review of Books* 31:16 (25 Oct. 1984) 31–2. However, it should be noted that Ellmann has made an incomplete sentence into a complete one.

5 Joyce's Irish Jew: Bloom

I "CALYPSO"

That Bloom may be the solution to Stephen's problem is suggested by the opening of "Calypso" with its emphasis upon the nominalistic world of experience: "Mr Leopold Bloom ate with relish the inner organs of beasts and fowls. He liked thick giblet soup, nutty gizzards, a stuffed roast heart, liverslices fried with crustcrumbs, fried hencods' roes. Most of all he liked grilled mutton kidneys which gave to his palate a fine tang of faintly scented urine" (U.55; IV.1–5). That we are in a radically different world is indicated by the syntax with its straightforward, vibrant progression from subject to predicate to object. As we read the passage aloud, hesitating at the consonant cluster and dwelling on the open vowels, we realize that the active voice and phonics stress Bloom's delight in his breakfast and savoring of his food. The emphasis on the "s" sound calls attention to the very different use of the "s" sound with which "Proteus" had been brought to a silent, mysterious close. Indeed, for the most part, Bloom takes pleasure in the simple routines of his morning, for the reason that they are enriched with genuine concern for his family and acquaintances. Joyce differentiates between, on the one hand, Bloom's enjoyment of experience and his pleasure in himself and, on the other, Stephen's egotistical and self-flagellating pride. That Joyce has Bloom close "Calypso" with his exclamation "Poor Dignam!", when his thoughts of himself and his family are suddenly interrupted by the church bells, indicates Bloom's generosity of spirit and contrasts strikingly with Stephen's bitter attitude toward Mulligan, crystallized by "Usurper", the final angry accusatory word of "Telemachus", which echoes Hamlet's judgment of Claudius.

While Stephen interprets or reads the world in terms of his abstractions, Bloom responds in terms of what he has learned from his experience. Within Joyce's hierarchy of values, Bloom is admirable because he responds to the not-I world more fully and in more varied circumstances.[1] What replaces the legends and myths of the first three chapters is actual experience. Bloom defines personal space in terms of the here and personal time in terms of the now. Unlike Stephen, who cannot escape the day to day condition of human life, Bloom is immersed in "the stream of life" and enjoys the physical body in which he lives (U.86; V.563). (Later, in the library, Stephen becomes less of a nay-sayer, when he defines his aspiration to achieve the immortality of God and Christ in terms of creating his own universe which will survive his mortality.) Milly, Molly, and Martha are Bloom's versions of Stephen's mythical Old Woman of Ireland. By using the first person plural pronoun, Molly speaks in the traditional Irish idiom: "O, rocks! she said. Tell us in plain words" (U.64; IV.343) or "Give us a touch, Poldy" (U.89; VI.80–1).

Bloom is not interested in theories and abstractions for their own sake. When he thinks of numbers, it is usually in relation-ship to money or to the age of people he knows. In contrast to Stephen, abstract numbers hold little interest for him: "Fifteen multiplied by. The figures whitened in his mind, unsolved: displeased, he let them fade" (U.58; IV.141–2. The Gabler edi-tion replaces fifty with fifteen; since multiplying fifteen is more difficult than multiplying fifty, Bloom's lack of interest in ab-stract mathematics – as opposed to practical and monetary numbers – becomes slightly less ostentatious.). For Bloom lives in the 'Ineluctable modality of the visible" on which Stephen philosophizes (U.37; III.1). He thinks of the East not, like Stephen, in terms of dancing numbers ("Across the page the symbols moved in grave morrice, in the mummery of their letters, wearing quaint caps of squares and cubes" [U.28; II.155–61]), but in terms of the promise of economic success for himself and in terms of the community benefits of fecundity: "*Agendath Netaim*: planters' company. . . . Orangegroves and immense melonfields north of Jaffa. . . . Every year you get a sending of the crop. . . . Crates lined up on the quayside at Jaffa" (U.60; IV. 191–7; IV.212). (Note the homophonic relationship between "Agenbite" and "Agendath".) Unlike Stephen, Bloom is not obsessed with discovering the right word, but rather has an analogistic mind that is willing to make substitutions for phrases with other apposite if slightly different phrases. Usually, the source of his analogies is his own experience; as Stephen says of Shakespeare, "All events brought grist to his mill" (U.204; IX.748). He associates Molly with Gibraltar, where she had been born. Both Bloom's extended fantasy of a desert in bloom in the holy land and his metaphorical substitutions remind us that Bloom is as much an artist figure as Stephen. As Joyce has Lenehan remind us in "Wandering Rocks", "There's a touch of the artist about old Bloom" (U.235; X.582–3).

Bloom's imagination and emotional resilience enable him to face the disappointments and frustrations of his life. Yet, as we become aware of his sexual life and Molly's adultery, we understand how partial a loaf he is accepting. Nevertheless, in contrast to Stephen's obsessive preoccupation with the Old Woman of Ireland – figured in his imagination by the milkwoman whom he imagines with "Old shrunken paps" and "wrinkled fingers", the midwives on the strand, and the old women of his parable in "Aeolus", Bloom, after similarly perceiving an old woman as the personification of his people, rejects the metaphor in favor of enriching personal memories and fantasies (U.13–4; I.398,401–2). No sooner does reality intrude on his fantasy of reviving the holy land ("No, not like that. A barren land, bare waste. Vulcanic lake, the dead sea: no fish, weedless, sunk deep in the earth. No wind would lift those waves . . . . Dead: an old woman's: the grey sunken cunt of the world"), than he turns to thoughts of the warmth of sharing his bed with Molly: "Be near her ample bedwarmed flesh. Yes, yes" (U.61; IV.218–20, 227–8, 238–9). Joyce is also contrasting a characteristic Jewish turn toward tomorrow and acceptance of today – even while being fully conscious of the frustrations of the present and disappointments of the past – with the Irish preoccupation with a romanticized version of the past and the Catholic obsession with dwelling on past sins and measuring every action according to a strict and narrow barometer of sins and grace.

We should note in the above passage the striking parallax in Bloom's echo of *Lycidas* – "sunk deep beneath the earth", and "No wind would lift those waves"; *Lycidas*, the poem which was part of Stephen's lesson in "Nestor", haunts Stephen's imagination in "Proteus" as the drowned man whose dead body would be discovered: "Found drowned. . . . A corpse rising. . . . Sunk though he be beneath the watery floor. We have him. Easy now" (U.25–6, 50; II.64–6, 79–80, III.471–5). Later, Bloom, too, thinks of drowning, and also – unwittingly – rejects the argument of *Lycidas* that death will be the birth of the eternal soul: "Drowning they say is the pleasantest. See your whole life in a flash. But being brought back to life no" (U.114; VI.988–9). But in "Eumaeus", Stephen's and Bloom's mutual, although quite different, familiarity with the poem becomes the grounding for the narrator's invoking the poem's optimistic ending – "dreaming of the fresh woods and pastures new as someone somewhere sings" and the more corrupt "dreaming of fresh fields and pastures new" (U.630, 660; XVI.632–3, 1727–8) – to suggest the possibility of renewal for both men and, in particular, Stephen the young artist who, like the poet of *Lycidas*, might perhaps overcome his mourning grief by means of writing about it.

What this modern Odysseus must do is cast off his thralldom to Molly as Calypso and, by displacing her suitors, restore himself to the position of husband of Penelope. For Bloom, however, Calypso is not so much an external person as a state of mind. The thralldom he must and, indeed, does for the most part overcome, is an obsessive preoccupation with the three concerns: his personal and racial past, his mortality, and his wife's and daughter's sexuality. His memories of Milly are not without the father's inevitable jealousy and barely suppressed incestuous impulses: "Molly. Milly. Same thing watered down. . . . Soon be a woman. Mullingar. Dearest Papli. Young student. Yes, yes: a woman too. Life, life" (U.89; VI.87–90). That he thinks of his own aging in terms of Lot's wife's looking back to Sodom, after God instructed her not to, is Joyce's way of showing the reader that self-conscious thinking of mortality – one of Stephen's subjects in the first three chapters – is a kind of narcissism and a dead end: "Cold oils slid along his veins, chilling his blood: age crusting him with a salt cloak" (U.61; IV.231–2). Stephen had also recalled a literary reference to "salt", the prediction by Dante's great- great-grandfather of Dante's future exile: "Now I eat his salt bread." But, unlike Bloom, Stephen does not turn from his bitterness or his fixation on the past; insofar as he is relying on Mulligan, who, as we noted, resembles Wilde in physical appearance and sexual preference, he is looking back with Lot's wife to Sodom (U.20; I.63).[2]

When Bloom transforms the serendipitous sight of a girl running into the fantasy of a girl running *to meet him*, we see in the resilience of his imagination the means by which he can break the thralldom of his psychological Calypso: "Quick warm sunlight came running from Berkeley Road, swiftly, in slim sandals, along the brightening footpath. Runs, she runs to meet me, a girl with gold hair on the wind" (U.61; IV.240–2). The perception of the girl bathed in sunlight is not only an optative fantasy, but a reverie of Molly's receptivity when she was younger and perhaps, more recently, of Milly's enthusiasm. Bloom is associated with the sun throughout the day. Perhaps Joyce wants us to recall the scene in *Portrait* where the bird-girl's beauty so profoundly affects Stephen that he feels "his soul . . . swooning into some new world" (P. 172).[3]

II "LOTUS-EATERS"

Just as we experienced the presence of *Portrait* in the first three chapters, we begin in the Bloom chapters to recall *Dubliners*; for Dublin's moral and spiritual paralysis becomes central and, indeed, some of the prior work's characters even reappear in minor roles. As *Ulysses* proceeds, we realize that our ideology for reading it must include an awareness that Joyce re-examines prior subjects in earlier chapters from a different perspective and style. Thus, the second three chapters dramatize the same hours of the same day in Bloom's life that had been the subject of the first three chapters. More importantly, these chapters show Bloom not only living in his unique manner through the same morning hours, but also thinking about the same subjects as Stephen had been doing in the first three chapters. Such iteration calls attention to the cyclical and synchronic nature of time.

"Lotus-Eaters" is the first of the three public chapters which take place between breakfast and lunch. As we make our way through "Lotus-Eaters", "Hades", and "Aeolus", we realize that most Dubliners seem to have very little work to do. Ironically, Bloom's sexual reveries throughout the day are the lotus leaves which retard his journey. That Joyce calls the technique of "Lotus-Eaters" "narcissism" indicates, among other things, that a certain amount of self-love is necessary to survive in the modern city. One has to be on guard against petty swindlers like M'Coy, potential adulterers like Blazes, and alert to the small pleasures of a public bath or a covert dalliance by correspondence. Befitting a chapter whose technique is narcissism, Bloom thinks rather more of his own interests than he does in "Calypso" and "Hades", the preceding and subsequent chapters. Bloom's pride and rationality enable him to resist the narcotics of sloth, gambling, male camaraderie, and Catholicism.

While Stephen's sexual reveries are adolescent, incomplete, narcissistic and abstract ("Touch me. Soft eyes. Soft soft soft hand. I am lonely here. O, touch me soon, now"), Bloom's memories of passion – drawing upon the first intercourse with Molly on the Howth – are personal and vibrant: "Lips kissed, kissing, kissed. Full gluey woman's lips" (U.49,67; III.434–5, IV.450). After Stephen's effort to escape the demands and responsibilities of his life by living in literary and personal abstractions, Bloom says "yes" to life. Thinking of the day Rudy might have been conceived he thinks "How life begins" (U.89; VI.81). Then, reluctantly accepting Milly's adolescence and the potential of her having sexual experience with a young student named Bannon, he thinks: "Yes, yes: a woman too. Life, life" (U.89; VI.89–90). (Are we not to contrast Bloom's wordly acceptance of sexuality and the phases of human life with Stephen's life-denying fixations which have been shaped by his pride, willed isolation, and his rigid Catholic upbringing?) While Bloom accepts his body, takes pleasure in bathing, and is fascinated by the possibility of a woman washing his navel, Stephen is repelled by the idea of someone else giving him a bath: "Bath a most private thing. I wouldn't let my brother, not even my own brother, most lascivious thing. Green eyes, I see you" (U.43; III.236–8).

"Eucharist" is the symbol of the chapter not merely because Bloom witnesses the taking of communion, but because for Bloom word and flesh, body and spirit, are one. That in "Lotus-Eaters", Bloom, too, goes into a Catholic Church and sees the Eucharist performed shows how the two principals are sharing common experiences on this vital day. But, because Joyce wanted us to understand that the rites and rituals of one culture iterate those of another – in metaphoric terms, signify or represent one another, Bloom perceives the Catholic rituals in terms of his Jewish experience: "Something like those mazzoth: it's that sort of bread: unleavened shewbread" (U.81; V.358–9). That he thinks of transubstantiation ("Hokypoky penny a lump") in terms of the child's corruption of *hoc est corpus* (this is [my] body) recalls

Mulligan's transformation of the Eucharist into a magic show; it also calls attention to the recurring needs for magic and rituals in all cultures (U.81; V.362).[4]

While the apostate Catholic Stephen accuses himself of being a "Chewer of corpses", the agnostic Jew comically accepts the logic of eating the body of Christ in words which recall Stephen's self-accusation: "Stupefies them first . . . . They don't seem to chew it: only swallow it down" (U.10,80; I.278; V.350–2). That he thinks of Martha's letter in the same breath as the concept of confession illustrates Joyce's strong belief that Catholicism depends on a perverse need in mankind to make itself suffer: "Penance. Punish me, please. Great weapon in their hands" (U.83;·V.426). Poignantly Bloom envies the sense of community that he thinks Catholicism provides: "Then feel all like one family party, same in the theatre, all in the same swim. They do. I'm sure of that. Not so lonely. In our confraternity" (U.81; V.362–4). But, ironically, he seems to find more continuity in the memories of the Jewish and Mason rituals ("in our confraternity", we learn, refers to Bloom's membership in the Masons) than Molly, Stephen, or anyone else finds in Catholic ones. He thinks of the Mass in terms of an anodyne or anesthetic and also in terms of the Haggadah service: "Blind faith . . . . Lulls all pain. Wake this time next year" (U.81; V.367–8). It is worth noting that while Bloom affirms the novel's emphasis on a cyclical theory of history, Stephen is tempted by the most pessimistic linear vision: "Life is many days. This will end" (U.214; IX.1097).

Unlike Stephen who lives in the world of ideas, Bloom lives in the world of experience. While Stephen is haunted by the past, Bloom, despite his nostalgia, is firmly turned towards the future. As James H. Maddox puts it, "It is a capacity to change the self according to circumstances – a supremely Ulyssean capacity – which is set in contrast to Stephen's stiff posing."[5] If necessary, Bloom can become Henry Flower without undermining his self-coherence. The pseudonym "Henry Flower" is the masque he wears in the thralls of Martha Clifford, a Calypso figure in the sense that she too retards his journey home; to recall Wilde's *The Importance of Being Earnest*, as Joyce would have expected us to do, "Henry Flower" is Bloom's Bunbury.

Yet in this chapter Bloom is a rather poignant figure. Writing soft porn to a pen pal whom he has never met, and engaging in fantasies of flagellation while his wife is preparing for adultery, he has symbolically left his key at home. He is preoccupied with a bath, in part because he might masturbate there. Anticipating a bath, he affirms – in contrast to the hydrophobic Stephen – his delight in his body: "He foresaw his pale body reclined in it at full, naked, in a womb of warmth, oiled by scented melting soap, softly laved. He saw . . . his navel, bud of flesh: and saw the dark tangled curls of his bush floating, floating hair of the stream around the limp father of thousands, a languid floating flower" (U.86; V.568–72). That the chapter ends with "flower", a metaphor for the fulfilment of his name "Bloom", at this point stresses the gap between the story of Bloom in Dublin and his historical and literary antecedents, between what seems at this point to the reader to be his rather ordinary life and any claims that might be made for his significance.

Thus Joyce is educating the reader to be aware of the fissure between Bloom's metaphorical role and his complex and contradictory role as character. For even while Joyce is establishing Bloom's importance as a twentieth century version of Ulysses, as the man of experience and putative father who provides contrasting sets of responses to the autobiographical portrait of the artist, and as an imaginative man with very human needs whose focus is on living horizontally in the here and now rather than, like Stephen, vertically in a world of Platonic ideals, his limp penis in the bath reminds us that he is a uxorious husband whose sexual potential is unfulfilled. Whether he will be able to achieve erection and intercourse with Molly is part of the novel's plot. The postcard "U.P". received by Breen is also applicable to Bloom (U.160; VIII.257). Notwithstanding his sexual problems, as the novel develops Bloom becomes the humanistic Everyman that a post-Christian age requires and a figure offering the values of love, generosity, and tolerance that a particular place, Dublin, and a particular time, the post-Christian era he lives in, require. For him, as for Stephen, paternity is a legal fiction. As the novel progresses the reader learns that Bloom is the father of us all because his physical responses are an integral part of how we make sense of the world and because his imaginative and sympathetic rendering of the responses of others is a lesson in how we can better make sense of *our* world.

III "HADES"

In "Hades", Bloom uses the occasion of Paddy Dignam's funeral to come to terms with his own mortality. A crucial issue for a post-Christian world is how one comes to terms with death. In the "Hades" episode we see that for Joyce the stream of consciousness is not merely a technique but a value, a value that affirms the interior space of the mind in contrast to the external world of the Homeric source. We recall that Odysseus descends into hell in search of Elpenor's ghost after the latter has fallen off a roof in a drunken stupor. That Bloom's descent into hell delves into his memories shows how the modern hero functions in interior psychological space. Haunted by memories of the dead, guilt, morbid associations, and feelings of social alienation from his companions, Bloom's hell is his own consciousness, and the means of extricating himself must also be found there.

In *Ulysses on the Liffey*, Ellmann argues that Stephen moves from abstraction to involvement in the physical world.[6] But while Stephen shows signs on this vital day of making a move from preoccupation with the vertical realm – the Platonic world of signs and symbols, of aesthetic distinctions and moral absolutes – toward interest in the empirical world, he has a very long way to go. For a comparison between "Proteus" and "Hades" shows that while Stephen accuses himself of killing his mother and then rouses himself from paralysis to make the most limited and narcissistic gestures (urinating, picking his nose, and writing a pastiche of a translated poem), Bloom creatively and imaginatively focuses his energy on coming to terms with his own life and the condition of being a mortal man in a world which offers no afterlife.

That Bloom's thoughts continue to echo Stephen's makes us aware of the transpersonal presence who is narrating the novel. Bloom, like Stephen, is concerned about his teeth: "Teeth getting worse and worse" (U.171; VIII.719). Milly, whose *joie de vivre* and acceptance of sexuality stand in contrast to the hyper-intellectual Stephen, does not bury her metaphorical grandmother but does bury a real bird: "Silly-Milly burying the little dead bird" (U.113; VI.952). Living more in an aesthetic world of signs than the world of experience, Stephen must symbolically bury his grandmother *because* he has failed in his actual life to bury properly his mother.

The emblem of mortality in "Hades" is the "obese grey rat" that Bloom sees in the graveyard at the end of the chapter: "An obese grey rat toddled along the side of the crypt, moving the pebbles. An old stager: greatgrandfather: he knows the ropes. The grey alive crushed itself in under the plinth, wriggled itself in under it. Good hidingplace for treasure" (U.114; VI.973–5). The passage echoes the solution to Stephen's riddle. While the Platonist Stephen thinks about an allegorical fox burying his figurative grandmother, the Aristotelian Bloom is both fascinated and repelled by the wily urge for survival exhibited by an ancient "greatgrandfather" rat who can chameleonically bury itself and its treasure.

Death is the antagonist of "Hades". Not only does the chapter mention various kinds of death – suicide, drowning, sudden death in one's sleep, infant death, even the death of a bird – but the texture of the language as in "The Dead" is imbued with death: "Dead side of the street this" (U.95; VI.316); "Give us a touch, Poldy. God, I'm dying for it" (U.89; VI.80–1). As Maddox has written, "This is the most terrible opiate in all of *Ulysses*; the living are drugged by their allegiance to the dead . . . . The statues and graves are signs of that essential element of Dublin life: the enervating allegiance to a past which is glorious but dead."[7] Not surprisingly in a scene that takes place in the graveyard, death is the subject on which conversation revolves and to which Bloom's mind returns. Humour is an important resource for Bloom: "Broken heart. A pump after all, pumping thousands of gallons of blood every day . . . . Lots of them lying around here: lungs, hearts, livers. Old rusty pumps: damn the thing else. The resurrection and the life. Once you are dead you are dead. That last day idea. Knocking them all up out of their graves. Come forth, Lazarus! And he came fifth and lost the job" (U.105; VI.673–9).

Bloom rejects the notion of an afterlife, a notion tentatively embraced by Simon, Stephen's real father, when he sees his wife's grave: "I suppose she is in heaven if there is a heaven" (U.105; VI.650–1). Indeed, Bloom has a naive view of the conservation of matter that implies that death is the source of new life: "Of course the cells or whatever they are go on living. Changing about. Live for ever practically. Nothing to feed on feed on themselves" (U.108–9; VI.780–2). In a metaphorical way, the novel does illustrate this principle that prior eras provide myths and paradigms by which we understand the present. As Bloom's stream of consciousness illustrates and as Stephen Dedalus believes, only the imagination can be the source of rebirth and regeneration.

Once again, the natural resilience of Bloom's imagination overcomes death. The chapter concludes with Bloom emerging from the hell of his own memories and fantasies: "Plenty to see and hear and feel yet. Feel live warm beings near you. Let them sleep in their maggoty beds. They are not going to get me this innings. Warm beds: warm fullblooded life" (U.115; VI.1003–5). Coupled with his small triumph over Menton, this affirmation returns him to his equanimity and self-esteem. If one recalls the links of "Life, life" with "Yes, yes" – "Yes, yes: a woman too. Life. Life" – and of "Yes, yes" with thoughts of Molly's warm body in bed, "Be near her ample bedwarmed flesh. Yes, yes", one sees that Bloom has made a strong affirmative turn towards his wife and home (U.89,61; VI.89–90, IV.238–9). In a world where, as Bloom puts it "Once you are dead you are dead", this is the only kind of resurrection that is possible – the resurrection achieved by the resilience of the mind and the capacity of the imagination to discover the necessary metaphors for hope (U.105; VI.677). That "next" and "life" are the leitmotifs of "Hades" – the chapter about death – is itself an affirmation; they are the words to which Bloom's mind returns to rescue him from depression.

To understand Bloom's interest in Stephen, one must appreciate the continuing impact of the death of Rudy, his infant son, who lived eleven days. If Bloom has one fixation, it is the loss of his son, a loss that reflects the characteristically Jewish desire for a male heir, but goes much deeper: "If little Rudy had lived. See him grow up. Hear his voice in the house. Walking beside Molly in an Eton suit. My son. Me in his eyes. Strange feeling it would be. From me" (U.89; VI.75–7). But Bloom's resilience is his greatest asset and a major feature of his energy and mental health. No sooner is he overcome by what might have been, than his creative imagination can transform past sorrows into future possibilities: "Our. Little. Beggar. Baby. Meant nothing. Mistake of nature. If it's healthy it's from the mother. If not from the man. Better luck next time" (U.96; VI.328–30). Yet the breathless, halting interior monologue, with its plethora of periods, poignantly renders Bloom's grief and loneliness. For as he rides in the funeral cortege with an assortment of anti-Semitic and insensitive Dubliners, including Simon Dedalus, all of whom themselves have severe domestic troubles, Bloom could not be more alone. Indeed, given the dramatic context, do not the periods orthographically stress how he is enclosed in his own thoughts and pain, separate from his fellows?

Both Bloom and Stephen keep alive the memory of the dead. "Hades" evokes "The Dead"; Bloom's dead son and father live, as Michael Furey does for Gretta Conroy in "The Dead", as a metaphor for the fullness of intense emotional commitment. As Gretta has kept Michael Furey alive in her memory, so Bloom keeps alive the memory of his son and father and the memory of his shared passion with Molly. For the most part, Bloom has rejected the sterile nostalgia and self-deception of Gabriel. Like Gretta, he has continued to live life in the present, but, as with her, the past haunts the present and creates a tension in his mind between experience as it seems to be occurring as external reality and experience as it is processed and transformed by his rich and powerful memories. As we read, we sometimes share this tension with Bloom, experiencing a double vision in which Bloom's subjective version of events is superimposed on an objective version to create a kind of photographic double exposure where a plenitude of contradictory data becomes an ironic comment on the possibility of coherence.

But we also experience an ironic gap between his perceptions – including his dialogue between past and present – and ours. As odyssean readers, we must come to terms with the discrepancy between the character's perception and our own perceptions, perceptions which sometimes are based on insight that the narrative presence shares with the reader, but which sometimes are based on qualifying or partially rejecting the narrator's interpretation. Thus the odyssean reader must come to terms with the ironic gaps between, on the one hand, metaphors that Joyce's narrator proposes for the twentieth century characters and, on the other hand, his perception that these characters may at times lack the resources, energy, and ability to live up to the literary or historical figures to whom they are compared. Put another way, the contemporary characters do not always fulfill their paradigms, but, upon rereading, we see that the historical and literary characters sometimes fall short of their successors.

"Hades" is a duet between an omniscient narrator who reports the narrative and the interior monologue of the isolated

Bloom with whom Joyce's narrator identifies; in much the same way, he will identify with Stephen in the latter parts of "Aeolus" and "Scylla and Charybdis". As Bloom overcomes morbidity and despair, the narrator abandons his neutrality and ironic detachment, and participates in Bloom's affirmation of the pleasures of life. The narrator and Bloom share the conclusion that Ireland's preoccupation with the dead, including its vast array of clerical and patriotic rituals, is a cause of its physical and moral sloth as well as its lack of national purpose: "Mr Bloom walked unheeded along his grove by saddened angels, crosses, broken pillars, family vaults, stone hopes praying with upcast eyes, old Ireland's hearts and hands. More sensible to spend the money on some charity for the living" (U.113; VI.928–31).

"Old Ireland's Hearts and Hands" was the kind of sentimental and nostalgic Irish song that, Joyce believed, deflected attention from the present realities.[8] Even before the grandiloquent speeches of Dawson, Burke, and Taylor in "Aeolus", and the burlesque of the Irish tendency to let style overwhelm substance in the romance voice of "Cyclops", this chapter explores the bankruptcy of the elegiac and nostalgic mode that dominates Irish life and literature; we shall see much more of this in the next chapter's windy comparisons of Ireland with the lost tribes of Israel.[9] Among other things, *Ulysses* is an implicit response to the kind of hyperbolic claims that Irishmen make for the past. In particular, Joyce had in mind the elegiac heroic poetry that Yeats sometimes wrote – such as "September, 1913" with its refrain "Romantic Ireland's dead and gone/It's with O'Leary in the grave" – in which the present is ironically juxtaposed to a romantic past. Joyce regarded Yeats as the figure with whose values he must wrestle; for Yeats was the Irish author of stature who, in his commitment to an Irish Renaissance and Celtic culture, had proposed an alternative to Joyce's view that Ireland must see itself as part of the European humanistic tradition.

Hynes, who in "Cyclops" is a friend of the bitter, cynical anonymous voice that complements the romance voice, represents the nostalgic mode: "Parnell will never come again . . . . He's there, all that was mortal of him. Peace to his ashes" (U.113; VI.926–7). Thinking of Stephen's riddle, we recall that the fox, a metaphor for Parnell, Stephen, and Ireland, had buried the past. And to a large extent, in "Hades", Bloom has shown the necessity of burying the past as a means of coping with the present. In this chapter, the novel is teaching us how to read it. Ultimately, Bloom's "reading" of his own past experience in "Hades" teaches us how to read the novel. For the reader learns, as Bloom must, that only the living – only those who can learn from the past and use it to experience the present and look toward the future – can ever return from a peregrination among the dead, from reminiscences about the past, from memories of what once was. Furthermore, the novel is insisting that the Irish look for a solution in the present. And the only solution proposed for Ireland, we begin to realize, is the humanistic Bloom who is committed to life in the face of death.

Rereading, we see Joyce carefully preparing us for Bloom as "the new Messiah for Ireland" (U.337; XII.1642). Of course, the Dubliners do not recognize Bloom's stature; they do not understand that his humanity, tolerance, decency, energy, and, indeed, enterprise in his pursuit of his personal and business goals are important examples of what Dublin requires from its citizens. When, in the next chapter, "Aeolus," Bloom inquires about his ad by phone, Myles Crawford, the editor, responds: "Tell him go to hell" (U.137; VII.672). We might recall that after Odysseus's men release the winds, Aeolus refuses to provide any further help for him. But Bloom, in an important difference from Homeric paradigm, has not received any help at all. And, unlike his epic prototype who descends to Hades after the "Aeolus" episode, Bloom has already been to hell.

IV   "AEOLUS"

In "Aeolus", Joyce uses the perspective of modern journalism to present a moral anatomy of Dublin; he builds on the satire of Dublin life in "Lotus-Eaters" and "Hades". In these three chapters in which Dublin becomes a character in the novel with its own collective character and personality, the organs – genitals ("Lotus-Eaters"), heart ("Hades"), lungs ("Aeolus") – are those necessary for life to continue from moment to moment and from generation to generation. To understand this chapter, it may be helpful to think of Stephen as the protagonist and Ireland as the antagonist. In "Ireland, Island of Saints and Sages", Joyce spoke of Ireland as a country from which the best must flee: "The soul of the country is weakened by centuries of useless struggle and broken treaties, and individual initiative is paralysed by the influence and admonitions of the church, while its body is manacled by the police, the tax office, and the garrison. No one who has any self-respect stays in Ireland, but flees afar as though from a country that has undergone the visitation of an angered Jove."[10]

As in *Dubliners*, the subject of *Ulysses* is the moral paralysis of Ireland, and Joyce's point in "Aeolus" is that the most paralyzed are the people who are speaking of Ireland in empty and hyperbolic rhetoric. Joyce's fixation on using the rhetorical devices so painstakingly catalogued by Stuart Gilbert is itself an ironic comment on the lack of content in the speeches.[11] Commenting on Joyce's calling the art of the chapter "rhetoric", Hugh Kenner has remarked: " 'Rhetoric', which is something less personal than pervasive talk and gives a collective identity to disembodied facility with words, corresponds as it blows through the episode's interstices, to a certain indifference on the part of the talkers, anonymous as the wind . . .".[12] Rather than using language to signify something beyond itself, Joyce uses language to weave intricate patterns of textures that resemble the formal non-mimetic patterns of Oriental rugs or abstract paintings. He not only places the action in the offices of the *Freeman's Journal* and the *Evening Telegraph*, but he uses the headline technique to expose how newspapers distort truth and debase language. Karen Lawrence has written: "The language of the headings is a language of common denominator . . . . This interest in the public resources of language rather than the particular speech acts of a persona is reflected in the inventory of rhetorical tropes . . . as well as in the set of received ideas."[13] But our interest in the plight of Stephen and Bloom distracts our attention from the stereotypical language and tropes and re-establishes the uniqueness of both characters' personalities and psyches, as they are revealed by Stephen's concluding parable and Bloom's stream of consciousness in the next chapter. As put by Professor MacHugh, with whose cynicism as a dramatized alternative to political rodomontade Joyce has some sympathy: "We mustn't be led away by words, by sounds of words" (U.131; VII.484–5).

The omniscient voice wears the masque of an editor who provides headlines for the chapter's vignettes. As the chapter proceeds, the headlines – in relation to the "story" they purportedly describe – increase in length even as they decrease in both sense and appropriateness to the story that follows. But this is not to agree with Arnold Goldman that the novel's style "becomes progressively *detached* from the mimetic action of the novel, from the primacy of the Dublin scene."[14] For just the opposite occurs; the Dublin scene is so powerful that it has the effect of transforming the style of the narrative presence and disrupting the narrator's efforts to maintain the objective omniscient style of the first six chapters. In this chapter, the narrator has a point of view distinct and separate from Bloom's.

What Goldman has called "the deliberately played-on gap between the narrative styles and the material which is their subject" is continually bridged by the reader's interest in making sense of the characters and their relationship to their metaphorical antecedents.[15] As will occur in several subsequent chapters, Bloom triumphs by winning our affection and admiration over a detached cynical style that is originally set against his values. Throughout the chapter he is bounced about like one of the "dullthudding barrels" of Guinness (U.116; VII.23). Along with the bombast and rubbish of modern journalism, the Catholic Church, the elegiac and nostalgic spirit, and the alcoholic stupor induced by Guinness and whiskey are responsible for Dublin's inertia. It is ironic that the Irish patronize and ignore Bloom in the very chapter where the Jews are invoked as the precursors of the Chosen People who, while temporarily in exile, will eventually be led to the Promised Land.

The chapter examines the relevance of the frequently proposed parallel between the Irish and the Jews, before ending with Stephen's bathetic debunking of the parallel in his "Parable of the Plums". "Aeolus" discredits the hyperbolic Irish rhetoric that depends on glib metaphors comparing the Irish with the Jews and the Egyptians with the English. In his 1907 lecture, "Ireland, Island of Saints and Sages", Joyce quoted approvingly Wilde's remark that the Irish " 'were the greatest talkers since the time of the Greeks' ", before adding his own codicil: "But though the Irish are eloquent, a revolution is not made of human breath and compromises."[16] As he defends the Celtic revival, John F. Taylor invokes Moses's refusal to accept the view of the Egyptian high priest:

But . . . had the youthful Moses listened to and accepted that view of life, had he bowed his head and bowed his will and bowed his spirit before that arrogant admonition he would never have brought the chosen people out of their house of bondage, nor followed the pillar of the cloud by day. He would never have spoken with the Eternal amid lightnings on Sinai's mountaintop nor ever have come down with the light of inspiration shining in his countenance and bearing in his arms the tables of the law, graven in the language of the outlaw. (U.143; VII.862–9)

Once again, by including these metaphors with their osten-tatious and bathetic gap between signifier and signified, Joyce demurs from granting his narrator ex cathedra authority over the novel's grammar of metaphors. Rather Joyce is insisting that the odyssean reader learn a grammar of metaphors by testing each one against the rest of his reading experience of *Ulysses*. Thus Taylor's rodomontade provides a rhetorical context – a rhetorical foil – which makes, by contrast, the comparison of Bloom to Moses, urged by the chapter's editorials, more credible.

Within the context of the chapter's hyperbole, Bloom becomes a credible Moses figure precisely because he suggests but does not fulfill the Moses paradigm. While speeches like Taylor's suggest a complete parallel, Joyce proposes a partial parallel – what we might call a half or partial metaphor. In the section headline, "AND IT WAS THE FEAST OF THE PASS-OVER", Bloom recalls the Passover service, which celebrates Moses leading the Jews out of the house of bondage: "Poor papa with his hagadah book, reading backwards with his finger to me. Pessach. Next year in Jerusalem. Dear, O dear! All that long business about that brought us out of the land of Egypt and into the house of bondage" (U.122; VII.203, 206–9). Notice how in the above passage prior to the "house of bondage", Bloom's gloomy thoughts about his home affect the prepositional change from "out of" to "into". Perhaps because he is thinking of the forty years in the wilderness, he confuses the lugubrious story of Diaspora with the glorious exodus from Egypt – the house of bondage – and the arrival in the Promised Land. Nor does he relate his memory of the phrase that signifies the prophesy of return, "Next year in Jerusalem", to either the Zionist dream of the Promised Land, or his personal version of it, signified by the phrase "Agendath Netaim".

Whem Bloom gloomily thinks of the song *Chad Gadya*, he recalls that one creature devours another before being in turn devoured by a third, but forgets that the final slayer in the chant is God, who kills the Angel of Death: "Justice it means but it's everybody eating everyone else. That's what life is after all" (U.122; VII.213–4). It may be that Bloom neglects this conclusion, because his characteristic ebullience has been somewhat undermined by the pervasive incivility that he has been experiencing all morning as well as by his memory of the rat in "Hades". Yet, as we shall see in "Lestrygonians", he rejects the "Eat or be eaten" credo that he derives from the *Chad Gadya* chant (U.170; VIII.703). In an interesting parallel, Stephen in the "Proteus" chapter had thought: "God becomes man becomes fish becomes barnacle goose becomes featherbed mountain" (U.50; III.477–9). This parallel itself illustrates how Bloom becomes Stephen becomes Bloom; it makes literal and actual the metaphoric movement by which one thing signifies another.

The word "Haggadah" means telling and the reading of the Haggadah celebrates both the continuity of the Jewish experience and the optimism for the future which takes more of an optative than a messianic form.[17] The technique of the Haggadah is to focus on the essence of the Jewish experience – the Passover narrative with the stress on the flight from Egypt – while using allusions to place the Passover narrative at the center of concentric circles which evoke the entire Jewish experience, including the Diaspora for which the forty years in the wilderness can be taken as prefiguration. Indeed, the Haggadah traditionally has assimilated to its telling new trials – the Holocaust, pogroms, the establishment of the State of Israel, persecution of the Jews in Russia or any other place. Joyce draws upon this elastic and protean tradition to imply that *Ulysses* is to be regarded as the Haggadah of the Irish experience.

What Kenner has called the "pervasive indifference" of the narrator, or adopting David Heyman's term, "the Arranger", is in the tradition of bearing witness to events which the teller fatalistically accepts, because he knows he cannot change them, even as he feels with grief and chagrin the moral weight of the events.[18] But I believe that the narrator is a far more congenial host than Kenner who writes, "The Arranger . . . treats us, when he deigns to notice our presence, with the sour xenophobic indifference that Dublin can turn upon visitors who have lingered long enough for hospitality's first gleam to tarnish."[19] Like Malachi, the speaker feels the "burden" of the prophecy – and we recall that "burden" is also a term for the principle idea of a narrative. What the narrator conveys throughout is not indifference, but deep concern for the moral sloth and hypocrisy of the Irish people who are imprisoned by the twin captivity of history's labyrinth. The Haggadah is thus as much a cyclical as a linear narrative. Indeed, the echo of past words from prior episodes is very much part of the Haggadah tradition. Stephen must develop from the self-immersed lyrical artist who writes about himself into an omniscient voice who can read the historical significance of events. The parable at the end of "Aeolus" is a step in the direction of Stephen's potential authorship of an Irish Haggadah.

Stephen's "Parable of the Plums" in "Aeolus" not only represents progress for him as an artist, but for us as readers because, we can, in contrast to the riddle in "Nestor", understand the parable." As Joyce must do if he is to write the Irish epic, Stephen addresses the political and moral health of Ireland. He also anticipates the movement in the later episodes to the "dramatic" form. In contrast to the speeches in the chapter which are merely part of a word-world woven from nostalgia and national self-delusion, Stephen's parable is based on transforming his own lived experience into more objective experience. For he bases the parable – or cartoon – of the old women spitting plum pits from Nelson's pillar on his view of the two old midwives on the strand. In terms of Stephen's aesthetic in *Portrait*, he has presented his image "in immediate relation to others" (P.214). The more Stephen thinks of the problem of creating a universal literary work and of the condition of Ireland, the less he is drowning in a welter of self-pity.

That Stephen's art progresses from the riddle and the plagiarized poem, that he uses the mythic method that is essential to the art of *Ulysses*, and that he takes public themes as his subject, imply that Stephen is developing towards the presence who is now telling the novel; he is closing the ironic gap between character and narrator. The reader comes to understand that, among other things, Stephen's development as an artist, although tentative and incomplete, is what makes 16 June 1904 a crystallizing day for Joyce's fictionalized voice, Joyce himself, and Ireland. At this point, the novel's speaker moves closer to Stephen's perspective than he has previously been; he does so to endorse Stephen's rejection of the bogus and sentimental idea that the Irish are the lost tribes of Israel or the spiritual descendents of the Chosen People. Of course, by showing the rampant anti-Semitism in Dublin, Joyce stresses the hypocrisy of this position. Because Stephen's parable indicates a progression of his art in responding to public themes and in observing the actual fabric of Dublin life, Stephen himself is a putative Moses figure whose visions will lead the Irish out of bondage. After all, like Moses, he reports on his Pisgah vision to his waiting listeners.

Moreover, Stephen's parable educates us to read the novel metaphorically. In Stephen's bitter parable, the midwives – his ironic version of the Old Woman of Ireland – spit plum pits on the barren ground, while fascinated with the statue of Lord Nelson: "They put the bag of plums between them and eat the plums out of it, one after another, wiping off with their handkerchiefs the plumjuice that dribbles out of their mouths and spitting the plumstones slowly out between the railings" (U.148; VII.1024–7). What Ireland needs is fertility and renewal; what these women do is spit potential seeds upon concrete where they cannot grow. Ireland's seers, the heirs to the Pisgah sight of Paradise, are two self-indulgent old women. That the phallic statue of the adulterous Nelson dominates Dublin emphasizes Ireland's illicit relationship with England. In a sensationalized and corrupt diction deliberately reminiscent of excesses of yellow journalism, the final headline stresses the lewd implications of the scene: "DIMINISHED DIGITS PROVE TOO TITILLATING FOR FRISKY FRUMPS. ANNE WIMBLES, FLO WANGLES – YET CAN YOU BLAME THEM?" (U.150; VII.1069–71).

Rather than assisting at a birth, the midwives are sexually aroused by the memory of Nelson's adultery. Unknown to Stephen, the parable refers to Bloom's plight and to Molly's sexual arousal by thoughts of adultery. For Bloom needs fertility to renew his life. The reader recalls the advertising jingle that fascinates Bloom:

What is home without
Plumtree's Potted Meat?

Incomplete.
With it an abode of bliss. (U.75; V.144–7)

The phallic "Plumtree" is, of course, a comic metaphor for an erect and functioning penis, which is essential to repair the broken relationship with Molly. Thus we have another instance of Stephen's or Bloom's mind fulfilling an image or completing or iterating a thought proposed by the other; while in this case Stephen's mind fulfills Bloom's, the reverse occurs more frequently. The effect of this transaction – a transaction manipulated by Joyce's transpersonal narrator or Arranger – is to make each the signifier for the other and to give us in linguistic terms a prolepsis of their ultimate union.

To stress their interchangeability, later Joyce has Bloom – after recalling his great moment on the Howth in contrast to the current day's adulterous relationship with Blazes – ironically echo Stephen's parable: "He gets the plums, and I the plumstones" (U.377; XIII.1098–9). To the rereader, aware of Molly's role as a fecund version of the Old Woman of Ireland, is Blazes not a metonymical comic replacement for Lord Nelson? Does not Molly replace the two aging midwives who sensuously savour the juice of their plums, while "peering up at the statue of the onehandled adulterer?" (U.148; VII.1017–8). Ireland has been diddled not only by outsiders but, as the betrayal of Parnell indicates, by its own indifference and self-indulgence.

While Bloom has had ties with Sinn Fein and the Masons and is committed to the welfare of others, Blazes Boylan is interested in his own sex life. It is true that when the British imperial viceroy passes, Blazes, to his credit, does not salute: "His hands in his jacket pockets forgot to salute but he offered to the three ladies the bold admiration of his eyes and the red flower between his lips" (U.254; X.1245–6). But is this because he is making a protest or simply because he has other concerns, namely his flirtations?

Joyce is educating his reader to understand the discrepancy between, on the one hand, Bloom's metaphorical role as the potential Moses figure whose values represent the departure from the land of bondage and at least a view of a promised land of Irish dignity and freedom and, on the other hand, his poignant position within the story as a victim of adultery. While

Bloom will point the way out of the land of bondage, and will get to Pisgah, Stephen, by growing into the artist, will write the Irish epic, will complete – as Joshua completed Moses's journey – Bloom's journey and lead the Irish out of their cultural bondage.

Bloom is not only what Dublin requires, but what Stephen requires. In "Hades," it is Bloom not Simon who notices Stephen passing the funeral carriage (U.88; VI.39ff). In "Aeolus", Stephen and Bloom almost meet in the newspaper offices and, later, in the library. When Myles tells Stephen "Your governor is just gone", the rereader smiles at the irony of the recent headline "EXIT BLOOM" (U.131,129; VII.510–1,429). That Stephen's parable is interrupted by Bloom's return to the editor's office, as the latter energetically seeks to complete the sale of his advertisement, stresses to the rereader that he is what Stephen requires. Because the completed novel establishes Bloom as the Moses figure which Ireland requires, the rereader of Stephen's parable is invited by the headline "RETURN OF BLOOM" to make a metonymical substitution of Bloom for the ineffectual and narcissistic old women who have the Pisgah vision (U.146;VII.962).

V   THE INFLUENCE OF FUTURISM

Living in Trieste from 1904–15 and immersed in its intellectual life, Joyce was more influenced by Futurism than Vorticism, its English counterpart. Although Ellmann acknowledges that Joyce attended "the most important exhibition of futurism", held in Trieste in 1908, he does not take seriously the influence of Futurism on Joyce because he thinks of Futurism as a movement in painting, not literature. Yet, as Ellmann himself notes, Joyce asked Budgen whether the "Cyclops" episode was not Futuristic?[20] That, of course, is not to deny that Joyce was influenced by Pound's call for objectivity in art and Pound's doctrine that art could provide order and stasis to a chaotic world. After all, Pound had placed *Portrait* in the *Egoist*.

To be sure, one can plausibly argue that Joyce's juxtaposition of scenes from the modern city, his alternation between close-up and distanced views, and his effort to dramatize both the physical motion of his characters as well as the rapid movement from one scene to another, particularly in "Wandering Rocks" and "Circe", all owe as much to the influence of cinematic montage as to that of Futurism. But in celebrating the excitement and bustle of modern life (although at the same time characteristically under-mining it with his customary irony and bathos), Joyce, I suspect, was very much influenced by Marinetti's 1909 "Futurist Mani-festo". Indeed, The Futurists' experiments in dramatizing mo-tion – the most notable of which is Marcel Duchamp's "Nude Descending the Staircase" (1912) – was influenced by Muy-bridge's stop-action photography; he had illustrated Paul Souriau's 1889 scientific study of motion, "The Aesthetics of Movement". We should remember that, unlike Cubism, Futurism began as a literary enterprise. Futurism insisted on the need for capturing the energy and motion of contemporary life and that included bodily sensations and physical movement.[21]

Depending on the idea that each perception is a function of the position of the perceiver, Joyce's idea of parallax owes something to Futurism and Cubism. For the "position" of the perceiver is not merely a function of his present temporal–spatial location, but of the entire past experience he brings to his perception. Not only did Cubist painting try to do justice to the multiple perspec-tives of any given perception, but it employed the collage to juxtapose seemingly incongruous experiences within one aes-thetic form. Marinetti, the prophet of Futurism, believed that art must express the fact that we simultaneously register many perceptual experiences; he believed that techniques had to be invented to do justice to the disparate elements that comprise our mental and emotional lives at any given moment. As Jane Rye has written, "the Futurist poets sought to convey the 'simultaneity' of impressions which characterized modern life. The stylistic devices by which they sought to achieve this aim were the abolition of traditional syntax, metre and punctuation and the introduction of mathematical and musical symbols, onomatopoeia and 'free expressive orthography' ".[22]

Futurism also sought to emphasize the visual potential of literature and stressed the importance of, as Grace Glueck has put it, "combining of onomatopoeic fragments, numbers, sym-bols and typographical effects in a format that stormed the viewer's eye".[23] Marinetti's phrase for this orthographic mode, "parole in liberta" or "words in freedom", would have appealed to Joyce, who clearly uses similar orthographic techniques in the opening of each of the three sections. Drawing upon the example of abstraction in painting, the literary Futurists wished to stress the spatial arrangement of language – what they thought of as a "supraconscious" verbal art, and what recent criticism has been calling a "subtext" – that superimposed itself on our linear reading process and our desires for chronological order and representation of a prior reality. In his famous article "Futurism" (1919), Roman Jakobson linked the defense of Cubism with the theory of relativity. As Joseph Frank has put it, "Since time and space no longer had fixed determinants, and the category of substance had lost all meaning, reality could only be represented, as the Cubists were showing it, from multiple points of view simultaneously."[24] Once one no longer believes it is possible to designate reality and once one believes that the arrangement of elements on a page itself becomes its own ontology, the focus shifts to the sounds and texture of the language itself.

Using the giant letters of Irish illuminated manuscripts, the best known of which is *The Book of Kells*, was another way of announcing the significance of his New New Testament. (Given that these giant letters appeared in every edition in his lifetime and, as far as I know, there is no evidence that Joyce objected to them, I am skeptical that Joyce would have approved of their omission in the Gabler edition.) The narrator in "Ithaca" specifically mentions *The Book of Kells* as one of the "points of contact" between the Jews and Irish (U.688; XVII.745,755). We see the influence of Futurism's "parole in liberta" in the capitalized first words of the first line of each chapter as well as, most notably, in the headlines of "Aeolus". We also see the influence of Futurism in Joyce's effort to fuse words and music in "Sirens", particularly the opening overture, in the dramatic interludes of "Scylla and Charybdis", in the play format of "Circe", especially the elaborate and often surrealistic stage directions, in the ironic scientific catechism in "Ithaca", and the punctuation and syntax of Molly's stream of consciousness in "Penelope".

To understand better the influence of Futurism in Joyce's technique, let us look briefly at a few passages in "Aeolus". When Joyce describes the movement of beer barrels in Dublin, a movement which becomes a metonym for the way Bloom is buffeted in the chapter, we should see the influence of Futurism's insistence on capturing motion itself and on celebrating the hustle and bustle of twentieth century life: "Grossbooted dray-men rolled barrels dullthudding out of Prince's stores and bumped them up on the brewery float. On the brewery float bumped dullthudding barrels rolled by grossbooted draymen out of Prince's stores" (U.116; VII.21–4). For the Futurists, the bodily smells and sounds of a modern city were, as Grace Glueck puts it, "fit subjects for poetic and visual exploration."[25] In the above passage from "Aeolus", we might also note how Joyce, by using chiasmus to reverse the syntax, orthographically implies Bloom's unique position as an Irish Jew since the left to right movement of English iterates the right to left movement of Hebrew.

In the section of "Aeolus" entitled "ORTHOGRAPHICAL", the phrase "sllt", made by the presses of the newspaper, recurs in Bloom's mind; but that phrase is also an orthographic prolepsis of the merging of Stephen and Bloom because the double "l" between "s" and "t", the first two letters of Stephen's name, signifies the recurring "l" in the names of "Leopold Bloom", as well as the two l's in "Leopold", and the "l" that is the second letter of both "Bloom" and "Ulysses" (U.121; VII.164. 174–7). That *Stephen* thinks of a "Sallust", a Roman historian whose name is composed of these very same consonants a few pages later is another powerful manifestation to the reader of the transpersonal presence who is illustrating the parallel thoughts of these seemingly diverse men who, although in the same place at virtually the same time, manage not to meet.

VI "LESTRYGONIANS"

I want to stress how the metaphoric and literal levels of "Lestrygonians" pull in opposite directions and undermine one another. In "Lestrygonians", Joyce uses his metaphors to expand Bloom's stature. The Reverend Dowie, a fundamentalist preacher of Messianic Christianity and the self-conceived "restorer of the church in Zion" is an ersatz Elijah figure – an Elijah pseudo-angelos just as D. B. Murphy in "Eumaeus" is a Ulysses pseudoangelos – who will offer nothing to Ireland's spiritual wasteland (U.151; VIII.8–9). In correcting Murphy's initials from "W. B." to "D. B.", Gabler has rendered obsolete the theory that Joyce had Yeats in mind. (See XVI.415). Dowie has predicted in his handout or throwaway that "Elijah is coming" in the form of Christ's return. When first glancing at the religious throwaway and seeing the the first four letters of one of the slogans, Bloom has mistakenly thought that the word "blood" in the phrase "Blood of the Lamb" was "Bloom":

> Bloo . . . Me? No.
> Blood of the Lamb. (U.151; VIII. 8–9)

Announcing the arrival of Elijah, with whom Bloom is increasingly identified, the throwaway is a mock annunciation of Bloom's putative identity as the saviour of Ireland. Bloom unwittingly prophesies the winner of the Gold Cup – the dark horse, Throwaway – when, giving Bantam Lyons his newspaper, he explains: "I was just going to throw it away" (U.86; V.534).

The chapter begins with the identification of Bloom with Elijah and shows how Bloom rejects moral cannibalism. While Elijah is fed by birds in the desert, Bloom feeds the gulls. In other words, he gives rather than receives Manna. But he feels unappreciated: "Lot of thanks I get. Not even a caw" (U.153; VIII.84). Indeed, Bloom even thinks of suicide: "If I threw myself down?" (U.152; VIII.52). In "Lestrygonians", Bloom is not, as some critics have remarked, condemning meat-eating; after all, "Calypso" opens with a carnivorous fantasy which leads to a trip to the pork butcher prior to *breakfast*. Rather, Joyce's target is the grim cycle of one creature eating another embodied in the song *Chad Gadya* from the Haggadah. What he rejects is epitomized by his momentary reduction of life to the grim alternative, "Eat or be eaten. Kill! Kill!" (U.170; VIII.703). But because the Haggadah is read at the Passover sevice, a service which promises the return of Elijah, we recall again the prophesy of Malachi and realize that the novel is proposing Bloom as the heir to Elijah. At the Passover service, a wine glass is always set for the expected return of Elijah, a return which will mark the end of the cycle of human misery.

In this chapter, when Bloom drinks his burgundy – a wine that could serve as the traditional Passover wine – he begins to assume his metaphorical role as an Elijah figure. In fact, after Bloom drinks the wine, two of the Dubliners, Nosey Flynn and especially Davy Byrne, speak of him with a warmth and charity that are uncharacteristic of the Dubliners' attitudes to Bloom, as if to imply that the very presence of Bloom might have a salutary effect on the quality of Dublin life. Speaking "humanely", Byrne calls Bloom a "Decent quiet man"; even the more grudging Nosey Flynn admits, "He's been known to put his hand down too to help a fellow" (U.177–8; VIII.947,976,983–4). Ironically, his metaphoric Elijah role takes the form of a humanistic sense of responsibility defined not by traditional Catholicism, but by its ancient enemy, Freemasonry, which, as comically reduced by Nosey Flynn, advocates the very same things as traditional Christianity: "Light, life, and love, by God" (U.177; VIII.963).

The dialectical struggle between Bloom's metaphoric role and his character is very much part of our reading experience. On one hand, Bloom rejects the credo "Eat or be eaten", a credo linking the contemporary Dubliners to their savage Letstrygonian prototype, and humanistically proposes a communal kitchen as an antidote to this cycle of moral and physical violence (U.170; VIII.703ff). But, on the other hand, that he cannot sustain this utopian fantasy which dissolves into a digression about who would wash up the plates in a community kitchen shows how the literal story undermines Bloom's metaphoric role as an Elijah figure. Joyce wants to emphasize that Bloom is very much a mortal man; like Stephen, Bloom's teeth are decaying, "Teeth getting worse and worse" (U.171; VIII.719). To make us hesitate before we apotheosize Bloom, Joyce has Bloom transform his mixture of fascination and disgust with eating rare meat ("Hot fresh blood they prescribe for decline. Blood always needed. Insidious. Lick it up, smokinghot, thick sugary" [U.171; VIII.729–30]) into a fantasy in "Sirens" of eating sperm – perhaps in combination with Molly's menstrual flow which he might suspect is soon to begin: "Flood of warm jamjam lickitup secretness flowed to flowin music out, in desire, dark to lick flow invading" (U.274; XI.705–6). Joyce, a sensual man with a very active sexual imagination, wanted us to think of Bloom as a sensual man with a very active sexual imagination.

The chapter continues to develop parallels between Stephen and Bloom. Bloom thinks of the gulls as spreading the "foot and mouth disease", which is the subject of Deasy's letter that Stephen delivers to Crawford (U.153;VIII.84–5). But Bloom had exited before Stephen's arrival. Like Stephen, Bloom uses poetry to respond to his experience with poetry; while Bloom's poem is not very distinguished, at least it is not, like Stephen's, plagiarized:

The hungry famished gull
Flaps o'er the waters dull. (U.152; VIII.62–3)

Later he thinks of another possibility:

The dreamy cloudy gull
Waves o'er the waters dull. (U.166; VIII.549–50).

A few minutes after Bloom sees the copulation of the buzzing flies in "Lestrygonians" ("Stuck on the pane two flies buzzed, stuck"), Stephen, recalling Hamlet's response to Polonius's foolish talk, ironically comments on his own monologue: "Buzz. Buzz" (U.175,189; VIII.896, IX.207).

By showing how the language of Bloom's stream of consciousness is transformed by hunger, Joyce emphasizes the importance of bodily needs in transforming our perceptions, the place of appetite in human behavior, and the necessity to control that appetite. According to Budgen, Joyce explained,

> Among other things . . . my book is the epic of the human body . . . . In my book the body lives in and moves through space and is the home of a full human personality. The words I write are adapted to express first one of its functions then another. In *Lestrygonians* the stomach dominates and the rhythm of the episode is that of the peristaltic movement . . . . If they *the characters* had no body they would have no mind . . . It's all one. Walking towards his lunch my hero, Leopold Bloom, thinks of his wife, and says to himself, "Molly's legs are out of plumb." At another time of day he might have expressed the same thought without any underthought of food. But I want the reader to understand always through suggestion rather than direct statement.[26]

To the evolving drawing of the anatomy of the human body, a drawing which traces itself as a visual image on our consciousness, Joyce adds "esophagus" as the organ of this chapter. But, as his technique "peristaltic" emphasizes, the chapter calls attention to the entire digestive system. Such an emphasis becomes for the reader a visceral event – what the futurists meant by supraconscious – apart from the linear process of understanding the words. Since the classical Greek era and the Renaissance are, along with the biblical era, Joyce's major historical archetypes, it is likely that in stressing the body as theme and subject he had in mind the scrupulous interest in physical anatomy of the classical Greeks, such as Phydias, or of such Renaissance painters as Leonardo and Michaelangelo.

Within Bloom's monologue, there is a struggle between the cannibalistic images of food and Bloom's benign, humanistic, and often humorous perceptions in terms of food images. This stylistic struggle is a miniature of the struggle between barbarism and humanism within Dublin on 16 June 1904. On one hand, we have anticipations of the "Cyclops" episode: "Perched on high stools by the bar, hats shoved back, at the tables calling for more bread no charge, swilling, wolfing gobfuls of sloppy food, their eyes bulging, wiping wetted moustaches. . . . A man spitting back on his plate: halfmasticated gristle: gums: no teeth to chewchewchew it" (U.169; VIII.654–6; 659–60). This kind of eating is a kind of metaphor for selfish and vicious behaviour that appears periodically throughout the novel, and is indeed the "food" for some of Bloom's most painful fantasies. But, on the other hand, once he chooses his light lunch, the pleasures of food become for Bloom a metaphor for the pleasures of sex.

Bloom's problem is to transform his memories of the past into possibilities of the future. Combined with his visit to the graveyard and the patronizing treatment he has received in "Aeolus", his hunger makes him prone to discouragement. On the literal level, "Lestrygonians" is composed of a dialectical struggle between two opposing terms, "Kill! Kill!" and "Yes." "Kill! Kill!" represents a negative strain in Bloom's psyche – his various impulses to depression, escape into the past, bitterness, and mortality. "Yes" becomes a metaphor for the memory of the climactic scene on the Howth and a metonym for "Agendath Netaim" with its association of possible renewal (U.168,183; VIII.635–6,1184); it encapsulates the various means by which he sublimates and represses Molly's adultery, including his interest in the physiology of the museum statues of the goddesses. "Yes" is a word associated with Bloom's affection for Molly and participation in life, but also with Molly's and Bloom's mutual memory of passionate intimacy. Since the book's argument addresses the way in which the artist is a divine figure who can create reality from words, it is appropriate that Bloom's major means of preserving his mental wholeness is to rely on verbal formulae ("Agendath" and "Yes") and charms – the soap and potato that he carries around all day – that are really metaphors for purity and fecundity.

Yet in this chapter "Yes" is associated with Blazes when he thinks of how Molly and Blazes first acknowledged one another. "He. Glowworm's la-amp is gleaming, love. Touch. Fingers. Asking. Answer. Yes" (U.167; VIII.590–1). Seeing the two flies copulating makes him think of Blazes and Molly. But, as he sips the wine, he recalls his first intercourse on the Howth with Molly, the very scene she recalls in her final reverie as she turns her passionate attention to Bloom:

> Ravished over her I lay, full lips full open, kissed her mouth. Yum. Softly she gave me in my mouth the seedcake warm and chewed. Mawkish pulp her mouth had mumbled sweetsour of her spittle. Joy: I ate it: joy. Young life, her lips that gave me pouting. Soft warm sticky gumjelly lips. Flowers her eyes were, take me, willing eyes. Pebbles fell. She lay still. A goat. No-one. High on Ben Howth rhododendrons a nannygoat walking surefooted, dropping currants. Screened under ferns she laughed warmfolded. Wildly I lay on her, kissed her: eyes, her lips, her stretched neck beating, woman's breasts full in her blouse of nun's veiling, fat nipples upright. Hot I tongued her. She kissed me. I was kissed. All yielding she tossed my hair. Kissed, she kissed me (U.176; VIII.906–16).

Recalling a moment of shared passionate intimacy and tender love, the above recollection gives new meaning to a series of thoughts that Bloom has had. For one thing, it is a kind of ironic Arcadia that momentarily pacifies his anxieties about social violence and allays his fixation on Molly's adultery. Moreover, he has associated satisfying his hunger with sexual fulfilment in "Calypso": "To smell the gentle smoke of tea, fume of the pan, sizzling butter. Be near her ample bedwarmed flesh. Yes, yes" (U.61; IV.237–9). Thinking of his precocious daughter, he associates "Yes" with "Life" but the repressed thought, the hidden agenda of his meditation, is her sexual maturity: "Yes, yes: a woman too. Life, life" (U.89; VI.89–90). And, since warmth is something his intimate life still retains, does not the memory of sharing a bed with Molly help him to overcome gloom in "Hades?": "Feel live warm beings near you. Let them sleep in their maggoty beds: . . . Warm beds: warm fullblooded life" (U.115; VI.1003–5). In her final reverie, Molly remembers Bloom's calling her "my mountain flower" (U.783; XVIII.1606). Yet Bloom's memory of the goat's defecating anticipates the analism of his hallucinations and his practice of licking Molly's behind. And, finally, Bloom has trouble sustaining his reverie of better days and poignantly returns to the copulating flies, his metaphors for the copulation of Molly and Blazes:

> Me. And me now.
> Stuck, the flies buzzed. (U.176; VIII.917–8)

On the metaphorical level, "Lestrygonians" crystallizes the dialectical struggle, within the odyssean reader's imagination as he makes his way through the novel, between two ways of reading – between, on the one hand, establishing Bloom's stature as Elijah, a figure whose significance relates to a teleology, and, on the other hand, allowing him to remain as Odysseus, whose struggle with the Lestrygonians has historical but not teleological importance. Of course, the striking parallel between Bloom and Odysseus has been the most obvious structural component for the past five chapters, beginning with "Calypso". It shapes the episodes and implies the cyclical view of history. But the biblical parallels in conjunction with the image of the artist as God the creator are just as important, if not more so, because they present the argument by which Bloom is transformed into a significant figure within Joyce's secular humanistic Bible.

Erich Auerbach's distinction between ancient and biblical conceptions of history helps us to understand the different kinds of significance in *Ulysses*. In biblical history, according to Auerbach, "the here and now is no longer a mere link in an earthly chain of events, it is simultaneously something which has always been, and which will be fulfilled in the future; and strictly, in the eyes of God, it is something eternal, something omni- temporal, something already consummated in the realm of fragmentary earthly event".[27] For the concept of God in the above passage, Joyce invites the odyssean reader to substitute the Creator of the imagined world. On the metaphorical level Bloom is part of the teleological pattern stretching from Genesis to the apocalypse, and must always be understood by reference to that larger pattern. As readers we engage in what Auerbach has called figural interpretation: "Figural interpretation 'establishes a connection between two events or persons in such a way that the first signifies not only itself but also the second, while the second involves or fulfils the first. The two poles of a figure are separated in time but both being real events or persons, are within temporality.' "[28]

More strikingly than any other novel I know, except *Finnegans Wake*, *Ulysses* depends upon Joyce's figurative interpretation of the world, and so must our reading of it. But Auerbach also proposes an alternative reading of history to the figurative one, a reading that Auerbach associates with the ancient classical world. This other mode of reading history depends on "externalized, uniformly illuminated phenomena, at a definite time and in a definite place, connected together without lacunae in a perpetual foreground; thoughts and feeling completely expressed; events taking place in leisurely fashion and with very little of suspense".[29]

Ulysses not only depends on both traditions, but uses extreme versions of both at the same time. On one hand, we are caught up in the nominalistic world of one day, a day whose events draw heavily on Joyce's own particular experience; on the other hand, the novel is urging us to see their lives as part of a larger pattern. Reading *Ulysses*, we participate in a dialectical struggle between these two views of history and events. (The criticism of *Ulysses* enacts this struggle; on one hand we have symbolic readings such as Ellmann's *Ulysses on the Liffey*; on the other we have John Henry Raleigh's transformation of *Ulysses* into a chronological family chronicle and a traditional story in his *The Chronicle of Leopold and Molly Bloom*.[30] And that struggle is crystallized in a chapter like "Lestrygonians," where a hungry and somewhat depressed Bloom is trying to repress his knowledge of Molly's adultery, while at the same time Joyce is proposing him as an Elijah figure.

Each of these readings, the literal and the metaphorical, undermines the other. A version of this dialectical struggle is the tension between, on the one hand, the Homeric pattern, which depends more on what Joyce himself calls "correspondences" within the horizontal dimension of linear time and, on the other hand, the teleological patterns that establish Bloom's vertical stature as a potential Elijah or Moses figure and propose Stephen, fertilized by the values of Bloom and Molly, as the successor to Shakespeare and the creative presence in *Ulysses*. We can see the difference between the Homeric and Biblical metaphors if we understand that Joyce's own reading of ancient and biblical authors basically follows the distinctions Auerbach proposed years later. For Joyce was educated in Ireland to read classical and biblical texts in radically different ways. Thus while the Homeric parallel is an extended historical and literary allusion that gives shape to, in Eliot's words in his *Dial* review of *Ulysses* "the immense panorama of futility and anarchy that is contemporary history", the biblical allusions establish the novel's teleology.

In "Lestrygonians", we can see how Joyce uses the Homeric parallel to signify within the horizontal linear world of Dublin in 1904, even as he draws upon the Bible as a paradigm for his teleological structure which transcends and subsumes the events of any one day or year into a larger synchronic pattern. Bloom's reluctance to eat meat may vaguely contribute to the Homeric correspondence; Ulysses, we recall, saves his crew from the cannibalistic Lestrygonians. But Bloom's reluctance is not a satisfactory image for his stature as a Ulyssean figure or even for sustaining the parallel to the Lestrygonian episode in the *Odyssey*. While we do not need this particular correspondence to make us understand that Bloom's morality is not that of the "Lestrygonians", it does show the problem – the quality of life in Dublin – that has to be solved by the putative successors to Parnell, Stephen and Bloom. Although criticism has paid vast attention to the parallel to the *Odyssey*, the Homeric patterns do not have much to do with establishing the major metaphoric correspondences that transform Stephen into an artist and Bloom into a humanistic Messiah. Nor do the Homeric parallels create the structure of effects to convince the reader of the potential merger of Stephen and Bloom into an artist who will offer the Irish a prophetic vision.

NOTES

1. Karen Lawrence ignores this hierarchy and diminishes Bloom's way of reading experience when she remarks: "In 'reading' the world, the characters rely on different tools of interpretation:

Bloom on clichés and bits of popular information, Stephen on abstruse allusion and esoteric philosophy" (Lawrence, p. 52).

2. Gifford and Seidman, p. 14, call attention to the passage in *Paridiso*, XVII:55–65, which Stephen has in mind.
3. See Ellmann, *James Joyce*, p. 55.
4. See Gifford and Seidman, p. 71.
5. James H. Maddox, Jr., *Joyce's 'Ulysses' and the Assault Upon Character* (New Brunswick, NJ: Rutgers University Press, 1978) p. 41.
6. Ellmann, *Ulysses on the Liffey*.
7. Maddox, p. 53.
8. See Gifford and Seidman, p. 96.
9. For a valuable discussion of Taylor's speech, based on Taylor's 1901 speech at a meeting of the Law Students Debating Society, see Ellmann, *The Consciousness of Joyce*, pp. 34–9.
10. *The Critical Writings of James Joyce*, p. 171.
11. See Stuart Gilbert, *James Joyce's 'Ulysses': a Study*, rev. edn (New York: Vintage Books, 1952) p. 7.
12. Hugh Kenner, *Ulysses* (London: Allen and Unwin, 1980) p. 63.
13. Lawrence, pp. 66–7.
14. Arnold Goldman, *The Joyce Paradox* (Evanston, Illinois: Northwestern University Press, 1966) p. 83.
15. Goldman, p. 83.
16. *The Critical Writings of James Joyce*, p. 174.
17. Goldman is mistaken to speak of the Passover service in terms of "the weariness of a yearly repetition". See Goldman, pp. 131–2.
18. Kenner, pp. 64–5; see David Hayman, *'Ulysses': the Mechanics of Meaning* (Englewood Cliffs, NJ, 1970).
19. Kenner, p. 66.
20. Ellmann, p. 430, see Frank Budgen, *James Joyce and the Making of Ulysses* (1934) repr. (Bloomington: Indiana University Press, 1960) p. 156.
21. Grace Glueck, "A Lively Review of the Futurist Experience", *The New York Times, Arts and Leisure* (1 May 1983) p. 29.
22. Jane Rye, *Futurism* (New York: Dutton, 1972) p. 111; also quoted in Jackson I. Cope, *Joyce's Cities: Archaelogies of the Soul* (Baltimore: The Johns Hopkins University Press, 1981) p. 104.
23. Glueck, p. 29.
24. Joseph Frank, "The Master Linguist", *The New York Review of Books*, 31:6 (12 April 1984) p. 30.
25. Glueck, p. 30.
26. Frank Budgen, *James Joyce and the Making of "Ulysses"* (1934). Reprinted Bloomington: Indiana Univesity Press, 1960.
27. Erich Auerbach, *Mimesis*, trans. Willard Trask (Princeton University Press, 1957), p. 65.

28. Auerbach, p. 64; he is quoting himself from *Romanische Forschungen*, Frankfurt am Main, 63 (1952).

What Auerbach calls figural interpretation is similar to what is called organic unity within the tradition of Anglo-American criticism. That Anglo-American criticism focuses on the text is characteristic of the New Critical ideology that dominated criticism in England and America; by contrast, Auerbach puts his stress on the interpretive act. But both Auerbach's figural interpretation and the concept of organic unity demonstrate that a pattern embodied within the text insists on a kind of reading. If we privilege organic unity as a value, then we can see that most great novels depend on the relationship of each part or strand to the major controlling thematic and structural principles. For a fuller discussion of Auerbach, see my *The Humanistic Heritage: Critical Theories of the English Novel from James to Hillis Miller* (London: Macmillan; Philadelphia, Pa. University of Pennsylvania Press, 1986).

29. Auerbach, p. 9.

30. John Henry Raleigh, *The Chronicle of Leopold and Molly Bloom* (University of California Press, 1977).

6 The Concept of Artistic Paternity in "Scylla and Charybdis"

I SHAKESPEARE AS METAPHOR

To suggest his own biographical relationship to *Ulysses*, Joyce has Stephen propose his expressive theory of the relationship between Shakespeare's art and life. What makes Shakespeare a man of genius is that he encompassed in his vision "all in all in all of us" (U.213; IX.1049–50). Joyce recreates Shakespeare according to his own experience of him and thus becomes the father of his own artistic father and the artist whose imagination is so inclusive and vast that it contains the "all in all" of Shakespeare plus the very substantial addition – or, in current terminology, the supplement – of his own imagination. Like Joyce, Shakespeare used the details of everyday life for his subject: "All events brought grist to his mill" (U.204; IX.748). The major creative artist discovers in his actual experience the potential within his imagination: "He found in the world without as actual what was in his world within as possible" (U.213; IX.1041–2). To activate that potential the artist must have as wide a range of experience as possible; to get beyond the limitations of his own ego in order to achieve the impersonality and objectivity that is necessary for dramatic art, his imagination must have intercourse – and the sexual metaphor is, I think, essential to understanding Joyce's aesthetic – with the world: "His own image to a man with that queer thing genius is the standard of all experience, material and moral" (U.195; IX.432–3).

At the same time Stephen uses Shakespeare as a standard to measure ironically his own present situation, Joyce would have us realize the hubris of the young artist who has yet to create any

138

major work comparing himself to Shakespeare. Yet Joyce's relationship to Stephen in "Scylla and Charybdis" reaches a turning point when he twice penetrates Stephen's mind to show Stephen briefly imposing dramatic form upon his experience by using the traditional typography of plays to organize his monologue (U.203, 209; IX.684ff, 893ff). In the second and longer instance, a play which lasts little more than a page, Stephen is the major character speaking to his friends about the same issues that he has been speaking about throughout the chapter. And the entire chapter puts the argument about the relationship between the author's life and his work in the form of a virtual monodrama. If, according to Stephen's theory, Shakespeare's transparently disguising his identity in his early work foreshadows *A Portrait of the Artist*, the more subtle disguises of biography in *Hamlet* anticipate the technique of *Ulysses*.

In this chapter Stephen makes some progress in defining himself as an artist and in aligning himself with Shakespeare, who, because he wrote of the world in which he lived rather than of his own experience, is for Stephen a paradigmatic Aristotelian. But Stephen is still locked in scholastic logic, particularly in his discussions of paternity which are defined by his Catholic education. His paradigms for paternity are not based on *his* experience but, rather, are ingenious recastings – imaginative "rereadings" – of abstractions that he has been taught. We understand that Stephen is still more of a Platonist than an Aristotelian. In his monologue he has, like the scholastic he still is, "Unsheath[ed his] dagger definitions" and has created his own version of the Nicene Creed, one that explains his relation to his artistic father, but he has not responded to the fabric of Dublin life in action – "what you damn well have to see" (U.186; IX. 84,86). He has not spoken of his own artistic mission in Dublin at all. Instead, he has sought nostalgic and playful refuge in a word world of his own making.

That Stephen playfully and hyperbolically proposes that Shakespeare precociously reached sexual maturity at the age of nine contrasts with his own inexperience at the age of twenty-two. In this regard, it is significant that Stephen talks only to men in this chapter and that the spectre of Wilde hovers over the chapter not only in the form of Mulligan's resemblance to him, but also as a subject to which the conversation returns several times. In fact, Wilde's *The Portrait of Mr. W. H.* (1889), in which he argues that Shakespeare's sonnets were addressed to Willie Hughes, a boy actor, establishes a model for the kind of forced, *willful* biographical argument that Stephen uses, even as it presents an example of the kind of relationship between a younger and older man that he must avoid. Not without malice, Mulligan jokingly raises the possibility of a homosexual relationship between Bloom and Stephen within the text when he sees Bloom and remarks: "He knows you. He knows your old fellow. O, I fear me, he is Greeker than the Greeks. His pale Galilean eyes were upon her mesial groove" (U.201; IX.614–5). "Pale Galilean", from Swinburne's "Hymn to Proserpine", not only evokes the spirit of Swinburne, who had a reputation for various forms of perverted sexuality, but also establishes Bloom's figurative messianic role; "old fellow" is both an allusion to Stephen's father and his penis.[1] That within Mulligan's anti-Semitic remarks Bloom replaces the Old Woman of Ireland as "collector of prepuces" is another example of how Joyce is using his Malachi figure to establish comically Bloom's stature (U.13; I.394). After Best recalls Wilde's biographical argument, Stephen thinks, "[Best's] glance touched their faces lightly as he smiled, a blond ephebe. Tame essence of Wilde" (U.198; IX.531–2).

Homosexuality is associated not only with Platonism but with art for art's sake, another doctrine that Stephen must avoid. Although his stress on the relation between art and life takes issue with Russell's evocation of Villiers de l'Isle Adam's epigram ("As for living our servants can do that for us"), the very abstraction and intellectual algebra of Stephen's remarks show that he has not put completely behind him the aestheticism of Pater, Swinburne, and Wilde and their continental counterparts (U.189; IX.186).

For Joyce, homosexuality represents sterile sexuality that must be avoided. He fervently believed that on 16 June 1904, the day he privileged in his imagination as the occasion of his first having walked with Nora, his artistic maturity began. It was, he believed, from that crucial day that he started to overcome paralysis and narcissism and began to move once and for all beyond the purely lyrical in his art, a movement demonstrated by the transformation of the extremely subjective and self-indulgent *Stephen Hero* into the more objective *A Portrait of the Artist*. And it was from this point that he eventually began the artistic journey that climaxed in the epical and dramatic form of

Ulysses. That he emphasized the crystallizing importance of Nora's willingness to walk with him on June 16, 1904, demonstrates the significance of the seemingly trivial in Joyce's aesthetic and provides a clue to understanding how the climactic meeting between Stephen and Bloom could have vast importance to Stephen's life, and perhaps also to Bloom's.

To understand the "Scylla and Charybdis" chapter, we have to realize the immense distance between Stephen, the character who is making the first steps to artistic maturity, and the retrospective narrator who is looking back many years later and seeing the folly of Stephen's behavior. In this chapter Stephen is having a somewhat more developed form of social intercourse with his male acquaintances than in prior episodes, but he is still self-immersed; put another way, he is still his own wife, as indicated by Buck Mulligan's title for an unwritten play: *"Everyman His own Wife or A Honeymoon in the Hand"* (U.216; IX.1171–3). Mulligan's facetious play title and cast of characters call attention to the intellectually onanistic quality of Stephen's Platonic dialogues, for, after all, isn't he pretending to be Socrates teaching his disciples?

Thinking of Wilde's *The Decay of Lying* and *The Critic as Artist*, Best specifically links Wilde to Platonism and the Socratic dialogues, when he tells Stephen, after the latter has delivered his theory of Shakespeare, "You ought to make it a dialogue, don't you know, like the Platonic dialogues Wilde wrote" (U.214; IX.1068–9). Isn't Stephen thinking specifically of Socrates and the dialogues in this chapter, including a passage which links Shakespeare's sonnet 126 with Socrates's fondling Phaedo's hair: "The dour recluse still there (he has his cake) and the douce youngling, minion of pleasure, Phedo's toyable fair hair" (U.215; IX.1138–9)?[2] (Joyce would have known Mann's *Death in Venice* where homosexuality and aestheticism are united in a tale in which the major figure ironically assumes a Socratic role to justify his own homosexuality.)

In a novel where heterosexual intercourse is a metaphor for artistic creativity, the narrator expects us to recognize the shortcomings of approaches to paternity that exclude sexuality and woman. Bloom's quest during the day – his horizontal quest through time as opposed to Stephen's vertical quest for controlling paradigms – and Molly's assertive and bawdy sexuality enact within the novel the alternatives to Stephen's epistemology. That the chapter returns frequently to homosexuality as a subject stresses, finally, the sterility of Stephen's Platonism, including the scholastic logic on which it is based. That ghosts are a frequent subject creates a subtext that undermines Stephen's belief that he is a full-fledged Aristotelian. Thus our epiphany and Stephen's are quite different; the chapter's final lines, taken from *Cymbeline*, have an ironic aspect. Their stress on spirituality and mysteries suggests the Platonism that Stephen must put behind him:

Cease to strive. Peace of the druid priests of Cymbeline: hierophantic: from wide earth an altar.

Laud we the gods
And let our crooked smokes climb to their nostrils
From our bless'd altars (U.218; IX.1221–5).

The narrator's telling and the behaviour of Bloom and Molly contradict the emphasis on sacred rites as the way to become an artist or a man.

In the first three chapters, we recall, Joyce calls attention to Stephen as a Hamlet figure. Haunted by the ghost of his mother, estranged from his father, dressed in black, and paralyzed by artistic inaction, Stephen himself identifies with Hamlet all day. It is in *Hamlet*, Joyce believed, that Shakespeare simultaneously writes about universal values even as he writes about himself; thus when Shakespeare "wrote *Hamlet* he was not the father of his own son merely but, being no more a son, he was and felt himself the father of all his race, the father of his own grand-father, the father of his unborn grandson . . ." (U.208; IX.867–9). Isn't this the position of the fictionalized Joyce who is recreating the life of his younger self as the son of his imagination and, at the same time, seeing himself as the artistic father of the Irish race? For Joyce wants to believe that, like Shakespeare's, his own youthful errors – dramatized in the life of the fictional Stephen Dedalus – "are volitional and are the portals of discovery" (U.190; IX.229). Indeed, does not Stephen's discovery of Bloom's significance at the end of "Circe" after the latter looks after Stephen, who is drunkenly exploring and disrupting the brothels of nighttown, illustrate this? But except in his creative capacity, the artist is no different from other men: "[H]e passes on towards eternity in undiminished personality, untaught by the wisdom he has written or by the laws he has revealed" (U.197; IX.476–8).

II   THE COSMOS AS METAPHOR

Joyce uses the cosmos to signify the events in the human world, and by implication to expand their importance. Put another way, as in the Bible and traditional epics, events in the cosmos are often metaphors for events in the human world of the novel. But in Joyce human events become metaphors for cosmological ones at the same time as they are images for them. An example of a cosmological metaphor is the heavenly disturbance at the end of "Cyclops", the purpose of which is to expand comically the significance of the Citizen's throwing a biscuit tin at Bloom. Recalling the earthquake at Christ's crucifixion, the disturbance is an example of Joyce's hyperbolic use of the cosmos to signify events within the human world: "The catastrophe was terrific and instantaneous in its effect. The observatory of Dunsink registered in all eleven shocks, all of the fifth grade of Mercalli's scale, and there is no record extant of a similar seismic disturbance on our island since the earthquake of 1534" (U.344; XII.1858–61). The passage is at once a parody of the Holy Scripture, a global perspective on trivial events, and Joyce's self-delighted display of verbal pyrotechnics.

That a star acknowledges Shakespeare at his birth, as a star acknowledged Christ, confirms Shakespeare's stature and his genius: "A star, a daystar, a firedrake, rose at his birth. It shone by day in the heavens alone, brighter than Venus in the night, and by night it shone over delta in Cassiopeia, the recumbent constellation which is the signature of his initial among the stars" (U.210; IX.928–31). It is crucial to Joyce's theory about the relationship between sexual maturity and artistic maturity that Shakespeare saw the star immediately after he had intercourse with Ann Hathaway; he saw it as he was "returning from Shottery and from her arms" (U.210; IX.933–4). Passion is the catalyst for Shakespeare's art: "There is, I feel in the words, some goad of the flesh driving him into a new passion, a darker shadow of the first, darkening even his own understanding of himself. A like fate awaits him and the two rages commingle in a whirlpool" (U.196; IX.461–4).

To be sure, the use of landscape to reflect the moods of characters and the significance of action is a common technique in literature. But the cosmological scope of Joyce's imagination is another means of urging the reader to see the characters as representative figures. The response of the cosmos to human events within Joyce's imagined world, albeit comic, has the effect of raising his character's stature. The style and narrative material confer stature that may be qualified by, but not nullified by, the irony.

Manipulating the heavens at will also calls attention to the creative presence who stands behind the various narrators and characters. But characteristically Joyce also keeps the reader from relaxing his attention by mocking his own epic and prophetic pretenses. Anticipating the serious cosmological perspective in "Ithaca", Bloom in "Wandering Rocks" is comically associated with the cosmological perspective. M'Coy recalls that Bloom once bought an astronomy book that contained plates with "the stars and the moon and comets with long tails" (U.233; X.527–8). Lenehan recalls that while he was flirting with Molly in a carriage to the point of ejaculation, Bloom – not unlike what Joyce is doing for the reader of *Ulysses* – "was pointing out all the stars and the comets in the heavens . . . But, by God, I was lost, so to speak, in the milky way" (U.234–5; X.567–70).

Let us consider how we can reconcile Joyce's vast cosmological perspective with his compulsive insistence on scrupulously rendering details of his own life and of the Dublin he knew. By choosing as a subject the recreation of aspects of his own life, Joyce is stressing his belief that the great artist cannot help but be an objective figure whose life takes on universal significance. Just as the heavens acknowledged Christ's birth with a star in the east and his death with an earthquake, so within the cosmology of Joyce's imagined world the man of genius is acknowledged.

Like D. H. Lawrence, with whom Joyce had much more in common than is usually realized, Joyce believed in the artist's prophetic function and saw himself as having a mission to awaken the world to his artistic and humanistic values. What M. H. Abrams has written about the Romantic Bard is applicable to both Joyce and Lawrence: "Whatever the form, the Romantic Bard is one 'who present, past, and future sees': so that in dealing with current affairs his procedure is often panoramic, his stage cosmic, his agents quasi-mythological, and his logic of events apocalyptic. Typically this mode of Romantic vision fuses history, politics, philosophy, and religion into one grand design, by asserting Providence – or some form of natural teleology – to operate in the seeming chaos of human history so as to effect from present evil a greater good."[3] Like Lawrence, Joyce wrote with a sense of mission, with a sense that he could awaken his fellows to see things differently. Like Lawrence and Blake, at times Joyce believed that he had heard the Holy Word. Ellmann writes, "Joyce not only binds fable to fact, but also fact to fable. He was forever trying to charm his life; his superstitions were attempts to impose sacramental importance upon naturalistic details. So, too, his books were not to be taken as mere books, but as acts of prophecy. Joyce was capable of mocking his own claims of prophetic power . . . but he still made the claims."[4]

By manipulating the heavens to endorse the importance of the action, Joyce establishes a kinship with the Romantic tradition – with Blake, Shelley, Byron, and Lawrence – and demonstrates the power of the creative imagination to recreate the cosmos in the author's own image and to give that world whatever temporal and spatial dimensions that he wishes. The reader feels the strong presence of a narrator who, like the Irish hero Cuchulain, can expand and contract at will.

III THE CONCEPT OF ARTISTIC PATERNITY IN "SCYLLA AND CHARYBDIS"

For Joyce, Shakespeare is the one writer in English who is a peer of the great European writers and hence the artistic father with whom he has to come to terms.[5] He identifies with Shakespeare as an artist whose great successes came late in life after severe personal and artistic tribulations. In *Ulysses* Joyce seeks, as he believes Shakespeare has done, to recreate his own life in his art and become the Creator of himself. Joyce sees himself in the role of the respectful artistic son of Shakespeare whom, as the Literary Genius in English, God-The-Father, Joyce loyally serves in *Ulysses* by speaking for the genius of his artistic father. But

Shakespeare is also God the Father whose position Joyce as rebellious Son – and as Lucifer and Faust – wishes to challenge. By making Shakespeare into a subject of his own twentieth century epic, and, in a sense, a function of the internal space of Joyce's mind, he not only pays Shakespeare homage, but shows his control over Shakespeare, and in what might be called a process of literary patricide, claims his place as his successor.

For Stephen, his argument about paternity as a "legal fiction" is psychologically necessary; it gives him a reason for his lack of filial feeling towards his father whom he despises and a justification for his search for an alternative – and suitably artistic – father figure. According to Stephen, "Paternity may be a legal fiction. Who is the father of any son that any son should love him or he any son?" (U.207; IX.844–5).

Stephen thinks of himself not only as Hamlet but as Shakespeare, the creator – or artistic father – of the character Hamlet. When, thinking of a gruesome Irish murder, Stephen recalled the ghost of Hamlet's father's words (*"And in the porches of mine ear did pour"*), which describe how Claudius, his false father, had murdered his real father, Stephen is an ironic Hamlet – the paralyzed, melancholy son (U.139; VII.750). Stephen characteristically identifies with Hamlet as a wronged son. In "Lestrygonians", when Bloom thinks of the same scene, he imagines the lines in which the ghost speaks paternally to Hamlet: "Hamlet, I am thy father's spirit/ Doomed for a certain time to walk the earth" (U.152; VIII.67–8). That Bloom and Stephen quote from the same scene in terms of their respective roles as surrogate father and son calls attention to the creative presence even as it anticipates their shared vision of Shakespeare. Since Bloom thinks of himself as the ghost in Hamlet, and he is a ghostly presence in "Scylla and Charybdis", we see how Joyce is urging us to think of Bloom and Shakespeare, Stephen's putative surrogate fathers, as interchangeable. Although Stephen does not yet know it, Bloom is the father he requires. His biological father, Simon, is the pretender father – the father pseudoangelos – who threatens within his imagination the position of Shakespeare as his real artistic father. For Simon, the father who demands allegiance by convention, represents service to traditional Ireland.

Shakespeare is a ghost-like presence in his own works, particularly as King Hamlet's ghost haunting his son: "[Shakespeare] is a ghost, a shadow now, the wind by Elsinore's rocks or what you will, the sea's voice, a voice heard only in the heart of him who is the substance of his shadow, the son consubstantial with the father" (U.197; IX.479–1). Since Stephen identifies with Shakespeare and Bloom is identified with Shakespeare, Shakespeare becomes the Holy Ghost in the artistic Trinity. Shakespeare is a ghost and a shadow, but he is also consubstantial with Stephen, his artistic and spiritual son. According to Stephen, the biographical figure – the figure "endowed with knowledge by his creator" in *Hamlet* – is the ghost (U.197; IX.470–1). Isn't Joyce also suggesting that the biographical figure in *Ulysses* is neither of the major figures who are present in the story, but the apparently absent ghostly voice – like Shakespeare, "heard only in the heart of him who is the substance of the shadow" – who has fathered both figures and is telling the story? Using his life as the secret agenda of his work, Joyce is the same kind of ghostly presence in *Ulysses*. More importantly, do not his literary and historical metaphors summon to the present ghostly figures from the past such as Telemachus, Ulysses, Moses, Elijah, Shakespeare, and Parnell – about whom he wrote, we recall, an essay called "The Shade of Parnell" in which he spoke of the ghost of the "uncrowned king"?[6]

But the reader understands that Stephen, who within the "Proteus" section has written a very derivative stanza and a few hours later in "Aeolus" spoken, but not written, a brief political parable, is far from deserving the mantle of Shakespeare. Stephen is to date more a legend in his own mind than a legend among his own kind. Joyce would have expected us to realize the hubris and bathos of the young artist, who has yet to create a major work, comparing himself to Shakespeare. Although he feels strongly that "Our national epic has yet to be written", he is a long way from the artist who might write it (U.192; IX.309). That he conceives himself as the spiritual son of Shakespeare anticipates his relation to Bloom: "He is in my father. I am in his son" (U.194; IX.390).

For Stephen paternity is a legal fiction because he believed that as an artist he is the Father – indeed God the Father – of all the reality he creates in his actual and his potential works. And this argument has particular importance to the form of Joyce's art in *Ulysses*, a form which recreates the identity of a younger self and implies the grounds of the potential maturation of the immature precocious artist into the artist who will write the major work of the era. In a very real sense, when the artist embodies his life in an imagined world, he creates the special child of his imagination, the privileged figure who in the imagined world represents himself; in other words, "the Father [is] Himself His Own Son" (U.208; IX.863). Since the creative genius was, in Joyce's mind, the truly divine man and since he believed that he himself, like Christ, had been persecuted by his unappreciative fellows, the identity of the artist as Christ appealed to him. Joyce believed that he had sacrificed pleasure in this world for his eternal survival as an artist. Like Christ and Parnell, he had lived his life for those people whom he would spiritually redeem.

The fusion of Christ and Parnell, in Stephen's perception of Shakespeare as "Christfox," anticipates the later union of Stephen and Bloom in Shakespeare. Joyce sees himself as "He Who Himself begot middler the Holy Ghost and Himself sent Himself, Agenbuyer, between Himself and others, Who, put upon by His friends, stripped and whipped, was nailed like bat to barndoor, starved on crosstree" (U.197; IX.493–6). The artist, like Christ, can return to where he had once been to settle accounts and pass judgments: "[He] shall come in the latter day to doom the quick and dead when all the quick shall be dead already" (U.198; IX.498–9). The term "Agenbuyer", referring to Bloom who is on the periphery of Stephen's consciousness during this monologue, calls attention to the creative presence of the ghostly Joyce who is fusing "agen", the first syllable of Agendath and Agenbite, with "buyer" to suggest that Stephen will be transformed by the intervention of a commercial traveller.

While "agen" carries the meaning of guilt and remorse for Stephen ("Agenbite of Inwit"), for Bloom it signifies renewal, coming as it does from "Agendath Netaim" – Bloom's version of the Zionist dream in the form of a colony of planters. "Agenbuyer", a punning metonym for Bloom, acknowledges Bloom's inherent potential to redeem not only the Christ figure – for us, both Bloom and Stephen, but for Stephen himself alone – who is being persecuted, but also Ireland, and thus represents a necessary step in the growth of Stephen's awareness. Put another way, Stephen takes another small step towards accepting Bloom's value system and acknowledging Bloom's metaphorical significance. Joyce uses the metaphorical potential of homophonic puns. These puns are phonic metaphors based on the substitution of a word that sounds like the original word but means something different ("pard/bard", "Agen/agon" – as in Stephen Agonistes), or the substitution of a different meaning for the same word ("Agen") to create significant relationships, in this case to persuade the reader that Stephen Agonistes must include Bloom Agonistes and vice versa.

If Shakespeare is the father figure who uses his life for his art, Bloom is the Holy Ghost that enables Joyce to write *Ulysses*. To a rereader, his presence is writ everywhere in the chapter, but even a first reader is aware of how descriptions of Shakespeare are applicable to Bloom. That the real sons of God were artists like Shakespeare is emphasized in "Scylla and Charybdis" by the back and forth movement from artist to God in Stephen's argument about creative paternity. It is central to the novel's values and techniques that the artist is the "father of all his race, the father of his own grandfather, the father of his unborn grandson" (U.208; IX.868–9).

That Stephen's discussion of Shakespeare is an expressive theory of art which views the works of an artist as an expression of the author's life defines Joyce's own aesthetic assumptions in *Ulysses*. The theory, located in the ninth of the eighteen sections, educates the reader on how to read the novel. Shakespeare's works are understood in terms of what we know of his life: "His own image to a man with that queer thing genius is the standard of all experience, material and moral" (U.195; IX.432–3). As I have argued elsewhere, expressionism is central to the transformation of the Victorian novel into what we think of as the modern novel.[7] Expressionism is also a central concept of modernity in the visual arts; for example, in a 1941 notebook entry, does not the following credo of Joan Miro express an essential premise of *Ulysses*, namely that he will find a responsive audience for his quirky combination of the nominalistic details of his own life and the scraps of information and knowledge which are of interest to his mind? "Act from the conviction that all these pure devisings of my mind will magically and miraculously find an echo in the minds of other men."[8]

By including himself as the character "Stephen" in his own playlet and having the character "Stephen" propose the expressive theory of Shakespeare for which he is arguing, the ambitious author Stephen Dedalus whose artistic aspirations are unfulfilled becomes – somewhat bathetically – the father of himself (U.209; IX.893ff). By imagining Shakespeare throughout the chapter as an Elizabethan figure, does not Stephen create Shakespeare as a character and thus become the father of his own grandfather? After all, Shakespeare has first fathered, in different senses, Hamlet and Bloom ("Himself sent himself, Agenbuyer"); Hamlet is Stephen's forbear in temperament and Bloom is Stephen's surrogate father. That Shakespeare created Hamlet from his own experience but then viewed him from an impersonal, objective perspective anticipates the kind of creative process that Joyce's dramatic mode requires for the creation of Bloom and for the movement of Stephen from the lyrical character of *Portrait* towards the epical character of "Scylla and Charybdis" and the dramatic character of "Circe", "Eumaeus", and "Ithaca".

The major action of the narrative presence is to reveal that the apparently different minds of Stephen and Bloom not only have a remarkable amount in common, but are in fact a confirmation of the premise that paternity is a mystical estate. The text urges their metaphorical union. In "Eumaeus", Bloom comically discovers what even a first reader has come to recognize: "Though they didn't see eye to eye in everything a certain analogy there somehow was as if both their minds were travelling, so to speak, in the one train of thought" (U.656; XVI.1579–81). While speaking of Shakespeare, Stephen imagines him walking amidst his peers in Stratford: "Do and do. Thing done. In a rosery of Fetter lane of Gerard, herbalist, he walks, greyedauburn. An azured harebell like her veins. . . . He walks. One life is all. One body. Do. But do" (U.202; IX.651–3). Later when Bloom is quoting Shakespeare, the narrative presence, urging us to identify Bloom with Shakespeare, applies Stephen's vignette: "In Gerard's rosery of Fetter lane he walks, greyedauburn. One life is all. One body. Do. But do" (U.280; XI.907–8; The Gabler edition's seemingly small correction of eliminating the hyphen between "greyed" and "auburn" stresses the iteration of the prior passage.) The use of Stephen's exact words shows us that Stephen is both a character and part of the authorial presence in whose mind, we are coming to learn, "one life is all". But, because the thoughts could also be ascribed to Bloom, whose thoughts of Shakespeare have been rendered in the prior paragraph, the parallel passages also show how Stephen and Bloom miraculously share the same perceptions. And this sharing of perceptions is one of the ways that Joyce urges the reader to see the consubstantiality of Bloom and Stephen. Like Stephen in "Scylla and Charybdis", Bloom "himself had applied to the works of William Shakespeare more than once for the solution of difficult problems in imaginary or real life" (U.677; XVII.385–7).

That Bloom has the very characteristics that Stephen attributes to Shakespeare and which he wants desperately to believe are applicable to himself anticipates the fusion of Shakespeare and Stephen in "Circe", for does not the reader recognize the applicability of the following to Bloom?

(1) "His errors are volitional and are the portals of discovery" (U.190; IX.228–9).
(2) "All events brought grist to his mill" (U.204; IX.748).
(3) "He found in the world without as actual what was in his world within as possible" (U.213; IX.1041–2).
(4) "[H]e was and felt himself the father of all his race" (U.208; IX.868–9). (At the end of "Ithaca" as Bloom drifts off to sleep in a fetal position, he is Everyman who contains "all in all in all of us" [U.213; IX.1049–50].)
(5) "He was himself a lord of language" (U.196; IX.454).
(6) "[H]e passes on toward eternity in undiminished personality, untaught by the wisdom he has written or by the laws he has revealed" (U.197; IX.476–8).

Like Shakespeare, but unlike Stephen or Molly, Bloom has the sexual experience, the openness and flexibility, the ability to learn from others, the capacity for growth, and the negative capability that enable him to see life from the perspective of others. Stephen can only be an artist of Shakespeare's stature when he assimilates the lessons of Bloom, the man who is physically a ghost-like presence in the library: "A dark back went before them, step of a pard" (U.218; IX.1214). Joyce rhymes "pard" with "bard" to reinforce phonically the parallel – indeed, the crucial metonymical relationship – between Shakespeare and Bloom.

NOTES

1. See Gifford and Seidman, p. 184.
2. See Gifford and Seidman, p. 205.
3. M. H. Abrams, "English Romanticism: the Spirit of the Age", in *Romanticism and Consciousness*, ed. Harold Bloom. (New Haven, Conn.: Yale University Press, 1970) p. 102.
4. Ellmann, *James Joyce*, p. 562, orig. ed; quoted in Jackson I. Cope, *Joyce's Cities: Archeologies of the Soul* (Baltimore, Maryland: The Johns Hopkins University Press, 1981) p. 67.
5. See John Richardson's discussion of Picasso's relationship to his precursors in "The Catch in the Late Picasso", *The New York Review of Books*, 36:13 (19 July 1984) 21–8.
6. *The Critical Writings of James Joyce*, eds Mason and Ellmann, p. 228.
7. See my "'I was the World in Which I Walked': the Transformation of the British Novel".
8. Quoted by Grace Glueck, "Joan Miro Exhibit, Sculpture and Ceramics", *The New York Times*, 4 May 1984, p. C24.

7 The Adventure of Reading: The Styles of the Odyssey and the Odyssey of Styles

I WANDERING ROCKS

"Wandering Rocks" dramatizes the spiritual and cultural sterility and the moral cannibalism that *Ulysses* must address. By presenting and implicitly discarding the Church, personified by Father Conmee, and the secular authority, personified by the Viceroy, the Earl of Dudley, Joyce is establishing the need for Bloom, the contemporary Elijah figure whose humanistic values offer hope; the need for Stephen, the putative artist whose creative imagination and prophetic vision will redeem Ireland and, in particular, Dublin, its morally paralyzed urban wasteland; and the need for Molly who will redeem Ireland through her sexuality, passion, and enjoyment of the physical. In its nineteen vignettes, it shows the specific effects of Ireland's position as a servant to England and Roman Catholicism. As we shall see, "Circe" re-examines much of the material in "Wandering Rocks" in terms of the hallucinations and nightmares of Stephen and Bloom, including material of which Bloom and Stephen were unaware within "Wandering Rocks".

The city of Dublin is the major character of "Wandering Rocks," a chapter with only the most indirect parallels to the *Odyssey*. The chapter emphasizes the purposeless movement of the city's population at three o'clock, a time when the day's work ought be reaching a climax. Not only are Conmee and the Viceroy, in the final analysis, aimless wanderers, but so are Bloom and Stephen. Mulligan's epithet "Wandering Aengus", apparently referring to Stephen's lack of equilibrium when he is tipsy, not only calls attention to the chapter's technique but to Stephen's putative fathers – Yeats ("The Song of Wandering

Aengus") and Bloom (U.249; X.1066–7). When in "Scylla and Charybdis" Mulligan – who is characteristically an unwitting prophetic figure – calls Bloom "The wandering jew", he is making, much more than he realizes, an important link between Bloom and Stephen, whom he had moments before called "wandering Aengus of the birds"; in the paragraph preceding Mulligan's phrase for Bloom, Stephen had silently thought of himself as "Aengus of the birds" (U.214, 217; IX.1093, 1206, 1209). Aengus, often portrayed with the birds of inspiration over his head, is a figure for the artist; in his search for an ideal mate, Aengus is an appropriate metaphor for Stephen.

The narrator seems to manipulate characters and events in an arbitrary and even, at times, a capricious manner as if to call attention to himself as magician. Doesn't Joyce's description of the technique as "mechanic" give away his ironic attitude towards the kinds of arbitrary connections the narrator makes in this chapter? At the very center of the epic, the major characters are relegated to minor roles as if to stress that no man in the modern world can be continually foregrounded as if he were an epic hero. But, as we shall see, even here Bloom overcomes this structural condescension.

For the reader, the chapter is a treacherous shoal that threatens to undermine his sense-making odyssey. Yet its symbol, "citizens", is as important to Joyce's political epic as its organ, "blood", – emphasizing the motion of circulation – is to Joyce's epic of the body. If the Liffey is the natural artery flowing through Dublin and carrying its life blood, water, and its metaphoric "Blood of the Lamb" in the form of the throwaway announcing Bloom, the tramlines are its human-made or mechanical artery linking the veins of the city (U.151; VIII.9). That the "Poddle river hung out in fealty [to the Viceroy] a tongue of liquid sewage" emphasizes at once both the pervasive corruption and potential for vitality of the Dublin landscape (U.252; X.1196–7). Doesn't this excremental activity of the Poddle River, a tributary of the Liffey, imply that the health of res publica, as well as the individual body, depends on the ability of the circulatory system to purge itself of waste products? Throughout the novel Joyce stresses that, with its internal waterways and proximity to the sea, Dublin has the geological potential to be a self-sufficient city and the heart of a more vital

Ireland if only it were left alone by England and the Catholic Church.

The chapter opens with the Jesuit Father Conmee – introduced by the brilliantly ironic description: "The superior, the very reverend John Conmee S.J." – recalling words of Cardinal Wolsey which remind us of the service motif: *"If I had served my God as I have served my king He would not have abandoned me in my old days"* (U.219; X.1; X.14–16; instead of the capitalized first line of each chapter in all prior editions, Gabler has restored normal typography.) Conmee has very little concern for the needs of the poor or the presumable damnation of the souls of the Lutherans who had drowned in the conflagration of the steamer *General Slocum* in New York Harbour.[1] Sequacious, complacent, self-satisfied, and hypocritical, he is bereft of real charity and concerned with his own interests in this world. That Father Conmee, the Jesuit priest, and the representative of the British empire, the ironically named William Humble, respectively begin and end the chapter emphasizes how Ireland is caught in the frame or vice of its two masters.

Father Conmee, who misreads what he sees because of his moral vacuity and complacency, is a lesson for the odyssean reader in how not to read. He is a model of a weak reader posing as a strong one, someone who, because he is not a genius, does not contain the "all in all" but only reflects his own narrow and myopic perspective. Conmee blandly neutralizes material that had prior significance. When Father Conmee thinks of a church-sponsored home "For aged and virtuous females", we may hear an echo of Stephen's parable in which he refers to Annie Kearns and Florence MacCabe as "elderly and pious" "Dublin vestals" (U.145, 221; VII.923, X.80). He reduces Stephen's arguments about paternity and creativity to the most simplistic formulations of Christian Platonism: "Those were millions of human souls created by God in His Own likeness to whom the faith had not (D. V.) been brought. But they were God's souls, created by God" (U.223; X.148–51). But his narrow, traditional, and reductive Platonism does call attention to the Platonic terms with which Stephen carried on his argument.

That Father Conmee fulfils Bloom's fantasy (in "Lotus Eaters") of priests as materialistic and voyeuristic fellows once again comically establishes Bloom's authority as a prophetic figure. Conmee is obsessed with sexual peccadilloes; the narrator mocks his preoccupation with "tyrannous incontinence", by transforming him into Don Giovanni: "Don John Conmee walked and moved in times of yore. . . . He bore in mind secrets confessed and he smiled at smiling noble faces in a beeswaxed drawing-room, ceiled with full fruit clusters" (U.223; X.171, 174–7). (Does not the passage also mock the metaferocity of the novel by which any character can be transformed instantly and glibly to another context?). We recall how Bloom had identified Martha Clifford's desire to hear of Bloom's private life with the curiosity of priests hearing confessions: "Wonderful organisation certainly, goes like clockwork. Confession. Everyone wants to. Then I will tell you all. Penance. Punish me, please" (U.82–3; V.424–6).

To show how "Wandering Rocks" is not an interlude but rather is as vital to reading *Ulysses* as any other chapter, let us examine the significance of a relatively neglected paragraph. That Stephen himself responds to Dublin's energy in spite of himself is indicated by his thinking of his heart throbbing in rhythm with the ahuman dynamos of the powerhouse:

> The whirr of flapping leathern bands and hum of dynamos from the powerhouse urged Stephen to be on. Beingless beings. Stop! Throb always without you and the throb always within. Your heart you sing of. I between them. Where? Between two roaring worlds where they swirl, I. Shatter them, one and both. But stun myself too in the blow. Shatter me you who can. Bawd and butcher were the words. I say! Not yet awhile. A look around. (U.242; X.821–7)

Influenced by the Futurists and perhaps, too, by Constructivists and Suprematists, Joyce was fascinated by the possibilities of machines; as Stephen responds to the energy and power of machinery, we realize that the technique of "mechanics" has a celebratory function. We recall, too, that Bloom had responded to the printing machines in "Aeolus" in terms which anthropomorphized them: "Almost human the way it sllt to call attention. Doing its level best to speak. That door too sllt creaking, asking to be shut. Everything speaks in its own way. Sllt" (U.121; VII.175–7). Isn't the pumping heart a metaphor for the throbbing dynamos of the Dublin Corporation Electric Light

Station which circulate – in the form of electricity and light – the necessary nourishment to the industrial city? That his heart responds rhythmically to the pulsations of the machine ("throb always without you and the throb always within") not only validates his aesthetic credo for the man of genius – "He found in the world without as actual what was in his world within as possible" – but stretches it to include experiences beyond encounters with other people (U.213; IX.1041–2).

By using the heart as signifier of machinery and vice versa, Stephen is growing into the writer who might write the Irish epic. In terms which echo Bloom's descent into hell, he imagines the imaginative writer as a figure who, like Orpheus, descends into the earth – an image both for a constructive probing of the past which, we recall from "Nestor", foxlike Stephen had tried to bury under the hollybush, and a descent into the unconscious self – and returns with the ingredients for literature: "And you who wrest old images from the burial earth?" (U.242; X.815). In another crucial echo that calls attention to the narrator's omniscience, Stephen's use of "swirl" as well as its homophone "whirr" suggest the song of Blazes which often echoes within Bloom's mind:

All dimpled cheeks and curls,
Your head it simply swirls . . .
Those girls, those girls,
Those lovely seaside girls. (U.67; IV.437–8, <u>442–3</u>)

Let us look further at the above paragraph. Isn't Stephen also modifying the self-image of Arnold's persona in "Stanzas from the Grand Chartreuse", who sees himself "Wandering between two worlds, one dead,/ The other powerless to be born"? And, our paragraph also contains the suggestion of Stephen's servitude to two masters, the Roman Catholic church and the British Empire, who are dominating this chapter as they have dominated his life and that of his fellow Irishmen. In this vein, he thinks of himself as Samson Agonistes who might pull down the twin pillars between which he is imprisoned: "Shatter them, one and both. But stun myself too in the blow. Shatter me you who can. Bawd and butcher, were the words." The iterated imperative "Shatter" recalls Stephen's vision of a secular apocalypse – based on a fusion of Blake's *The Marriage of Heaven and Hell* with the fall of Troy – at the beginning of "Nestor:" "I hear the ruin of all space, shattered glass and toppling masonry, and time one livid final flame" (U.24; II.8–10).[2] The imperative is directed at the fusion of Shakespeare and Christ that Stephen had created in "Scylla and Charybdis" where he had imagined that the prototypical literary genius Shakespeare contained "all in all in all of us, ostler and butcher, and would be bawd and cuckold too" – an image that looks forward to the similar inclusiveness of Bloom's more passive imagination as he dozes off to sleep at the end of "Ithaca" (U.213; IX.1049–50).

In the paragraph we are discussing, Stephen plays on the homophonic relationship between "worlds" and "words". (In "Nausicaa," Bloom misremembers Martha's request in her letter, "Please tell me what is the real meaning of that word" as "What is the meaning of that other world" [U.77, 381; V.245–6, XIII.1262–3].) Playing upon the idea that God's Word *is*, among other things, the creation of the world from divine substance and that the artist wresting images is iterating the principle of divine creation, this homophonic relationship whereby "word" becomes "world" (or reality) in any way that the artist wishes is central to the meaning of *Ulysses*. But the converse principle, that the world or reality is no more than a sequence of words in a catalogue of terms that undermine meaning, is always present as a lurking challenge to the novel's dominant patterns of signification.

It has been argued by Clive Hart that the purported objectivity of "Wandering Rocks" "is a fraud, a deliberate trap. . . . While almost everything *the narrator* says is, strictly speaking, true, there are many lies of omission, the narrator failing to provide essential connective information which we have to extrapolate for ourselves".[3] But throughout our reading of *Ulysses*, doesn't the reader have to weave together his or her own connection? Aren't the perils of false assumptions part of the challenge facing the odyssean reader?

The technique is called "labyrinth" by Joyce in part, I think, because the chapter provides an intensified version of the reader's wandering through a maze as he desperately tries to figure out what is going on. As we discussed in Chapter 1, when Stephen looks in the jeweller's window, his thoughts – "Born all in the dark wormy earth, cold specks of fire, evil, lights shining in the darkness" (U.241; X.805–6) – play on the conceit with which he had ironically recalled the Jews of Paris in terms of traditional descriptions of the coming of Christ: "darkness shining in brightness which brightness could not comprehend" (U.28; II.160). But the prefiguration of Bloom is inappropriately linked to "fallen archangels" beneath the earth (U.241; X.806). Thus the labyrinth includes false clues that must be discarded: Bloom the dentist, Parnell's brother, and Artifoni as father. By rapidly moving from incident to incident as he cinematically scans the streets of Dublin – as, for example, Antonioni will scan Milan in *Red Desert* – Joyce places readers in the position of having actively to seek their way out of the labyrinth of incomplete understanding. Indeed, doesn't the movement of the chapter – with its partial integration of some material and its willful disregard of other material – become a figure for the reader's activity?

Karen Lawrence and others have insightfully noticed the lack of connections between the events in "Wandering Rocks". According to Lawrence, "[The] narrative mind exhibits . . . a 'lateral' or paratactic imagination: it catalogues facts without synthesizing them. It documents the events that occur but fails to give the casual, logical, or even temporal connections between them".[4] But I would argue that this seeming lack of an integrating imagination is in the service of presenting a mindscape of contemporary Dublin in a style which captures its wasted potential and its absence of direction. Neither this style nor any other prevents Joyce or the reader from privileging the events that occur to the characters who are central to the novel's plot. Just as we in our lives separate those people whose stories interest us from the plethora of data that we encounter each day, we as readers separate the agons of Stephen and Bloom from the plethora of factual information in this chapter. In this chapter the narrator leaves us to synthesize or discard the minor vignettes and descriptions of Dublin.

As the chapter progresses the syntax does become more circumlocutious, the diction more windy, and the meaning of the episodes that do not involve major figures less precise as if to imply that the speaker cannot sustain the kind of satiric energy that reduced Conmee to a caricature even as it established him as a representative figure for the hypocrisy of the Roman Catholic Church. Yet amidst the rodomontade of the final paragraphs that describe William Humble's procession, the narrator reasserts his energy and stylistic control as he turns to the secular cause – British imperialism – for Dublin's mediocrity. Does not the narrator emphasize a relationship between the quality of life in Dublin and the dominance of these two predatory authorities by calling attention in the penultimate paragraph to the invidious Reuben J. Dodd, the repulsive and patronizing Haines, the destitute Dilly Dedalus, and the adulterer Blazes? Indeed, does not Blazes remind us of the adulterous Nelson of Stephen's parable, the English imperialistic hero who took advantage of Ireland's ingenuous but somewhat complicit women? Aren't the "three ladies" to whom Blazes "offer[s] . . . the bold admiration of his eyes and the red flower between his lips" versions of the passively perverse old Irish midwives who, in Stephen's parable, let themselves be used by the British Empire (U.254; X.1245–6)?

The narrator presents a remarkable coincidence in the book stalls of Dublin. When Bloom comes upon a putative volume by Aristotle, and Stephen finds a secret book of the Pentateuch, it seems as if each has discovered a book central to the other's interest. But upon examination, the reader realizes that each has discovered an apocryphal version of the other's focus. That Bloom notices Aristotle's *Masterpiece* is a false sign that Stephen and Bloom are on a converging course. For the *Masterpiece* is not a book by Aristotle, but a bogus book (*Aristotle's Masterpiece Completed*) about medical matters pertaining to sexuality.[5] Similarly, Stephen comes across a bogus book about Bloom's Jewish tradition, one that embroiders upon the Pentateuch or Five Books of Moses: "Eighth and ninth book of Moses. Secret of all secrets. Seal of King David. Thumbed pages: read and read. Who has passed here before me? How to soften chapped hands. Recipe for white wine vinegar. How to win a woman's love. For me this" (U.242; X.844–7).

The phrase "read and read" is another example of Joyce – even while maintaining the verisimilitude of his story – self-consciously intruding into the reader's consciousness. Joyce is using a character's sense-making to admonish his odyssean readers to pay attention in their journey through the text. That Stephen and Bloom each discover a book that apparently represents interests of the other suggests the possibility of convergence, a convergence stressed by our knowing that the answer to the question "Who has passed here before me?" is Bloom who moments before had been in the book stalls. But, by debunking the substance of the particular parallax, Joyce shows the reader the danger to his or her sense-making of being overly eager for parallels. Like D. B. Murphy, the figure in "Eumaeus" whom Joyce regarded as Ulysses pseudoanglos, such an ersatz parallel keeps the reader alert to the need for examining every possible metonymy and metaphor before accepting its suggested analogy.

Whether the book, containing elements of the Cabbala or at least material mentioned in the Cabbala such as the eighth and ninth books of Moses, is something Joyce once saw or, as is just as likely, an invention of Joyce's is unimportant. What does matter is that the book continues his satire on the Irish propensity for magic and mysticism, a propensity which deflects Dublin – the subject of this chapter – from *its* journey homeward toward a viable culture and freedom from Roman Catholicism and Britain. Both the bogus Aristotle and the apocryphal biblical text represent reasons that the citizens of Dublin are metaphorically wandering rocks rather than fulfilled humans.

The book that most engages Bloom's attention in the book stalls is the pornographic novel, *Sweets of Sin*. Ironically, for Bloom, such a book, in its discovery of secret sexual desires and possibilities, becomes a kind of Cabbala; in its revelation of Bloom's character – his resilience and imaginative energy – *Sweets of Sin* becomes a Cabbala for the reader. For he transforms the story about how an adulterous wife and her lover betray a husband – with whom Bloom initially identifies – into a fantasy in which husband and lover merge into a sexually successful beloved with whom he can identify: "Melting breast ointments (*for him! for Raoul!*). Armpits' oniony sweat. Fishgluey slime (*her heaving embonpoint!*). Feel! Press! Chrished! Sulphur dung of lions!)" (U.236; X.621–3; Gabler's substitution of "Chrished" for "Crushed" seems doubtful). Not only does the merging of food and sex, of taste and passion, recall Molly's and Bloom's great moment on the Howth, but "fishgluey" recalls his nickname "Mackerel" and Molly's "gumjelly lips" (U.162, 176; VIII.405, 909). And the analism of "dung of lions", recalling the goat droppings in his reverie of the Howth, anticipates his anal fantasies in "Circe" and his licking Molly's behind in "Ithaca" as his way of paying her sexual tribute. That this episode featuring *Sweets of Sin* occurs in the middle or tenth section of "Wandering Rocks" underlines its importance.

"Wandering Rocks" shows us how far Stephen still has to come before he will be the mature artist and experienced man who could write *Ulysses*. Unlike Molly, who generously flings a coin to the needy one-legged sailor, and unlike Bloom, who gives five shillings to the fund for Dignam's family (the exact sum that Father Conmee has in his pocket when he ignores the same one-legged sailor), Stephen does not offer to share his salary with his sister. (Five shillings is the sum that the Dedalus curtains yield at the auction [U.237; X.647–8].) Rather he prefers to drown in self-pity; thus he paranoidally savors his family's miserable plight and merges his fear that he will destroy his sister with the morning's traumatic memory of his mother's death: "She is drowning. Agenbite. Save her. Agenbite. All against us. She will drown me with her, eyes and hair. Lank coils of seaweed hair around me, my heart, my soul. Saltgreen death" (U.243; X.875–77). The echoes in this reverie mime the original combination of iteration and transformation – notably, the association of the sea outside the tower home to which he had fled with the green vomit in the bowl by his mother's bedside – that formed a central subject of chapter one. Moreover, the process of iteration and transformation is itself a model of how Joyce's text is about itself and therefore needs be read – like traumas and dreams – for the recurring clues of iteration and variation embedded in its tightly woven texture. Unlike Mulligan who physically rescues a drowning man and Milton who immortalizes his drowned friend by imagining that Christ will restore his soul to heaven, Stephen fails as a man and as an artist, and he retreats into his own emotional indulgence. At this point he not only seems spectacularly unready to write the major Irish epic, but unable to create even lyrical or kinetic art. Rather, he seems to be the predatory "pale vampire" of his poetic pastiche (U.132; VII.524). Indeed, as a brother does he not replicate the role of Simon as an unresponsive father figure, and suggest inadvertently that perhaps paternity is not a legal fiction? For Boody Dedalus's sacrilegious remark, "Our father who art not in heaven", also is applicable to Stephen, the consubstantial son of Simon (U.227; X.291).

That the arrival of the *Rosevean* is associated with Malachi Mulligan's prophecy that Stephen "is going to write something in ten years" is another instance of how *Ulysses* is, among other things, self-consciously about the writing of itself. Indeed, among the subjects of the later chapters is an examination of the way that the earlier chapters were written. It is appropriate that Bloom's arrival is predicted in a chapter which presents new versions of the false father. Like Professor McHugh in "Aeolus", both Artifoni (Arti/foni [phony]), the singing teacher, and Conmee (Con/me) suggest versions of what Stephen might become had he not rejected these alternatives.

Joyce expected his reader to recall the conclusion of the prophecy of Malachi – whose presence hovers over the novel in the form of his ironic namesake Malachi Mulligan – foretelling the reconciliation of fathers and sons. "I shall send you Elijah the prophet. . . . And he shall turn the heart of fathers to the children and the heart of the children to their fathers" (*Malachi*. 3:23ff). The increasing emphasis on Elijah-Bloom in "Wandering Rocks" stresses that he is what both Dublin and Stephen require. Between Father Conmee's walk and the Viceroy's procession is the throwaway announcing Bloom's arrival. Aware that Bloom is what Stephen and Dublin require, the narrator at this point immediately calls attention to Bloom's metaphoric possibilities: "A skiff, a crumpled throwaway, Elijah is coming, rode lightly down the Liffey" (U.227; X.294–5). The throwaway, discarded by Bloom, passes the "threemasted schooner *Rosevean*" which predicts the eventual union of the three major figures, denoted by the three giant letters "S", "M", and "P" (U.249; X.1098; I am skeptical about Gabler's omission of these giant letters which appear in every edition published in Joyce's lifetime and to which, as far as I know, he never objected). That two pages later the favorite adjective of Dignam's son, the unknowing object of Bloom's charity, is "blooming", comically calls attention to Bloom's significance.

"Wandering Rocks" also contains verbal echoes that call attention to the consubstantiality of Stephen and Bloom. For example, in "Scylla and Charbydis" when Stephen thinks, "I am tired of my voice, the voice of Esau. My kingdom for a drink", he is not only identifying with Richard III ("A horse! A horse! My kingdom for a horse!" [V.iv.7, 13]) and Esau who would exchange his earthly possessions for food and drink, but also correcting Bloom's memory of the Old Testament and his confusion of the Bible with Mosenthal's play *Deborah* (U.211; IX.981).[6] We recall that the dying and blind Isaac had been deceived by Jacob, pretending to be the first born son, into giving him his blessing. This is after Esau had sold his birthright to Jacob for some pottage. Isaac recognizes that something is amiss: "The voice *is* Jacob's voice, but the hands *are* the hands of Esau."[7] In his version, Bloom had substituted Abraham for Isaac and Nathan for Esau: "I hear the voice of Nathan who left his father to die of grief and misery in my arms, who left the house of his father and left the God of his father" (U.76; V.203–5). Bloom has skipped the crucial middle generation of the traditional triad, Abraham, Isaac, and Jacob, and thus called attention to the disruption of the Jewish heritage that his own history represents, including his father's conversion and the death of his son. When Bloom thinks that "Blazes is a hairy chap", the reader is invited to think of the hairy Esau; but this is a false metaphor because Blazes is not Esau to Bloom's Isaac (U.173; VIII.807–8). Is Bloom not playing the role of Isaac searching for his real son and anticipating his discovery of Stephen whom, among other things, he later thinks of substituting for Blazes in Molly's bed? Without realizing it, Stephen in "Wandering Rocks" verbally re-establishes the lineage when he identifies himself with "the voice of Esau". By identifying himself with the wronged Esau – the missing son in the original story and in Bloom's faulty recollection of the story – Stephen becomes metaphorically linked to Bloom.

II SIRENS

In terms of the reader's odyssey, "Sirens" is really the first chapter in which we become conscious of the narrative presence as a strong persona who is arranging his material for purposes that go beyond the requirements of presenting the lives of his characters or the cityscape of Dublin. "Sirens" tests and, on the whole, discards the possibility that language can use the techniques of music. According to Joyce's schema, the organ is the ear and the symbol is music; that he called the technique "Fuga per Canonem" had generated some abstruse commentary analyzing the chapter's fugal structure. Joyce, who in 1904 was still thinking of a singing career, explores whether the universal language of music can tell us something about the paradigmatic family relationships – father and son, husband and wife – that, he believed, were common to all cultures and civilization. Karen

Lawrence has remarked that the chapter "is Joyce's experimental and, I think, parodic answer to Walter Pater, the tutelary genius of the chapter, who said that all art constantly aspires to the condition of music".[8]

For Joyce does not fully succeed in transforming words into sounds or in creating a musical texture of experience that supplements the representational qualities of language. It would be an overstatement to claim that at times the overture of "Sirens" proposes, in the form of a musical trope, pure self-referential textuality – where words lack referents – as a substitute for mimesis. But we must acknowledge that even while we take pleasure in the way that Joyce's ingenious and painstaking imitation of sounds recalls a Bach prelude or a Wagnerian overture or even an orchestra tuning up, we lose our focus on the story of Bloom and Stephen and what they imply. Gradually and not without some hesitation we readers reject the overture's deflection of our interest in character and theme, in part because we realize that Joyce is using the substance of the songs' lyrics to establish necessary contexts (or "grounding") for the reader's sense-making. Put another way: as soon as the words or lyrics are introduced, the universality of music dissolves into another instance of the nominalism of language since the words refer to something other than themselves. The result is that, whatever Joyce intended, in "Sirens" the reading, rather than the hearing of songs, dominates our experience.

In its efforts to condense the chapter into metaphors – in terms of phonic substitutions – for the action that follows, the overture is a *tour de force*. It contains the sounds in association with what the body of the chapter reveals as the source of the sounds. Clearly the source of these sounds is not Bloom but the narrator who had foreknowledge of the events that follow. The recurring variations of "Bloom" ("Blew. Blue bloom"; "Bloo"; "blooming"; "Bloom. Old Bloom") in the overture establish him at the outset as the major figure in the chapter (U.256–7; XI.6, 19, 32, 49). Since "jingle" is associated with the creaking of Bloom's marital bed (when he first sees Molly in "Calypso", she "set the brasses jingling") and, in particular, Bloom's imagining Blazes and Molly having intercourse in it, "Jingle. Bloo" phonically and musically indicates the incompleteness of Bloom's marital relationship (U.63, 256;; IV.303; XI.19). To emphasize how Bloom has become separated from his jingling bed, the next line begins with a phonic resemblance to Bloom which dissolves into the sounds of aggressive, masculine behaviour – apparently miming the orgasmic rhythms of Blaze's consummation: "Boomed crashing chords. When love absorbs. War! War! The tympanum" (U.256; XI.20).

As the New Testament fulfils the Old, the rest of the chapter "fulfils" – in the sense of giving significance to – the overture. Indeed, in its fulfilment by later events which give meaning to earlier obscure references, "Sirens" is both a miniature and a self-conscious parody of the entire novel. In the stress on asking the reader to imagine events that actually take place offstage, such as the meeting at four-thirty between Blazes and Molly, "Sirens" also teaches us how to read the novel. That Blazes arrives at Eccles street in Bloom's imagination before the actual events take place is a comic foreshadowing of the structural principle that potential or implied events such as the reunion of Molly and Bloom – or the fusion of Bloom, Molly, and Stephen – have significance. Does not reading *Ulysses* teach the reader that, just as many anticipated or foreshadowed events – such as the meeting of Bloom and Stephen and the appearance of Molly – do occur later in the day within the imagined world of the novel, so other proposed events – Stephen's maturation, the sexual reconciliation of Molly and Bloom – may occur even if they are deferred beyond the crucial day of the novel's action?

The narrator's function is to use songs and sounds to place Bloom's emotional problems in an ironic context. The narrator becomes an encyclopedic resource of musical knowledge; his intrusive efforts to perceive behavior and attitudes in terms of aural perceptions order the chapter and threaten to deflect the reader's attention from Bloom. In distancing himself from Bloom in "Sirens", he achieves an ironic perspective but sacrifices the empathy achieved by focusing the action within his character's stream of consciousness. According to C. H. Peake, "[T]he process in *Ulysses* is away from the more representational conventions of interior monologue, where the style is tied to the thoughts and feelings of the central characters, towards styles and techniques which present in more and more complexity the author's judgment of and insights into the essence of his characters, their situations and their relationships, and his vision of the life of the city in which they move."[9]

While the narrator who is proposing the musical metaphor

calls attention to himself, and while the focus of verbal pyro-technics poses a serious threat to the characters' agons, our interest once again returns to Bloom and responds to his di-lemma. (Even Karen Lawrence, who complains that in "Sirens" "the drama of the writing usurps the dramatic action", grudg-ingly acknowledges that Joyce does not completely abandon his subject: "In 'Sirens', our sense of the emotional as well as the empirical reality is stubbornly maintained throughout the ver-bal machinations of the prose."[10]) I am doubtful whether the sounds really deflect us for long from poignant awareness of Bloom's isolation, frustration, or depression in this chapter. Do we fully respond *aurally* – as opposed to intellectually and even synesthetically – to written signs that may evoke the suggestion of our experience of the text but which as sounds signify neither complete thoughts or recognizable fragments of them? Indeed, in terms of the action, Stephen's rejecting the bizarrely named Artifoni's proposal of a musical career anticipates the narrator's rejection of the possibility of using musical patterns as substi-tutes for language.

"Sirens" is about what happens when metaphors replace reality in one's sexual life. Joyce's use of music as a substitution or metaphor for language emphasizes this theme. Perhaps the most obvious sirens are the barmaids, Miss Douce and Miss Kennedy, and the unfulfilled promise of real sexual fulfilment that their unselective, bawdy flirtation represents. But to Bloom, Martha Clifford, who occupies a good deal of his attention in this chapter and to whom he writes a letter – which, it should be noted, he never mails – is the most substantial siren who might deflect his attention from Molly. It is surely significant that the major song in the chapter, sung by Simon Dedalus, is from Flotow's opera *Martha*.

In "Hades" we saw how, in the modern epic, the descent into hell is within the interior space of the mind and is rendered in terms of our nightmares, fears, and depression. Here the reader learns that modern sirens are less external forces or other people than they are the obsessions, fixations, grim memories, and temptations that prey upon our sense of purpose and deflect us from our best impulses. The ultimate sirens are not people or songs, but feelings of loss, self-pity, depression, and petty vindic-tiveness that interfere with passionate relationships with others and become a kind of self-indulgent emotional correlative to the sterility of homosexuality. These feelings are the sirens that the suffering Bloom must resist. Thus, for Bloom, a major siren is his obsession with Blazes whom Bloom follows into the Ormond Bar and whose rendezvous with Molly tortures him within the chapter. Although, as we have seen, he characteristically oscillates between hopefulness and gloom, in "Sirens", the latter emotion dominates; yet the chapter is not without hopeful signs that he can escape the sirens. For example, when he imagines the consummation of the affair between Molly and Blazes, and thinks of abandoning Molly – "Forgotten. I too. And one day she with. Leave her: get tired. Suffer then. Snivel" – we see in his thoughts of the effects of his withdrawing his love, his customary resilience, and appealing egotism (U.277; XI.807–8).

Thus Bloom's anxieties, fantasies, and evasions, rather than external figures, are the most important sirens that keep Bloom from returning to Molly and his proper sexual role in his home. These internal sirens take the form of his imaginative transformations of external sexual stimuli: the letter from Martha Clifford, the playful anonymous sexuality of the bar girls Misses Douce and Kennedy, the pornographic *Sweets of Sin*, and the approach of Blaze's and Molly's rendez-vous. His imaginative transformation is a version of misreading that Joyce is warning us readers to avoid, even while knowing such misreading in terms of our own hopes and fears is inevitable.

Certainly Bloom's thoughts of licking Blazes's semen are a dead end because they represent a continuation of the self-abasing sexual homage – indeed, masochistic subservience – which deflects him from coition and the possibility of a son. The narrator not only emphasizes the applicability of the song of the apparently jilted Lionel by calling Bloom "Lionelleopold", but in the same passage also mocks his sexual futility by referring to the various sirens that are wooing him from his quest to restore himself: "Up the quay went Lionelleopold, naughty Henry with letter for Mady, with sweets of sin with frillies for Raoul with met him pike hoses went Poldy on" (U.288; XI.1187–9). Does not "Lionelleopold", by recalling "dung of lions" in Bloom's masochistic and anal fantasy response to *Sweets of Sin*, continue the sequence of Bloom's savoring of the misery of Molly's adultery? Notice how the word "quay" echoes Bloom's first hyperbolic fantasy of reviving the holy land through an investment in "Agendath Netaim": "Crates lined up on the quayside at Jaffa"

(U.60; IV.212). Isn't the narrator reminding us that Bloom's imagination is both a great resource and a siren that deflects him from reality?

The inclusion in the above passage of Molly's misreading of metempsychosis ("met him pike hoses") alongside thoughts of his pathetic correspondence with Martha and the pornographic fantasies of *Sweets of Sin* emphasizes Molly's place in the masochistic sexual sequence that is defining his sexuality. But its inclusion also stresses that Bloom must break her uxorious hold on him and stop his submissive service if he is to regain his proper position in his home. Indeed, as we shall see in "Circe", he has become within his subconscious the victim of the sadomasochistic novel, *Ruby: the Pride of the Ring*, that Molly had been reading in "Calypso". We should note the homophonic relationship between "Ruby" and "Rudy". Because Bloom has assigned himself the guilt for *Rudy*'s loss and the failure to replace him, he has allowed himself to take on *Ruby*'s role.

Closely related to the siren of psychological depression is the siren of male camaraderie represented by the lonesome, homeless, and hopeless men in the bar: Ben Dollard, Father Cowley, and Simon Dedalus. Just as Stephen must turn his back on the homoerotic possibilities suggested in "Scylla and Charybdis", Bloom must avoid the less sexual male bonding of Dublin's bars where, for some, singing about disrupted passionate relationships becomes a substitute for heterosexual relationships. Like Stephen in "Scylla and Charybdis", Bloom must resist allowing himself to be shaped by paradigms, must resist fully accepting metaphors that are not quite relevant to his needs. Corresponding to the Platonism of the earlier chapter are the songs which, as Bloom perceives, are all variations on the pattern of unfulfilled love: "Thou lost one. All songs on that theme" (U.277; XI.802). Joyce understood that if we allow our metaphors to become rigid, controlling patterns that shape how we respond rather than flexible parallels that suggest to us how our behavior is part of a general iterative pattern with specific individualizing variations of how humans behave, then we are controlled by the past. When we allow metaphors to "freeze" or ossify our perceptions, then they become sterilizing Platonic forms rather than tools of inquiry.

Thoughts of becoming a widower like Simon or a widow like Mrs Dignam recall the darker moments of "Hades": "Let people get fond of each other: lure them on. Then tear asunder. Death. Explos. Knock on the head. Outtohelloutofthat. Human life. Dignam. Ugh, that rat's tail wriggling!" (U.277; XI.803–5). In the above passage, we have another example of how the book is not only about the lives of its major characters, but about the reading of itself. In "Scylla and Charybdis," when Stephen says "There can be no reconciliation . . . if there has not been a sundering" (U.195; IX.397–8), he not only prefigures Bloom's above comment, but prophesies, or at least proposes one important mode of reading the novel. The tension between "sundering" and "reconciliation" is not only thematically relevant to the relationship of Bloom and Molly and to the discrete worlds inhabited by the three major characters that are reconciled within the narrator's presentation, but is also essential to the relationship between discrete chapters. Recollections of prior chapters becomes an important structural principle; in a sense, a few phrases echoing a prior chapter can become a metonymical substitution for the style and substance of the passage and to a lesser extent the entire chapter. By metonymically bringing past chapters into the reader's present, the book enacts its own stress on metaphorically bringing past eras into the reader's synchronic focus.

Yet, in a counter-movement that resists the claims of the novel to free itself from traditional characterization and signification, the reader overcomes the narrator's ironic distancing and reestablishes his focus on Bloom's point of view. Let us examine an instance of this phenomenon. In an anticipation of the ironic distance of the next three chapters – "Cyclops", "Nausicaa", and "Oxen of the Sun", the narrator turns his irony upon Bloom, echoing the words and rhythms of Dawson's Celtomania in "Aeolus" in order to describe the note with which Simon sings the word "*Come!* . . ." in the final line of Lionel's song: "It soared, a bird, it held its flight, a swift pure cry, soar silver orb it leaped serene, speeding, sustained, to come, don't spin it out too long long breath he breath long life, soaring high, high resplendent, aflame, crowned, high in the effulgence symbolistic, high, of the etherial bosom, high, of the high vast irradiation everywhere all soaring all around about the all, the endlessnessness" (U.275–6; XI.744–50). In "Aeolus", Dawson had used this rodomontade to conclude a silly nationalistic speech in which, as in the case of songs in "Sirens", the sound of words threatens to take precedence over their sense (U.126; VII.327–8). Yet what follows makes clear not merely that the flight of the note is a metaphor for the soaring tumescence of Blazes's consummation, but that the speaker is being crass and insensitive to Bloom's plight:

– *To me!*
Siopold!
Consumed. (U.276; XI.750–2)

Paradoxically, because of the narrator's tastelessness and because he has adopted a discredited style to emphasize crudely Blazes Boylans's sexual triumph, our sympathies are with Bloom as victim of the narrator. As the reader understands that the speaker's breathlessness and confusion are the voyeuristic result of describing sexual excitement, he resents the speaker's condescension and his effort to reduce Bloom's stature.

Bloom overcomes the narrator's patronizing style to triumph both as a character on the literal level and as a significant figure in the novel's teleology. As a character he triumphs because his imaginative resilience enables him for a moment to see himself as the successful lover Lionel. To be sure, Bloom originally identified with Lionel, the hero of Flotow's *Martha*, because Lionel had gone mad after apparently losing his love, Lady Harriet, after she had disguised herself as a servant girl, Martha. The major thrust of Joyce's use of the song "*M'appari* or "Come Thou Lost One" from Flotow's opera is to demonstrate the parallel between Bloom's loss and Lionel's. But we should not forget how while reading *Sweets of Sin* Bloom's ebullience, optimism, and energetic sexuality enabled him to participate empathetically in Raoul's sexual conquest. Does not Bloom's response to Lionel's song in orgasmic terms anticipate Lionel's later triumph when Harriet's return restores his sanity and his love is fulfilled in marriage to her? Knowing that Lionel's poignant cries, climaxing in "Come to me!", are answered by Harriet's return, but also perhaps thinking of the estrangement between them which suggests his relationship with Molly, Bloom identifies in his imaginative epiphany, "Siopold!", with both the real singer, Simon, and the fictional one, "Lionel".

The chapter, finally, confirms Joyce's interest in and respect for Bloom's humanity. For Bloom thinks – because he has not had intercourse with Molly since Rudy died – of Blazes and Molly in association with the son he lacks.

> He bore no hate.
> Hate. Love. Those are names. Rudy. Soon I am old (U.285; XI.1068–9).

Is not the union of Stephen and Bloom anticipated by "Siopold?" After Simon Dedalus finishes his song the narrator and the rereader, aware of what will follow, understands that "Siopold" anticipates not only the father-son relationship in which Leopold substitutes for Simon, who has been singing *M'appari* from an opera about hidden and mistaken identities, but also the potential union of Stephen and Leopold in "Blephen" and "Stoom" and, ultimately, in the new entity who is telling the tale and has written the novel (U.682; XVII.549, 551). The "S" of Siopold suggests also Shakespeare, who resembles both Bloom at rest in a fetal position at the end of "Ithaca," and the mature artist ("the father of all his race") who is telling the reader the epic not merely of Ireland but of the recurrent patterns of human history (U.208; IX.868–9). "Consumed" is not merely a pun on consummated, inspired by the presence of Blazes, but a comment by the narrative presence calling the reader's attention to the metonymical process by which one figure can be substituted for another.

The other major song, sung by Ben Dollard, "The Croppy Boy", is about the betrayal of a young rebel by a loyalist officer disguised as a priest. The song somewhat deflates the expectations that Bloom will fully escape the sirens within this chapter and sets a distance between Bloom and his Homeric archetype. For Bloom identifies with the betrayed boy and thinks of Blazes as "a false priest" (U.283; XI.1016). When the song speaks of the boy's arrival at the entrance of what he thinks is the priest's house, Bloom is thinking of Molly greeting Blazes in the entrance of his Eccles street home. Bloom also identifies with the croppy boy because the latter has lost his family; when in the song the croppy boy says to his listener: "I alone am left of my name and race," Bloom thinks: "I too. Last of my race" because he lacks a son to carry on his name. (U.285; XI.1066).[11] The narrator expects us to realize that the croppy boy also resembles Stephen, not only in his betrayal by false friends – Mulligan,

Deasy, Simon – but also in his failure to pray for his mother. Since Stephen within the novel has no brother or son, he, too, until and unless he conceives a manchild or, alternatively, gives birth to the putative Irish epic, is the last of his race.

III CYCLOPS

"Cyclops" is the climax of the public theme of the novel. The twelfth chapter, it is sandwiched between "Sirens" and "Nausicaa", two chapters in which Bloom is in danger of being diverted by sexual reveries and self-pity not only from his private mission to return home and to re-establish his conjugal relationship with Molly, but also from demonstrating his humanistic community values. It takes place at 5 p.m. in Barney Kiernan's pub, which is presided over by an anonymous boor called the Citizen and "that bloody mangy mongrel" dog, Garryowen (U.295; XII.119–20). The pub is inhabited by a group of bigoted, xenophobic, self-styled patriots whose violent aggressive behavior contrasts with the humanism and androgyny of Leopold Paula Bloom. Its art is "politics" and its technique is "gigantism". After this chapter, the book returns to its emphasis on the interrelationships among the three major characters and between them and the narrative presence.

In this chapter the Irish are not only intolerant of any nation other than their own, but are lost in a welter of ineffective rhetoric. Joyce might have expected the reader to recall Homer's description of the Cyclops in section IX of *The Odyssey* as "an overweening/ and lawless people, who. . . . /Do not sow plants with their hands and do not plow. . . . /They have neither assemblies for holding council nor laws. . . . [E]ach one dispenses the laws/ For his children and his wives and is not concerned for the others".[12] Indeed, the talk of the horse race reminds us that the Citizen and his colleagues are Yahoos. In this chapter, Bloom establishes his credential as a hero. It is his courageous behavior within this hostile environment and the credo he articulates that make him a humanistic successor to Parnell, Moses, Elijah, and Christ. (Using as his clue an earlier schema that Joyce sent to Carlos Linati, Ellmann has argued that Shelley's Prometheus should also be included in the cast of this chapter's archetypes.)[13] That Bloom's role as a successor in this series is evoked in a cynical way by the Citizen and in a mocking way by the omniscient voice actually prepares the reader for the expectation that such an analogy is possible.

The Citizen is the most obvious Cyclops figure, a Polyphemus who would physically attack Bloom. While Odysseus gets Polyphemus drunk in order to blind him, Bloom, "the prudent member" fails to buy a round of drinks (U.297; XII.211). But the Citizen becomes blind with rage. We recall that Odysseus tells Polyphemus that his name is "No-man"; when Odysseus and his men burn out Polyphemus's eye in retaliation for cannibalizing six of Odysseus's followers, the other Cyclops are deceived by Odysseus's words, "No-man is attacking me". The marginal Jewish outsider Bloom is "No-man" to the Citizen and his bar patrons. Just as after his escape Ulysses can not refrain from revealing his identity to Polyphemus and enraging him, Bloom provokes an attack when he declares "Christ was a jew like me" (U.342; XII.1808–9); before throwing the biscuit tin at him, the Citizen responds: "By Jesus . . . I'll brain that bloody jewman for using the holy name. By Jesus, I'll crucify him so I will" (U.342; XII.1811·12).

Joyce uses the later chapters to comment on earlier ones. Thus, *Ulysses* becomes, among other things, a novel about its own styles and ways of writing and perceiving as well as about the anterior worlds of Joyce's life and the quality of life in Dublin at the turn of the century. "Circe" makes use of what has preceded in the novel. According to A. Walton Litz, "The 'reality' to be processed into art is both the imitated human action and the rich artistic world already created in the earlier and plainer episodes."[14] For example, in Joyce's hilarious pastiche of the kind of folk poetry espoused by the Celtic Renaissance and represented within the novel by Hyde's translation of the *Love Songs of Connaught* – which, we recall, is the inspiration of the poem Stephen wrote in "Proteus" – the ill-tempered Garyowen has the facility to deliver a poem in Welsh:

> The curse of my curses
> Seven days every day
> And seven dry Thursdays
> On you, Barney Kiernan,
> Has no sup of water
> To cool my courage,

And my guts red roaring
After Lowry's lights. (U.312; XII.740–7)

That Garryowen assumes a nearly human voice anticipates the metamorphism in "Circe".

While in "Cyclops", the subject of writing may on occasion compete with the characters for our attention, I believe that the focus always returns to the characters, the imagined Dublin in which they live, and their significance. We should not forget that, for Joyce, ways of writing are ways of perceiving reality and understanding significance. With the snarling personal perspective of a bar denizen alternating with the vast omniscient historical perspective of an even more hyberbolic voice than those of the xenophobes that Stephen mocked in his parable, "Cyclops" is a sequel to "Aeolus". Indeed, "Cyclops" is "Aeolus" without the headlines and rhetorical tropes, but with a similar hyperbole that is disproportionate to the facts that it describes. If the first narrator abuses the spoken word, reducing it to an angry, malicious weapon of aggression, the second narrator abuses the written word with his convoluted and circumlocutious prose. Comically and poignantly, each narrator speaks with splendid indifference to the words of the other. In the sense that both narrators are lacking in perspicacity, they are one-eyed Cyclopean narrators; indeed, doesn't the anonymous bill collector's first word "I" suggest the homophone "eye" of his fellow Cyclops?

Each voice pretends to speak for Ireland. Each voice exposes the pretense and insincerity of the other. Both narrators speak in tones of male aggressiveness that befit a chapter that takes place in a male bar and in a chapter whose organ is "muscle". Indeed, "Cyclops" offers another version of the asexual male camaraderie that both Stephen and Bloom must avoid; Bloom's exchanges with the Citizen and his companions are a parody of the Socratic dialogue in "Scylla and Charybdis". The snarling narrator reinforces the Citizen's point of view and credentials. But the other speaker assumes a grandiose voice, derived from epic and romance, that by its very excesses undermines the Citizen and his fellows. Because his hilarious exaggerations have a point of reference within the novel, particularly in the windy rhetoric of "Aeolus", Joyce uses him to make satirical points. Within the binary rhetorical system of "Cyclops", he often implicitly speaks on Bloom's behalf, if only by contrast to the other speaker. But given the moral urgency of Bloom's position, the ventriloquist's seeming indifference to the implications of what he describes, including a hanging before the trial, raises questions about the quality of his moral discrimination. Isn't his position frequently one of cynical and reductive mockery? Do not the very excesses of his satire often turn on him, as his catalogues and exaggeration undermine the force of his remarks and align him with the rodomontade of "Aeolus?" This chapter has the effect of making even more attractive the satiric energy of Stephen's concluding parable in that episode.

Throughout *Ulysses* Joyce teaches his reader that style signifies more than the individual words and sentences that it renders. In "Sirens", "Cyclops", "Nausicaa", and "Oxen of the Sun", Joyce uses styles as metaphors for particular states of mind. In "Cyclops", "Nausicaa", and "Oxen of the Sun", the use of parody is a stylistic metaphor for values that are being discredited, while in "Sirens" the style is trying to evoke the aesthetic values of music. In "Cyclops", when the omniscient narrator speaks from his mock romance and historical perspective, usually relatively few of his words establish the meaning of a passage, while the rest of the words do not signify something beyond themselves. Rather, the words weave a texture – rather like the design of a Persian rug – which depends upon a formal pattern of relationships within itself. (We should not forget the pervasive influence in Europe of Cubism, Fauvism, and other non-representational kinds of visual art; these approaches redefined art as something that need not have an anterior subject or be *about* anything, even as they opened up the possibility of art as formal design and abstract relationships.) I think this is how the reader responds to the relation of the overture to what follows in "Sirens" as well as to the passages containing encyclopedic catalogues in "Cyclops". Of course, even within these catalogues some words mean more than others. In fact, within any passage there are infinite gradations between the poles of signification, one pole of which is the major signifying words, such as "Agenbite of inwit", "agenbuyer", or "throwaway", and the other pole of which is passages or phrases which, like the catalogues of "Cyclops", merely disseminate ungerminated seeds for the reader's sense-making or, to use another metaphor, strands for the warp and woof of a decorative texture.

To understand how the cataloguing affects our reading, let us briefly look at the following passage in which Joyce is using his omniscient speaker to mock the Irish propensity for self-inflation and hyperbole and specifically to parody Standish O'Grady's and Yeats's belief that an Irish mythology can be the root of a Celtic revival:

> The figure seated on a large boulder at the foot of a round tower was that of a broadshouldered deepchested stronglimbed frankeyed redhaired freelyfreckled shaggybearded widemouthed largenosed longheaded deepvoiced barekneed brawnyhanded hairylegged ruddyfaced sinewyarmed hero. From shoulder to shoulder he measured several ells and his rocklike mountainous knees were covered, as was likewise the rest of his body wherever visible, with a strong growth of tawny prickly hair in hue and toughness similar to the mountain gorse . . .
>
> From his girdle hung a row of seastones which jangled at every movement of his portentous frame and on these were graven with rude yet striking art the tribal images of many Irish heroes and heroines of antiquity, Cuchulin, Conn of hundred battles, Niall of nine hostages, Brian of Kincora, the ardri Malachi, Art MacMurragh, Shane O'Neill, Father John Murphy, Owen Roe, Patrick Sarsfield, Red Hugh O'Donnell, Red Jim MacDermott, Soggarth Eoghan O'Growney, Michael Dwyer, Francy Higgins, Henry Joy M'Cracken, Goliath, Horace Wheatley, . . . Charlemagne, Theobald Wolfe Tone, the Mother of the Maccabees, . . . William Tell, Michelangelo Hayes, Muhammad, . . . Dick Turpin, Ludwig Beethoven. . . . (U.296–7; XII.151–8, 173–94)

Although Joyce's 1922 Irish readers would have recognized far more of the names than we do, the fact remains that even after, with the help of Gifford and Seidman, we have done our scholarly homework, we are overwhelmed with information that we cannot weave into our own interpretation. We are left with a performance – an enactment of the hyperbolic mode, a metaphor for a way of looking at things – more than a sense of the things themselves. Isn't Joyce using style to equate the speaker with Cuchulain, the Irish hero who, although an effective figure, is often conceived as a little man who puffs himself up and changes shape by filling himself with air? Isn't Joyce mocking a style that would substitute catalogues for metaphors? Indeed, doesn't the Citizen himself use a version of this hyperbole and thus become a Cuchulain pseudoangelos, even as the omniscient narrator – who has encyclopedic knowledge, but who is unable to impose significant form on his material – becomes an artist pseudoangelos? In contrast to the elaborate historical metaphors on which the book depends, the names are merely names; the speaker cannot summon them by merely listing them.[15]

I am very skeptical about the claim of Michael Groden, a claim supported by other recent critics, that "Joyce changed his focus of interest from his characters to his styles, knowing that the first nine episodes provided support to sustain the characters as much as necessary through the successive elaborations."[16] It is a mistake to think that Joyce is interested in style for its own sake. By showing in this chapter how the two speakers create a word world, Joyce is creating a moral context for Bloom's forceful eloquent responses and decent, human, courageous behavior. Bloom survives the attempts to mock and undermine him.

One can say that in "Sirens", "Cyclops", "Nausicaa", and "Oxen of the Sun", Joyce is fascinated (one might even say fixated) with what happens when the prose violates the conventions of utility – what we call significant form – and when language and action take different paths. The romance voice comments on the action in such a way as to create his own parodic version of events. He also parodies the self-inflation of Irish rhetoric, the self-inflation that leads to the kind of self-deceptions illustrated in "Aeolus" by both the headlines and the comparison of the Irish with the lost tribes of Israel. As Karen Lawrence writes: "Almost every verbal expression of feeling or belief on the part of the characters automatically generates its own parody."[17] Thus from time to time the omniscient voice abandons his characteristic romance voice and becomes a third distinct voice, as, for example, when he wears the masque of one of the cynical denizens of the bar – perhaps the masque of the first narrator – as if to imply stylistically the trace of a metonymical relationship between the two speakers. For example, the omniscient voice intrudes to belittle Bloom's forceful, impassioned and energetic defense of love: "Love loves to love love. . . . Gerty MacDowell loves the boy that has the bicycle. M. B. loves a fair gentleman. . . . You love a certain person. And this person loves that other person because everybody loves somebody but God loves everybody" (U.333; XII.1493–501). That the narrator attempts to reduce love to verbiage and that the narrator not merely mocks sentimentality and clichés, but human emotion and eloquence, discredits him. Does the narrator really succeed in reducing to oversimplifications and nonsense the universal need to be loved, a need that is dramatized by the behaviour of Gerty and Molly ("M. B.") and the poignant reality that love is often unrequited? The answer, of course, is negative. For, finally, Bloom triumphs over both speakers' attempts to denigrate and trivialize his credo.

The romance voice, with its propensity for myth-making for its own sake, misses the point of Bloom's significance; he does not realize the immorality of publicly hanging a victim *before* trying him. Nor, of course, is the snarling Thersites figure any more reliable. In its plenitude and randomness, the language of "Cyclops" is in danger of being devalued. It seems at times to be self-indulgently oblivious to what it is describing. Furthermore, as Arnold Goldman has written, "As in the *Wake* the incipient encyclopaedism promotes a sense of randomness and arbitrariness of any one particular 'interpretation' of the action, or direction of the narrative."[18]

The trial of Bloom is a development of the accusation that Ireland is being swindled by strangers and Jews. Because there is no evidence against Bloom, the narrator's description of the execution, trial, and resurrection of Bloom has the effect of establishing him as a Christ figure. When Joe Hynes calls him, "a bloody dark horse himself", he has in mind Bloom's Jewishness and Freemasonry as well as his being dressed in black (U.335; XII.1558). Since "Throwaway", the dark horse that Bloom purportedly backed, is a comic prefiguration of Bloom's triumph, Joyce is using Hynes to suggest comically the promise held by disregarded and underestimated outsiders. This promise also suggests the legend of the Just Men, whose identities are often hidden even from themselves (See my Chapter 2). Like Parnell, Bloom is a neglected and ostracized hero who is unrecognized and finally crucified. When in his characteristically bitter, cynical tone the Citizen says of Bloom, "A new apostle to the gentiles" and "That's the new Messiah for Ireland", he is unwittingly announcing Bloom's importance (U.333, 337; XII.1489, 1642). As we shall see, Molly's reacceptance of Bloom in the final paragraph, as her menstruation begins, makes possible the birth of a male child who might be the Messiah in the form of a figure – either hero or artist – who would effectively espouse the humanistic Bloomian values on which Ireland's redemption depends.

Bloom's articulate, eloquent, and courageous response gives an affirmative answer to John Wyse's question, "why can't a jew love his country like the next fellow?" (U.337; XII.1628–9). Indeed, it is in this chapter that Bloom publicly affirms his identity as a Jew, something he deliberately refrained from acknowledging when he encountered his fellow Jew, the pork butcher: "And I belong to a race too . . . that is hated and persecuted. Also now. This very moment. This very instant" (U.332; XII.1467–8). Are we not to assume that this courageous speech to the Citizen, at the risk of physical attack, is one major reason that for Bloom 16 June 1904 is not merely a gratuitous day but rather a crystallizing day? Bloom is acknowledging his Jewish identity in such a way that it becomes a return to his racial heritage. That Bloom asserts himself and his values in a hostile environment is part of his growth. His answer also affirms the potential of language – in the face of the attacks on meaning and coherence by the two principle narrators – to communicate values and feelings.

Thus language and Bloom both triumph. Later, when proudly retelling the story to Stephen in "Eumaeus", his narrative – even though in the retelling he hedges on his Jewishness for fear of losing the chance of Stephen's affection – testifies to its importance to him: "I . . . told him his God, I mean Christ, was a jew too and all his family like me though in reality I'm not" (U.643; XVI.1083–5). The story of his triumph also demonstrates the role of language in giving life to past experience – in Stephen's words, "call[ing] . . . into life across the waters of Lethe . . . the poor ghosts" (U.415; XIV.1113–14). If he does not quite embrace his Jewish identity, the reason for his diffidence is not lack of pride but embarrassment about his two Christian baptisms, his lack of a Jewish mother (which Joyce knew would have prevented his being Jewish in the eyes of the orthodox tradition), and his uncircumsized penis (U.373; XIII.979).

Bloom's self-respect, concern for others, courage, and tolerance undermine the twin mockery of the snarling, bitter Thersites figure and the hyperbolic blarney of the Irish folk legend. He presents a humanistic alternative to the sterility and paralysis of Dublin. Despite the mockery of the begrudging, petty denizen of the Citizen's pub and the romantic speaker's grandiloquent bathetic style, Bloom emerges as vessel of value. His language and values are strikingly different from the two narrators and the other characters. In his dialogue with the Citizen and his cohorts, Bloom's syntax and diction affirm the value of a language of direct statement, a language that reflects the speaker's attitudes and values – in this case, Bloom's humanity, integrity, and sincerity – with clarity and precision.

IV   BLOOM AS ELIJAH

Joyce uses metaphor to define a space or plane of meaning which supplements that of the action. In this space, he presents his characters in a timeless perspective in which they co-exist with their literary and legendary predecessors. Put another way, all the cycles of human history exist simultaneously in concentric circles radiating outward from the present moment. As an historical or literary metaphor is proposed, the reader becomes attentive to correspondences. As he discovers these correspondences, the metaphor becomes more established as part of his reading experience. This is another way *Ulysses* teaches us how to read itself.

It is appropriate that "Cyclops", the chapter in which Bloom actively embraces his Jewishness, returns to the subject of the Passover story and the Haggadah. While the Haggadah tells the Exodus story, the focus is on the captivity in Egypt as a metaphor for the Diaspora in general and for specific pogroms, ghettos, and institutionalized bigotry. Bloom owns "An ancient haggadah book in which a pair of hornrimmed convex spectacles inserted marked the passage of thanksgiving in the ritual prayers for Pessach (Passover)" (U.723; XVII.1877–80). Not being circumsized aligns the exiled wandering Jew Bloom with the uncircumsized Jews wandering in the wilderness after their exodus from Egypt.[19] In "Nausicaa," he thinks of the Passover story again in confused terms: "That brought us out of the land of Egypt and into the house of bondage" (U.378; XIII.1158–9).

But he never forgets its optimistic strand – the hope of return embodied in "Next Year in Jerusalem" – which applies to his hope of regaining Molly.

The Haggadah rarely mentions Moses, who had taken the Jews out of Egypt, but rather looks forward to the promise of Elijah's coming which will relieve current misery. (We should recall that in versions of the turn-of-the-century Haggadah and to the European Jews whom Joyce knew, the Zionist dream of return to Palestine and of a Jewish state was only slightly less remote than Elijah's coming.) That the technique of "Cyclops" is gigantism is appropriate since the Haggadah – which means "the telling" – depends upon exaggerations and illuminating distortions; this befits a telling meant to impress and educate Jewish children at the Passover Sedar as a way of perpetuating the Jewish tradition. An example of the Haggadah's hyperbole is the place where the ancient Rabbis, while discussing the Exodus story, deduce – without textual evidence in the Bible but with a kind of scholastic and Platonic logic not unlike Stephen's in "Scylla and Charybdis" – that in reality there were not ten plagues visited upon the Egyptians, but two hundred and fifty plagues. Their enthusiasm is in the service of illustrating the Haggadah's exclamation, "How many abundant favours the Omnipresent has performed for us!"

Within Joyce's secular, humanistic universe Bloom, the Just Man, is what the modern world requires. Since in the Haggadah Elijah is the figure who will deliver the Jews from bondage, Bloom is presented as an Elijah figure. For Christians, Malachi's prophecy of the coming of Elijah has been fulfilled in Christ, who will return for the last days; for the Jews Elijah's coming is still to take place. Since it supported Joyce's belief for an ideology of history that assumed repetition rather than progress, he stressed the kinship between Christian and Jewish customs and between the traditions of Easter and Passover. After all, Christ was crucified during Passover. Not only was the Last Supper a Sedar meal, but also the Eucharist recalls the ritual of eating matzah and drinking Passover wine.

Joyce comically refers to details of the Passover Sedar. Within the chapter, isn't the bigoted, persecuting Citizen a modern Pharaoh who would, if he could, violate the principles of hospitality and harass if not enslave the Jews? But, as we shall see, he and his fellows are, like the Egyptians in the Exodus story, visited with plagues. Indeed, one can locate in "Cyclops" elements of a parodic version of the Passover Sedar, one in which the inhabitants of the bar ironically take part. The Cyclops drink their beer four times, corresponding to the four cups of wine, and the dog biscuit is a comic version of the unleavened bread or matzah. Corresponding to the bitter herbs, Joe Hynes speaks "from bitter experience" (U.298; XII.233). Like Elijah, for whom a cup is always set but never drunk, Bloom does not drink with the rest of the company. And yet metaphorically a special cup, the Gold Cup, the winner of which Bloom prophesies, belongs to him even though he does not partake in the monetary feast that results from the victory of "Throwaway".

With a little effort and some ingenuity, one can locate the ten plagues: blood (the continual repetition of "bloody" which characterizes the speech of the Citizen and his companions); vermin – metaphorically, those multitudes, who, in the paranoid minds of the denizens of the Citizen's bar, prey upon Ireland's well-being (prominent among these "vermin" are Jews, including the "bloody big foxy thief", the Jew Moses Herzog [U.292; XII.13]); beasts (Garryowen, although in some Haggadahs beasts are "flies", in which case "playful insects" is the more likely parallel [U.294; XII.82]); murrain ("foot and mouth disease" [U.293; XII.62]; also, "syphilisation" [325; XII.1197]); boils (the result of typhoid fever); hail (Surely the thunder and lightning before the hanging of the malefactor could be the prelude to a hailstorm: "The deafening claps of thunder and the dazzling flashes of lightning which lit up the ghastly scene testified that the artillery of heaven had lent its supernatural pomp to the already gruesome spectacle" [U.306; XII.528–31]); locusts ("filling the country with bugs" [U.323; XII.1141–2]); darkness ("On which the sun never rises" [U.329; XII.1351]); slaying of the first born males (Rudy's death and talk of "the slaughter of human animals who dare to play Irish games in the Phoenix park" [U.316; XII.870–1]). While no frogs – the second plague – appear in the chapter, there is a plethora of fish ("silvery fishes, crans of herrings, drafts of eels, codlings, creels of fingerlings" [U.294; XII.81–2]), and Joyce would have enjoyed the difficulty such a partial omission presents to the odyssean reader in his quest to complete the parallel.

Joyce is turning upside down the comparisons in"Aeolus" which conceived of the Irish as the lost tribes in Israel and showing us that, at worst, the xenophobic Irish may become not only "Cyclops", but Egyptians who would keep the Jews in captivity. Isn't that the thrust of Bloom's accusation that at "This very moment. This very instant" he is being "Insulted. Persecuted" by the Irish (U.332; XII.1467, 1470)? Before the Irish can be compared to the persecuted Jews who successfully freed themselves from Egyptian bondage, they must recover their own best human impulses; put another way, they must acknowledge Bloom as a potential heroic figure, as the humanistic successor to Parnell, whose values might lead them out of bondage. Finally Bloom will merge with Stephen at a point beyond the novel to form the text entitled *Ulysses*, the humanistic Haggadah as well as the New New Testament which enacts the values that will lead the Irish from bondage.

"Cyclops" establishes Bloom's stature as a contemporary version of Elijah. Elijah is a significant prototype for Bloom in several ways. God sent Elijah as his messenger to remind the Jews that they had strayed from his Commandments, and replaced him with the worship of foreign gods. Similarly, Joyce created Bloom as his messenger to remind the Irish and modern man how they have strayed from humanistic values; the "foreign gods" they have adopted are, of course, the England monarchy and the Roman Catholic Church. Just as God has ravens feed Elijah in the desert as a reward for courageously representing God's values and announcing God's punishment to the corrupt idol-worshipping Ahab, so Joyce, the Creator within his imagined world, enables Bloom's psyche to have the vision of Rudy as a reward for his humane and selfless response to Stephen.

Elijah's generosity is the quality on which Joyce focuses his comparison between Bloom and the biblical archetype. We might recall that after God sends Elijah to seek refuge with a destitute widow and her son, God prevents the three of them from going hungry. So that Elijah may live with them without using their food, God miraculously renews their supplies. Perhaps the restoration of the child's health through prayers anticipates the salutory effect that Bloom will have on Stephen. Elijah's charity anticipates Bloom's concern for Mrs Dignam and her family as well as for Stephen. The important difference is that God works his charity through Elijah, while Bloom performs his own charitable acts without divine intervention.

Bloom's debate with the denizens in the pub recalls Elijah's victory over the prophets of Baal. But, while Elijah slays the prophets with his sword, Bloom's only weapons are his righteous words. The iconoclastic Joyce seems to have understood the Old Testament concept of the "righteous" man – the concept best illustrated by a leader or prophet speaking as if he knows God's will and has been chosen to speak it. Particularly when he eloquently defends the Jews, Bloom's zealous words in the pub have the tone of a "righteous" man: the man who believes it is his mission to teach others what is morally upright and correct. That Bloom speaks with forceful, lucid, straightforward diction and syntax – in contrast to the prolixity, hyperbole, and grandiloquence of the romance speaker and the snarling innuendos and cynical implications of the anonymous Thersites figure in the pub – emphasizes his position as the righteous man in Dublin. As a man whose heroism, like Elijah's, takes the form of just and wise words, Bloom is a version of the Old Testament prophet who has a sense of mission.

After slaying the idolaters, Elijah goes to the wilderness and sits under a broomtree to die. (Wouldn't Joyce have enjoyed the rhyme with "Bloom?") After forty days and nights in the desert, the Lord calls him. As he ascends in a whirlwind, he drops his mantle on Elisha, who has watched Elijah's ascent and inherits his spirit in "double portion" (II Kings 2:9). In II Kings 2:11 12, it is Elisha who seeing Elijah's chariot rise into the parting heavens cries, "My father, my father, the chariots of Israel and the horsemen thereof!" Just as Elisha acknowledges Elijah as father, so must Stephen acknowledge Bloom. Elisha's use of language to cure bad water ("So the waters were healed unto this day according to the word of Elisha" [II Kings 2:21]) suggests that he, like Stephen, is a prototype of the artist.

Joyce is teaching his reader that the fictionalized presence who is telling *Ulysses*, and who is trying to awake the Irish to the moral and spiritual dangers of their bondage to the false gods of Roman Catholicism and the British Empire, is a figure who combines the metaphorical prophet (Elijah) with the metaphorical artist (Elisha). In the Haggadah, Moses is a precursor for the even more miraculous coming of Elijah, but in Joyce's humanistic haggadah they are both proleptic figures for Bloom's fulfilment. Thus, in a sense, the mature artist, the creative presence who is telling *Ulysses*, combines into one the figure of Moses, God's man of action, the figure of Elijah, God's prophet, and the figure of Elisha, God's artist.

The apotheosis at the end of "Cyclops" is one of the book's climaxes. Echoing Elijah's ascent in a whirlwind, the final paragraph confers stature upon Bloom only ironically to undermine it:

> When, lo, there came about them all a great brightness and they beheld the chariot wherein He stood ascend to heaven. And they beheld Him in the chariot, clothed upon in the glory of the brightness, having raiment as of the sun, fair as the moon and terrible that for awe they durst not look upon Him. And there came a voice out of heaven, calling: Elijah! Elijah! And He answered with a main cry: Abba! Adonai! And they beheld Him even Him, ben Bloom Elijah, amid clouds of angels ascend to the glory of the brightness at an angle of fortyfive degrees over Donohoe's in Little Green Street like a shot off a shovel (U.345; XII.1910–18)

That this does not happen at the literal level, but rather at the level of metaphor is emphasized by the bathetic intrusion ("like a shot [a turd] off a shovel") of pedestrian events in the streets of Dublin. Put in other terms that are essential to the values of *Ulysses*, the nominalistic concluding phrases – illustrating that reality is the Aristotelian "what you damn well have to see" – undermine the Platonic apotheosis of Bloom into Elijah and remind the reader that Bloom's divinity in a Post-Christian world depends on his nobility within chronological time where God, in the sense of a providentially ordered world, does not exist and can be no more than "A shout in the street" (U.186, 34; IX.86, II.386).

We should notice the extent to which Bloom's apotheosis is a fulfillment of Stephen's argument in "Scylla and Charybdis." If Elijah is the son of Bloom ("ben Bloom Elijah"), then Bloom, like Shakespeare, is the father of his own father. Indeed, if Bloom is the father of the prophet Elijah, does he not become – as the timeless spirit of man seeking meaning in an amoral cosmos – Joyce's version of the divine principle in the universe? In "Sirens," Bloom recalled seeing the throwaway in association with feeding the gulls: "Penny the gulls. Elijah is com" (U.279;

XI.866–7). While Elijah is miraculously fed by ravens, Bloom had given the gulls food and thinks: "They never expected that. Manna" (U.153; VIII.78–9). Thus, ultimately, Bloom transcends Elijah's stature. "Manna" is a term which is usually applied to the miraculous feeding in the wilderness during the Exodus, and which is thus prominent in the Haggadah. It is worth noting that, throughout the day, Bloom – without any intervention from God – does what he can, as a decent, concerned human being, to dispense spiritual and monetary manna to Stephen, Mrs Dignam, and Mrs Purefoy.

Just as the Old Testament prefigures the New Testament and is in turn fulfilled by the New Testament, *Ulysses* is prefigured both by the Old and New Testaments and fulfils both of them. Elijah, who at his death rises into the heavens, is a traditional precursor to Christ. As we saw in our discussion of "Wandering Rocks", the final words of the prophet Malachi, the last prophet in the Old Testament, contain God's promise to send Elijah. That the prophecy is in the book of Malachi, the first name of Mulligan, the dominant figure in the opening chapter, forges an ironic relationship between the Old Testament and Joyce's humanistic Newest Testament. For Christians, the passage from *Malachi* that predicts the coming of Elijah – "I will send you the prophet Elijah before the coming of the great and terrible day of the Lord" – establishes a typological connection between Elijah and Christ. Indeed, the language of the second sentence in the climax of "Cyclops" describing Elijah's ascent echoes a passage in *Matthew* 17:1–5 in which Jesus is transfigured in front of his followers, and they see him speaking to Moses and Elijah.[20] Bloom fulfils the typological language of the early chapters; as the mysterious but disregarded Jew who will, when acknowledged, bring light to the morally confused Gentiles, he is "a darkness shining in brightness which brightness could not comprehend" (U.28; II.160).

The hyperbolic narrator of the last paragraph subsumes both voices into a medley that takes Bloom's metamorphosis seriously only to undermine it.[21] In the context of what precedes, the comic hyberbole with which "Cyclops" concludes raises Bloom's stature. Finally the narrator's ventriloquy presents the acknowledgement of Bloom as Elijah and Bloom's recognition of and submission to God the father as if Bloom were not merely Elijah but Christ the son of God. By transferring to Elijah the words of

Elisha in which he acknowledges Elijah as father, Joyce transforms Bloom into a Christ figure. The narrator's hyperbolic
description of the execution, trial, and resurrection comically
equates Bloom with Christ, for Bloom, too, is both ostracized
outsider and victim.

V NAUSICAA

Just as Joyce tests and discards styles and metaphors in his quest
for the appropriate form, Bloom throughout the day tests and
discards a number of pretenders to Molly's place. The most
notable ones, aside from Martha, are Gerty MacDowell and the
whores in nighttown, particularly Bella Cohen. Martha Clifford,
Gerty MacDowell, and Bella Cohen are comic and poignant
versions of Penelope pseudoangelos. Bloom's masturbation is a
significant digression from his journey home because it diminishes his chances of having a son that night were he to have
carnal intercourse with Molly after all these years. (He does not
seem aware that her period is about to begin.) His masturbation
makes him less vulnerable to the whores in nighttown and more
alert to Stephen's plight. Masturbating on the strand is not only
a violation of the Jewish law against onanism, but, after the
triumphant conclusion of "Cyclops", is also a bathetic act that
deprives Bloom of some of the reader's esteem. The reader is
reminded again of the gulf between Bloom as metaphor and
Bloom as character; exploring and partially resolving that gulf is
one of the subjects of the remainder of the novel.

The Homeric parallel is based on Odysseus's meeting the
virgin Princess Nausicaa after he has been shipwrecked. The
novel explores a dialectic between linear and cyclical time, and
this chapter, as we shall see, makes a case for cyclical time. By
aligning Nausicaa with the Virgin Mary and Gerty, this chapter
explores the reiteration of the totemized virginal figure in Western civilization. While Nausicaa turns her back on the sexual
possibilities and arranges for Odysseus to continue his journey
home and the Virgin Mary (and in Dante, Beatrice, the figure of
spiritual purity for whom the Virgin Mary is an archetype)
intercedes for the lapsed soul and helps him on the journey to
Paradise, Gerty comically does a little of both. But the gap
between Gerty and the characters who signify her – what we

might call the half-metaphoricity – raises questions about the claims that *Ulysses* makes for historical repetition. In part, Joyce is mocking his own metaphoricity. Joyce knew that the reader experiences the teller's quest to establish the cyclical view of history and the process of trying to find the style and metaphors to align Gerty with the Virgin Mary and Nausicaa. Part of the chapter's humour derives from the inability of the teller to close the gap. Indeed, the final "cuckoo" could be poking fun at the glib metaphoricity of the entire chapter.

To undermine the quality of Gerty MacDowell's self-righteous and hypocritical behavior and Gerty's and Bloom's response to one another, Joyce invented a style that parodies sentimental romantic fiction. In an oft-quoted remark about this chapter, Joyce described the style as "a namby-pamby jammy marma-lady drawersy . . . style with effects of incense, marliolatry, stewed cockles, painter's palette, chit chat, circumlocution, etc., etc".[22] As Karen Lawrence puts it, "[Joyce] parodies her senti-mental mind by parodying the second-rate fiction that has nurtured it".[23] As if she were reading a novel, Gerty thinks of herself as a character in a romance. Put another way, by experi-encing her life in terms of the perceptions that she has learned from others, Gerty reduces herself to an aesthetic object in a third rate romance. She is a warning to the reader to beware of seduction by simplistic texts. For she has been created – or, better, re-created – by the clichés of romantic and sentimental fiction into a carbon figure whose narcissistic life imitates me-diocre and reductive art: "[S]he could have a good cry and relieve her pentup feelings though not too much because she knew how to cry nicely before the mirror" (U.351; XIII.191–2). Her narcissism and her failure to sustain a coherent self cause her to misread her experience and make her a lesson of how not to read *Ulysses*.

The exaggerated third person feminine style of "Nausicaa" – anticipating Molly's breathless, digressive, self-immersed first person narrative of "Penelope" – is the counterpart of the reductive masculine styles in "Cyclops". The third person style is appropriate for Gerty's mind; unlike Molly whose sexual pride enables her to transcend cultural stereotypes and retain an independent identity, Gerty's mind is so steeped in cultural stereotypes that it has lost its capacity for independence. Twenty-two, like Stephen, the virginal but very sexual Gerty is desperate for sexual experiences and, lacking them, substitutes her own poignant fantasies. (In Joyce's schema, the chapter's symbol is "virgin", while its "technic" is – in an ironic comment on Gerty's pretensions to the symbol of "virgin" – "tumescence detumescence.") Because her mind always solipsistically turns back on herself, she is a parody of Stephen's mind. She is trying to turn her reading of sentimental magazine stories into her life, but she is also trying to align those sentimental romances with her Catholicism. Using indirect discourse and letting her indict herself by revealing her myopic perspective, the narrator establishes an ironic discrepancy between the quality of her mind and how he wants the reader to understand that mind. But he also frequently steps aside to create a style that by its very exaggeration and distortion undermines Gerty's perspective.

Yet Gerty is a far more sympathetic figure than most critics allow. For she refuses to be confined by the clichés of her style, and subconsciously, by asserting her right to her fantasies, comes to terms with, even if she does not quite overcome, the restraints of her Roman Catholicism. Notwithstanding the severe limitations of her perspective, she gradually becomes more complex as she strays from her virginal romantic ideals of the first paragraphs and begins to express her real emotions and, in her act of defiant exhibitionism, her sexual needs. Her impressions of Bloom show the universal need to love and be loved and her desperate effort to discover the common grounds of a possible relationship: "[S]he wanted him because she felt instinctively that he was like no-one else" (U.358; XIII.429–30); "Passionate nature though he was Gerty could see that he had enormous control over himself" (U.361; XIII.539–40). While the language with which she thinks is conditioned by what she has read and deprives her of individuality, her perceptions, although clothed in stereotypes, are not without sensitivity: "He was in deep mourning, she could see that, and the story of a haunting sorrow was written on his face" (U.357; XIII.421–2). Because she takes cultural signs such as Bloom's wearing black for Dignam more seriously than she should, and thus assumes – in a parody of the ingrained logic of her Catholic schooling – that she can logically reduce culturally produced effects to rigidly defined prior causes, it does not occur to her that the main cause of Bloom's sorrow could be something other than the reason he wears black.

The first section is a duet shared by a voice rendering Gerty's thoughts in indirect discourse and an ironic voice, who is facetiously merging Gertrude and the Virgin Mary as a way of undermining the cult of virginity to which Irish single women are supposed to subscribe. Of course both voices are created by the ventriloquy of the fictionalized voice who is telling *Ulysses*. The ironic narrator repeats the shibboleths of the religious epistemology in which Gerty was educated: "Through the open window of the church the fragrant incense was wafted and with it the fragrant names of her who was conceived without stain of original sin, spiritual vessel, pray for us, honourable vessel, pray for us, vessel of singular devotion, pray for us, mystical rose" (U.356; XIII.371–4).

Roman Catholicism is one of the novel's major antagonists, in part because it makes sex and the physical body a problem. In contrast to Gerty and Stephen, the fifteen-year-old Milly and her father accept sexuality and the body. In Joyce's epic, the bodily functions and the physical life are celebrated. Not only does Bloom require sexual intercourse to regain his home, not only does Stephen require a passionate relationship, but Joyce presents as part of the fabric of life the bodily functions – urinating, farting, even defecating – that are unmentioned in Victorian novels. While hardly an heroic act, Bloom's acceptance of sexuality stands in contrast to the cult of the virgin.

In the second half of "Nausicaa" the narrator gradually restores Bloom to his stature as a character. For one thing, Bloom's perspective makes his masturbation seem natural, human, and harmless; he rationalizes that he "[m]ight have made a worse fool of myself however" (U.372; XIII.942–3). For another, he now seems to be able to resume his focus on the problems of others – especially Mrs Purefoy – and on Molly. Moreover, the narrator re-establishes the metonymical relationship between Bloom and Stephen by calling attention to parallels. For example, Bloom half-echoes and half-parodies Stephen's endorsement of Maeterlinck's theory – "*If Socrates leave his house today he will find the sage seated on his doorstep. If Judas go forth tonight it is to Judas his steps will tend*" – that each man finds confirmation of himself in his experiences and encounters: "When you feel like that you often meet what you feel" (U.213, 369; IX.1042; XIII.828–9).

Bloom experiences one of his day's low points. He thinks that the appropriate metaphor for himself is Rip Van Winkle, the man who awoke after twenty years only to be not recognized by his wife: "Twenty years asleep in Sleepy Hollow. All changed. Forgotten. The young are old. His gun rusty from the dew" (U.377; XIII.1115–16). In the above passage Bloom uses the short breathless phrases punctuated by complete stops that he frequently uses when depressed. The frequent periods mime a mind that is resisting the words his consciousness provides and that is having difficulty coming to terms with his experience. The rusty gun is a bitterly ironic joke about his own potency.

It is when he recognizes that Molly is both the solution to his problem as well as his problem that he can complete his voyage. This occurs at the end of "Nausicaa" when his monologue re-emphasizes how Gerty and Martha are merely surrogates for Molly:

> O sweety all your little girlwhite up I saw dirty bracegirdle made me do love sticky we two naughty Grace darling she him half past the bed met him pike hoses frillies for Raoul de perfume your wife black hair heave under embon *señorita* young eyes Mulvey plump bubs me breadvan Winkle red slippers she rusty sleep wander years dreams return tail end Agendath swoony lovey showed me her next year in drawers return next in her next her next. (U.382; XIII.1279–85)

(Gabler's restoration of "bubs me breadvan Winkle red slippers she rusty sleep wander" emphasizes the relationship between Bloom's feelings of sexual inadequacy, especially his self-image as a sexually dormant Rip Van Winkle figure, and his wanderings far from home; but Joyce also wants the reader to understand that, like Rip Van Winkle, Bloom might awaken.)

The above passage crystallizes the increasing ascendency of Molly in his thoughts after his ejaculation. "Naughty", with its pun on naught or zero, recalls the fantasy relationship with Martha which offers nothing. Gradually thoughts of Molly become more prominent. Images associated with Molly ("met him pike hoses", "wife black hair", "young eyes", "plump bubs",) increasingly displace fantasies of other women; even the drawers, at first associated with Martha and Gerty, become associated in the second part of the monologue – as "Circe" will make clear – more with Molly than Gerty: "Felt for the curves inside her *deshabillé*. . . . Pinned together. O, Mairy lost the pin of her. Dressed up to the nines for somebody" (U.368; XIII.796, 803–4).

The motif of return and renewal ("next" and "Agendath") is associated with Molly. "Return" also raises Bloom's hope that life is cyclical and not linear and thus will return to a previous points; as he puts it: "The year returns. History repeats itself" (U.377; XIII.1092–3). And he thinks of metempsychosis not merely in terms of Molly's bawdy misunderstanding but in terms of the actual concept: "Metempsychosis. They believed you could be changed into a tree from grief. Weeping willow" (U.377; XIII.1118–19). "Next" and "Agendath" stress the Zionist dream of return ("Next year in Jerusalem") which is associated with Elijah's return. As the novel progresses, Bloom aligns himself more and more with the cyclical view of history to which the novel in the main subscribes, although he certainly never abandons the linear progressive view that is always turned to the future.

At first it may seem that Bloom's moment of personal and metaphorical triumph in "Cyclops" is ironically framed by two chapters, "Sirens" and "Nausicaa", that deprive him of stature. It is as if the struggle to establish Bloom's metaphorical significance in the face of personal behavior that undermines that significance is part of the novel's drama. It is as if two modes of meaning – the literal and metaphorical, the story and discourse – are competing with one another. After gaining self-esteem in the public arena in "Cyclops", Bloom's stature is considerably reduced, but gradually "Nausicaa" takes a somewhat sympathetic view of Bloom's and Gerty's interlude, for each gives and receives pleasure without causing pain. By returning in the second half of "Nausicaa" to the technique of his characteristic interior monologue and by increasingly acknowledging the centrality of Molly, Bloom signifies that he is ready to resume his journey homeward, a journey threatened by various kinds of sirens, and to fulfil his potential as father and husband. In the above monologue, has he not finally slain the suitors in his mind?

"Nausicaa" takes place on the strand where Stephen had been during "Proteus". Bloom, too, is aware of the tide, and his moods seem to follow the fluctuations of the tide. He even finds a piece of paper that Stephen may have left there: "Page of an old copybook" (U.381; XIII.1248). He finds a "bit of stick" which reminds us of Stephen's ashplant. With his stick, he writes "I . . . AM. A" which, I think, emphasizes both his incompleteness and his forward thrust: his sense of self as someone who has a coherent "I" but is always growing, developing and becoming (U.381; XIII.1258, 1264). Bloom in the imagined world of the novel is trying to complete this sentence. That four times Bloom is unable to complete phonically the word "bat" ("ba") stresses that the dark mysterious creature is a metonym for his own quest to complete himself (U.377–8; XIII.1117–43). Now that he has come to terms with his experience in the above monologue, he is able to complete the word "Bat". At the climax of "Circe", when Stephen acknowledges Bloom, dressed in black all day as "Black panther. Vampire", we recall that in folklore bats are associated with vampires and other occult principles (U.608; XV.4930). As a homonym with "Pat" (Dignam), "Bat" suggests the mortality that all humankind shares and looks forward to the homonymical series with which "Ithaca" ends and which contributes to universalizing Bloom's significance. Put another way: after establishing his public stature at the end of "Cyclops", Joyce tests Bloom in the private realm and exposes him as ridiculous before showing him in a more sympathetic light. "Circe" re-examines his actions, with considerable stress on looking at the events and conscious thoughts of "Cyclops" and "Nausicaa" from the interior and unconscious perspective of fantasy and hallucination.

That Bloom's characteristic style – the dominant style of sections four through six and eight – progressively reasserts itself in the second half of the chapter as he regains his composure and self-worth and turns his attention to Molly and his dreams of renewal indicates that he has survived another assault on his dignity and integrity. The passage I cited above is Bloom's last major direct interior monologue in the novel, and is thus the first of the series of climaxes to the novel, one that occurs, in terms of total pages, at the very center of the novel. With its absence of punctuation and its stress on the mind's free association, the passage anticipates the conclusion of Molly's monologue.

Because we have not been in his mind since "Sirens," and have been listening to the myopic voices of "Cyclops" and Gerty, Bloom's sincerity and humanity are all the more compelling. By enacting how style itself can become a value, the passage demonstrates the problem with Karen Lawrence's claim that: "The succession of styles in 'Cyclops' and the different styles in the book as a whole imply that all language is, in a sense, inherently stupid, that all styles are arbitrary."[24] I believe that by using style as a metaphor for the characters and the kind of behaviour he is describing, Joyce establishes the potential of style as a method of discovering values. The diverse styles demonstrate the flexibility and variety not only of Joyce's language, but the potentiality of all language. He shows that style – especially the parodic styles of "Cyclops" and "Nausicaa" which are spoken by a ventriloquist who knows that the styles are ersatz – can have an intelligence that transcends that of the characters.

VI OXEN OF THE SUN

In "Scylla and Charybdis" and "Oxen of the Sun", the reader learns that a principle metaphor for artistic creativity in *Ulysses* is sexual intercourse leading to fruition. In Joyce's epic, the bodily functions and the physical life are celebrated. Joyce believed that his passionate sexual relationship with Nora had helped him mature as an artist. But Stephen, like Shakespeare, had to come to terms with the possibility of homosexuality, a possibility suggested by Mulligan's identification with Wilde in "Telemachus". We recall that, in the library, as Stephen listens to Best propose that the sonnets were written for William Hughes and comment "the very essence of Wilde", Stephen takes Best's remark to be less about Wilde's scholarly method than about Best's identification with Wilde's sexuality: "a blond ephebe. Tame essence of Wilde" (U.198; IX.529–32). In this chapter, the presence of Mulligan, who has from the outset been identified with Wilde; the sensual drunken male camaraderie (iternating the camaraderie of the older men in "Sirens" and the atavistic barroom crowd in "Cyclops"); and the parody of the Platonic dialogues on the subject of art once again call attention to the sterility of Stephen's emotional life (U.415–6; XIV.1110ff).

Like the encylopedic catalogues in "Cyclops", the pastiche of styles in "Oxen of the Sun" engages the reader's quest for significance at the same time as it teases and undermines that quest. At first the very imprecision of "Oxen of the Sun" resists

our attempts to organize it into patterns of meaning, causing
Kenner to remark that Bloom and Stephen are presented as
"barely visible and wholly inaudible. Much as in the crucial
chapter of Bloom's cuckolding we are almost continually dis-
tracted by tricksy imitations of musical effects, so now in the
crucial chapter after two near misses – at the newspaper office,
in the library – he and Stephen meet at last, we are debarred
from scrutiny of either man's thoughts and prevented from
hearing one word that is spoken by anybody, so enamoured is
the narrator of his system of stylistic impersonations".[25] The
rereader understands that the dynamic and evolving nature of
language is itself a subject, a subject that complements the
seventeen other chapters which place more focus on rendering
events and characters. It is as if Joyce felt that *Ulysses* required a
chapter that examined the extent of the available stylistic resources and traditions with which to write his modern epic. Yet, as
we shall see, the action – Bloom's growing interest in Stephen –
resists appropriation by style. The narrator is educating us to
understand that just as Odysseus and Bloom resist the various
obstacles and temptations to abandon their homeward journey,
so we as readers – armed with something of Bloom's consistency
of purpose – must resist stylistic efforts to deflect us.

Marilyn French has written of "Oxen of the Sun": "The
subject of the chapter is dual: coition between people leading to
conception parallels coition between mind and reality leading to
expression, otherwise called literature."[26] What French neglects
is the fertilizing function of Bloom on Stephen's imagination.
That Joyce conceived the chapter in part as one in which Bloom
metaphorically fertilizes Stephen as an artist is clear from a
letter written on 13 March to Budgen: "Am working hard at
Oxen of the Sun, the idea being the crime committed against
fecundity by sterilizing the act of coition. . . . Bloom is the
spermatozoon, the hospital, the womb, the nurse the ovum,
Stephen the embryo."[27]

The emphasis on sexuality that fails to lead to fruition calls
attention not only to Bloom's eleven year abstinence from intercourse with Molly, but to Stephen's failure to consummate his
aesthetic aspirations. Joyce uses the evolution of English prose as
a metaphor for the birth of the Purefoy child to show how the
word becomes flesh and the flesh word: "In woman's womb
word is made flesh but in the spirit of the maker all flesh that
passes becomes the word that shall not pass away" (U.391;

XIV.292–4). By using the conception, embryonic development, and birth of the Purefoy child as a metaphor for Stephen's birth as an artist, Joyce is stressing the organic quality of the language.

Speaking of Purefoy's fertilizing act, Joyce writes in sexual terms which suggest what the artist must do to create an imagined world from the infinite possibilities that the artist confronts: "In her lay a Godframed Godgiven preformed possibility which thou hast fructified with thy modicum of man's work" (U.423; XIV.1412–14). In the chapter in which Mrs Purefoy gives birth to her child, Stephen speaks of the artist as creator of life: "You have spoken of the past and its phantoms, Stephen said. Why think of them? If I call them into life across the waters of Lethe will not the poor ghosts troop to my call? Who supposes it? I, Bous Stephanoumenos, bullockbefriending bard, am lord and giver of their life" (U.415; XIV.1112–16). But Joyce, ever alert to the potential bathos of the artist's claims, has Vincent remind Stephen that his remarks would be more "fitting" "when something more, and greatly more, than a capful of light odes can call your genius father. . . . All desire to see you bring forth the work you meditate, to acclaim you Stephaneforos" (U.415; XIV.1118–21). It is this dialogue, a parody of the Socratic dialogues about beauty and art, that calls attention to the disparity between Stephen's aspirations and performance. That Stephen is so poignantly frustrated in his sexual or artistic life is what gives the encounter with Bloom its significance if only as a possibility for transforming Stephen's potential into actuality.

The very self-consciousness of the chapter calls attention to the relationship between the 1922 teller and the 1904 putative artist. We realize that the 1904 Stephen might have been able to have written the pastiche of styles, but it is the fictionalized Joyce of later years who could have appreciated Bloom's stature. However, before Stephen can father "this chaffering allincluding most farraginous chronicle" that we read as *Ulysses* (U.423; XIV.1412), he must meet Bloom, the enterprising commercial traveller, the middle-aged father and cuckolded husband, the marginal Jew in Irish society. For Bloom is the man who embodies, to the fictionalized presence, the world that Stephen needs to know. He must also have the kind of experience with women that Purefoy has had and, indeed, Bloom had before Rudy's death.

In calling attention to its antecedents, the chapter establishes the lineage of Joyce's book and insists on its importance. In a sense, it claims that the history of English literature is itself a long gestation period for his novel. Put another way, the chapter gives birth to itself and its multiple styles. The chapter shows that artistic paternity is a legal fiction. For it dramatizes the way prior writing affects an author's imagination and the way an author inevitably reads his successors by "misreading" them – that is, reading them not as the author intended or as the text rhetorically demands but perversely and willfully for his own purposes. (In other words, the chapter is about what Harold Bloom has been calling "the anxiety of influence".)

In "Oxen of the Sun", the distinction between signifier and signified blurs, and writing does indeed become more the subject than elsewhere in *Ulysses*. Whereas in "Wandering Rocks", each vignette gave a tiny fragment of life in Dublin, here each style renders one perspective upon the action. "Oxen of the Sun" is a chapter that calls attention to the infinite possibilities of the word to reinvent the world. As Iser notes, "[E]ach style reveals a latent ideology, constantly reducing the reality to the scope of individual principles."[28] In that sense, it is a chapter about writing. Joyce is showing that the history of a language is not mere philology but the history of a culture. That the styles evolve to greater sophistication and precision only to devolve back to chaos stresses the Viconian cyclical view of history rather than the more traditional concept – subscribed to in general by both English Victorians and Celtic Romantics – that history, under the auspices of Divine Providence, inevitably progresses upward toward fulfilment of a teleology.

Style can never be neutral; even if it does not represent in its every word a reality anterior to the novel or even the page, it signifies or, put another way, is a metaphor for, values. Style – the soul of language – is metempsychotic; while it always imposes its order and perspective, it changes shape in response to the values and cultural conventions of its time. While it is true that style manipulates and distorts, it also discovers and intensifies. Style is a function of point of view, and point of view, by selecting and arranging what it presents, determines what we read.

Perhaps Iser oversimplifies the function of Joyce's use of multiple styles in "The Oxen of the Sun": "By parodying the styles, Joyce has exposed their essentially manipulative character. The reader gradually becomes conscious of the fact that style fails to achieve its ends, in that it does not capture reality but imposes upon it an historically preconditioned form."[29] But Joyce has shown throughout *Ulysses* that one end of style is to present a *perspective on reality* that is not historically conditioned but synchronic. Furthermore the ends of style include the discovery of the values inherent in each perspective and in what is being described. For that reason, we should conceive of style as a dynamic process which engages in actively discovering the aforementioned values.

Of course, "Oxen of the Sun" does have a self-parodic aspect. As he rapidly changes his stance by changing his style, the narrator parodies the method of the novel. Isn't Joyce, by means of the rapid changes in styles, mocking Stephen's failure – and his own youthful failure – to complete major projects, and does not the pastiche of styles imply perhaps his own failure as yet to achieve his own voice? Even if we agree with C. H. Peake that the diverse styles are not sufficiently functional in terms of their presentation of theme and story, we must also acknowledge that Joyce consciously or unconsciously embodied that very effect – the recalcitrance and overabundance of stylistic alternatives – in the chapter's form.[30]

Joyce delighted in his virtuosity. But for the odyssean reader the plethora of styles are a verbal action, a speech-act, if you will, that collectively dramatizes that Stephen must achieve something more than a pastiche of styles if he is to achieve the living reality of multiple points of view – rather than the surface *tour de force* of "Oxen of the Sun" – that the modern epic requires. In much the same way that "Wandering Rocks" is a bathetic version of the novel's structure, so "Oxen of the Sun" is a bathetic version of the novel's efforts to use ventriloquy to achieve multiple points of view. Thus "Oxen of the Sun" stands in relation to the multiple points of view of the completed novel as a negative example that has been tested and discarded. Furthermore, quite frequently the individual styles are inefficient, elusive, and even incomprehensible as if to stress that language without subject – or what Deconstruction calls anterior grounding – is a self-consuming artifact of limited interest.

That, as "Oxen of the Sun" proceeds, Bloom gradually replaces Stephen as the object of attention, affirms the movement of the narrative from literary and stylistic values to human ones.

Karen Lawrence has argued that the chapter provides "a classic demonstration of the provisional nature of any one style", but does it not also show how inevitably mankind in the form of Bloom becomes the necessary subject of stylistic play?[31] That the recollection of material from prior chapters provides strands of content associated with the major figures urges their attention upon us. Aren't we moved to sympathy by Bloom's lack of the son he so intensely desires? "No. Leopold. Name and memory solace thee not. That youthful illusion of thy strength was taken from thee – and in vain. No son of thy loins is by thee. There is none now to be for Leopold, what Leopold was for Rudolph" (U.413–4; XIV.1074–7). Does not this passage, in the sentimental and gentle melancholy tone of Charles Lamb, anticipate the climax of "Circe" and the relationship between Bloom and Stephen that develops in "Eumaeus" and "Ithaca"?

In the very next passage, the rendering of Bloom's gloom in De Quincey's style recalls his introspective descent into an interior hell in "Hades": "They fade, sad phantoms: all is gone. Agendath is a waste land, a home of screechowls and the sandblind upupa. Netaim, the golden, is no more" (U.414; XIV.1085–7). The substitution of the neologism "upupa" for "utopia" suggests the cause of Bloom's wasteland. "Upupa" not only suggests the anonymous postcard "U.P." received by the Breens – implying Mr Breen's inability to maintain an erection (and thus the impotence Bloom fears for himself), but also suggests in its homophonic resonance "papa", the identity that Bloom seeks to redeem his wasteland. Furthermore, "Upupa" suggests "pupa", a transformation stage for an insect between the larva and the imago, and thus calls attention to the embryonic growth of both the Purefoy heir and language as well as the possible metamorphosis of Bloom into a suitable father or "papa".

I must also take issue with Lawrence's contention that, "at least some of the reader's uncertainty is caused by the rapid succession of styles, which prevents him from adjusting to one style long enough to concentrate on the dramatic events reported".[32] For the evidence of Bloom's humanity defeats attempts to patronize him, as in the following passage: "And sir Leopold that was the goodliest guest that ever sat in scholars' hall and that was the meekest man and the kindest that ever laid husbandly hand under hen and that was the very truest knight of the world one that ever did minion service to lady gentle pledged him courtly in the cup. Woman's woe with wonder pondering" (U.388; XIV. 182–6). Because the novel's action has established the grounds of the comparison, the style effectively urges us to recognize that Bloom is the heir to the knightly ideals of concern for others, bravery, and selfless service. Bloom remains in the room with Stephen and the medical students because he is concerned about the drunken Stephen: "And sir Leopold sat with them for he bore fast friendship to sir Simon and this to his son young Stephen" (U.388; XIV.197–9). Evoking a chivalric code of courtesy and honor, the medieval style confers value on Bloom's behavior. And yet, by exaggerating the bonds of friendship between Bloom and both Simon and Stephen, Joyce playfully reminds the reader that style distorts even as it illuminates.

The diverse styles not only become metaphors for epistemologies and value systems, but cumulatively they become a metaphor for Joyce's basic premise that reality is relative and a function of the observer. The styles do not merely parody forms of writing but also invoke the value system with which they are associated. In this case the medieval romance style does not merely suggest Malory, but the ideals of a chivalric tradition which his work privileges: "But sir Leopold was passing grave maugre his word by cause he still had pity of the terrorcausing shrieking of shrill women in their labour and as he was minded of his good lady Marion that had borne him an only manchild which on his eleventh day on live had died and no man of art could save so dark is destiny" (U.390; XIV.264–8).

Parody is a form of homage and an acknowledgement of paternity. Joyce's parodic use of Bunyan's style to define Stephen's problem is his tribute to the value and energy of that seemingly mannered style. Bloom becomes the allegorical Calmer who tries to ease the anxious and bitter Stephen's fear of thunder, a fear which Joyce attributes to his failure to fill the gap left by his loss of religious faith. It is not Bunyan's orthodox Protestant beliefs that are invoked, but his epistemology; and Joyce shows that an epistemology which allegorizes unacknowledged thoughts and emotions is not irrelevant to other systems of beliefs. In the first paragraph of the following passage which seems to be as much a parody of the scientific explanations of the Royal Academy as of Thomas Browne, thunder is hilariously described in sexual terms; Joyce may even have in mind Swift's famous joke about Master Bates in *Gulliver's Travels*:

> Master Bloom, at the braggart's side, spoke to him calming words to slumber his great fear, advertising how it was no other thing but a hubbub noise that he heard, the discharge of fluid from the thunderhead, look you, having taken place, and all of the order of a natural phenomenon.
>
> But was young Boasthard's fear vanquished by Calmer's words? No, for he had in his bosom a spike named Bitterness which could not by words be done away. . . . But could he not have endeavoured to have found again as in his youth the bottle Holiness that then he lived withal? Indeed no for Grace was not there to find that bottle. Heard he then in that clap the voice of the god Bringforth or, what Calmer said, a hubbub of Phenomenon? (U.395; XIV.424–36).

In the second paragraph of the quoted passage, Joyce invokes Bunyan's values that focus on death as the birth of the eternal soul and the salvation of the soul through good works, only to discard those values. For Bloom's counsel and Stephen's thoughts are secular and pragmatic; in terms that recall Hamlet's soliloquy on suicide ("To sleep, perchance to dream"), he thinks of the mortality of man: "[H]e must for a certain one day die as he was like the rest too a passing show. And would he not accept to die like the rest and pass away" (U.395; XIV.439–40). But as the last sentence indicates, because he views himself as the artist who can create immortality, Stephen does not fully acknowledge the inevitability of death.

As the Bunyan pastiche continues, it turns to the subject of the characters' sexual practices and begins to allegorize them:

> Yes, Pious had told him of that land and Chaste had pointed him to the way but the reason was that in the way he fell in with a certain whore of an eyepleasing exterior whose name, she said, is Bird-in-the-Hand and she beguiled him wrongways from the true path by her flatteries that she said to him as, Ho, you pretty man, turn aside hither and I will show you a brave place, and she lay at him so flatteringly that she had him in her grot which is named Two-in-the Bush or, by some learned, Carnal Concupiscence. (U.395–6; XIV.447–54)

Has not the discrepancy between Bunyan's values and what the pastiche of his style describes become even more pronounced and outrageous? Iser would have it that, "The personification of sexual urges, carried to extremes by Joyce, destroys the whole principle of the form as it had been used up to and including Bunyan."[33] But Joyce is smiling at how piety and chastity, even in their allegorical personifications, are mere words, are pretensions posing as truths, and cannot displace sexual desires. Since mankind has not fundamentally changed, Bunyan's epistemology has always been, as far as Joyce is concerned, an allegory based on misreading man's nature. In a final irony, Joyce has impertinently revivified Bunyan's style to show that it is *more* pertinent to a less repressed era where sexuality can be discussed humorously and boisterously, and where thoughts that were formerly hidden can now be openly acknowledged. Within the paragraph that we have been discussing Joyce progressively works his magic to transform the values for which the style is a metaphor. He first implies somewhat different values than Bunyan's; he then suggests values that are fundamentally distinct from Bunyan's; and, finally, he proposes diametrically opposite values.

Thus in "Oxen of the Sun", Bloom's humanity triumphs over the self-conscious artistry of the narrator's ventriloquism and resists the attempts of the diverse styles to deprive him of stature. Bloom's concern for Mrs Purefoy and Stephen strikingly contrasts with the chapter's obsessive interest in stylistic matters. The chapter establishes Bloom's humanity on the literal level and his potential on the metaphorical level. Bloom imagines himself as Stephen's father: "Now he is himself paternal and these about him might be his sons. Who can say? The wise father knows his own child" (U.413; XIV.1062–3). And, in a comic version of Isaiah's prediction of the coming of the Messiah to judge the world, Bloom is metaphorically apotheosized: "Whisper, who the sooty hell's the johnny in the black duds? Hush! Sinned against the light and even now that day is at hand when he shall come to judge the world by fire. . . . Elijah is coming! Washed in the blood of the Lamb" (U.428; XIV.1575–6; 1580). By transforming Bloom from "the sooty . . . johnny in the black duds" into Elijah, Joyce metaphorically reinforces Bloom's concern for Mrs Purefoy and Stephen.

One could argue that this kind of transformation, dependent

on establishing the validity of a series of metaphors in which
Bloom and Stephen are compared to various precursors, is the
major action of the book. It is particularly important that "Oxen
of the Sun", the chapter on language, concludes with the novel's
principle linguistic technique – namely, the metaphoricity by
which Bloom becomes an heir to the Judeo-Christian tradition. In spite of the dissolution of style into twentieth century
American jargon and in spite of the speaker's crude metaphors
in which the quenching of spiritual thirst is equated with a swig
of liquor ("He's got a coughmixture with a punch in it for you,
my friend, in his back pocket"), the prior metaphors and
Bloom's actions urge us to accept at least partially Bloom's metaphorical apotheosis (U.428; <u>XIV.1590–1</u>). Yet we are much
more conscious of a gap between signifier (Christ) and signified
(Bloom) than we are of the metaphor that proposes Bloom as a
knight in the courtly tradition. Bloom is not God, Moses, or
Christ, but Bloom's human kindness and sense of justice are the
closest thing to divinity that we can expect: "The Deity aint no
nickel dime bumshow. . . . He's the grandest thing yet and don't
you forget it" (U.428; <u>XIV.1585–7</u>). And of course this kind of
typology by which the importance of prior generations is seen in
the fulfilment of subsequent ones is central to the typological
readings of the Old Testament by Christians.

Finally, the chapter resists local interest in style for its own
sake by including material that engages the reader to eschew the
pleasures of word play and pastiche and to continue his interpretive odyssey. Following "the reverberation of the thunder" –
formerly described as "A black crack of noise in the street",
recalling Stephen's definition of God as "a shout in the street" –
the rainfall, in contrast to Eliot's *The Waste Land*, ends "drought"
and "barrenness" and arouses expectations of fertility and renewal (U.34, 394, 422; II.386; XIV.408, 1388). When Bloom
and Stephen leave the hospital, Joyce parodies Carlyle to stress
the significance of the rain: "The air without is impregnated
with raindew moisture, life essence celestial. . . . God's air, the
Allfather's air" (U.423; XIV.1407–9). But in the novel's imagined world, where God is a figure of the artist, the passage is a
prophecy of the novel to be written as well as the human
relationships to be discovered. In this regard, it is important that
the thunder not only echoes the apocalyptic fantasies of Stephen
but is heard also by Molly after intercourse with Blazes: "that

thunder woke me up . . . as if the world was coming to an end"
(U.741; <u>XVIII.134–7</u>).

Nor should we ignore how "Oxen of the Sun" anticipates the
future relationship between Stephen and Bloom; rereading, we
see how Joyce uses the style of Macaulay to emphasize the
human and domestic aspect of their encounter in the hospital.
Their mutual acknowledgement looks forward to their friendship
in "Eumaeus" and "Ithaca" and their drinking beer together
anticipates the ritualistic sharing of cocoa in Bloom's house:
"Eventually, however, both their eyes met and as soon as it
began to dawn on him that the other was endeavouring to help
himself to the thing he [Bloom] involuntarily determined to help
him himself and so he accordingly took hold of the neck of the
mediumsized glass recipient which contained the fluid sought
after and made a capacious hole in it . . ." (U.417; <u>XIV.1190–5</u>).

NOTES

1. See Gifford and Seidman, p. 150.
2. See Gifford and Seidman, p. 20.
3. Clive Hart in Hart and Hayman, eds *James Joyce's 'Ulysses'*, 1974, quoted in Kenner, *Joyce's Voices* (University of California Press, 1978), p. 103.
4. Lawrence, p. 83.
5. See Gifford and Seidman, p. 221.
6. See Gifford and Seidman, p. 67.
7. Quoted in Gifford and Seidman, p. 200.
8. Lawrence, p. 91.
9. C. H. Peake, *James Joyce: the Citizen and Artist*, p. 231.
10. Lawrence, pp. 93, 100.
11. The song is reprinted in Gifford and Seidman and in Weldon Thornton's *Allusions in Ulysses*.
12. *The Odyssey*, trans. and edited by Albert Cook (New York: Norton, 1967).
13. See Ellmann, *Ulysses on the Liffey*, p. 115.
14. A. Walton Litz, "Ithaca", in *James Joyce's 'Ulysses': Critical Essays*, ed. Hart and Hayman, p. 386.
15. I am taking issue with Karen Lawrence who claims: "As if by incantation, the dead heroes of the past are summoned in the epic catalogues" (Lawrence, p. 107).
16. Michael Groden, *'Ulysses' in Progress* (Princeton University Press, 1977) pp. 50–1.

17. Lawrence, p. 114.
18. Arnold Goldman, *The Joyce Paradox: Form and Function in His Fiction* (London: Routledge & Kegan Paul, 1966) p. 93.
19. *The Pentateuch and Haftorahs*, ed. Dr J. H. Hertz (London: Soncino Press, 1980) see p. 1010.
20. See Gifford and Seidman, p. 311.
21. In *Ulysses on the Liffey*, Ellmann notes that in the last paragraph the chapter's "two historians . . . each having stared from his one eye in magnificent disregard of the other, combine their dictions with a sudden click" (Ellmann, p. 115).
22. *Letters*, I. 135.
23. Lawrence, p. 120.
24. Lawrence, p. 122.
25. Hugh Kenner, *Joyce's Voices* (University of California Press, 1978) p. 79.
26. Marilyn French, *The Book as World: James Joyce's 'Ulysses'* (Cambridge, Mass.: Harvard University Press, 1959), p. 17.
27. *Letters*, I, 138–9.
28. Wolfgang Iser, *The Implied Reader* (Baltimore & London: The Johns Hopkins University Press, 1974), p. 190.
29. Iser, p. 192.
30. See C. H. Peake, pp. 262–3.
31. Lawrence, p. 144.
32. Lawrence, p. 124.
33. Iser, p. 189.

8 "Circe" as the Climax of Joyce's Humanistic Vision

I THE FORM OF "CIRCE" AND THE FANTASIES OF BLOOM

One could argue that beginning with Bloom's pursuit of Stephen into nighttown, the human values displace the aesthetic ones as a focus. For in the final four chapters, the form – no matter how innovative – is in the service of meaning. In "Circe", Joyce uses the technique of omniscient narration to explore the subconscious lives of Stephen and Bloom. As Lawrence indicates, the chapter dramatizes aspects of experience that the stream-of-consciousness represses: "his father's suicide, his son's death at eleven days old, and his wife's adultery".[1] Frequently, Joyce provides metaphors – hyperbolic metaphors – for the repressed experiences of Stephen and Bloom rather than new perspectives on their actual past experience.[2] However, "Circe" is not merely the dramatization of the conscious and subconscious lives of Bloom and Stephen, but the revelation of the narrative presence, the fictionalized Joyce, as he searches for meaning and fulfilment. Indeed, the increasingly radical metaphors demonstrate the fulfilment of the quest to find the necessary technique to write *Ulysses*. By refusing to separate clearly the surface events from the hallucinations and fantasies, Joyce demonstrates for us that external events and unconscious life cannot be meaningfully distinguished. But by including the life of fantasy and dream, the climax of the "Circe" becomes all the more convincing; surely, a reader does not step back and experience this climactic scene, as Lawrence would have it, in terms of "where the climax *would have been* in a more conventional novel".[3]

That the fantasies and hallucinations of Stephen draw upon the experience of Bloom and vice versa makes us aware of the strong presence – indeed, the metaferocity – of the fictionaliz-ing Joyce. Thus within Bloom's fantasy Marion (Molly) Bloom knows the talisman – "Nebrakada! Femininum!" – for winning a woman's love that Stephen has read in a book in "Wandering Rocks" (U.242, 440; X.849, <u>XV.319</u>). Does not Joyce descend into the hell of his own imagination as well as Bloom's and present the grotesque material that dwells there? Isn't "night-town" a state of mind inhabited by fears, anxieties, sexual obsessions, guilt, and doubt? Marilyn French has aptly noticed that in "Circe", "The hallucinations are production numbers staged by the author for the audience."[4] These hallucinations are performances of fantasies that haunt the imagination of the presence whose words we experience as we read the book. (As we have discussed, Joyce would have been exposed to such perform-ances in the paintings of Cubism and the paintings and writ-ings of Futurism.)

Because Stephen and Bloom share "Circe", the chapter in which Joyce probes their subconscious fears and obsessions even as they mutually experience nighttown, our expectations are aroused for the kind of union with which "Circe" concludes. The prolonged fantasies in "Circe", imagined in dramatic form, illustrate the validity of Stephen's theory of Shakespeare and the applicability of that theory to reading Ulysses. For reading *Ulysses* the first time is a process of learning how to read the novel; it argues and demonstrates its own aesthetic principles. And we realize that these hallucinations express the personal lives of the characters in ways that have significance for all of us. Throughout "Circe", then, the merging of the identities of Bloom and Stephen – a merging which climaxes in their shared vision of Shakespeare – is actually taking place.

That "Circe" is written in the dramatic form with which Stephen ended his monologue confirms the technique of "Scylla and Charybdis". Indeed, Stephen's monodrama in which Ste-phen imagines that Shakespeare, after he has made love with Ann Hathaway, sees the star that rose at his birth is a strong imaginative act that prefigures the fantasies and hallucinations of "Circe". The use of the dramatic form shows Joyce calling attention to his own artistic growth. Does not the dramatic mode of "Circe" recall Joyce's privileging of the dramatic form over the lyrical and epical because in the dramatic mode "life is purified in and reprojected from the human imagination"

(P.215)? We know from Joyce's letters and biography that "Circe" has its expressive aspect in its mirroring of Joyce's own sexual fantasies and anxieties. "Circe" also draws upon Joyce's encounter with a Jew named Hunter whose concern for him one night became in Joyce's imagination a crystallizing incident with teleological significance to his growth as an artist.[5]

In an interesting passage, the narrator emphasizes the importance of seemingly insignificant incidents: "I have often thought since on looking back over that strange time that it was that small act, trivial in itself, that striking of that match, that determined the whole aftercourse of both our lives" (U.140; VII.763–5). By using language that recalls the prose rhythms of *Matcham's Masterstroke*, which Bloom had been reading in "Calypso", the omniscient narrator seems to be intruding his parodic presence into Stephen's mind and drawing our attention to his role in creating parallels or "matches" that bring together his two diverse characters. Indeed, our process of reading includes an awareness of how Joyce playfully stands in the marginalia of his text in much the same way that Renaissance painters, such as Fra Lippo Lippi, painted diminutive portraits of themselves into the lower corner of their works.

One of Bloom's major problems is that he is a Platonist when it comes to women. Like Stephen, he perceives woman according to a binary vertical standard in which women are either spiritualized beings or whores. He thinks of Martha and Gerty in idealized terms as if they were statues or pictures. For Martha and Gerty are for Bloom virginal figures – inaccessible, spiritual, absent in terms of real sexual possibility – posing as whores. It is important that he never speaks one word to either of them. Neither Martha nor Gerty offers the passionate sexual intercourse that he requires before he can join with Stephen in a point beyond the end of the novel to become the artistic presence.

Within the world in which Bloom lives only one woman inhabits for him the ineluctable modality of the visible, and that is Molly. In "Circe", the nymph – "eyeless, in nun's white habit, coif and hugewinged wimple, softly, with remote eyes" – represents the spiritualization of sex (U.552; XV.3434–5). The nymph is a version of the traditional Mariolotry which Joyce believed had degraded sexuality by wearing the guise of spirituality: "No more desire. . . . only the ethereal" (U.552; XV.3436–7). Her transformation of Bloom's little lyric on gulls also associates her with the Neo-Platonism of George Russell (AE): "Where dreamy creamy gull waves o'er the waters dull" (U.552; XV.3437–8). Joyce was particularly amused that the ethereal Russell had the pedestrian and highly visible job of delivering dairy products on his bicycle. A little earlier in the episode "Mananaun Maclir", a comic version of Russell who had written the "Children of Lir," had announced: "I am the dreamery creamery butter" (U.510; XV.2262, 2267, 2275–6). Since the nymph is a figment of Bloom's imagination, Bloom is linked ironically to AE. And, we realize, that, in his bent for elaborate intellectual paradigms and systems. Bloom – like his creator – does have a Platonic aspect.

That Bloom breaks the nymph's spell with the word "Nebrakada", a word noticed by Stephen in the book stalls, shows how the narrator is manipulating the minds of his two seemingly different central characters to show us their mutuality. Put another way: "Coming events cast their shadows before" (U.165; VIII.526). We realize that like Stephen, Bloom, too, is looking for a magic formula for winning a woman's love. That the charms for this exercise are found in a book by "the most blessed abbot Peter Salanka" reinforces Joyce's satiric thrust at the clergy for their alleged preoccupation with sexual matters, a preoccupation that Bloom assumes in "Lotus Eaters" and that Father Conmee illustrates in "Wandering Rocks" (U.243; X.850–1).

In "Circe" Bloom's political program no sooner arouses our expectations of a serious if vague Utopian vision, than it bathetically degenerates into a hedonistic fantasy that undermines his pretensions to leadership: "Union of all, jew, moslem, and gentile. Three acres and a cow for all children of nature. . . . General amnesty, weekly carnival with masked licence. . . . Free money, free rent, free love and a free lay church in a free lay state" (U.489–90; XV.1686–7, 1690–3). Within Bloom's fantasy, he becomes a buffoon and a sexual athlete prior to his imagining his denunciation. Must we not acknowledge in our account of how *Ulysses* means that at the level of story Bloom is inadequate to his intent, as perhaps the most well-meaning of us must be? Yet, at the level of metaphor, Joyce is insisting on his stature by showing us that he is denounced by discredited and irrelevant figures, including Theodore Purefoy, Alexander J. Dowie, and Dr Mulligan.

II JOYCE'S METAPHORICAL BESTIARY

A bestiary is a moralized tale of animal behaviour in which animals are implicitly metaphors for humans. An example is the fox who decides that the grapes he cannot reach are sour. Joyce has this tradition in mind, I think, in his insistent comparison of humans to dogs. Joyce's bestiary is an important part of what is, among other things, Joyce's epic of the physical aspect of human life. The bestiary emphasizes the role in human life of libidinous needs and appetite, considered to be "lower" animalistic behavior not only by most prior novelists, but by the Catholic clergy and by most of the Irish public which was a major aspect of his intended audience. For Joyce, although an exile, was more concerned with the parochial problems of Ireland than with what we vaguely define as "the modern world" or "the contemporary *Zeitgeist*".

Throughout the novel, Bloom carries with him the supplement of metaphoricity and the trace of anonymity. Or, as Elijah puts it in "Circe", the novel asks of Bloom, "Are you a god or a doggone clod?" (U.507; XV.2194). Wonderfully and exotically human, Bloom exemplifies the odd combination of the bestial and godlike, and, for the reader, of the poignantly irrelevant and highly significant. Intercourse inspired by Molly's watching two dogs copulate results in Rudy's birth: "Give us a touch, Poldy. God, I'm dying for it. How life begins" (U.89; VI.80–1). That god and dog are inversions of one another suggests the paradoxical relationship between the beastly and divine in man. Since the Irish Catholics believed that the Black Mass – performed variously by Satanists, Freemasons, and even Protestants – worshipped dogs, Joyce used dogs to represent what is ungodlike in man: mortality, irrationality and appetite. Mulligan introduces this theme in relation to Stephen when he addresses him as "poor dogsbody" (U.6; I.112), a phrase that Stephen recalls when he sees and identifies with a dead dog in "Proteus". Indeed, he plays on the inversion by recalling Deasy's view of history as an upwardly evolving process which fulfills God's goal: "Dogskull, dogsniff, eyes on the ground, moves to one great goal. Ah, poor dogsbody! Here lies poor dogsbody's body" (U.46; III.350–2; Gabler's restoration of the exclamation point stresses the impact of Mulligan's exact words, "Ah, poor dogsbody!" [U.6; I.112]). Later, Bloom's recollection of his father's suicide, triggered by his seeing a section reserved for dogs in the graveyard in "Hades", again associates dogs with mortality. He recalls the "last wish" in his father's suicide note that he care for his father's dog: "Be good to Athos, Leopold" (U.90; VI.125–6).

Obsessed with his mother's death, and also recalling Mulligan's insensitive words to his mother, "*O, it's only Dedalus whose mother is beastly dead,*" the cynical Stephen is proposing that the great goal is inevitably death (U.8; I.198–9). Searching for a coherent identity, Stephen oscillates between thinking of himself, on one hand, as God the Father and Christ, and on the other hand, in bestial terms, as in his riddle of the fox burying his grandmother. As Stephen enters nighttown, "A liver and white spaniel on the prowl slinks after him, growling" (U.432; XV.100–1). Later in "Circe", "a stout fox, drawn from covert, brush pointed, having buried his grandmother, runs swift for the open, brighteyed, seeking badger earth, under the leaves. The pack of staghounds follows, nose to the ground, sniffing their quarry, beaglebaying, burblbrbling to be blooded" (U.572; XV.3952–6). In terms of the bestiary of *Ulysses*, Stephen is the fox chased and caught by the blessed hound Bloom; his capture is the novel's version of the Fortunate Fall.

Stephen has been associated in "Aeolus" by Professor Mac-Hugh with Antisthenes, the cynic, who in "Circe" is called by Stephen "the dog sage" (U.523; XV.2642); the Greek word *kynikos* means doglike and was chosen to categorize philosophers who turned their backs on traditional customs and values.[6] Although the professor, whose own bitter cynicism makes him as much a follower of Antisthenes as any other character in "Aeolus", is another example of what Stephen must avoid, the professor pointedly defines a major problem inhibiting Stephen's creative potential: "You remind me of Antisthenes. . . . It is said of him that none could tell if he were bitterer against others or against himself" (U.148–49; VII.1035–7). To follow a cynic is – Joyce (who was himself prone to cynicism) is implying – to reduce oneself to the bestial level.

Yet very few allusions evoke purely negative examples, and few distinctions in *Ulysses* are black and white. For Antisthenes also provides a positive example when he, anticipating Joyce's own stress on the significance and potential of humans, took "the palm of beauty from Argive Helen", a goddess, and gave it the human Penelope (U.149; VII.1038–9). According to Gifford and Seidman, "Antisthenes apparently had argued [in the lost volume *Of Helen and Penelope*] that Penelope's virtue made her more beautiful than Helen, whose virtue was somewhat less solidly demonstrated."[7] While this is another instance where the novel suggests Molly's stature, it is a passage fraught with irony; for within *Ulysses*, the Penelope figure is hardly virtuous and Stephen's response ("Penelope Rich") calling attention to the Elizabethan parallel in a rather oblique way unweaves the metaphorical pattern that the reader is weaving based on the Odyssean parallel within "Aeolus". Yet the rereader sees the humour in Stephen's non sequitur. For in identifying Penelope Rich as the beautiful, virtuous Penelope figure, Stephen is oblivious to Molly, the rotund and hardly innocent Penelope of *Ulysses*. For first readers, when "Coming events cast their shadows before", it may be in ironic terms.

In "Circe", Bloom is, following the Homeric model, appropriately transformed into a swine as befits his self-accusations. But he also has doglike characteristics; at one point, he "creeps under the sofa and peers out through the fringe" (U.531; XV.2871). Bloom is followed by a metamorphosizing dog, undoubtedly the spaniel slinking after Stephen, which is at one moment a "retriever . . . nose to the ground" (U.437; XV.247) and at another a "sniffing terrier" (U.441; XV.356). Soon, it is Alf Bergan who "dogs him to left and right" (U.446; XV.482), and then Richie Goulding who "marches doggedly forward" (U.447; XV.513). After changing back into a retriever (U.452; XV.659), the dog becomes Garryowen, who is comically called not a sheepdog or a wolfhound but a "wolfdog" as well as a "mastiff" who "gluts himself with growling greed" (U.453; XV.663, 673–4) and, finally, a bulldog devouring the remnants of a pig [Bloom]: "a gobbet of pig's knuckle between his molars through which rabid scumspittle dribbles" (U.454; XV.693–4).

Being besieged and victimized by dogs anticipates Bloom's trial for sexual peccadilloes where he is figuratively devoured by his accusers. As he is about to be hanged, Paddy Dignam, another example of the bestial and mortal in man, intervenes in the form of a beagle, to corroborate Bloom's assertion that he was at a funeral and could not be guilty of the crimes of which he is accused: "The beagle lifts his snout, showing the grey scorbutic face of Paddy Dignam. He has gnawed all. He exhales a putrid carcasefed breath. He grows to human size and shape. . . . Half of one ear, all the nose and both thumbs are ghouleaten"(U.472; XV.1204–8). Thus Bloom is saved by Dignam, the man for whom he cared and for whose family he contributed generously. Kindness to Paddy, like his kindness to animals from dogs to gulls, illustrates Bloom's essential humanity. As if in reward for assuming the role of surrogate father to Dignam's family, Bloom's imagination corrects his confused version – in "Lotus-Eaters" – of the story in which Esau unsuccessfully disguised himself as Jacob: "The voice is the voice of Esau" (U.76,473; V.203–5, XV.1220).

Paradoxically, by assuming the role of generous father, he is restored to the role of son, for it is in the role of King Hamlet's ghost that Paddy speaks to Bloom: "Bloom, I am Paddy Dignam's spirit. List, list, O list!" (U.473; XV.1218). That Bloom, as is characteristic of Jewish people, takes seriously the continuity of generations and his role as son is illustrated by his recurring and guilt-ridden memories of his father's suicide – memories surely brought into focus by Paddy's funeral; Bloom, who undoubtedly knew the Jewish custom of honoring the anniversary date of a parent's or child's death, would have been particularly aware of his father's suicide since the anniversary date of 27 June 1886 is only eleven days away. But if Paddy is the ghost who has returned from the grave, then Bloom becomes the guilty Hamlet who frets that he has not done his duty towards his father. And this is precisely the point. Bloom is anxious about his own role of son; as Just Man and Wandering Jew, he bears a feeling of guilt disproportionate to any crime or sin. He is continually taking on himself the burdens of humanity, including the plight of the Dignam family. Bloom, like Shakespeare, contains the "all in all" both as an artist and as a man. Prior to their mutually seeing Shakespeare in the mirror, Joyce stresses again the parallel between Stephen and Bloom. After all, in "Lestrygonians" Bloom had thought: "Hamlet, I am thy father's spirit/Doomed for a certain time to walk the earth" (U.152;VIII.67–8); meanwhile, Stephen has been thinking of the ghost's first appearance to Hamlet all day and in "Scylla and Charybdis" had quoted the same lines that Paddy parodies: "Hamlet, I am thy father's spirit," (U.188; IX.170). By identifying Paddy with Hamlet's ghost and Esau, Joyce uses his evocation of the dead Paddy, whom he has summoned across "the waters of Lethe", to call attention to the resemblance between the literary transformations of metaphors and the physical transformations of metamorphosis and metempsychosis. When Paddy attributes his appearance and multiple identities to "metempsychosis", we understand that metempsychosis is, at the verbal level, another name for the artist's metaphorical process.

Isn't Joyce using the bestiary to call attention to the artist's ability to use the metaphorical potential of language to transform, like Circe, man into whatever he wishes? And at the same time he stresses in "Circe" the impossibility of having a single coherent identity. The rapid metamorphosis of the dog from one species into another becomes itself a metaphor for the process by which one thing becomes another, by which the most literal nominalistic facts momentarily take on representative meaning only, quite often, to be replaced by subsequent terms which may or may not sustain the meaning of the original term. Just as the reader seeks to locate the common denominator of the dog analogy, and to discover the common thread that links the Protean dog with the Circean dog, the reader participates in a process of sorting out identities, of trying to locate the consistent term of a metaphorical system.

III THE SHARED VISION OF SHAKESPEARE

"Circe" fulfils the aesthetic theory of "Scylla and Charybdis" in an unexpected form. Rather than dramatizing the conscious lives of Stephen and Bloom, the two halves of his putative artist figure, Joyce presents in dramatic terms their unconscious lives. Are we not supposed to see that these characters are as much an expression of their artistic creator as Shakespeare's characters are of him? Is not the dramatic form of the chapter a deliberate effort to achieve the "dramatic form" described in *Portrait* where the artist impersonalizes himself and regards his characters from a distance? We should think of "Circe" as the fulfilment of the author's odyssey of style – as the kind of turning point that Shakespeare achieved in *Hamlet* – when the artist moves from kinesis to stasis, moves conclusively from a lyrical to a dramatic mode.

The union of Stephen and Bloom in the vision of Shakespeare

has been anticipated by another of Stephen's riddles: "What went forth to the ends of the world to traverse not itself, God, the sun, Shakespeare, a commercial traveller, having itself traversed in reality itself becomes that self. . . . Self which it itself was ineluctably preconditioned to become" (U.505; XV.2117–21). That the riddle is asked to a "cap" in "Circe" recalls Stephen's sphinxian riddle in "Nestor" to the class of young schoolboys, but this time the riddle lacks a question mark and contains its own answer. For the "what" of the declarative sentence is the Joyce-presence who is dramatizing the subconscious hallucinations of his characters and ultimately narrating the words we read. Within Joyce's theology of metaphors, the Holy Ghost that brings Stephen and Bloom together is Shakespeare, but the Holy Ghost is also the narrative presence who is rendering their experience in terms that could not have occurred to the imagination of either of them.

Within "Circe", by recreating the past from the privileged perspective provided by greater knowledge than the characters in the present could have, Joyce is illustrating a major aesthetic principle of the novel. In "Scylla and Charybdis", he has defined this aesthetic principle: "As we, or mother Dana, weave and unweave our bodies . . . from day to day, their molecules shuttled to and fro, so does the artist weave and unweave his image. And as the mole on my right breast is where it was when I was born, though all my body has been woven of new stuff time after time, so through the ghost of the unquiet father the image of the unliving son looks forth" (U.194; IX.376–81). Among other things, this passage defines how Stephen as artist reiterates the life of Shakespeare, his apostolic father, whose life he as the spiritual son repeats. It also reminds us that the artist, by proposing a metaphor in which a figure in an imagined work is prefigured by a historical, mythic, or literary predecessor, can weave and unweave any father figure he might choose. Thus, in his own mind, Stephen is signified by Shakespeare and Christ. In every allusion "the image of the unliving son" – unliving because displaced by the imaginative creation of the artist (who fathers him) – "looks forth" "through the ghost of the unquiet father." That Stephen himself thinks in terms of Shakespeare and Christ shows how he is moving towards the metaphorical method of *Ulysses*. But that he is unaware of the potential of this technique for giving shape and meaning to his life and contemporary Dublin and that he is oblivious to the novel's fundamental parallel to *The Odyssey* shows that he still has a long way to go (U.149; VII.1039–40; recall that when in "Aeolus" the Professor mentions Penelope, Stephen thinks of Penelope Rich). That within Bloom's fantasy Bello applies Stephen's term "secondbest bed" for the bed of the cuckolded Shakespeare to Bloom (a term which Bloom probably did not hear in the library) emphasizes not only their kinship, but the narrative presence who is creating this extraordinary parallel: "You have made your secondbest bed and others must lie in it" (U.206,543; IX.800; XV.3198–9). In "Circe" as they simultaneously look into the mirror in the whorehouse, "The face of William Shakespeare, beardless, appears there, rigid in facial paralysis, crowned by the reflection of the reindeer antlered hatrack in the hall" (U.567; XV.3821–4). The reader's epiphany is that the artist who, like Shakespeare, will be truly universal, must include both Stephen and Bloom – intellect and experience – even if as a man in the actual world he may be ridiculous. Living in poverty and deeply involved in the details of a very pedestrian life, Joyce enjoyed imagining the vast, even bathetic distinction between Shakespeare the artist and Shakespeare the man. That Shakespeare speaks "in dignified ventriloquy" is an endorsement of the ventriloquism that Joyce adopts as he moves from style to style after "Lestrygonians" (U.567; XV.3826).

That Stephen and Bloom share a vision of Shakespeare shows the reader that these seemingly very different figures – the inexperienced ("beardless") artist and the cuckolded man of experience – have the potential to merge in the figure of the artist. The image of Shakespeare that they see mirrors their artistic frustration (we recall Bloom's literary aspirations) and sexual paralysis. Shakespeare's oracular words speak to Stephen's guilt for not praying at his mother's bedside, but Bloom also hears a resonance of the guilt he feels for his father's suicide: "How my Oldfellow chokit his Thursdaymornun" (U.567; XV.3828–9; Gabler's correction of "Thursdaymomun" to "Thursdaymormun" seems to blur the thrust of this passage). Shakespeare mocks Bloom's role as putative father, even as he recalls the analogy between Bloom's ghostlike presence in the library and his ghostly presence in the life of Hamlet-Stephen: "Thou thoughtest as how thou wastest invisible" (U.567;

XV.3827). By adding "est" to "was," and at the same time adding "st" to the verb "waste", "wastest" becomes a humorous form of ersatz Elizabethan language that punningly emphasizes Bloom's estrangement from his role of husband, father, and son.

The variations on "Iago" – "Iagago" and "Iagogogo" – emphasize that both Stephen and Bloom feel that they have been betrayed (U.567; XV.3828–9). Bloom suffers betrayal by Molly and Blazes; the rereader is aware that the hostility of Dublin's citizens towards him, despite his love and generosity for them, is the very kind of betrayal Parnell suffered. Moreover, Stephen feels deeply that he has been betrayed by Mulligan, his father, and Dublin, his native city which refuses to recognize his artistic potential. Moreover, to the extent that both major figures also carry the heavy psychological baggage of seeing themselves as betrayers – Stephen of his mother and his commitment to art, Bloom of his Jewish heritage and his father – the Iago allusion reflects the guilt that they both feel; as we have seen, the anniversary of his father's suicide is very much on Bloom's mind: "Poor papa! Poor man! I'm glad I didn't go into the room to look at his face. That day! O, dear! O, dear!" (U.76; V.206–7).

In his expressive theory of Shakespeare, Stephen had spoken of how Shakespeare in *Othello* had divided himself between the title character and "the hornmad Iago" who is obsessed with sexual betrayal: "[Shakespeare's] unremitting intellect is the hornmad Iago ceaselessly willing that the moor in him shall suffer" (U.212; IX.1023–4).[8] That the "him" refers to both Shakespeare and Iago emphasizes how each character contains aspects of his own opposite, while the author contains aspects of both a character and the same character's opposite. This is a structural principle of the book that the reader gradually learns and which climaxes with the epiphanic moment when Bloom and Stephen simultaneously see each other in the mirror.

In his next speech, Shakespeare gives a garbled and degenerate version – "Weda seca whokilla farst" – of the Player Queen's line in *Hamlet*: "In second husband let me be accurst/ None wed the second but who kill'd the first" (U.568; XV.3853; *Hamlet* III.ii.189–90). Because Shakespeare's soul contains "all in all" and because he had been betrayed by his wife, Shakespeare's face in the mirror is replaced by the face of Martin Cunningham – whose face in "Hades" is to Bloom "Like Shakespeare's face" and with whom Bloom empathizes as another man wronged by his wife (U.96; VI.345). Like his creator, Bloom is a maker of metaphors. We realize that it is his imagination as much as Stephen's that is the source for their shared vision.

IV THE APPEARANCE OF STEPHEN'S MOTHER

In "Circe", recalled events and phrases play a metonymical function for the reader by bringing into his present focus the scene and emotions from which they are taken. This recurrence of past episodes has the rhetorical effect of urging the reader to understand that there is no such thing as the pastness of the past.

Stephen experiences his "Hades" when the ghost of his mother appears in "Circe". As he confronts her ghost, he recalls his apostasy and guilt in terms of specific impressions from "Telemachus," including phrases from the requiem for the dead (*"Liliata rutilantium te confessorum . . . iubilantium te virginum . . .*) and Mulligan's crass remarks ("She's beastly dead") (U.10,8,580; I.276–7, 198–9; XV.4164–5,4170). But Stephen recoils against the grip of his mother's ghost and refuses to accept the charge that he killed her by refusing to pray. When he smashes the chandelier with his ashplant, he, like Hamlet, is acting in such a way as to exorcise the grip of his mother and is taking a step to overcome the paralytic self-consciousness that interferes with his personal and artistic growth: "He lifts his ashplant high with both hands and smashes the chandelier. Time's livid final flame leaps and, in the following darkness, ruin of all space, shattered glass and toppling masonry" (U.583; XV.4243–5). Echoing his Blakean hope in the opening of "Nestor" for a secular apocalypse ("I hear the ruin of all space, shattered glass and toppling masonry, and time one livid final flame"), which will purge his mind of the haunting "daughters of memory", this Viconian vision in which he symbolically destroys the imprisonment of space and time looks forward to a new cycle in Stephen's life (U.24; II.7–8).

The subsequent appearance of Lord Tennyson and Edward the Seventh represent the English artistic and political heritage that Stephen must reject. In his bizarre dress "and with the halo of Joking Jesus", Edward the Seventh is associated with Wilde and Mulligan as a frivolous sexual and artistic alternative that

must be avoided (U.591; XV.4476). Once we recall the association of the old milkwoman with Ireland and by extension with
his mother in "Telemachus", we realize that in this scene his
mother represents the Irish heritage with which he must come to
terms. She also represents the debilitating hold of his personal
past and the fixed and paralysing Platonic conceptions – including Christianity – that Stephen's intellectual imagination
substitutes for the here and now; she assures him, "Prayer is
allpowerful. . . . I pray for you in my other world" (U.581;
XV.4197, 4202). When he asserts ostensibly to Private Carr,
but really to himself, "Let my country die for me. Up to the
present it has done so. I didn't want it to die. Damn death. Long
live life!", he is turning his back on the deathgrip of the past
(U.591; XV.4473–4). Since "Life" is an affirmative value that
has been identified with Bloom (U.61,89,115; IV.239–40,
VI.89–90, 1003–5), Joyce is urging us to see that Stephen is
progressing. In a sense Stephen is exhuming the grandmother
(Ireland and his mother) that he had buried under the hollybush.

But the reader experiences a schism between story and metaphorical significance. At the level of meaning, Stephen's break-
ing the chandelier with an ashplant that is compared to
Nothung, the magic sword of Siegfried, from Wagner's *Der Ring
des Nebulungen*, is an important event in his progress; "*Nothung*" in
German means "Needful". But at the level of story the evocation
of Siegfried's sword, as Stephen drunkenly destroys the property
of others, exposes him as an adolescent writer with a long way to
go to reach maturity. Until fertilized by experience and transformed by love, he will not be able to "kill the priest and the
king" that haunt his mind, and his intellectual imagination will
inhibit his growth as an artist (U.589; XV.4437).

Before growth is possible, Stephen must come to terms with
the debilitating effect of his personal past. He must assimilate
Bloom's values and break the inhibiting effects of his "intellectual imagination", a quality which Joyce associates with Lucifer's refusal to serve: "The intellectual imagination! With me all
or not at all. *Non Serviam*" (U.582; XV.4227–8). (I am taking
issue with Ellmann, among others, who argues, "In Stephen the
saving grace is . . . 'the intellectual imagination'."[9]) The intellectual imagination is not Stephen's solution but his problem;
it is a large factor in his cynicism, arrogance, iconoclasm,
and inability to respond humanely to others. In contrast to the

affirmations and Yesses of Bloom's imagination, Stephen's intellectual imagination is aligned with negations; after invoking the "intellectual imagination", the next speech begins "No! No! No!" and the one after that contains the one word "*Nothung!*" (U.582–3; XV.4235,4241). Thus even if his intellectual imagination is a factor in his refusal to submit to his past, it is also a quality that causes his fixation on the past. A few moments later, Stephen reveals another problem in relying too much on the life of the mind: "Personally, I detest action" (U.589; XV.4414). Joyce has the Citizen reappear to growl a xenophobic curse to point up the contrast between Bloom's assertion of values in the face of personal danger in "Cyclops" and Stephen's drunken behavior and ineffectual responses to Private Carr's and Private Compton's challenge.

This episode leaves the reader with a double effect – one from the literal story, the other from the metaphorical implications. It prepares the reader for the conclusion of "Circe" where, as we shall see, Joyce resolves story and significance. Stephen is more open to new experience and, in particular to Bloom's offer of friendship. He separates himself from the hostesses and patrons of the whorehouse and aligns himself with Bloom: "Why should I not speak to him or to any other human being who walks upright upon this oblate orange? . . . I'm not afraid of what I can talk to if I see his eye" (U.589; XV.4426–7). This passage recalls the moment in "Oxen" when "both their eyes met" and looks forward to their mutuality in "Eumaeus" (U.417, 656; XIV.1191, XVI.1579–81). But, since Stephen never indicates in the subsequent chapters his awareness of this vision, one cannot codify the effects of the hallucination on Stephen's behavior.

V THE CONCLUSION OF "CIRCE"

Let us examine how the narrative presence establishes the significance of the relationship between Stephen and Bloom at the end of "Circe". We recall that Bloom is in nighttown because of his concern for Stephen in "Oxen of the Sun": "The stranger still regarded on the face before him a slow recession of that false calm there, imposed, as it seemed, by habit or some studied trick, upon words so embittered as to accuse in their speaker an unhealthiness, a *flair*, for the cruder things of life" (U.422; XIV.1356–9). We should notice that Bloom at this point has more insight into the plight of another human being than Stephen has exhibited all day. We should also notice that the distance between Bloom and the narrator continues to narrow and that Bloom's interpretation of Stephen is close to that of the narrative presence, the fictionalized Joyce who is narrating the novel.

At the conclusion of "Circe" Stephen acknowledges Bloom as his spiritual father and Bloom responds to Stephen as his spiritual son. Bloom assumes the role of a protective father when he pays the whores for the chandelier that Stephen has broken, and he comes to Stephen's aid after Stephen has passed out. That Bloom calls Stephen by his first name shows Bloom's desire for intimacy as well as his specific concern for the young man lying prostrate before him: "Mr. Dedalus! . . . the name if you call. Somnambulist . . . . Stephen! . . . Stephen!" (U.608; XV.4925–28). Bloom's concern for Stephen, in contrast to the neglect of his Catholic compatriots and his own father, makes an ironic point about the Freemasons, to which Bloom belongs; the Roman Catholic religious establishment despised and vilified the Freemasons as the personification of Anti-Christ and accused them of practicing the Black Mass. Because the Masons were committed to each other, regardless of their nation or religious affiliation, they were perceived as a threat to the authority of a universal Church. (Somewhat paradoxically, because their loyalty was presumed to be more to each other than to a nation-state, Freemasonry was also perceived as a dangerous menace to nationalism.) Because their focus seemed to be on the events of this world, they were perceived as a threat to orthodox Catholicism which preached that this world was a mere prelude to the next.

That in Bloom's quest for the advertisement for the merchant Alexander Keyes, he searches in the library for the emblem of the "House of Keys", the parliament of the Isle of Man, metaphorically affirms his Masonic commitment to mankind rather than to any one nation or sect. We should note the reference in "Circe" to "the Three legs of Man", the heraldic insignia of the Isle of Man, immediately before Bloom's appearance as the secular Elijah. Bloom, as a Mason, would have been committed to help fellow Masons and their families, but he extends that mandate to include Dignam, Mrs Purefoy, and, especially Stephen. It may be that Joe Hynes's reference to Bloom as "the prudent member" refers both to his Jewishness and to his membership in the Masons (U.297; XII.211). Within "Circe", Bloom reveals that his consciousness is saturated with Masonic lore and that the rites of Masonry have partially usurped not only his secular Judaism but his Irish nationalism. Gifford and Seidman remind us that the masons felt a mystic identity with Jews: "The Knights of the Red Cross are also known as the Knights of Babylon as a reflection of their mystic identity with the Jews who rebuilt Jerusalem and the temple after the Babylonian captivity."[10] Certainly both groups were regarded as outsiders if not ostracized by the Catholic majority in Dublin.

Bloom frequently thinks of Masonic lore, and imagines that even Major Tweedy, Molly's father, is a mason (U.596; XV.4615–6); indeed, Bloom gives one of the Masonic signs of distress to the First Watch: "plucking at his heart and lifting his right forearm on the square, he gives the sign and dueguard of fellowcraft" (U.456; XV.758–9). Since Masonry was prominent in the Protestant Anglo-Irish establishment (Edward VII was an important member of the Masonic hierarchy until he became king), Bloom's Masonry stresses his universality in yet another way. He not only has mysterious ties to Sinn Fein and Parnell, but perhaps also as a fellow Mason to influential Anglo-Irish. In another important instance of the parallelism of their minds, Stephen, too, thinks of Masonry, but he associates if with the decadence of Edward VII and the Black Mass. For it is Stephen's hallucination which comically evokes the bizarre figure of Edward VII in Masonic garb, but holding the tools of a stonemason (U.590; XV.4454–6). And in his vision of the Black Mass, the dead of Dublin "exchange in amity the pass of knights of the red cross" (U.598–9; XV.4681–2). When Stephen is lying prostrate on the ground, Bloom responds in terms of the Masonic code: "[S]wear that I will always hail, ever conceal, never reveal, any part or parts, art or arts" (U.609; XV.4951–2). Since Masons cannot speak about Masonry except to fellow Masons, it is appropriate that it becomes important in a chapter dramatizing Bloom's repressed and unspoken fantasies and hallucinations.[11]

VI PATERNITY AND METAPHOR IN THE EPIPHANY
    OF "CIRCE"

Stephen's drunken perception of Bloom is in terms of "Who Goes With Fergus", the Yeats poem that haunts his imagination and which he associates with his response to his mother's death. If we recall that Joyce chanted this melancholy poem, originally a song from *The Countess Cathleen*, to his dying brother, George, we realize that Bloom is not only a surrogate father to Stephen but also a surrogate brother. Because Joyce omitted a version of a fictionalized Stanislaus Joyce in *Ulysses*, and because he shows that Stephen lacks any rapport with his sisters (although Joyce had warm if intermittently tense relationships with his sisters), Stephen's requirement for an empathetic other is all the more compelling. Among other things, Bloom provides a fraternal figure in the face of Stephen's isolation and alienation from his family.

For the odyssean reader, Yeats is a central metaphor of the artist through whom spiritual father meets spiritual son. But, in contrast to the reader, neither the drunken Stephen nor the uneducated Bloom know that their mutual invocation of Yeats as a figure who embodies imaginative energy and artistic patrimony creates a necessary bond. Stephen's perception of Bloom in terms of "Who goes with Fergus" may imply that Bloom will replace or at least complement Yeats's role as Stephen's spiritual father (and that of the younger Joyce for whom Stephen is a metaphor). Yet the Irishman Yeats is not as important a metaphor for the fulfilled artist as Shakespeare, although Joyce would have been aware that Yeats's difficulties with Maud Gonne made him another sexually betrayed artist. For Yeats, with his allegiance to the Celtic Renaissance, magic, theosophy, and symbolism, is an artistic father that Joyce must partially reject if he is to write *Ulysses*. Clearly, the hyperbole of the romance voice in "Cyclops" is a satire on Yeats's glorification of Irish Gods and heroes. And so is Stephen's reference to folk literature in "Telemachus:" "Five lines of text and ten pages of notes about the folk and the fishgods of Dundrum. Printed by the weird sisters in the year of the big wind" (U.12–13; I.365–7). (The big wind was the colophon for books printed by Yeats and his sisters.)

Isn't Rudy a supreme fiction, the kind of figure Yeats would have created to illustrate the power of the imagination? Certainly Bloom's fantasy of Rudy as a changeling suggests Yeats's faeryland poems, particularly "The Stolen Child" and "Who Goes with Fergus". The latter is about escape to an imaginary place where the painful emotions of human life are absent. Within the poem, the man who accompanies Fergus will "brood on hopes and fears no more", and will "no more turn aside and brood upon love's bitter mystery". A mythical king who gave up his throne to the son of his bride as the price of marriage, Fergus, for Yeats, is a metaphor for the man who seeks wisdom instead of personal gain. He is, like Bloom, a figure for whom passionate love within the commitment of a marriage is the central value. Bloom misunderstands Stephen's abstruse mind, as he will quite frequently in the subsequent two episodes, and thinks that Fergus is short for a woman named Ferguson: "Best thing could happen him" (U.609; XV.4951). (The "best" contains an echo of both Shakespeare's and his own "Secondbest Bed" [U.203; IX.698–9]). The reader understands not only that Bloom's sympathetic response is far more important than his response to Stephen's literary reference, but that Bloom's comment affirms a central premise of the novel, a premise articulated in Stephen's aesthetic in "Scylla and Charybdis", namely that passionate sexual experience is crucial to the development of the mature artist.

For the inexperienced, paralytically self-conscious, and hyper-intellectual Stephen, Bloom is the necessary complement required to fertilize his soul and transform his unrealized and unfulfilled artistic potential into reality: "[Stephen] stretches out his arms, sighs again and curls his body" (U.609; XV.4944). Stretching out his arms implies his acceptance of Bloom. That Stephen is curled in the foetal position indicates not only Stephen's potential for rebirth, but also that the fictionalized Joyce is recreating Stephen. It also anticipates Bloom's fetal position at the end of "Ithaca" when, as he dozes off, "the childman weary, the manchild in the womb", he contains within himself the "all in all" (U.737; XVII.2317–8). Stephen's encounter with Bloom fulfills his stature as a Shakespeare figure, for his life is illustrating the basic premises of "Scylla and Charybdis".

Doesn't the encounter with Bloom dramatize that for Stephen, as for Shakespeare, "His errors are volitional and are the portals of discovery" (U.190; IX.228–9)? In meeting and getting to know Bloom, hasn't Stephen "found in the world without as actual what was in his world within as possible" (U.213; IX. 1041–2)? Establishing that Stephen is moving in the direction of Shakespeare on the crucial day when the novel occurs, 16 June 1904, enables us to believe that the distance between Stephen and Shakespeare has between then and the time of the telling considerably narrowed and that Stephen has grown perceptively closer to the retrospective fictionalized Joyce who is our teller and our exegetical guide through Dublin. Urging the reader to believe that this perceptible movement signifies a larger pattern of development that will take place over a period of years is another version of Joyce's metaferocity.

Perceived by Stephen as "Black panther. Vampire", Bloom is a comic version of the Christ figure anticipated within the text by the typological tradition (U.608; XV.4930.4930). For in "Nestor" Jews had been associated with darkness by Stephen in terms which traditionally describe the coming of Christ: "dark men in mien and movement, flashing in their mocking mirrors the obscure soul of the world, a darkness shining in brightness which brightness could not comprehend" (U.28; II.158–60). More comically, the angel of Bloom's annunciation is Haines the Englishman at the Martello tower who raved in his sleep about killing a black panther. Joyce has Stephen the apostate allude to the anti-Christian tradition that a Roman soldier named Panther was Christ's real father.[12] Panther foreshadows Leopard or Leopold; Joyce would have enjoyed the punning resonance of "bard" in the second syllable of "Leopard".

The vision of Rudy is the grace and benediction of Bloom's humanity. Put in other terms, after Bloom has exorcised his guilt and anxieties, his imagination is receptive to transforming his actual role as Stephen's guide into the imaginative one as father of his deceased son, Rudy. His son would now be eleven years old, and eleven is the traditional number – with its repetition of 1 – of renewal. As he stands diligently over Stephen – "Silent, thoughtful, alert" – Bloom has a vision of his son Rudy who died at the age of eleven days: "Against the dark wall a figure appears slowly, a fairy boy of eleven, a changeling, kidnapped, dressed in an Eton suit with glass shoes and a little bronze helmet, holding a book in his hand. He reads from right to left inaudibly, smiling, kissing the page" (U.609; XV.4955–60).

While the typography suggests that the final speaking part in "Circe" is assigned to Rudy, he speaks no words:

RUDY

(gazes, unseeing, into Bloom's eyes and goes on reading,
kissing, smiling. He has a delicate mauve face. On his suit he
has diamond and ruby buttons. In his free left hand he holds a
slim ivory cane with a violet bowknot. A white lambkin peeps
out of his waistcoat pocket.) (U.609; XV.4964-7)

Rudy's "unseeing eyes" emphasize an inevitable gulf between
Bloom's reality as a character in Joyce's Dublin and Rudy's
existence as a fiction of Bloom's imagination. The lambkin
suggests both Christ the lamb and the traditional equation of
child and lamb, both of which are the basis of Blake's "The
Lamb". And we recognize that the rebellious and iconoclastic
Blake is one of Stephen's favourite poets. The identification of
Rudy with a lamb also recalls Stephen's sense of himself as
Christ the son and Christ the victim.

Marilyn French has argued that Bloom's vision is rather
pathetic: "Noble Leopold Bloom can find a purpose to his life
only in a fairy-tale/ nursery rhyme symbol – a fact that is at
once ludicrous, pathetic, outrageous, comic, and true to human
experience".[13] But hasn't Bloom been rewarded for his response
to Stephen with a vacation from his daytime self? To be sure, as
Karen Lawrence contends, "The sense of irretrievable and prema-
ture loss is expressed in the incompleteness of the dialogue."[14] Yet
the importance of the scene as climax is not affected by Rudy's
silence; indeed, conceived as the benediction to Bloom's concern
for Stephen, as a fantasy of what might have been that power-
fully informs Bloom's response to what is – Stephen's plight and
his own psychic needs, doesn't Rudy's silence touch us deeply?
The reader is being urged to understand that such a moment of
vision, such a moment out of time, is its own reward. This vision
testifies to the power of Bloom's imagination and shows that he
is, in his own way, as much a Shakespeare figure as Stephen. For
Bloom, as father and artist, has summoned his son "into life
across the waters of Lethe" (U.415; XIV.1113-4). (Ironically,
as soon as Bloom's ephemeral vision disappears, Rudy, like
Yeats's Fergus, must cross back over Lethe into faeryland.)
Joyce is implying here that we readers are different from the
creative artist in degree not kind and that we all can and should
recreate reality. Finally, do we not understand that by using the

words "Silent, thoughtful, alert", Joyce is using Bloom to modify his concept of the artist who in *Portrait* stands apart, inconoclastically detached from his fellows, "using for my defence the only arms I allow myself to use – silence, exile, and cunning" (P.247)?

Bloom thinks of an eleven year old Rudy, wearing his yarmulke, following in the Jewish tradition of his own forefathers and reestablishing the tradition he feels guilty for having abandoned. In "Lotus-Eaters", and again in the first part of "Circe", Bloom had imagined his father rebuking him for leaving "the house of his father" and leaving "the god of his father", although it is his father who had changed his name from Virag and abandoned his religion. That Bloom imagines the yarmulke as a "bronze Helmet" may indicate that he has forgotten the word "yarmulke". But it may also indicate that he realizes that the Jews need a helmet to protect them against the kind of anti-Semitism, which, as we saw in "Hades", Bloom presumably experiences daily if not so dramatically as in the climax of "Cyclops".

The helmet may also suggest Mercury–Hermes who will finally summon Bloom, the narrator, and the reader back over the river Lethe to join Rudy in death. It is after all Hermes who gives Ulysses the magic herb, moly, to guard him against Circe's magic. Are not dignity, humanity, and self-worth the "moly" necessary for Bloom's survival in Dublin – in the indifferent, amoral cosmos of *Ulysses* which contains people who are pursuing their own selfish aims? (Is not the odyssean reader urged to see in "Circe" not only a heightened and intensified metaphor of the prior ontology of the novel, but also of his own world?) In his metaphorical role of Hermes, Rudy gives Bloom the "moly" of realizing his value to others and thus his sense of self-worth. According to Gifford and Seidman, Rudy has a lambkin because Hermes was often represented as a shepherd.[15] While the Eton suit suggests Bloom's traditionally Jewish dreams of his son's success as scholar, the glass shoes suggest Cinderella and the ephemeral quality of Bloom's midnight fantasy.

Bloom's vision confirms the metaferocity of his imagination and shows his continuities with the imagination of his creator. Metaphorically, within this scene, Stephen becomes a figuration of Rudy because Stephen has to some degree taken Rudy's place in Bloom's imagination. That Bloom could not possibly know that in "Proteus" Stephen had thought of himself as a change-ling shows the kinship between Stephen and Bloom and thus calls attention to Joyce as the father of meaning and patterns, including foreshadowing and fulfilment, on which the reader depends. Finally, the bard who is the "lord and giver of their life" is the creative presence who presides over the entire novel (U.415; XIV.1116).

In his fantasy version of his son, Bloom the watchful, thoughtful, humanistic Mason evokes a figure that is his opposite, his anti-self, his masque. The bizarre vision of his deceased son is the kind of extravagant figure Wilde would have imagined. The ivory cane suggests Stephen's ashplant which Bloom is holding, but the bizarre costume suggests to the reader Oscar Wilde. Just like the epical and biblical prototypes, Wilde and Yeats – since being evoked in "Telemachus" – are signifiers to whom the reader refers; specifically they are never completely absent from the reader's mind as they hover over the story of Stephen's develop-ment as an artist. In this scene, Joyce affirms his ties not only to the Romantic tradition of Blake and Yeats, but to the decadent Romanticism of Wilde. For does not the vision of Rudy enable Joyce to establish a link with Wilde, another of Ireland's artistic pariahs? For just as Yeats was crucified for his literary noncon-formity because of *The Countess Cathleen*, Wilde was ostracized for nonconformity in personal and sexual matters. Joyce identified with both his fellow victims of middle class parochialism.

That Bloom recognizes Stephen as a spiritual son in terms of the major writers Stephen quoted in the first two episodes – Blake, Yeats, and Wilde – shows the folly of Stephen's desire to escape from the past. Joyce shows us that Stephen – indeed, all major artists – are signified by their predecessors or artistic fathers; or as Eliot put it, "no artist has his meaning alone". Like Yeats, Wilde, because of his frivolity and homosexuality, is a potential artistic father that must be rejected. But rejection of artistic patrimony requires the kind of redefinition that implicitly acknowledges the stature of the rejected figure.

The patrimony of Blake, Yeats, and Wilde reminds us that notwithstanding his obsession with realism and naturalism, Joyce has strong ties to the Romantic tradition. For Joyce, the Romantic tradition is something which becomes a supplement to and a qualification of his nominalistic realism. That tradition provides another perspective and becomes part of the "all in all" he seeks. Isn't *Ulysses* an attempt to reconcile the claims of realism and romanticism by privileging realism without neglecting romanticism? We know from Stephen's discussion about Irish art in "Telemachus" that Joyce has in mind Wilde's Preface to *The Picture of Dorian Gray*, where Wilde writes: "The nineteenth century dislike of Realism is the rage of Caliban seeing his own face in a glass. The nineteenth century dislike of Romanticism is the rage of Caliban not seeing his own face in a glass."

NOTES

1. Lawrence, p. 153.
2. As Lawrence puts it, "we are given *conceits* or expressive equivalents for the characters' psychic secrets rather than actual replays of past scenes in their lives" (Lawrence, p. 154; her emphasis).
3. Lawrence, p. 161; her emphasis.
4. French, p. 187.
5. See Ellmann, *James Joyce*, pp. 161–2, 375.
6. See Gifford and Seidman, p. 409.
7. See Gifford and Seidman, p. 120.
8. See French, p. 93.
9. Ellmann, *Ulysses on the Liffey*, p. 146.
10. Gifford and Seidman, p. 431.
11. Gifford and Seidman have useful comments on the Masonic references in *Ulysses*.
12. Gifford and Seidman, pp. 408–9.
13. French, p. 206.
14. Lawrence, p. 160.
15. Gifford and Seidman, p. 433.

9 Metaphoricity in "Eumaeus" and "Ithaca"

I THE SIGNIFICANCE OF THE RELATIONSHIP BETWEEN STEPHEN AND BLOOM

Perhaps if we apply the recent terminology of story (the chronological sequence of actions or events, independent of artistic form) and discourse (the formally organized discursive presentation or narration of events), we can understand how the metaphorical union of Stephen and Bloom which is established by the discourse is not sustained by the story; for Stephen and Bloom form no lasting bond, and they separate at the end with little possibility of renewing their relationship. Stephen declines Bloom's offer of lodging and disappears into the night. Is it too much to say that while the discourse or metaphorical level affirms Stephen's acceptance of Bloom as the necessary father figure and implies his future maturation, the story does not substantiate this?

In "Circe", it is possible that much of the drama exists mostly at the level of discourse because the characters in their subsequent thoughts are unaware of its taking place; after all, neither Stephen nor Bloom ever recollects his visions. In a sense, if these hallucinations are outside the consciousness of the characters, it is inevitable that we think of the narrator – whose presence we feel through the stage directions – as performing them for the reader. It is as if the meaning and significance of the action increasingly become the subject of the narrator's interest. The relation between story and discourse – between the nominalistic details of diurnal life and the possibility that those details may be part of a larger pattern – becomes in "Eumaeus" and "Ithaca" more and more a major subject of the novel and of the odyssean reader's sense-making. In the conflict between those who have stressed the naturalistic aspect of *Ulysses* and those who have stressed its symbolic aspect, the criticism of *Ulyssses*

231

has enacted the dialectic experienced by its readers between story (content) and form (discourse); roughly, the naturalistic critics have emphasized what I am calling story and the symbolic critics have focused upon what I am calling discourse. Of course we must remember that story and discourse are no more separable than form and content, and that, since the selection and arrangement of the actions and events reflect the intervention of form, nothing in the text precedes discourse. Put another way, to quote Tzvetan Todorov, "a discourse has superior autonomy for it assumes its entire signification starting from itself, without the intermediary of an imaginary reference".[1] Certainly the correspondences in Stephen's and Bloom's thoughts imply a transpersonal narrator ordering the narrative into a pattern of discourse. But at the level of story, one could contend that beginning with their shared vision of Shakespeare and their mutual recognition at the end of "Circe", and continuing until they part in the middle of "Ithaca", both Stephen and Bloom have a series of epiphanies of the other's significance, epiphanies which will have a lasting effect on both of them. These epiphanies are the way in which Bloom and Stephen give significant form to their experience; that is, the epiphanies create the meaning or discourse that they discover in the "stories" that they are living.

"Eumaeus" depends upon the episode in which Odysseus disguises himself as an old man to visit Eumaeus, a conscientious swineherd. In a sense the narrator is an Odysseus figure, while the reader is the Eumaeus figure. For, by adopting a verbose, clichéd, and often enervated style, the narrator, like Odysseus, is disguising himself as an old man; and he does this presumably to involve the less sophisticated reader – the conscientious Eumaeus figure – in Bloom's and Stephen's quests. In the more obvious plot parallel, Bloom disguises himself as Stephen's father and advises Stephen, who plays the role of his son. Their relationship depends upon each seeing through the disguise of conventional identity and realizing that they are, indeed, spiritual father and son. Each character sees the other as a radical metaphor. It is in their shared mythmaking that they become metonyms for one another, become "Bloom Stoom" and Stephen Blephen" (U.682; XVII.549, 551). Put another way, they are each signifiers in search of signifieds, and in the zeal of their needs they each apotheosize the other. In particular, Stephen,

the Catholic apostate who disbelieves the way only a former
believer can, allows his search for an artistic hierarchy and for a
paternal principle to come to rest in his hazy perception of
Bloom as Christ.

Joyce ironically shows that the common style of pulp fiction is
as intrusive as any other style and calls attention to itself as
much as any literary style. Thus "Eumaeus" adds another
chapter to Joyce's inclusive epic of contemporary writing. It is
an indictment of a particular kind of pretentious sentimental
fiction. But it is also a performance by the virtuoso Joyce who
shows how he can appropriate *any* language to the service of
meaning. The narrator assumes a double disguise. According to
Kenner, "we are meant to suppose that Bloom might be execu-
ting [the style of 'Eumaeus'] had he the time and freedom from
distraction".[2] Disguising himself as Bloom, the narrator writes
as someone with Bloom's education and pretensions might. But
he also assumes the disguise of Bloom's literary fantasy –
namely of Philip Beaufoy writing for a a penny magazine such as
Matcham's Masterstroke.

The reader responds to the differences between "Eumaeus",
the first chapter in the third part, and "Telemachus", the first
chapter in the first part. To emphasize the progress in the
characters' journeys and the parallel to Odysseus's homeward
journey, Joyce called the art "navigation", a term which emphasizes the linear and Aristotelian nature of experience in the
here and now as opposed to the vertical and Platonic implications of "theology", the art of "Telemachus". Further emphasis upon the experiential basis of the chapter's values is the
choice of the horizontally oriented "sailors" for the symbol in
contrast to the designation of the vertical and patristic symbol
"heir" of "Telemachus," a symbol which defined the terms in
which Stephen thought of paternity in the Telemachiad. While
"Telemachus" has no organ, Joyce called the organ of "Eumaeus"
"nerves" – the fibres that convey emotional impulses between the
brain and the entire body – to suggest the physical and emotional
intensity of Bloom's and Stephen's mutual response to one another.

Joyce expected the reader of "Eumaeus" to be attentive to
echoes of both "Telemachus", the first Stephen chapter, and to
"Calypso", the first Bloom chapter. For "Telemachus", "Calypso", and "Eumaeus," Joyce's elastic term "technic" seems to be
closely related to what we usually mean by literary style – as

opposed say to the "narcissism" of "Lotus-Eaters", which thematically describes temptations that Bloom must avoid; or the "labyrinth" of "Wandering Rocks", which rhetorically describes the reader's position as much as or more than it thematically places the characters in Dublin. In contrast to the vitality, liveliness, and vivaciousness of the "narrative (young)" style in "Telemachus", and the enegy, assertiveness, and specificity of "narrative (mature)" in "Calypso", the "narrative (old)" style of "Eumaeus" is clichéd, fatigued, and unfocused. But the striking contrast in style underlines the fact that one major action of this chapter is the replacement of Mulligan by Bloom as Stephen's advisor and mentor. Throughout the novel the narrator stresses a kind of competition between the two for Stephen's attention as if Stephen were, not unlike Prince Hal, a character in a morality play who must decide between True and False staffs on which to lean. Characteristic of Mulligan's irresponsible use of language – talk for the sake of onanistic dissemination of sound but not meaning, Mulligan accuses Bloom of the very homosexuality that Mulligan represents, while Bloom generously refers to Mulligan, in the context of warning Stephen, as an "allround man", the very term Lenehan used to praise him (U.235, 620; X.581, XVI.288).

In this chapter in which Bloom conclusively replaces Mulligan, we realize, too, that the clichéd, circumlocutious but sober and sincere writer has a much different attitude towards language than Mulligan, who speaks without thinking of the consequences of what he says or to whom he is saying it. Given that Joyce's choice of techniques urges us to compare "Telemachus" and "Eumaeus", should we not recall that the dominant figure of what some critics stress as the normative style of chapter one was Mulligan, whose self-indulgent wit and narcissism threaten to overshadow the paralysed Stephen? Sincerity and decency, like the style with which Joyce in "Eumaeus" embodies these values, may have their unexciting and pedestrian aspects. What the chapter does is question the hierarchy of literary style by which elegance rather than sincerity is the authoritative value. It questions vertical and Platonic conceptions of style and raises the possibility of a pragmatic conception of style which defines effectiveness in terms of whether a style is suitable to the subject and values it is presenting. In doing so, the chapter anticipates the non-conventional styles of "Ithaca" and "Penelope".

Yet the chapter also warns us of the elusiveness of language and the difficulty in establishing meaning, of reading the "Signatures of all things" (U.37; III.2). As Stephen puts it, "Sounds are impostures . . . likes names"; and he thinks that "He could hear . . . all kinds of words changing colour like those crabs about Ringsend" (U.622, 644; XVI.362–3, 1142–4). While Stephen doubts whether words can evoke absent reality, the narrator's circumlocutions, clichés, and stereotypes interfere with the reader's ability to get a clear picture of what is being presented. For example, note how the narrator refuses to commit himself to the truth or falseness of Murphy's story: "[I]t was quite within the bounds of possibility that it was not an entire fabrication though at first blush there was not much inherent probability in all the spoof he got off his chest being strictly accurate gospel" (U.635; XVI.826–9). Throughout this oxymoronic and evasive telling, the narrator refuses to commit himself to a strong reading of events.

Lawrence persuasively writes, "There is something vaguely senescent about this writing, from the wandering sentences to the half-remembered idioms. It is as if all the allusions, clichés, and idioms of a lifetime floated somewhere in the memory and were summoned forth for the sake of the story."[3] But I would add that although the speaker is not Bloom, who is a character within the third person narrative, he is someone who very much respects Bloom as a human being and who wants to tell a story that establishes his stature. On the whole, he is more prolix and clichéd than Bloom who, as we saw in "Cyclops", speaks with dignity, clarity, and concise eloquence, and whose probing if comic originality is one source of our delight in him. And throughout the novel Bloom's interior monologues often reveal sensitivity, precision, intellectual energy, and insight.

Thus, if this is the story as Bloom would have written it, Joyce would have expected us to realize that Bloom's literary talents do not do justice to his quality of mind. Within the chapter the speaker eloquently if somewhat circumlocutiously articulates his humanistic credo for solving national problems:

It is hard to lay down any hard and fast rules as to right and wrong but room for improvement all round there certainly is though every country, they say, our own distressful included, has the government it deserves. . . . I resent violence and intolerance in any shape or form. It never reaches anything or

stops anything. A revolution must come on the due instal-
ments plan. It's a patent absurdity on the face of it to hate people
because they live round the corner and speak another vernacu-
lar, in the next house so to speak. (U.643; XVI.1095–103).

Just as in the above passage, the reader overcomes his resistance
to the anesthetizing clichés of Bloom's first sentence to respond
to the eloquence of Bloom's powerful reading of history, so as he
reads the chapter he sees that the action challenges and overcomes the speaker's homogenizing and inelegant telling.

In both "Eumaeus" and "Ithaca" Bloom's stature triumphs
over the use of a style, the purpose of which seems to be to
trivialize him. In "Eumaeus" he not ony survives the clichés,
but shows that for all its inadequacies and circumlocutions, the
language cannot disguise his heroism: "Mr Bloom actuated by
motives of inherent delicacy inasmuch as he always believed in
minding his own business moved off but nevertheless remained
on the *qui vive* with just a shade of anxiety though not funkyish in
the least" (U.616; *XVI.116–9*). Although the syntax and diction
are undistinguished, the content often reflects knowledge of the
novel's prior pattern and intimations of Bloom's significance.
Thus when the speaker confers on Bloom the identity of "[Ste-
phen's] *fidus Achates*", evoking the faithful friend of the wandering Aeneas, he is echoing Simon Dedalus's comment on
the funeral carriage in "Hades:" "Was that Mulligan cad
with him? His *fidus Achates*!" (U.614, 88; XVI.54–5; VI.49).

The rhetorical tentativeness and circumlocutions are appropriate for a chapter that is addressing the problem of finding the
conceptual framework and terminology to define a unique male
friendship that not only lacks precedent in the characters' experience, but which has little literary precedent for Joyce to draw
upon. The style is also appropriate for a chapter in which
Stephen's and Bloom's fear of commitment struggles with their
desire to communicate. Because the syntax refuses to take a
position, because it deflates meaning even before proposing it,
and defers it prior to announcing it, the reader of "Eumaeus"
becomes aware of the doubtfulness of significance. Typical of the
endless qualification and inability to ground a sentence in certainty is the following: "Though this sort of thing went on every
other night or very near it still Stephen's feelings got the better of
him in a sense though he knew that Corley's brandnew rigma-

role on a par with the others was hardly deserving of much credence" (U.617; XVI.172–5). That the alcoholic Corley has become a vagrant is a comic but not irrelevant warning to the odyssean reader of the dire fate that awaits those who, like Stephen, have not yet developed a coherent identity and who desperately need an advisor to look out for their interest.

"Eumaeus' establishes the father-son relationship both by developing Bloom's paternal attitude towards Stephen and by showing similarities between Stephen and Bloom.Their minds illustrate a kind of parallax, because, as the scene where they simultaneously see Shakespeare in the mirror illustrates, despite differences in perspective they are often seeing the same things: "Though they didn't see eye to eye in everything a certain analogy there somehow was as if both their minds were travelling, so to speak, in the one train of thought" (U.656; XVI.1579–81). Bloom sees a parallel between his political views at age twenty-two and Stephen's current ones. Bloom has poetic aspirations and, like Stephen, loves music. Like Stephen has tried to do in "Scylla and Charybdis", Bloom reads Shakespeare to solve "difficult problems in imaginary or real life"; like Stephen, he has "derived imperfect conviction from the text, the answers not bearing in all points" (U.677; XVII.387, 390–1; that, after "bearing", Gabler's Critical and Synoptic edition proposes the obviously unidiomatic and inappropriate substitution "in" for "on" should give us pause in accepting every correction as if the Gabler edition had descended from the heavens.)

While the question in "Ithaca" about the numerical relation between Stephen's and Bloom's ages gives Joyce a chance to poke fun at the numerological nonsense of theosophy and other versions of mysticism, it does call attention to the special relationship between the two men (U.679; XVII.446ff). Bloom has utopian plans for the summer of 1882, the year Stephen was born. Dramatizing the parallel between these seemingly dissimilar figures establishes the validity within the text of the novel's metaferocity, for the novel depends upon Joyce convincing the reader that there is a "certain analogy . . . in the one train of thought" (U.656; XVI.1579–81). Isn't that the basis for the comparison between Ulysses and Bloom, Stephen and Shakespeare, and, indeed, between Joyce's fictionalized presence and both Stephen and Bloom?

Bloom and Stephen achieve a significant human relationship.

They develop an intimacy that neither achieves in his other
personal relationships during the day. Seeing that Stephen is
having trouble walking, Bloom invites him to "Lean on me"
(U.660; XVI.1720). Does the Anglo-American culture have a
paradigm for a non-sexual relationship between two males of
different ages who are not related? Joyce knew perfectly well that
readers would see homosexual possibilities in Bloom's befriend-
ing Stephen and teasingly proposes such a possibility: "[I]t
would afford him very great personal pleasure if he would allow
him to help to put coin in his way or some wardrobe" (U.657;
XVI.1618–9). After all, we recall that in "Scylla and Charybdis"
Mulligan, who is so closely identified with Wilde, had suggested
that Bloom was sexually interested in Stephen. Once the reader
understands that sixteen symbolizes homosexuality, he sees the
importance of their relationship developing in the sixteenth
episode on the sixteenth of June. Joyce would have expected his
reader to remember that Wilde was born on the sixteenth of
October. Sixteen is further stressed by the sailor's showing
Stephen and Bloom that he has tattooed on his chest "the figure
16 and a young man's sideface" – the face of the Greek tattooer
(U.631; XVI.675–6).[4]

But the narrative, told in a wordy, colloquial style that is so
different from the pretensions of Wilde and his fellow aesthetes,
insists on rejecting the simplicity of a symbolic reading in favor
of coming to terms with the more complex realities of Stephen's
and Bloom's human relationship. In contrast to the aesthetes
and symbolists who, Joyce believed, created abstruse symbols
for trite ideas, the narrative of "Eumaeus" shows that a seemingly insipid style can create meaning. Within the novel, as we
have seen, homosexuality becomes aligned with the self-
referentiality of symbolism and Platonism, and heterosexuality
becomes aligned with reality and Aristotelianism. Thus Bloom's
inelegant remarks become significant, as when he misconstrues
Stephen's quotation from Yeats: "A girl. Some girl. Best thing
could happen him" (U.609; XV.4950–1); or when he tells
Stephen that he must cast off Mulligan: "I wouldn't personally
repose much trust in that boon companion of yours who contributes the humorous element, Dr Mulligan, as a guide, philospher
and friend if I were in your shoes" (U.620; XVI.279–81).
Do we not recall both Stephen's efforts to separate himself from
the Platonists in "Scylla and Charybdis" and Bloom's view of

the symbolists and aesthetes: "Those literary etherial people they are all. Dreamy, cloudy, symbolistic. Esthetes they are" (U.166; VIII.543–4)? In a sense, the narrative style of "Eumaeus" as well as Bloom's somewhat pedestrian way of telling throughout the novel are Joycean comments upon the artistic pretensions of Joyce's recent literary precursors.

What is most attractive about Bloom to Joyce, himself extremely shy, is that, without being overly concerned with embarrassment or rebuff, he takes chances in personal relationships. Stephen's response emphasizes his need to believe that this is a significant experience: "[H]e thought he felt a strange kind of flesh of a different man approach him, sinewless and wobbly and all that" (U.660; XVI.1723–4). Within this most garrulous of chapters, the major communication between Bloom and Stephen is non-verbal and takes the form of looks and touches. After Bloom shares his memories of the "Cyclops" chapter with Stephen – and with the reader whose focus is redirected to Bloom's triumphant moment, the two communicate by means of eye contact until Stephen sees in Bloom the possibility of Christ: "*Ex quibus*, Stephen mumbled in a noncommittal accent, their two or four eyes conversing, *Christus* or Bloom his name is or after all any other, *secundum carnem*" (U.643; XVI.1091–3; as Gifford and Seidman note, this passage echoes the Vulgate, Romans 9:5: "*et ex quibus est Christus secundum carnem*" which means "and from that race [the Israelites] is Christ, according to the flesh").[5] Perceiving Bloom as something other than an ordinary man, as a divine principle – as Fergus, as a black panther, a vampire, as a man of strange flesh, and finally, as Christ – is an indication that Stephen is in the process of becoming the Joyce who will write *Ulysses*.

The conclusion of the chapter stresses their companionship; as a driver watches them, they continue "their *tête à tête* . . . about sirens, enemies of man's reason, mingled with a number of other topics of the same category, usurpers, historical cases of the kind . . ." (U.665; XVI.1889–91). We realize that the subjects of their conversation are the subjects of *Ulysses*, the book that results from their metaphorical union. The line "*to be married by Father Maher*" from the song that Stephen is singing, "The Low-Backed Car", surely suggests the possibility of union and fulfilment (U.665; XVI.1887–8). We recall that at the end of "Cyclops" Bloom as Elijah ascends to heaven in a chariot where his immortal status presumably is confirmed. While the story urges the reader to see the union of Stephen and Bloom as important at the human level, the metaphorical implications point toward their respective roles as artist and hero. Bloom and Stephen find in each other the intimacy that eluded them all day in their relationships with others. For in this scene, it is the carriage driver who is the outsider, rather than Stephen, who has been thinking of following the example of Fergus and turning his back on the real world, or Bloom, who had been the outsider in the carriage at Dignam's funeral.

But does the action of the novel justify the metaphorical union? The association of cars with death hints at another meaning, too. Given that Bloom first sees Stephen from the funeral carriage in "Hades", and that their intimacy increases while discussing the authenticity of Fitzharris as a driver in the Phoenix Park murders, and given that Fergus, who in "Telemachus" *"rules the brazen cars"* and transports his followers away from the real world, the metaphorical union is not without a hint of the mortality that awaits them both (U.9; I.241).[6]

II THE STYLE OF "ITHACA"

In "Ithaca", Joyce chooses to present his characters by means of a purportedly scientifically objective catechism: "I am writing Ithaca in the form of a mathematical equation. All events are resolved into their cosmic, physical, etc. equivalents . . . so that the reader will know everything and know it in the baldest and coldest way, but Bloom and Stephen thereby become heavenly bodies, wanderers like the stars at which they gaze."[7] The phrase "thereby become" suggests the metaphoricity of Joyce's imagination. When he all but declares, "Let the characters be heavenly bodies", he is affirming a belief in the power of the creative imagination to act as the copula and create, in the face of the claims of logic and realism, what it will. Such an affirmation places him within the Romantic tradition along with Blake, Shelley, and Lawrence.

The catechistic style often oversimplifies as when it reductively categorizes Bloom as representing "The scientific" temperament and Stephen as representing "The artistic" one (U.683; XVII.560). And the cataloguing tendency of the scientific style recalls that of the romance speaker in "Cyclops"; thus, while Bloom is at first identified with the "universality" as well as the "democratic equality and constancy" of water, the sheer plethora of information about water undermines the comparison and reduces it to bathos (U.671; XVII.185). The questions and answers are often, but not always, outside the minds of the characters. Yet, as in the prior chapter, the humanity of the characters triumphs over the style as we watch Stephen and Bloom find metaphorical significance in each other and discover the friend each needs. The reader understands that human emotions triumph over efforts to patronize or de-emphasize them. Indeed, as the chapter progresses the narrator becomes increasingly interested in the characters' feelings. When Bloom focuses on Stephen in the oral chronicle of his day that he gives to Molly, his human needs to overcome loneliness and to communicate – the needs that created the mutual relationship with Stephen and which are informing the intimate bedroom scene – are confirmed for the reader as the essence of the novel's values:

> Which event or person emerged as the salient point of his narration?
> Stephen Dedalus, professor and author. (U.735; XVII. 2269–70)

Gradually, as the reader becomes accustomed to the question-answer format, his attention returns to the characters. The reader thus joins with Bloom as "a conscious reactor against the void incertitude", and against a style which would align itself with the scientific perception of a cosmic void (U.734; XVII.2210–11).

I agree with Karen Lawrence that "Ithaca" parodies "the idea of a taxonomic system itself" and "shows the arbitrariness of any system of classification, either of the book or, by implication, of the world".[8] But she fails to realize that Joyce's novel, by parodying and undermining systems of knowledge and by discarding them in favor of its focus on central characters, dramatizes a hierarchy of values that establishes the pre-eminence of human relationships. Her problem is that she does not understand that Joyce is not and could not be discarding plot (the selection and arrangement of the story into a narrative that is perceived by the reader in the linear process of reading); rather, Joyce is supplementing the kind of plot that tells the story of the characters' actions and thoughts with another "metaphorical plot" that tells the story of how two men of different backgrounds can become significant for us. Like a final examination in which attention is directed to the major issues, the questions are often a formal means of directing our attention to the issues that are crucial: "What points of contact existed between these languages and between the peoples who spoke them?" (U.688; XVII.745–6). By continuing the process of defining the parallels between the two characters and their relationship as well as establishing their significance for the reader, the answers serve the needs of both plots.

III THE COSMOLOGICAL PERSPECTIVE IN "ITHACA"

"Ithaca" creates a cosmic context for the characters and points toward a possible resolution in the deferred future. As Stephen and Bloom emerge from Bloom's house after establishing their friendship, they share a mutual vision, before Stephen departs into the night: "The heaventree of stars hung with humid nightblue fruit" (U.698; XVII.1039). But Bloom finally rejects the concept of "heaventree" and responds to the aesthetic rather than the religious implications of this spectacle. For he believes:

> That it was not a heaventree, not a heavengrot, not a heaven-beast, not a heavenman. That it was a Utopia, there being no known method from the known to the unknown: an infinity renderable equally finite by the suppositious apposition of one or more bodies equally of the same and of different magnitudes: a mobility of illusory forms immobilised in space, remobilised in air: a past which possibly had ceased to exist as a present before its probable spectators had entered actual present existence. (U.701; XVII.1139–45)

Within the nominalistic world of 16 June 1904, Bloom's logical mind rejects the entire vertical dimension of experience, the very notion that the heavens can signify. Yet within Joyce's metaphorical universe informed by the teleology of his fiction, the stars do exactly that. But does not the preceding passage define the relationship between past and present in the novel, define how Bloom relates to the absent past, how Joyce moves from the known of the present to the unknown of the past, and how the characters do the same thing when they realize the significance of one another? In fact, Joyce's use of his historical and literary models provides a method for moving "from the known to the unknown" by means of "the suppositious apposition of one or more bodies equally of the same and of different magnitudes" (U.701; XVII.1140–3). Does this not define the relationship between Bloom and Odysseus, Shakespeare, and Elijah and between Stephen and Telemachus, Shakespeare, and Elisha? Does it not also define the relationship of the characters to each other and to Joyce?

By providing the cosmological geography and defining the terms of human life as they exist within the novel, "Ithaca" defines the conditions in which the action of *Ulysses* takes place. In a sense, "Ithaca" provides a center to which we can refer for essential data. Indeed, Bloom not only responds to time and space in the very objective, scientific terms which Joyce proposes in his novel as replacements for the traditional Christian interpretation of the universe, but he does so in terms which see the cosmos in a metaphorical relation to mankind. Thus, the answer to the question, "With what meditations did Bloom accompany his demonstration to his companion of various constellations?", concludes: "of our system plunging towards the constellation of Hercules: of the parallax or parallactic drift of socalled fixed stars, in reality evermoving wanderers from immeasurably remote eons to infinitely remote futures in comparison with which the years, threescore and ten, of allotted human life formed a parenthesis of infinitesimal brevity" (U.698; XVII.1040–1, 1051–6; Gabler's restoration of the word "wanderers" tightens the metaphorical relationship between Bloom the wanderer and the cosmos which, because it contains wandering stars and human wanderers, is conceived of as dynamic rather than fixed). That Bloom's own cosmological perspective parallels one major aspect of Joyce's vision in the finished novel is one of the ways that he is, like Stephen, a prefiguration of the presence who is telling the novel.

But in perceiving the world from the anthropocentric vantage point of one man's position as a mortal man within the vast universe, Bloom also shares Joyce's perspective. For in the next paragraph Bloom–Ulysses returns from his imaginative odyssey in space to the infinitesimal point that each man must occupy.

Put another way, after his multiplying takes him towards infinity
in the prior passage, Bloom divides infinitely the "eons of
geological periods recorded in the stratifications of the earth"
until he approaches but – in a version of Zeno's paradox –
never reaches zero: "nought nowhere was never reached" (U.699;
XVII.1058, 1068–9). Bloom's oscillation between vast imaginative leaps and the minute details of pedestrian reality is characteristic of his mind throughout the day. Indeed, his alternation
between a hawk's and frog's perspective illustrates the concept of
parallax and mirrors Joyce's own alternation between a Brog-
dingnagians and Lilliputian perspective – an alternation illustrated most vividly in "Cyclops" by the alternation between the
omniscient voice who usually speaks from a romance perspective
and the voice of the snarling, cantankerous Thersites figure.

Unlike Stephen, Bloom accepts time and mortality: "There
remained the generic conditions imposed by natural, as distinct
from human law, as integral parts of the human whole: the
necessity of destruction to procure alimentary sustenance: the
painful character of the ultimate functions of separate existence,
the agonies of birth and death: . . . the fact of vital growth,
through convulsions of metamorphosis, from infancy through
maturity to decay" (U.697; XVII.995–9; 1005–6). But just as
Bloom's resilience puts behind him personal disappointment, so it
enables him to turn from depressing contemplation of the inevitability of mortality, to "desist from speculation": "Because it
was a task for a superior intelligence to substitute other more
acceptable phenomena in the place of the less acceptable
phenomena to be removed" (U.697; XVII.1007–10).

Shortly after sharing the vision of "the heaventree of stars",
Bloom and Stephen observe simultaneously a "celestial sign":
"A star precipitated with great apparent velocity across the
firmament from Vega in the Lyre above the zenith beyond the
stargroup of the Trees of Berenice towards the zodiacal sign of
Leo" (U.703; XVII.1210–3). The "celestial sign" – a shooting
star moving from "Vega in the Lyre" to "the zodiacal sign of
Leo" – implies the movement of Stephen toward Bloom. This
cosmological sign also predicts the union of Bloom and Stephen
into the persona of the maturing artist who will be able to write
Ulysses. The narrator stresses that this movement in the heavens
has been anticipated by a similarity in the movement of the stars
at the births of Shakespeare and Bloom:

[T]he appearance of a star (1st magnitude) of exceeding brilliancy dominating by night and day (a new luminous sun generated by the collision and amalgamation in incandescence of two nonluminous exsuns) about the period of the birth of William Shakespeare over delta in the recumbent neversetting constellation of Cassiopeia and of a star (2nd magnitude) of similar origin but of lesser brilliancy which had appeared in and disappeared from the constellation of the Corona Septentrionalis about the period of the birth of Leopold Bloom and of other stars of (presumably) similar origin which had (efectively or presumably) appeared in and disappeared from the constellation of Andromeda about the period of the birth of Stephen Dedalus, and in and from the constellation of Auriga some years after the birth and death of Rudolph Bloom, junior . . . (U.700–1; XVII.1118–130)

After Stephen departs, Bloom remains to view the rising sun: "The disparition of three final stars, the diffusion of daybreak, the apparition of a new solar disk" (U.705; XVII.1257–8). On the metaphorical level, are not the three fixed stars that Bloom sees disappearing the characters of Bloom, Stephen, and Molly and is not the "new solar disk" the mature Joyce who will write *Ulysses*? Isn't there a teasing possibility, too, that the "new solar disk" is not the sun, but a spectacular astronomical phenomenon? After all, in the movement of the shooting "star . . . from Vega in the Lyre" towards "the zodiacal sign of Leo", the heavens have objectively acknowledged the genius of Stephen–Bloom–Joyce who, like Shakespeare, has progressed from lyrical art to dramatic art and who "was and felt himself the father of all his race, the father of his own grandfather, the father of his unborn grandson" (U.208; IX.868–9).

IV *ULYSSES* AS PROPHECY: THE IMPLICATIONS OF "ITHACA" FOR 17 JUNE AND THEREAFTER

Bloom understands that the generic laws of human life make the perfectability of human existence impossible. Nevertheless, as the Just Man and the twentieth century version of Moses, Elijah, and Christ, he has an infinite desire to try to improve the human situation: "Because at the critical turningpoint of human existence he desired to amend many social conditions, the product of inequality and avarice and international animosity" (U.696; XVII.990–2). He is depressed because he knows he cannot fulfil his Utopian plans – and that knowledge had informed the fantasy of his own crucifixion that followed the creation of the new Bloomusalem in "Circe". Yet at the very moment when Bloom is most depressed, he seems to have influenced Stephen who, within the limits of his own intellectuality and scholastic training, accedes to the limits of his own position in the human world: "He affirmed his significance as a conscious rational animal proceeding syllogistically from the known to the unknown and a conscious rational reagent between a micro and macrocosm ineluctably constructed upon the incertitude of the void" (U.697; XVII.1012–15). Does not the word "ineluctably" call attention to the progress Stephen has made in defining his place in space and time and since, at the outset of "Proteus", he had meditated upon the "Ineluctable modality of the visible" (U.37; III.1)?

It is central to Joyce's method to show that apparent dissimilarities can be resolved into actual parallels. By substituting Stephen for Bloom and Bloom for Stephen to establish that "Jewgreek is greekjew. Extremes meet" (U.504; XV.2097–8), Joyce is urging the reader to see a metonymical relationship between his two principle characters; each becomes a signifier for the other. Thus the climax of the novel is their momentary union in "Ithaca" when, under the influence of the invisible Molly ("denoted by a visible splendid sign, a lamp"), the muse who will fertilize their union in the last chapter, they have a mutual epiphany of recognition: "Silent, each contemplating the other in both mirrors of the reciprocal flesh of theirhisnothis fellowfaces" (U.702; XVII.1178, 1183–4). Their union has not only been anticipated, but at a subconscious level been made possible, by their mutual perception of Shakespeare in the mirror and by Stephen's sense in "Eumaeus" that he has been touched by a strange kind of flesh. Moreover, despite their very different perspectives, they do share a mutual need for friendship in a world where mortality is the only certainty. In Bloom's backyard, no longer the wasteland that he had imagined in "Calypso", but now a garden where renewal and rebirth are possible, "At Stephen's suggestion, at Bloom's instigation both, first Stephen, then Bloom, in penumbra urinated" together

(U.702; XVII.1186–7). It hardly needs saying that this moment puts to rest any possibility of misconstruing their friendship as homosexual, even as it shows the need in our culture for fresh language to describe male bonding.

That, as Bloom and Stephen separate, both respond to the bells of the church of Saint George with thoughts of death reminds us that death is a major antagonist in *Ulysses*. Of course, Stephen thinks of the prayer for the dying which he refused to say at his mother's deathbed, while Bloom thinks of the earlier association of the bells with the death of his acquaintance Dignam, whose death and its effects on his survivors Bloom characteristically feels as if Dignam were a member of his own family. Does not their mutual silent recognition of one another pointedly substitute social values for artistic ones and thus qualify the silence, cunning and exile that Stephen proposed for himself as artist at the end of *Portrait*? Indeed, is not the necessity for the artist to participate in social interaction in terms of family, passionate sexual relationships, and friendships, and to develop mature social values, including the ability to sympathize with the points of view of others, a major point of *Ulysses*? Bloom, the somewhat ostracized Irish Jew, is the paradigm for the social values that Stephen must learn. On one hand, Stephen has little affection for family or acquaintances and no palpable prospect of passionate love. On the other hand, Stephen is a poignantly divided self who has not reconciled various personal, social, and artistic claims he feels. Until he meets Bloom, he is in danger of fleeing from himself into an uncomfortable exile of aestheticism and narcissism and turning his back on the potentially socially and morally mature artistic self that is struggling to define itself.

Bloom and Stephen discover in one another significance – or, in our terms, metaphorical meaning – that confirms the kind of meaning proposed by the novel. Seeking an epiphanical experience, Stephen finds one. In "Ithaca", Stephen sees Bloom in terms of others who had befriended him. We recall his desperation even during his intellectual *tour de force* in the library: "I believe, O Lord, help my unbelief. That is, help me to believe or help me to unbelieve? . . . Life is many days. This will end" (U. 214; IX.1078–9, 1097). In his perception of Bloom in "Ithaca", Stephen is using the metaferocity – the poetic bard (Stephen) fused with the aggressive energy of the pard (Leopold) to produce the kinds of striking and bold metaphors which will be the essence of *Ulysses*. In Bloom Stephen hears "in a profound ancient male unfamiliar melody the accumulation of the past" (U.689; XVII.777–8). By accepting Bloom as a paradigm of historical iteration, of the very concept of metaphoricity, Stephen modifies his cynical rejection of history epitomized by his remark to Deasy in "Nestor" that "History . . . is a nightmare from which I am trying to awake" (U.34; II.377). When Stephen discovers in Bloom a metaphor for "The traditional figure of hypostasis" (in other words, the underlying substance of the trinity which makes the Word flesh) "with winedark hair" (an Homeric epithet for the sea fused with the heroic figure he requires for his art), is he not discovering the essential components of Joyce's art (U.689; XVII.783, 785)?

Stephen is a man who lives and dies by the metaphors he creates. Fusing spiritual father and mother (do we not recall the association of the sea with his mother?), Bloom becomes Stephen's "androgynous angel" (U.213; IX.1052). That in "Eumaeus" and "Ithaca", Stephen recognizes and acknowledges Bloom as "Christfox" – the fusion of Parnell and Christ into one figure – implies that Stephen might become "Christfox", the fusion of Christ and Parnell in the artist whose work will redeem Ireland (U.193; IX.336). Put another way, Stephen can begin exhuming the grandmother that he had buried "under a hollybush" (U.27; II.115). As Bloom lights the fire for his guest, Stephen thinks "Of others elsewhere in other times who, kneeling on one knee or on two, had kindled fires for him . . ." (U.670; XVII.135–6). Isn't this search for prior members of a series of signifiers the major technique of *Ulysses*? Our reading confirms the epistemological and teleological significance of the search for "others elsewhere in other times", whose behaviour resembles that of his characters in contemporary Dublin.

Bloom also lives in terms of metaphors – to name a few, Agendath Netaim, *Sweets of Sin*, the potato he carries around all day. Bloom lives in his imagination as surely as Stephen does, and it is this quality of imagination, more than any other, that enables him to be the artistic figure who will fuse with Stephen to write the novel. For his part, Bloom sees "in a quick young male familiar form the predestination of a future" and hears "The traditional accent of the ecstasy of catastrophe" – in other words, he imagines Stephen's walking into the future, but a future which to Bloom the Jew and bereaved father inevitably contains its undoing, "the ecstasy of catastrope" (U.689; XVII. 780, 786).

To patronize Bloom is to misread *Ulysses*, for Joyce is in awe of the man he calls Mr. Bloom. But to fail to recognize Joyce's gentle, good-natured irony towards Bloom is also an error. Thus Joyce believes that Bloom has the right to feel reasonable satisfaction for his day's work:

> What satisfied him?
> To have sustained no positive loss. To have brought a positive gain to others.
> Light to the gentiles. (U.676; XVII.351–3).

The gentiles are not merely Dignam's family, Mrs. Purefoy, Stephen, or the denizens of the bar in "Cyclops", but also the readers whose values Bloom's paradigmatic humanism is amending. Yet Joyce also smiles at Bloom's tendency to live in the optative case, where he finds refuge in his fantasies of perfecting both his own future and all humankind's: "[H]e desired to amend many social conditions, the product of inequality and avarice and international animosity" (U.696; XVII.990–2).

It is as much an error to think that, after meeting Bloom, Stephen is ready to become the mature artist as it is to ignore the implications of their meeting. For even after the crucial meeting the distance between Stephen and Shakespeare remains vast. The narrator has shown significant parallels that enable the reader to have an epiphany of a metaphorical union that transcends the action or its logical implications. Stephen's perspective has been modified and fertilized by that of Bloom, but we, not Stephen, have met Molly. On the literal level, we have scant evidence that he is ready to write *Ulysses*. At most, Stephen has begun a movement towards the voice that is telling the novel, but as the novel ends he has a very long way to go.

Indeed, one can argue that Stephen and Bloom barely respond to one another. That Stephen's cynical song ("Little Harry Hughes") about predestined fate awaiting the trusting and innocent has an anti-Semitic aspect shows how oblivious he is to Bloom's feelings; for the song evokes the Christian fear of Jews as mysterious figures whose sacrificial rites require that they prey on their children. Perhaps in the recesses of his imagination Stephen, who does not know Jews and whose mind has been inculcated from childhood by prejudice, is the potentially innocent victim being preyed upon by the wiliness of Jews. Joyce knew a great deal about Jewish tradition, and he may be using the song to laugh at the matchmaking tradition and at Bloom's efforts to find suitors for his wife and daughter. For the last stanza evokes sexual captivity and castration even as it mocks circumcision: "She took a penknife out of her pocket/ And cut off his little head./And now he'll play his ball no more/For he lies among the dead" (U.691; XVII.825–8).

Surely the dialogue between Stephen and Bloom at times reveals their intellectual estrangement, as when in "Eumaeus" Bloom and Stephen discuss the subject of intelligence (U.633–4; XVI.748ff). That Bloom and Stephen are urinating when they share a vision of the star shooting from the Lyre to Leo may undermine the symbolic significance insisted upon by the discourse. In reading *Ulysses* as a symbolic novel, we sometimes are in the position of taking signs for wonders, of turning the bread and wine of life into the Eucharist of meaning. While the novel's "discourse" or form insists that Stephen and Bloom see the star under the aegis of the missing member of the necessary trinity ("the mystery of an invisible attractive person, his wife Marion [Molly] Bloom, denoted by a visible splendid sign, a lamp"), its "story" or content reminds us that the men are simply and necessarily under her window and that the light is a "paraffin oil lamp" (U.702; XVII.1173–4; 1177–8). And the story provides neither a muse nor a symbol of the potential of woman, but a stereotypical, frustrated, lower middle class woman obsessed with sexuality at the expense of intellect and feelings.

On one hand, Bloom is the necessary principle that Stephen requires and must assimilate before he can become a mature artist – before Joyce can become the new Messiah of Ireland by combining in his transpersonal presence the values of Bloom, Stephen, and Molly. On the other hand, he is a middle-aged man who is fundamentally different in attitudes and values from Stephen, and the brief personal intimacy achieved for a few hours is based on very thin reeds. Given that their communion is based on drinking cocoa and urinating together, should we wonder whether their relationship and its significance may prove ephemeral?

V BLOOM ALONE: THE HUMAN DRAMA AFTER STEPHEN DEPARTS

Joyce wants the reader to understand that the story – the human situation of Bloom – does not support the metaphorical implications of the movement of Stephen's star towards that of Bloom. When, in a brief vignette recalling Stephen's and Bloom's shared vision of Shakespeare, Bloom looks into his mirror after Stephen departs, he does not see anything but a solitary mutable man:

> What composite asymmetrical image in the mirror then attracted his attention?
> The image of solitary (ipsorelative) mutable (aliorelative) man. (U.707–8; XVII.1348–50)

The riddle that answers the next question emphasizes both the theme of paternity and, in the context of Bloom's dead father and son, Bloom's poignant isolation and his desperate need to return to Molly:

> Why solitary (ipsorelative)?
>
> *Brothers and sisters had he none*
> *Yet that man's father was his grandfather's son.* (U.708; XVII.1351–3)

The solution to the riddle – a riddle which recalls Stephen's self-indulgent and insoluble riddle to his pupils – is Bloom himself. The next question calls attention not only to Bloom's growing resemblance to his father but also his artistic creator, Joyce.

> Why mutable (aliorelative)?
> From infancy to maturity he had resembled his maternal procreatrix. From maturity to senility he would increasingly resemble his paternal procreator.
> (U.708; XVII.1355–6)

The question and answer thus refocus our attention on the aesthetic theory of "Scylla and Charybdis" and the novel that insists on the relationship between an artist and his work.

Bloom knows that life is serendipitous and that signs should not be taken for wonders. In a comic version of the paternity theme, specifically of the theme that paternity is a legal fiction and that fatherhood depends on a mutually acknowledged relation between father and son and on the power of the imagination to create whatever hierarchical patterns that one wishes, a clown had declared to the audience that Bloom was his father: "an intuitive particoloured clown in quest of paternity had penetrated from the ring to a place in the auditorium where Bloom, solitary, was seated and had publicly declared to an exhilarated audience that he (Bloom) was his (the clown's) papa" (U.696; XVII.976–9). But, of course, the clown's claim is not true. As a figure who can create reality according to his own fantasy, the clown is an artist figure; but because of the association with Mulligan and Wilde, he is a jester whose one-dimensional story is irresponsibly narcissistic and fey.

In a comic version of the hope to return to the past, Bloom recalls how a coin that he had marked had never returned to his possession: "[O]nce in the summer of 1898 he (Bloom) had marked a florin (2/-) with three notches on the milled edge and tendered it in payment of an account due to and received by J. and T. Davy, family grocers, 1 Charlemont Mall, Grand Canal, for circulation on the waters of civic finance, for possible, circuitous or direct, return" (U.696; XVII.980–4). Only as readers can we return to past time, can we experience again the full thrust of an author's "marks" on a page or words, but as living humans we face the same inevitable conditions of life as the characters, and we can never retrace the steps we take and the marks we make. The necessary qualities and skills for reading books – perspicacity, sensitivity, memory, judiciousness – are the same as our tools for "reading" our experience. Yet, in one very important way, our lives as readers are at odds with our "real" lives. As readers we have the ability to re-enter time when and where we please by returning to prior places in the work and hence in the novel's imagined world. By contrast, in our lives, even when memory or trauma gives us the temporary illusion of returning to the past and even when passion or faith gives us the illusion of suspending the tick-tock of chronological time, the present continues inevitably forward to become the past.

The disjunction between man's putative patterns of significance and actuality is as much the point as the fulfilment of

Bloom's and Stephen's human quest and Joyce's own artistic quest. The vague plans for an epic novel that Joyce recalls having in mind in 1904 is hardly the novel that Joyce publishes eighteen years later as a forty-year-old exile who has lived two decades in Europe with his wife and family. Nor, as he recreates a version of the past in Stephen's characterization, is he rendering the actual life that he led on 16 June 1904. Despite perceiving prophetic signs of the potential artist, Bloom and Stephen are, like all of us, trapped in their mortality. Immediately before seeing the "new solar disk", which implies among other things the renewal of human life and its cyclical nature, Bloom had felt, as Stephen retreated, "The cold of interstellar space" along with "the incipient intimations of proximate dawn" (U.704; XVII.1246–8). These conflicting images enact the oscillation of Bloom's mind from despair to hope. But it is significant that following his feelings of coldness and loneliness, Bloom remains outside held by the dawn – "the diffusion of daybreak" – heralding the promise of a new beginning (U.705; XVII.1257).

But that he soon goes inside becomes a metonym for the way the book concludes, for the reader never sees the fulfilment of the prospects that are suggested. Like the Haggadah, the prayer book used at Passover, the holiday which haunts Bloom's imagination, and in particular, like the vital word "next" from the pivotal phrase in the Passover service "Next year in Jerusalem", the novel depends on thrusting our expectations beyond the text of the book. Put another way, Joyce's humanistic premise, like the Jewish promise of return to the Holy Land, and the Christian promise of Christ's second coming, depends upon presenting the *promise* and on postponing the *presence* of fulfilment. Isn't God's specific promise to Moses on Pisgah mount – that while the Jews will settle in the promised land, Moses will not live to lead them there – a prototype for the kind of reading experience where fulfillment remains as a future possibility rather than as a realized actuality?

VI THE EXPANSION OF BLOOM AT THE CONCLUSION OF "ITHACA"

Notwithstanding the deflating effect of Bloom's isolation and the focus on him as a mutable human being, the ending of "Ithaca" also continues Joyce's transformation of Bloom into a significant figure. But it does so without sacrificing his claims to our attention as a sympathetic human being who, rather than slaying Molly's suitor, *thinks* anxiously and enviously of his rival, kisses her bottom, briefly chats with his wife, and finally curls up and goes to sleep. Although he incorrectly imagines that Molly has frequently betrayed him, he accepts his plight. As Bloom climbs into bed, the narrator provides a question and answer that focuses on Bloom's complex emotional response to Molly's adultery:

> With what antagonistic sentiments were his subsequent reflections affected?
> Envy, jealousy, abnegation, equanimity. (U.732; XVII.2154–5).

The four one word questions – "Envy?", "Jealousy?", "Abnegation?", "Equanimity?" – parody psychoanalytic inquires into the causes of emotions and the kinds of rationalizations that psychoanalysis provides for accepting these emotions (U.732–3; XVII.2156, 2162, 2169, 2177). The answers analyse Bloom's emotions in terms that both mock the scientific claims of such inquiries and raise the question of whether it is possible for complex emotions to be understood in terms of formulaic linguistic formations. That the first two – "envy" and "jealousy" – are different names for the same thing verbally enacts how difficult it is for the cuckolded Bloom to move beyond envy. But the stress finally falls on, "equanimity", the last of the series of the emotions, just as at the end of "Penelope" it falls on Bloom as the last of the series of men in Molly's mind:

> Equanimity?
> As natural as any and every natural act of a nature expressed or understood executed in natured nature by natural creatures in accordance with his, her and their natured natures, of dissimilar similarity. As not so calamitous as a cataclysmic annihilation of the planet in consequence of a collision with a dark sun. (U.733; XVII.2177–82)

Although the reflexive repetition of "nature" shows how difficult it is for Bloom to rationalize adultery, nevertheless his equanimity is a necessary precondition if Molly's final "yes" is to imply the possibility of renewing their relationship.

As he rests in a fetal position (recalling Stephen's position at the end of "Circe",) "the childman weary, the manchild in the womb", he, like Shakespeare, contains all men and becomes the father of his race (U.737; XVII.2317–8). In a sense, as he rests, his imagination gives birth to an endless series of potential successors.

Womb? Weary?
He rests. He had travelled.

With?
Sinbad the Sailor and Tinbad the Tailor and Jinbad the Jailer and Whinbad the Whaler and Ninbad the Nailer and Finbad the Failer and Binbad the Bailer and Pinbad the Pailer and Minbad the Mailer and Hinbad the Hailer and Rinbad the Railer and Dinbad the Kailer and Vinbad the Quailer and Linbad the Yailer and Xinbad the Phthailer.

When?
Going to a dark bed there was a square round Sinbad the Sailor roc's auk's egg in the night of bed of all auks of the rocs of Darkinbad the Brightdayler.

Where?

(U.737; <u>XVII.2319–31</u>)

(Editions prior to 1961 had nothing after "Where?"; since 1961 most but not all editions have had a far larger orthographic dot after "Where?") That the chapter ends with an orthographic mark indicates that Joyce can take the ordinary language of conscious syntax no further and prepares us for Molly's stream of consciousness, or, perhaps more accurately, stream of unconsciousness.

Varying the first two letters of the two principle words in the series that begins with "Sinbad the Sailor", while keeping the rest of the sequence the same is an orthographic way of indicating Bloom's status as Everyman. In "Oxen of the Sun", Joyce had established Bloom as Everyman in the temporal dimension by describing him in a sequence of styles beginning with Celtic and Latin and climaxing in bastardized modern English. At the close of "Ithaca", Bloom is established as Everyman spatially, for he is at the center of a series of concentric circles from which human life radiates outward. Everyman is the Wandering Jew and the Wandering Jew is Everyman. Sinbad the Sailor recalls D. B. Murphy and the one-legged sailor, two nearly anonymous marginal men in Dublin, who along with the man in the macintosh, Bloom the dentist, and the orthographic error L. Boom are metonyms for Leopold Bloom. Joyce considered D. B. Murphy to be "Ulysses Pseudoangelos", an invalid Ulysses whose tale is apocryphal and who is a con man. Put in other terms, he is a signifier who, despite his pretensions to meaning, including the number sixteen tatooed on his chest in this the sixteenth chapter, signifies almost nothing.

The reader participates in a dialectical process that establishes Bloom's identity. "Darkinbad the Brightdayler" fulfils the typological pattern that associates Bloom with Christ. Notwithstanding the identification of Bloom with "Black panther", and, more ambiguously, with the light and dark spots of the leopard, Bloom gradually becomes more and more associated with light until the final chapter associates Bloom with the sun. Stephen had thought of the Jews in Paris in terms that echo John 1:45: "a darkness shining in brightness which brightness could not comprehend" (U.28; II.160); later he uses this phrase to describe worlds that are hidden beyond his capacity to see in terms of the very star that shines at the birth of Shakespeare, and which shone at Stephen's and Bloom's birth: "Darkly they are there behind this light, darkness shining in the brightness, delta of Cassiopeia, worlds" (U.48; III.409–10). Deasy's anti-Semitism speaks to the association of Christ with light and Jews with darkness: "They sinned against the light. . . . And you can see the darkness in their eyes. And that is why they are wanderers on the earth to this day" (U.34; II.361–3). In "Circe", the yellow soap had sung, "We're capital couple are Bloom and I./ He brightens the earth. I polish the sky" (U.440; XV.338–9). Yet the reader simultaneously recalls that Bloom is suffering the pain and loneliness of adultery which despite his rationalization has much more personal significance to his emotional life than the abstract possibility of cosmic events, including "a cataclysmic annihilation of the planet in consequence of a collision with a dark sun" (U.733; XVII.181–2). That Bloom's significance depends upon nonsensical syntax bathetically implies the possibility that our rage for order is creating significance where none exists; perhaps it also implies Joyce's own doubts about the ability to make the word flesh. *Ulysses* establishes a double vision of mankind. It implies that we all are potential Leopold Blooms, noble and decent and able to make a difference in the quality of life. Yet as anonymous creators of insignificant gestures we are also potential Blooms. But the possibility of nobility and decency is the dominant effect of our reading and the more pessimistic implication about man's meaninglessness and ineffectuality is subservient to it.

NOTES

1. Tzvetan Todorov, *The Poetics of Prose*, trans. Richard Howard (Ithaca, New York: Cornell University Press, 1977).
2. Hugh Kenner, *Joyce's Voices*, p. 47.
3. Lawrence, p. 168.
4. See Ellmann, *Ulysses on the Liffey*, p. 155.
5. See Gifford and Seidman, p. 449.
6. I want to acknowledge Barbara Heusel's unpublished work on "Eumaeus"; Ms Heusel was a participant in my Summer 1984 NEH Seminar entitled *Critical Perspectives on the Early Twentieth Century British Novel*.
7. *Letters*, I, 159–60.
8. Lawrence, pp. 195, 197.

10 "Penelope": Molly as Metaphor

Joyce concludes his epic of the body with Molly Bloom's monologue. Joyce wrote:

> Penelope is the clou/nail of the book . . . . It begins and ends with the female word yes. It turns like a huge earth ball slowly surely and evenly round and round spinning, its four cardinal points being the female breasts, arse, womb and cunt expressed by the words *because, bottom* (in all senses bottom button, bottom of the class, bottom of the sea, bottom of his heart), *woman, yes.* Though probably more obscene than any preceding episode it seems to be perfectly sane full amoral fertilisable untrustworthy engaging shrewd limited prudent indifferent *Weib.*[1]

After presenting a plethora of perspectives, and dramatizing his two principle characters in unusual detail and then bringing them together, Joyce turns to Molly: "The last word (human, all too human) is left to Penelope."[2] In terms of the story, he thought of "Penelope" as something of a coda: "The Ithaca episode . . . is in reality the end as Penelope has no beginning, middle or end."[3] But in terms of the novel's significance the presentation of Molly's perspective is essential. For Molly is the necessary ingredient, the Holy Ghost, necessary for him to complete the novel that is at once the story of how he moved beyond the limitations of his younger self, represented by Stephen; the anatomy of modern Ireland with its unlikely Jewish hero, Bloom; the discovery of the essential patterns which unite the major epochs of European civilization; and the epic of the body, epitomized by Molly.

While the plot does not require her characterization, the rhetoric – the fulfillment of the reader's expectations – does. For the reader of *Ulysses*, Molly is the deferred and anticipated presence; for the odyssean reader to complete his story of read-

258

ing, he must experience what Joyce calls "the indispensable countersign to Bloom's passport to eternity".[4] Molly deflates the reader's expectations of cosmic significance in terms of story, while at the same time expanding the novel's pretenses to cosmic significance in terms of metaphor. On one hand, she is a bawdy, sexually alive, uneducated woman intent on her own pleasure but appreciative of her husband's qualities; her point of view and style challenge the very process of organizing our reading of her monologue into metaphors or – in de Man's term – interpretative allegories. But, on the other hand, she completes the metaphorical and formal patterns of the novel. Most obviously, she is a way of expanding the novel spatially to include the prehuman, or at least pre-self-conscious world, that preceded modern man. Like Lawrence, Joyce is trying to find verbal equivalents for the physiological experience of the body. Molly is amoral, unconscious, and libidinous; her monologue is a lyrical explosion that comments on the prior intellectuality of the novel – upon the collecting sensibility of Bloom's imagination, upon Stephen's abstruse display of learning, and, yes, upon the fictionalized Joyce's obsessions with inclusiveness of subject matter and formal patterns.

Thus Molly represents values that are an important part of *Ulysses*. Her spontaneity represents an alternative to the contrivance and artificiality of style that we experience in some of the more mannered chapters such as "Oxen of the Sun" and "Sirens". It is true, as French writes, that "Joyce's point in 'Penelope' as well as elsewhere in *Ulysses* is that the unremitting intellect is the cause of much human torment."[5] Like Stephen, Joyce struggled within himself to overcome *his* unremitting intellect. Molly's "stream" of consciousness stands in contrast to the self-consciousness of Stephen and fragmentation of Bloom. Her immersion in life contrasts with Bloom's and Stephen's self-conscious Hamletizing, embodied in the phrase that each thinks of separately: "One life is all. One body. Do. But do" (U.202, 280; IX.653, XI.907–8); we should note how the second appearance of the phrase – in Bloom's monologue in "Sirens" – is preceded by "To be or not to be" (U.280; XI.905). Doesn't Molly live in her body? Doesn't Molly *do* sexually what Stephen and Bloom only imagine? Not unlike Stephen's, her view of the world is solipsistic, but she is not paralysed by her perceptions.

As a Penelope figure, Molly is a kind of artist unweaving at night what she has woven by day. Penelope had promised to marry one of her suitors when she finishes weaving an enormous web that will supposedly be a shroud for Ulysses's father, Laertes; the web is also metonymically a shroud for her missing husband and her marriage to him. To forestall the marriage day to her lucky suitor, she cunningly unravels at night what she weaves by day.[6] What Molly has woven by day is an affair with Blazes, but her reverie in bed reaffirms her commitment to Bloom. Her spontaneous, sexual, and lyrical voice unweaves what Maddox calls the "intricate tapestry of rationality which Bloom and Stephen have woven all day."[7] Untroubled by contradictions, she is an artist who weaves a pattern of her satisfactions and passion, her frustrations and dislikes, into an affirmation of her position on earth as human being who is entitled by her existence to pleasure and satisfaction.

The chapter begins with her acceding to Bloom's request to get him breakfast: "Yes because he never did a thing like that before as ask to get his breakfast in bed with a couple of eggs since the *City Arms* hotel" (U.738; XVIII.1–2). That she accedes to his assertive request indicates that the characteristic pattern of uxorious submission will be reversed on 17 June 1904. Her recalling that she had nourished him prior to their first intercourse by giving him seedcakes out of her mouth establishes the possibility that similarly nourishing him now will lead to the re-establishment of their sexual relationship.

By recasting the thoughts of Stephen and Bloom in her own terms, Molly not only unweaves what the novel has woven, but calls attention to the technique whereby a transpersonal presence reveals how three separate persons are linked by parallel thoughts. Thus she thinks of the bogus medical book *Aristotle's Masterpiece* – hilariously confusing Aristotle with Aristocrat – which Bloom had seen in the book stalls of "Wandering Rocks" and apparently once brought her: "if its the truth they don't believe you then tucked up in bed like those babies in the Aristocrats Masterpiece he brought me another time as if we hadnt enough of that in real life without some old Aristocrat or whatever his name is disgusting you more with those rotten pictures children with two heads and no legs" (U.772; XVIII.1237–41.) The real Aristotle holds no interest for Molly, who disdains the abstract thinking which characterizes Stephen's "intellectual

imagination" and who eschews Bloom's concern with the plight
of other people; that concern was the reason for his interest in
Aristotle's Masterpiece: "infants cuddled in a ball in bloodred
wombs like livers of slaughtered cows. Lots of them like that at
this moment all over the world. All butting with their skulls to
get out of it. Child born every minute somewhere. Mrs Purefoy"
(U.235; X.586–90). (Bloom is thinking not only of his once and
putative son, and of Mrs Purefoy, but of the cycle of human
regeneration that the energy and fecundity of Molly's monologue
– its style and subject matter – enact.)

Nor does Molly have any interest in Irish politics, a subject
which engages Bloom's attention: "he was going about with
some of them Sinner Fein lately or whatever they call themselves
talking his usual trash and nonsense he says that little man he
showed me without the neck is very intelligent the coming man
Griffiths . . . . I hate the mention of their politics after the war
that Pretoria and Ladysmith and Bloemfontein . . ." (U. 748;
XVIII.383–8). Drawn by the place name Bloemfontein, her
mind turns to the Boer War, not in terms of politics but in terms of
the memory of a former boyfriend who had apparently died of a
fever while stationed there. The Boer War, hated by the Irish as
an example of the rampant and threatening British imperialism,
is a subject to which both Stephen and Bloom had alluded;
Stephen had mentioned Kipling's propaganda poem, "The
Absent-Minded Beggar", and in one of Bloom's fantasies of
persecution in "Circe", he had defended himself with the argument that as a "staunch . . . Britisher" he had loyally fought in
the "absentminded war" under the apostate Irish-born General
Gough at "Spion Kop and Bloemfontein" (U.187, 457–8;
IX.125, XV.793–6).[8] That, while affirming the values of family
and private life, the novel has both discredited the politics of
Irish nationalism and established Bloom as the coming man
gives credence to Molly's position as a sexual, private person
concerned with her personal life. The reader of "Penelope" is
placed in the position of Stephen and Bloom when they look into
the mirror and see the image of Shakespeare; looking at Stephen
and Bloom as "Ithaca" fades out, the image of Molly appears to
the reader and demands to be understood in terms of what
precedes.

That Molly menstruates indicates that she has not been
impregnated by Blazes and that, if Bloom and she resume

intercourse, the possibility exists of her having the son Bloom desperately desires. Indeed, Stephen's analogy between the process of life and art is particularly applicable to her, for her body is the subject of art: "As we, or mother Dana, weave and unweave our bodies . . . from day to day, their molecules shuttled to and fro, so does the artist weave and unweave his image" (U.194; IX.376–8). As an artist, who speaks without self-consciousness of her memories and experience and uses her creative imagination to define herself, she provides a lesson for the fictionalized Joyce who will write *Ulysses*. Like Bloom, she has "found in the world without as actual what was in [her] world within as possible" (U.213; IX.1041-2). As she speaks, Word becomes flesh and flesh becomes Word in the divine process of art, and this finally is the ultimate metaphoricity upon which Joyce's art depends.

In terms of the metaphorical structure, Molly has several purposes. She is the goal of Bloom's Odyssean quest to return home and Stephen's quest for mature sexuality to complete himself. She is what Joyce's retrospective presence requires to complete both the Irish epic and his nominalistic fictionalized account of the crucial day in his life. In this sense, she plays the role of the traditional muse who must inspire the artist's creative process. Within the novel she may be a metaphor for the various Homeric archetypes, but she is also a metaphor for Nora. As Ellmann has written, "*Ulysses* is an epithalamium; love is its cause of motion."[9] The final chapter is a tribute to the role that Joyce believed Nora played in the creation of the artist. He wrote: "O take me into your souls . . . and then I will become indeed the poet of my race. I feel this, Nora, as I write it. My body will soon penetrate yours, O that my soul could too! O that I could nestle in your womb like a child born of your flesh blood, be fed by your blood, sleep in the warm and secret gloom of your body."[10] Reading this passage in which Joyce imagines that Nora gives birth to him, do we not recall Bloom's fetal position at the end of "Ithaca" and realize that Bloom requires Molly to recreate him? The little black dot after "Where?" is the potential seed of Bloom that might fertilize Molly, but it is also the seed from which Bloom might flower.

Molly is the fulfilment of the long-awaited expectations aroused in the reader that he might come to know the woman who haunts Bloom's imagination. As "flesh", following the chapters in which the organs were "nerves" ("Eumaeus") and "skeleton" ("Ithaca"), she weaves together the discrete parts of the body. Lying in bed preoccupied with sexuality, Molly completes for the reader the epic of the body. Molly represents hope for Ireland. It is as if, finally, her libidinous self-renewing energy puts aside the problems of Ireland's twin occupation by England and the Roman Catholic Church by implying that she will survive and transcend them. She becomes the symbolic Old Woman of Ireland and replaces the milkwoman of "Telemachus", as well as the midwives whom Stephen saw on the strand in "Proteus" and who became the catalysts for his ironic Parable of Plums.

For Bloom, Molly is also the New Jerusalem promised by the Passover Sedar. Indeed, her final reverie represents the conclusion of the Sedar when the door is opened for Elijah, the presence that has been awaited throughout the ceremony and indeed for centuries. At the close of the Sedar, verses depicting Jerusalem in the form of a beloved young maiden who is associated with flowers – "a rose of sharon, a lily of valleys" – are sung from the "Song of Solomon". Bloom associates Molly with flowers (the "rose of Castille" and the rhododendrons on the Howth), and Molly embraces this association: "[H]e said I was a flower of the mountain" (U.782; XVIII.1576).

Because Molly represents the sexuality Stephen requires, she is the ironic fulfillment of Stephen's dream of being led by a man with melons: "That man led me, spoke. I was not afraid. The melon he had he held against my face. Smiled: creamfruit smell" (U.47; III.367–8); "A creamfruit melon he held to me" (U.217; IX.1208). When Bloom kisses Molly's backside, described metaphorically as melons, hasn't Bloom not only returned to the promised land but also pointed the way for Stephen? "He kissed the plump yellow smellow melons of her rump, on each plump melonous hemisphere, in their mellow yellow furrow, with obscure prolonged provocative melonsmellonous osculation" (U.734–35; VII.2241–3). We recall that the prospectus for Agendath Netaim promised "immense melonfields" and that Bloom associates the commercial enterprise of investing in the Holy Land with, among other places, Gibraltar, Molly's birthplace: "Coming all that way: Spain, Gibraltar, Mediterranean, the Levant" (U.60; IV.194, 211–2). Just as Jerusalem is the symbolic light for the long suffering Jews, Molly's "paraffin oil lamp" becomes for both Bloom and Stephen a "visible luminous sign" of the absent Molly:

> What visible luminous sign attracted Bloom's, who attracted Stephen's, gaze? (U.702; XVII.1171–4)

In one sense, Joyce has tested Molly in the roles of Calypso, Circe, and even Nausicaa, before discarding these false roles and defining her in her proper role as Penelope. In another sense, Joyce shows us that Molly contains all these figures and is not only Everywoman, but the principle of sexuality which is an essential part of the "all in all in all of us" (U.213; IX.1049–50). She is also an alternative to the ersatz sexuality of Martha Clifford and Gerty MacDowell as well as to the various forms of perversion in "Circe". Indeed, Molly becomes Mother Danu, the Celtic goddess of plenty and fertility, and thus provides an alternative to the sterility of prior female images of Ireland. That Bloom has once asked her to provide the milk for Bloom's tea ("I had to get him to suck them they were so hard he said it was sweeter and thicker than cows then he wanted to milk me into the tea") underlines her metaphorical role as a potential fecund replacement for the Old Woman of Ireland (U.754; XVIII.576–8). Do we not recall the old milkwoman who had brought milk for the tea in "Telemachus?" While Stephen had perceived her in terms of the ironic metaphor of the Old Woman of Ireland, she had, to his dismay, acknowledged Mulligan while slighting him. Molly's love of flowers contrasts with the sterility of the midwives in Stephen's parable who spit the plum pits onto the concrete beneath Nelson's pillar.

That Molly is of indeterminate rather than Celtic blood makes her, for Joyce, an appropriate image for the Ireland that he imagines would be based on internationalist principles and would acknowledge the variety of the Irish people. In his essay, "Ireland, Island of the Saints and Sages", Joyce mocked the idea of racial purity, pointed out that most of the Irish heroes of recent centuries were not of Irish stock, and argued that "Nationality . . . must find its reason for being rooted in something that surpasses and transcends and informs changing things like blood and the human word."[11]

Given the novel's focus on the equation of Israel and Ireland, we realize that the putative reunion of Molly and Bloom within the novel represents the potential restoration of Ireland. We recall that Molly has been identified throughout with the Zionist dream of renewing the Holy Land; perhaps the climax of this motif is Bloom's meditation at the end of "Nausicaa" which concluded: "dreams return tail end Agendath swoony lovey showed me her next year in drawers return next in her next her next" (U.382; XIII.1283–5). Joyce is drawing upon a tradition which conceived of Israel as a woman; as M. H. Abrams puts it, she is "the beloved but faithless, and therefore divorced and exiled, bride of the Lord, to whom is held out the promise, when she shall repent, of reunion with the bridegroom".[12] As the Wandering Jew, the exile, the man in search of a return home, Bloom is part of the tradition which sees the goal of the quest as the New Jerusalem, conceived in terms – as in the famous passage from *Revelation*, 22:17 – of a woman inviting the wanderer to an eternal wedding: "And the Spirit and the bride say, Come. And let him that heareth say, Come. And let him that is athirst come."[13] Parodoxically, as in the *Odyssey*, what seems a linear voyage becomes, finally, a circular return. And this, for Joyce, is an apt model for human history.

Since Joyce was familiar with Bruno and Boehme as well as with the contemporary theosophists and mystics in Ireland, especially Yeats and Russell, he would have known the Hermetic tradition that conceives of man as an androgynous figure who "has disintegrated into the material and bisexual world of alien and conflicting parts, yet retains the capacity for recovering his lost integrity".[14] Stephen introduces this tradition when he thinks in "Proteus" of "Adam Kadmon", the primordial unfallen, complete, and androgynous One Man of the Kabbalah, and Heva, the Eve figure in the Kabbalistic tradition who, because she was not mothered, has no navel. As Leopold Paula Bloom and as the man who contains within his imagination in "Circe" the female and male experiences of Bella and Bello Cohen, isn't Bloom a version of the androgynous man? Since Bloom is – to recall Stephen's description of Shakespeare in "Scylla and Charybdis" – the "all in all" as "Adam Kadmon" and as Christ, another androgynous figure according to Hermetic tradition, Molly must be thought of as an objectification or, in theosophic terms, a manifestation of Bloom. She is the *Shekkinah* or "the feminine principle which is both antithesis and complement to the masculine principle within the divine unity."[15]

But Molly also has androgynous impulses and fantasies. Androgyny, we realize, is not only a metaphor for Bloom, the paradigmatic figure on whom Ireland depends for revival, but also for reconciliation after sundering – a key recurring motif that, finally, becomes a dominant (but not monolithic) principle as the book concludes. Androgyny is a metaphor for resolving the pervasive binary opposition that confronts the reader, whether it be the aesthetic opposition between the digressive claims of individual nominalistic passages and chapters and the contrary claims of the whole for organic unity, or the thematic opposition between the often conflicting claims of national and personal values. Containing within himself – as Stephen claimed for Shakespeare – "all in all in all of us", the epic novelist for Joyce is the successor to Adam Kadmon and Christ; hence, he is androgynous and contains the female muse (U.213; IX.1049–50).

Joyce felt that only under the profound influence of Nora could he make the Word flesh. Molly is both fictionalized Nora and the muse Joyce had to create before he could write the profane epic of the body. Writing of Molly enables Joyce to demonstrate that his fictionalized self, the narrative-presence, has, like Shakespeare but unlike the twenty-two-year old Stephen on 16 June 1904, had mature sexual experience, has had the necessary intercourse with the world. As Stephen puts it in "Oxen of the Sun", "In woman's womb word is made flesh but in the spirit of the maker all flesh that passess becomes the word that shall not pass away" (U.391; XIV.292–4). Or, in our terms, metaphoricity – the word made flesh – depends on sexuality. For Joyce, sexual experience is a necessary precondition of the artist's ability to make the Word become flesh; it is the precondition which would enable Stephen's abstractions to become the praxis of *Ulysses*. Thus Joyce is replacing the tradition that Christ's incarnation without intercourse is the appropriate model for the transformation of the Word into flesh.

Molly is essential for Joyce's idea that the possibility of mature art, art that depicts a complex knowledge of the world, depends upon the artist's experiencing a pasionate sexual relationship. Such a relationship, although frustrating and difficult, becomes, as the lives of Shakespeare and Bloom illustrate, a passport to experience. It enables the artist to remake the "[s]ignatures of all things" – a phrase that comes from Boehme and shows

Joyce's awareness of the Hermetic tradition – into a pattern
that will have meaning for others; put another way, it makes
possible the novel's progressive movement from the lyrical to the
epical and, finally, the dramatic (U.37; III.2). Molly is what
Stephen requires. Yet we should recall that as Stephen leaves
Bloom's house and walks into the night he remains unfulfilled,
and the questions, "And my turn? When?", that he asked
himself while thinking of how Ann Hathaway – like Molly, a
sexually experienced older woman – seduced the young Shakespeare, remain unanswered (U.191; IX.261).

To some readers, including French, Molly does not seem a
complete person because of her indifference to politics, disregard
for both mortality and morality, and neglect of the feelings of
others.[16] But is Joyce's creative impulse for Stephen and Bloom
always realistic? They, like Molly, are at times illuminating
distortions, defined by the context of Joyce's world and themes
to signify something beyond their identity as characters. Moreover, Molly's monologue reveals her as a rather complex,
albeit unsophisticated, woman who is coming to terms with what
is probably her first act of adultery: "anyhow its done now once
and for all with all the talk of the world about its people make it
only the first time after that its just the ordinary do it and think
no more about it" (U.740;XVIII.100–2). Not immune to the
values of middle class respectability, she is not able to provide
sufficient rationalization to assuage her feelings of guilt: "that
thunder woke me up God be merciful to us I thought the heavens
were coming down about us to punish us when I blessed myself
and said a Hail Mary like those awful thunderbolts in Gibraltar
as if the world was coming to an end and then they come and tell
you theres no God what could you do if it was running and
rushing about nothing only make an act of contrition" (U.741;
XVIII.134–9. Gabler's corrections – particularly moving "as if
the world was coming to an end" from after "woke me" to its
present position – both clarify the antecedent of the "it" and
sharpen the parallel between Molly's fear of thunder, which she
can articulate to herself, and Stephen's nearly catatonic response
in "Oxen of the Sun"). Her simple faith, of course, contrasts
with Stephen's apostasy and Father Conmee's hypocrisy. As she
turns increasingly away from the adultery with Blazes towards
re-establishing her relationship with Bloom, she unweaves by
night what she has woven by day.

Ellmann contends that "The narrative level of the book has by this time become less important."[17] But I believe it is the odyssean reader's experience of Molly's nominalistic, idiosyncratic, and eccentric narrative that confirms the values of the novel – namely that life, with all its frustrations, incomprehensibility, quirks, and contradictions must take precedence over the categorizing sensibility of both Bloom and Stephen and over the rigidity of Platonic formulations, whether they be religious and political solutions or even the kind of artistic patterns on which *Ulysses* is based. Ellmann brilliantly writes of the significance of the menstrual blood in the chamberpot: "In allowing Molly to menstruate at the end Joyce consecrates the blood in the chamberpot rather than the blood in the chalice, mentioned by Mulligan at the beginning of the book. For this blood is substance, not more or less than substance. The great human potentiality is substantiation, not transubstantiation, or subsubstantiation. It is this quality which the artist has too, in that he produces living human characters, not ethereal or less than human ones."[18] For menstrual blood is menstrual blood, just as urine is urine, and the epic of the body – with its attention to the physicality of the body – resists and undermines abstract allegories of reading and insists upon the reader's immersion in the functions and substances of life. Molly's obsessive sexuality is an expression of Joyce's conception of Nora, perhaps a conception that only a man with his religious background could have had. As artistic "father" of her uninhibited sexual energy – in the sense of creator – Joyce thus has a kind of control over the physiological life of Molly-Nora that, we know from his letters, he feared he might lose in life.

Yet we do need to take seriously the experience of some readers that Molly is less of a character than Stephen or Bloom. Perhaps at times Joyce's desire to give Molly metaphorical significance undermines her credibility as a character. Put another way, the needs of discourse or significance undermine the demands of story. Moreover, it is a feature of Joyce's imagination – think of Gretta in "The Dead" or the various women in *Portrait* – that men are in motion, while women are at rest. Men generate experience, women are the recipients. In Joyce's world, the men move and the women remain stationary because the men provide the movement and energy in the modern world. We see Molly at home, Gerty on the strand, Bella in nighttown, Miss

Douce and Miss Kennedy in the bar, but we never see them outside their characteristic setting. Once women are *placed*, they do not move. For despite the rapid motion of her stream of consciousness, Molly lies stationary in bed. That Molly's life is composed of bits and snips of experience and revolves around her sexual life and fantasies may reflect Joyce's recreation of Nora, but it also indicates for us, far more than Joyce realizes, the way women could be assigned to the cupboards of male authors' worlds.

If we recall the end of *Portrait*, we can see how Joyce has chosen a subject and technique for Molly that enacts the movement of his imagination from the Daedalean or Apollonian impulse to an Orphean or Dionysian one. The former had dominated the presentation of Stephen in the Telemachiad, and had played an important if decreasing role in the presentation of Bloom as the novel progressed. In Molly's ability to recreate reality in her own imagination, she represents the latent romantic strand within Joyce's sensibility and within *Ulysses*. Her monologue enacts the essence of her present life, even as it recaptures her past. Even if she arises to get Bloom breakfast and even if she resumes her sexual relationship with Bloom and turns her back on Blazes, her potential for growth and development is, in contrast to Stephen and Bloom, limited. She is actuality to their potentiality.

Crucial to Molly's acknowledgement of Bloom's stature is her identification of Bloom with the sun; for her identification confirms, in terms of her personal needs and in terms of the novel's evolving significance, the metaphorical value of Bloom that both the cosmos and Stephen have recognized. No sooner does Molly inquire about the First Cause of creation and associates it with the mystery of the daily sunrise ("who was the first person in the universe before there was anybody that made it all who ah that they don't know neither do I so there you are they might as well try to stop the sun from rising tomorrow . . . "), than she recalls Bloom's and her climactic day on the Howth: "[H]e said I was a flower of the mountain yes so we are flowers all a womans body yes that was one true thing he said in his life and the sun shines for you today yes that was why I liked him because I saw he understood or felt what a woman is . . . " (U.782; XVIII.1569–71, 1576–9).

In a sense Bloom is Molly's sun, described in "Ithaca" as "a solar disk" which refers both to the miraculous star that appeared at the birth of Bloom and Stephen and Shakespeare as well as to the sun that appears each morning at daybreak (U.705; XVII.1257–8). Bloom is her first cause, and she inevitably turns to him. When she concludes, "yes I said yes I will Yes", does not the movement from past to future imply that she will acknowledge him, just as each morning Gea Tellus, the earth, must acknowledge the sun in whose orbit it rotates (U.783; XVIII.1608–9)?

That the cosmos by producing a new sun responds to Bloom's birth is Joyce's way of signifying Bloom's artistic and moral potential. The sun, of course, traditionally implies renewal. In "Calypso," Bloom had proposed to follow the sun for a day as a way of forestalling time (U.57; IV.85ff). In "Nestor" Stephen had inadvertently prophesied the coming of a new sun in terms of the traditional pun for Christ – sun/son – when thinking of the biblical "darkness shining in brightness which brightness could not comprehend" (U.28; II.160). We recall that in "Scylla and Charybdis", Stephen is thinking of the supernova that was discovered above Delta in 1572 (and which outshone all the stars for a brief time) when Shakespeare was eight and one-half, and which Elizabethans thought, like the Star of Bethlehem, heralded Christ's coming. Since Delta is a star at the bottom of the left-hand loop of the constellation of Cassiopeia which forms a "W" in the northern skies – representing, in Stephen's metaphorical imagination, Shakespeare's first name, Stephen may have in mind that the next supernova above Delta would foreshadow an artist whose name begins with "D", namely "Dedalus".[19]

The ascendency of Bloom at the climax of Molly's reverie emphasizes his triumph:

O and the sea the sea crimson sometimes like fire and the glorious sunsets and the figtrees in the Alameda gardens yes and all the queer little streets and the pink and blue and yellow houses and the rosegardens and the jessamine and geraniums and cactuses and Gibraltar as a girl where I was a Flower of the mountain yes when I put the rose in my hair like the Andalusian girls used or shall I wear a red yes and how he kissed me under the Moorish wall and I thought well as well him as another and then I asked him with my eyes to ask again yes and then he asked me would I yes to say yes my mountain flower and first I put my arms around him yes and drew him down to me so he could feel my breasts all perfume yes and his heart was going like mad and yes I said yes I will Yes. (U.783; XVIII.1598–1609)

Within her mind Molly slays the suitors; she recalls when Bloom was, as Blazes is now, a lusty young man who wore a straw hat. Even though Blazes is a vigorous lover, she prefers Bloom: "I dont know Poldy has more spunk in him" (U.742; XVIII.167–8).

By transforming the sea into a positive sexual image (as opposed to Stephen's hydrophobia and obsessive association of the green sea with his mother's death), and appropriating flowers to her sexual reveries (as opposed to the sterile figure of the pseudonymous Henry Flower), her crescendo is a means of exposing for the reader what has been nay-saying and life-denying in Stephen and Bloom. Does not the breathless movement of her language – emphasized by the increasing frequency of the resoundingly affirmative "Yes", which is associated with her original intercourse with Bloom on the Howth – itself mime their mutual orgasm? Isn't Joyce's point that Molly's orgasm and epiphany are one? Recreating her memory of the first intercourse with Bloom on the Howth, the very moment that haunts and pleasures Bloom's memory, the ending is a performance, a celebratory enactment, a passionate explosion, of her sexuality. As she says "Yes" to Bloom, she joins Stephen, the various voices created by Joyce, the real Joyce who creates those voices to represent his fictionalized self, and the reader in saying "Yes" to Bloom's humanistic values and the potential effectiveness of those values. Within the lives of Molly and Bloom, "Yes" suggests the power of the imagination to evoke the presence of the past and the potential fulfilment of the future. Very much in the tradition of Wordsworth, Proust, and Wallace Stevens, Joyce uses Molly to affirm the power of the imagination to isolate a past moment out of time. Just as she provides the seed for Bloom in the Howth scene, androgynously reversing the expectations that the male fertilizes the female, as muse she fertilizes the imagination of the artist.

In her final passage, Molly acknowledges Bloom's stature in terms which dramatize how, within her mind, Bloom as a metaphor triumphs over Bloom as metonymy. For recognition of

Bloom's supremacy shows that he is not merely part of an endless series of interchangeable males – along with Mulvey, Boylan, d'Arcy and a series of fantasy lovers – as the indeterminate "he" of her sexual reveries; nor is he part of an endless series of putative fathers for Stephen – along with Mulligan, Deasy, Artifoni, and, indeed, Simon. In other words, he is not a metonymical figure based on contiguity who can be thought of as interchangeable with the other members of the series. That Bloom achieves vital metaphorical stature for Stephen and Molly is part of Bloom's triumph and part of the reason that the novel persuades us to confer significance upon him. In terms of the novel's typological or metonymical structure, Molly's punning thought "a flower that bloometh" (U.759; XVIII.775) echoes a phrase from his hallucination in "Circe": "There is a flower that bloometh" (U.517; XV.2489–90), and thus shows the affinity between herself and her husband. For Molly, and, indeed for the reader, Bloom's very name has "an origin and a force which are themselves 'metaphorical'".[20] By contrast, Blazes is reduced to metonymically representing Bloom's absent penis, before he is finally displaced within Molly's mind by the whole for which he stood as a part.

Molly's simple and stark, yet lyrical and performative, iteration of "yes" contrasts with the digressive minds of Stephen, Bloom, Joyce's presence, and, of course, herself. It is a rejection of Stephen's negativism, epitomized by "*Nothung*", his punning invocation of Siegfried's sword in "Circe" (U.583; XV.4242). "Yes" is an affirmation of Bloom's and Molly's mutual acceptance of one another on the Howth. Despite her spitefulness, she affirms her belief in passionate love.

In addition to the diachronic dimension of the final affirmation, in which the reader is urged to look forward to the possibility of a restored relationship in the future, the last passage also makes a crucial synchronic affirmation. By beginning and ending the chapter with the capitalized "Yes", and thus reversing the letters "y", "e", and "s" of the opening word "*Stately*", Joyce typographically affirms his cyclical and synchronic view of history. He also implies the continuity of human life, indeed, the stream of life represented by the presence of the Liffey which has flowed through Dublin prior to human history. Thus "yes" is, finally, a word that stands at the very center of the novel's concentric circles rippling outward to the various cultures and historical and literary personae that are metaphorically evoked and returning again to their present day sources. The "stream of life" is a metaphor within the novel for the processes of the body as well as for the perpetuation of crucial similarities within history, similarities that belie the notion that history is progressive and moves toward one great goal (U.153; VIII.95.) Like Bloom, Molly affirms the continuity of human life as a value and turns her back on "Eat or be eaten. Kill! Kill! (U.170; VIII.703).

Do not the constant motion and energy of Molly's prose enact the triumph of "the stream of life?" Associated with renewal in nature, mountains, flowers, fecundity, and sexuality, Molly becomes a metaphor for the stream of life: "I love flowers Id love to have the whole place swimming in roses God of heaven theres nothing like nature the wild mountains then the sea and the waves rushing then the beautiful country with the fields of oats and wheat and all kinds of things and all the fine cattle going about that would do your heart good to see rivers and lakes and flowers all sorts of shapes and smells and colours springing up even out of the ditches primroses and violets nature it is . . ." (U.781; <u>XVIII.1557–63</u>). Her stream of consciousness becomes the ultimate metaphor for the energy that makes intellectual, spiritual, and artistic growth possible. To use the metaphor that Stephen uses for Shakespeare, her imagination turns everything into grist for her mill.

Since, as we have seen, the novel resists one-dimensional stories of reading, we should be attentive to the secondary and marginal implications of the ending. Although within her mind, Bloom becomes more and more predominant, he still retains a touch of the uxorious husband; she imagines herself as the active figure reaccepting the compliant lover. And in a kind of pentimento, the memory of the earlier relationship with Mulvey on Gibraltar intrudes and metonymically suggests the sexual variety – in the form of, specifically, Blazes – that poses a threat to Bloom's return and thus a qualification of the prophecy implied by Molly's reacceptance of Bloom. The superimposition of the earlier reverie reminds the reader that in *Ulysses* sexual desires are often at odds with the needs for more permanent and stable relationships.

In terms of both our local response to the moment in time when Molly speaks and our placing the conclusion in the context of our interpretive quest, the concluding affirmation requires a pluralistic reading that accounts for its ambiguous implications. For one thing, Molly's monologue contains sexual relationships that are incomplete. For another, the putative renewal of the Bloom–Molly relationship exists at best in potentiality. But it is not dramatized within the novel. Nor is there any rational reason to suppose that the restoration of Molly to Bloom will have any effect on the quality of life in Dublin. Finally, her monologue shows that each of us lives life within his or her own mind. As an affirmation that each of us lives within our own perceptions (that, as Conrad's Marlow puts it in *Heart of Darkness*, "We live, as we dream – alone"), her monologue challenges the novel's major implication that history repeats itself; how can history *really* repeat itself if everyone is really unique? If each of us lives in our own perceptions, can we have any confidence that any created vision (including, for all his historical range and ventriloquism, that of the narrative presence of *Ulysses*) is able to see the entire pattern? Indeed, Molly's monologue reminds us that parallax – different perspectives on the same data – always undermines pattern and that neither Molly nor the artist can weave a holistic pattern whose meaning completely transcends the idiosyncrasies of the characters or imposes itself on the diverse readers.

Standing for the passionate sexual intercourse which Stephen requires, "Yes" is the ultimate metaphor. For sexual intercourse signifies the artistic intercourse which Stephen–Joyce must have to write the novel. But within the context of the novel, "Yes" paradoxically also becomes a word that says "No" to the reader who seeks significance from every detail on this crucial day, to the reader who seeks – as Molly urges of Bloom in "Calypso" – to have *Ulysses* "Tell us in plain words", and even to the reader who requires that the conclusion be a metaphor for a resolution to the problems of Stephen, Bloom, and the teller (U.64; IV.343). For, notwithstanding the potential value of "yes", the passionate heterosexual experience that both Bloom and Stephen desperately need – and which Odysseus presumably has on his return home and Shakespeare had before becoming a mature artist – eludes them both on 16 June 1904. And 17 June remains an unwritten script. Perhaps the inconclusiveness of the action is itself a metaphor for – a signification of – Joyce's awareness that his own quest to render his fictionalized life as the ingredients of an epic and to discover styles adequate to his intent must always fall short. Within the imagined world of *Ulysses*, the failure of Stephen to begin writing as well as of Bloom to sleep with Molly implies formally that the reader's quests for fulfilment and meaning – in both life and texts – are likely to be partial and incomplete.[21]

Finally, metaphoricity is a process, not a fulfilled goal. Bloom is proposed as a signifier for Ulysses, Moses, Christ, Shakespeare, and Parnell; he is examined in that metaphorical context, and in turn used to examine his predecessors. But does not the conclusion with its unfulfilled expectations drive a fissure between signifier and signified, and create the possibility that Bloom the man has been inadequate to the style, even as the style has been inadequate to the man? We realize that metaphoricity is as much part of Joyce's quest for meaning as the epistemological quest of Marlow is for Conrad. In the terms I have used, does not the novel discover that metaphoricity can only approach, but never quite reach, the historical and moral significance of Bloom? With its multiple styles and its consequent failure to establish the authority of any one style, *Ulysses* enacts the Zeno's paradox of much modernist literature: words always must fall short of their intent and subject. For the reader understands that, for all its brilliance and imaginative energy, Joyce's language must prove partially inadequate to the grace of Bloom's zest for life and feeling for humanity, must prove partially inadequate to the grace and benediction of Bloom's passionate love for Molly.

NOTES

1. *Letters*, I. 170.
2. *Letters*, I. 159–160.
3. *Letters*, I. 172–3.
4. *Letters*, I. 159–60.
5. French, p. 250.
6. See *The Odyssey*, II. 91 ff, trans. by Albert Cook.
7. Maddox, p. 231.
8. See Gifford and Seidman, p. 380.
9. Ellmann, *James Joyce*, p. 379.
10. *Selected Letters*, p. 169; quoted in Rader, p. 16.
11. *The Critical Writings of James Joyce*, eds. Ellmann and Mason, p. 166.
12. M. H. Abrams, *Natural Supernaturalism* (New York: Norton, 1971) p. 155.

13. Quoted in Abrams, p. 165.
14. Abrams, p. 155.
15. Abrams, p. 156.
16. See French, *The Book as World.*
17. Ellmann, *Ulysses on the Liffey*, p. 174.
18. Ellmann, *Ulysses on the Liffey*, p. 171.
19. See Gifford and Seidman, p. 198.
20. Quoted in Culler's *On Deconstruction*, from *Marges*, p. 321.
21. While sympathetic to Ellmann's eloquent reading of the concept of love in his "The Big Word in 'Ulysses,'" *The New York Review of Books*, 31:16 (25 Oct. 1984) 31–2, I am doubtful that *Ulysses* "is one of the most concluded books ever written" (p. 31).

Appendix: Joyce's Schema for *Ulysses*

Title	*Scene*	*Hour*	*Organ*	*Art*	*Colour*	*Symbol*	*Technic*	*Correspondences*
I *Telemachia*								
1 "Telemachus"	The Tower	8 a.m.		Theology	White, gold	Heir	Narrative (Young)	*Stephen*: Telemachus, Hamlet; *Buck Mulligan*: Antinous; *Milkwoman*: Mentor
2 "Nestor"	The School	10 a.m.		History	Brown	Horse	Catechism (Personal)	*Deasy*: Mentor; *Sargent*: Pisistratus; *Mrs O'Shea*: Helen
3 "Proteus"	The Strand	11 a.m.		Philology	Green	Tide	Monologue (Male)	*Proteus*: Primal Matter; *Kevin Egan*: Menelaus; *Cocklepicker*: Megapenthus
II *Odyssey*								
4 "Calypso"	The House	8 a.m.	Kidney	Economics	Orange	Nymph	Narrative (Mature)	*Calypso*: The Nymph; *Dlugacz*: The Recall; *Zion*: Ithaca

continued on page 278

Appendix: continued

Title	Scene	Hour	Organ	Art	Colour	Symbol	Technic	Correspondences
II Odyssey								
5 "Lotuseaters"	The Bath	10 a.m.	Genitals	Botany, Chemistry		Eucharist	Narcissism	*Lotuseaters:* The Cabhorses, Communicants, Soldiers, Eunuchs, Bather, Watchers of Cricket
6 "Hades"	The Graveyard	11 a.m.	Heart	Religion	White, black	Caretaker	Incubism	*Dodder, Grand, & Royal Canals, Liffey:* The 4 Rivers. *Cunningham:* Sisyphus *Father Coffey:* Cerberus. *Caretaker:* Hades. *Daniel O'Connell:* Hercules *Dignam:* Elpenor. *Parnell:* Agamemnon. *Menton:* Ajax
7 "Aeolus"	The Newspaper	12 noon	Lungs	Rhetoric	Red	Editor	Enthymemic	*Crawford:* Aeolus *Incest:* Journalism *Floating Island:* Press
8 "Lestrygonians"	The Lunch	1 p.m.	Esophagus	Architecture		Constables	Peristaltic	*Antiphates:* Hunger *The Decoy:* Food

	Scene	Hour	Organ	Art	Colour	Symbol	Technic	Correspondences
9 "Scylla and Charybdis"	The Library	2 p.m.	Brain	Literature		Stratford London	Dialectic	*The Rocks:* Aristotle Dogma, Stratford *The Whirlpool:* Plato Mysticism, London *Ulysses:* Socrates, Jesus, Shakespeare
10 "Wandering Rocks"	The Streets	3 p.m.	Blood	Mechanics		Citizens	Labyrinth	*Bosphorus:* Liffey *European Bank:* Viceroy. *Asiatic Bank:* Conmee *Symplegades:* Groups of Citizens
11 "Sirens"	The Concert Room	4 p.m.	Ear	Music		Barmaids	Fuga per Canonem	*Sirens:* Barmaids *Isle:* Bar
12 "Cyclops"	The Tavern	5 p.m.	Muscle	Politics		Fenian	Gigantism	*Noman:* I. *Stake:* Cigar *Challenge:* Apotheosis
13 "Nausicaa"	The Rocks	8 p.m.	Eye, Nose	Painting	Grey, blue	Virgin	Tumescence, detumescence	*Phaeacia:* Star of the Sea *Gerty:* Nausicaa
14 "Oxen of the Sun"	The Hospital	10 p.m.	Womb	Medicine	White	Mothers	Embryonic development	*Hospital:*Trinacria *Nurses:* Lampetie, Phaethusa. *Horne:* Helios. *Oxen:* Fertility. *Crime:* Fraud
15 "Circe"	The Brothel	12 Midnight	Locomotor Apparatus	Magic		Whore	Hallucination	*Circe:*Bella

III *Nostos*							
16 "Eumaeus"	The Shelter	1 a.m.	Nerves	Navigation	Sailors	Narrative (Old)	*Skin the Goat:* Eumaeus. *Sailor:* Ulysses Pseudangelos. *Corley:* Melanthius
17 "Ithaca"	The House	2 a.m.	Skeleton	Science	Comets	Catechism (Impersonal)	*Eurymachus:* Boylan *Suitors:* Scruples *Bow:* Reason
18 "Penelope"	The Bed		Flesh		Earth	Monologue (Female)	*Penelope:* Earth *Web:* Movement

Selected Bibliography

The following list includes all critical and scholarly studies cited in the notes plus works that have been particularly significant in the development of my argument.

Abrams, M. H., *Natural Supernaturalism* (New York: Norton, 1971).

Adams, Robert M. *Surface and Symbol: the Consistency of James Joyce's Ulysses* (New York: Oxford University Press, 1962).

———, *James Joyce: Common Sense and Beyond* (New York: Random House, 1966).

Atherton, James S., *The Books at the Wake: a Study of Literary Allusions in James Joyce's Finnegans Wake* (New York: Viking, 1960).

Auerbach, Erich, *Mimesis: the Representation of Reality in Western Literature*, trans. Willard Trask (Princeton University Press, 1953).

Blackmur, R. P., "The Jew in Search of a Son", *Virginia Quarterly Review*, XXIV (1948) 109–12; rpt. in *Eleven Essays on the European Novel* (New York: Harcourt, Brace World, 1964).

Bloom, Harold, ed., *Romanticism and Consciousness* (Baltimore, Md: The Johns Hopkins University Press, 1970).

Budgen, Frank, *James Joyce and the Making of 'Ulysses'* (1934; rpt. Bloomington: Indiana University Press, 1960).

Burgess, Anthony, *Joysprick: an Introduction to the Language of James Joyce* (London: Andre Deutsch, 1973).

Chace, William M., *Joyce: a Collection of Critical Essays* (Englewood Cliffs, NJ: Prentice-Hall, 1974).

Cope, Jackson I., *Joyce's Cities: Archaeologies of the Soul* (Baltimore, Md: The Johns Hopkins University Press, 1981).

Culler, Jonathan, *On Deconstruction: Theory and Criticism after Structuralism* (Ithaca, NY: Cornell University Press, 1982).

Eliot, T. S., "Ulysses, Order, and Myth", *The Dial*, 35 (1923) 480–3; repr. as "Myth and Literary Classicism" in *The Modern Tradition*, eds Richard Ellmann and Charles Fiedelson, Jr (New York: Oxford University Press, pp. 679–81).

Ellmann, Richard, *James Joyce* (New York: Oxford University Press, 1959).

———, *Ulysses on the Liffey* (New York: Oxford University Press, 1972).

———, *The Consciousness of Joyce* (New York: Oxford University Press, 1977).

———, "The Big Word in 'Ulysses'", *The New York Review of Books*, 31:16 (Oct 25, 1984) 31–2.

Epstein, Edmund L., *The Ordeal of Stephen Dedalus* (Carbondale: Southern Illinois University Press, 1971).

Fogel, Daniel Mark, "Symbol and Context in *Ulysses*: Joyce's 'Bowl of Bitter Waters' and Passover", *ELH*, 46 (1979) 710–21.

Frank, Joseph, "Spatial Form in Modern Literature", *Sewanee Review*, 53 (1945); rev. in *The Widening Gyre: Crisis and Mastery in Modern Literature*, pp. 3–62 (Bloomington: Indiana University Press, 1963).

———, "The Master Linguist", *The New York Review of Books*, 31:6 (12 Apr. 1984).

French, Marilyn, *The Book as World: James Joyce's Ulysses* (Cambridge, Mass.: Harvard University Press, 1976).

Gifford, Don and Robert J. Seidman , *Notes for Joyce: an Annotation of James Joyce's 'Ulysses'* (New York: Sutton, 1974).

Gilbert, Stuart, *James Joyce's Ulysses: a Study* (1930; rev. New York: Random House, 1952).

Givens, Seon, *James Joyce: Two Decades of Criticism* (New York: Vanguard Press, 1948).

Glueck, Grace, "A Lively Review of the Futurist Experience", *The New York Times, Arts and Leisure* (1 May 1983).

———, "John Miro Exhibit, Sculpture and Ceramics", *The New York Times* (4 May 1984) p. C24.

Goldberg, S. L., *The Classical Temper: a Study of James Joyce's Ulysses* (New York: Barnes & Noble, 1961).

Goldman, Arnold, *The Joyce Paradox: Form and Freedom in his Fiction* (London: Routledge & Kegan Paul, 1966).

Gottfried, Roy K., *The Art of Joyce's Syntax in Ulysses* (Athens: University of Georgia Press, 1980).

Gould, Stephen Jay, Review essay of Evelyn Fox Feller, "A Feeling for Organism: the Life and Work of Barbara McClintock", *New York Review of Books*, 31:5 (20 Mar. 1984) pp. 3–6.

Groden, Michael, *'Ulysses' in Progress* (Princeton University Press, 1977).

Gross, John, *James Joyce* (New York: The Viking Press, 1970).

Harari, Josue, ed. *Textual Strategies* (Ithaca, NY: Cornell University Press, 1979).

Hart, Clive and David Hayman, eds, *James Joyce's 'Ulysses': Critical Essays* (Berkeley: University of California Press, 1974).

Hart, Clive, *Structure and Motif in Finnegans Wake* (Evanston, Ill.: Northwestern University Press, 1962).

——, "James Joyce's Sentimentality", *Philosophical Quarterly*, 46 (Oct. 1967) 516–26.

Hartman, Geoffrey H., "The Culture of Criticism," PMLA, 99:3 (May, 1984) 371–379.

Hayman, David, *'Ulysses': the Mechanics of Meaning* (Englewood Cliffs, NJ: Prentice-Hall, 1970).

Herring, Phillip F., ed., *Joyce's Notes and Early Drafts for Ulysses* (Charlottesville: University of Virginia Press, 1977).

Hodgart, Matthew J. C. and Mabel P. Worthington, *Song in the Works of James Joyce* (New York: Columbia University Press, 1959).

Hofstadter, Douglas, *Godel, Escher, Bach: an Eternal Golden Braid* (New York: Basic Books, 1979).

Homer, *The Odyssey*, trans. and ed. Albert Cook (New York: Norton, 1967).

Hyde, Montgomery H., *The Trials of Oscar Wilde* (New York: Dover Publications, Inc., 1962).

Iser, Wolfgang, *The Implied Reader: Patterns of Communication in Prose Fiction from Bunyan to Beckett* (Baltimore: The Johns Hopkins University Press, 1974).

Joyce, James, *The Critical Writings*, ed. Ellsworth Mason and Richard Ellmann (New York: Viking, 1959).

——, *Dubliners: Text, Criticism, and Notes*, eds Robert Scholes and A. Walton Litz (New York: The Viking Press, 1969).

——, *The James Joyce Archives: Ulysses* vols., ed. Michael Groden (New York: Garland Publishing, Inc., 1978).

——, *Letters of James Joyce*, vol. I, ed. Stuart Gilbert (New York: The Viking Press, 1957). Vols. 2 and 3. Edited by Richard Ellmann (New York: The Viking Press, 1966).

——, *A Portrait of the Artist as a Young Man* (1916), text corrected by Chester G. Anderson and ed. Richard Ellmann (New York: The Viking Press, 1964).

——, *Selected Letters of James Joyce*, ed. Richard Ellmann (New York: The Viking Press, 1975).

——, *Stephen Hero* (1944); rev. edn. Edited by Theodore Spencer (New York: New Directions, 1963).

——, *Ulysses* (1922; rev. edn. New York: Modern Library – Random House, 1961).

——, *Ulysses: a Critical and Synoptic Edition*, ed. Hans Gabler with Wolfhard Steppe and Claus Melchior (New York and London: Garland, 1984).

Joyce, Stanislaus, *The Dublin Diary of Stanislaus Joyce*, ed. George Harris Healey (London: Faber & Faber, 1958).

——, *My Brother's Keeper: James Joyce's 'Early Years'*, ed. Richard Ellmann (London and New York, 1958).

Kain, Richard, *Fabulous Voyager: a Study of James Joyce's Ulysses* (New York: Viking, 1947; rpt. 1959).

———, "The Significance of Stephen's Meeting Bloom: a Survey of Interpretations", *James Joyce Quarterly*, 10:1 (Fall 1972; rpt. in *Fifty Years: Ulysses*. ed. Thomas Staley. Bloomington: Indiana University Press, 1974).

Kenner, Hugh, *Joyce's Voices* (University of California Press, 1978).

———, *Ulysses* (London: Allen & Unwin, 1980).

———, "Molly's Masterstroke", *James Joyce Quarterly*, 10:1 (Fall 1972; rpt. in *Fifty Years: Ulysses*, ed. Thomas Staley. Bloomington: Indiana University Press, 1974).

———, *Dublin's Joyce* (1956; rpt. Boston: Beacon Press, 1962).

———, *The Stoic Comedians: Flaubert, Joyce, and Beckett* (University of California Press, 1962).

Kermode, Frank, *The Genesis of Secrecy* (Cambridge, Mass.: Harvard University Press, 1980).

Lawrence, Karen, *The Odyssey of Style in "Ulysses"* (Princeton University Press, 1981).

Levin, Harry, *James Joyce: a Critical Introduction* (rev. edn. New York: New Directions, 1960).

Litz, A. Walton, *The Art of James Joyce: Method and Design in Ulysses and Finnegans Wake* (New York: Oxford University Press, 1961).

———, "The Genre of *Ulysses*", in *The Theory of the Novel: New Essays*, ed. John Halperin (New York: Oxford University Press, 1974).

———, "Pound and Eliot on Joyce: the Critical Tradition", *James Joyce Quarterly*, 10:1 (Autumn 1972); rpt. in *Fifty Years: Ulysses* (Bloomington: Indiana University Press, 1974).

Lord, George DeF., "The Heroes of *Ulysses* and Their Homeric Prototypes", *Yale Review*, 62:1 (Oct. 1972) 43–58.

Maddox, James H. Jr., *James Joyce's Ulysses and the Assault Upon Character* (New Brunswick, NJ: Rutgers University Press, 1978).

Magalaner, Marvin, and Kain, Richard M., *Joyce: the Man, the Work, the Reputation* (New York University Press, 1956).

Noon, Father William, S. J., *Joyce and Aquinas* (New Haven, Conn.: Yale University Press, 1957).

O'Brien, Darcy, *The Conscience of James Joyce* (Princeton University Press, 1968).

Peake, C. H., *James Joyce: the Citizen and the Artist* (Stanford University Press, 1977).

Pentateuch and Haftorahs, ed. J. H. Hertz (London: Soncino Press, 1980).

Rader, Ralph W., "Exodus and Return: Joyce's *Ulysses* and the Fiction of the Actual", *University of Toronto Quarterly*, 48 (Winter 1978/79) 149–71.

Raleigh, John Henry, *The Chronicle of Leopold and Molly Bloom: Ulysses as Narrative* (University of California Press, 1971).

Reynolds, Mary, *Dante and Joyce* (Princeton University Press, 1980).

Richardson, John, "The Catch in the Late Picasso", *The New York Review of Books*, 36:13 (19 July 1984) 21–8.

Rye, Jane, *Futurism* (New York: Dutton, 1972).

Schiffer, Paul S., " 'Homing, Upstream': Fictional Closure and the End of *Ulysses*", *James Joyce Quarterly*, 16:3 (Spring 1979) 283–98.

Schwarz, Daniel R., " 'I Was the World in Which I Walked': the Transformation of the British Novel", *The University of Toronto Quarterly*, 51:3 (Spring 1982) 279–97.

———, *The Humanistic Heritage: Critical Theories of the English Novel from James to Hillis Miller* (London: Macmillan; Philadelphia: University of Pennsylvania Press, 1986).

Schwarz-Bart, André, *The Last of the Just*, trans. Stephen Becker (New York: Atheneum, 1961).

Staley, Thomas F., ed. *Fifty Years: Ulysses*. (Bloomington: Indiana University Press, 1974), rpt. of *James Joyce Quarterly* 10:1 (Fall 1972).

Stanford, W. B., *The Ulysses Theme* (Oxford: Blackwell, 1954).

Steinberg, Leo, *The Sexuality of Christ in Renaissance Art and Modern Oblivion* (New York: Pantheon, 1984).

Sultan, Stanley, *The Argument of Ulysses* (Ohio State University Press, 1964).

Thickstun, William, *Visionary Closure in the Modern Novel*, unpublished Cornell University Ph.D. dissertation, 1984.

Thornton, Weldon, *Allusions in Ulysses: a Line-by-Line Reference to Joyce's Complex Symbolism* (Chapel Hill: University of North Carolina Press, 1968; rpt. New York: Simon & Schuster, 1973).

Tindall, William York, *A Reader's Guide to James Joyce* (New York: Farrar, Straus & Giroux, 1959).

———, *James Joyce: His Way of Interpreting the Modern World* (New York: Scribner, 1950).

Todorov, Tzvetan, *The Poetics of Prose*, trans. Richard Howard (Ithaca, NY: Cornell University Press, 1977).

Tolemeo, Diane, "The Final Octagon of *Ulysses*", *James Joyce Quarterly*, 10:4 (Summer 1973) 439–54.

Trilling, Lionel, *The Opposing Self: Nine Essays in Criticism* (New York: The Viking Press, 1955).

Warner, William B., "The Play of Fictions and Succession of Styles in *Ulysses*", *James Joyce Quarterly*, 15:1 (Autumn 1977) 18–35.

Wilson, Edmund, "James Joyce" in *Axel's Castle* (New York, 1931; rpt. in *Joyce: a Collection of Critical Essays*, ed. William M. Chace. (Englewood Cliffs. NJ: Prentice-Hall, 1974).

Index

Abrams, M. H., 144–5, 152n, 265, 275n–76n.
Aquinas, Thomas, 25, 49, 95, 102
Adams, Villiers de L'Isle, 140
AE (George Russell), 64, 140, 210, 265
  "The Children of Lir", 210
Andrewes, Lancelot, 93
Antonioni, Michelangelo, 159
Antisthenes, 212–13
Aristotle, 47, 98, 112, 139, 142, 160, 186, 233, 238, 260
Arius, 94, 102n
Arnold, Mathew, 56n
  Culture and Anarchy, 56n
  "Stanzas From the Grand Chartreuse", 157
Auerbach, Erich, 46, 57n, 133–5, 136n–137n

Bach, Johann Sebastian, 165
Barnacle, Nora (Mrs James Joyce), 11, 140–1, 195, 262, 266, 268–9
Beardsley, Aubrey Vincent, 84
Bible, The, 20, 23, 131, 133–5, 143, 163
  Abraham, 164
  Ahab, 184
  Christ Story, 17–18, 31–2, 41–2, 52, 55, 85, 87–91, 93–4, 104, 109, 128, 143–4, 148, 158–9, 162, 173–4, 179–80, 187–8, 204, 212, 216, 226–7, 233, 239, 245, 253, 256, 265–6, 270, 275
  Deuteronomy, 42–3, 45
  Elijah, 17–19, 23–4, 31, 51, 56, 63, 66, 81, 87–8, 90, 127–9, 133–5, 147, 153, 163, 173,
  181–3, 193, 203, 222, 239, 243, 245, 263
  Elisha, 185–6, 188, 243
  Exodus, 18
  Haggadah, 42–3, 109, 119–21, 128, 181–7n, 253
  Isaac, 164
  Isaiah, 203
  Jacob and Esau, 163–4, 214
  Judas Maccabee, 42
  II Kings, 185
  Lot, 106
  Malachi, 87, 121, 128, 140, 163, 182, 187
  Mathew, 93, 187
  Moses, 40–3, 45, 52–3, 63, 81, 118–19, 122–4, 135, 147, 160–1, 173, 182, 185–7, 204, 245, 275
  Nathan, 164
  New Testament, 2, 9, 53, 63, 87–8, 166, 187
  Old Testament, 2, 53, 63, 87, 89, 163, 166, 187, 204
  Passover Story, 17, 23, 40, 42–3, 118–24 *passim*, 128, 136n, 181–3, 253, 263
  Revelation, 84, 265
  Romans, 239
  Talmud, 9
  Torah, 9
Blake, William, 2, 63, 98, 145, 157, 219, 227, 229, 240
  The Marriage of Heaven and Hell, 157
  "The Lamb", 227
Bloom, Harold, 33, 152n, 198
Boehme, Jacob, 265
Book of Kells, The, 126

Booth, Wayne, 14, 19, 36n
Brodsky, Joseph, 38
"Odysseus to Telemachus", 38
Browne, Thomas, 201
Bruno, Giordano, 58, 265
Budgen, Frank, 9, 69n, 124, 130,
    136n, 196
Bunyan, John, 201–3
Byron, Lord George Gordon, 38,
    145

Cabbala (Kabbalah), 161, 265
Cambridge Ethnologists, 26
Carlyle, Thomas, 204
Celtic or Irish Rennaissance, 1, 37,
    115, 118, 174, 177, 224
Cohen, Ted, 67, 70n
Columbanus, 84, 94
Conrad, Joseph, 20, 75, 82, 274–5
    Lord Jim, 75, 82
    "The Secret Sharer", 75
    Heart of Darkness, 274
Constructivists, 156
Cope, Jackson I., 136, 152n
Cubism, 125–6, 176, 208
Cuchulain, 37, 145, 177–8
Culler, Jonathan, 24, 34, 36n, 68–9,
    70n, 276n

Daedalus, 66, 74, 86, 269
Dante, Alighieri, 2, 31, 33, 38–9,
    44–5 *passim*, 56n–57n, 63, 65,
    70n, 90, 98, 106, 188
    The Divine Comedy, 44–50 *passim*,
        56n–57n, 65
    Inferno, 44–50 *passim*, 56n–57n
Darwin, Charles Robert, 16
Deconstruction, 4, 14, 34, 68
de Man, Paul, 14–15, 36n, 259
De Quincy, Thomas, 200
Derrida, Jacques, 14, 23, 35n–36n,
    276n
Dickens, Charles, 39, 61
    Alan Woodcourt (*Bleak House*), 39
Douglas, Lord Alfred, 77
Duchamp, Marcel, 125

Edward the Seventh, 219, 223

Egoist, The, 124
Eliot, George, 72, 101n
Eliot, T. S., 16, 20–2, 29, 36n, 42,
    93, 135, 204, 229
    Dial Review of "Ulysses, *The*", 20,
        36n, 135
    Gerontion, 22, 93
    "Journey of the Magi, The", 42
    Waste Land, The, 20, 204
Ellmann, Richard, 8–9, 11, 18, 23,
    35n–36n, 57n, 58, 69n, 84,
    102n, 124, 136n, 145, 150n,
    173, 205n–6n, 220, 230n, 257n,
    262, 267–8, 275n–76n
    Consciousness of Joyce, The, 102n,
        136n
    ed. (with Ellsworth Mason), *The
        Critical Writing of James Joyce*,
        57n, 101n, 136n, 152n, 275n
    James Joyce, 8–9, 11, 18, 35n–36n,
        136n, 152n, 230n, 276n
    Ulysses on the Liffey, 36n, 69n, 111,
        134, 136n, 205n–206n, 230n,
        257n, 262, 267–8, 276n
Emmet, Robert, 50
Expressionism, 149

Fauvism, 176
Faulkner, William, 18
Faust, 45, 85, 146
Fenians, 54, 67
Fergus, 27, 78, 81, 224–5, 227,
    239–40
Fitzgerald, Lord Edward, 50
Flotow, Friedrich Von, 32, 167–72
    passim
    Martha, 32, 167–72 *passim*
Fogel, Daniel Mark, 102n
Forster, E. M., 16, 20
Frank, Joseph, 126, 136n
Frazer, Sir James George, 16
    The Golden Bough, 16
Freemasonry, 30, 109, 123, 129, 211,
    222–3, 229
French, Marilyn, 196, 206n, 208,
    227, 230n, 267, 275n–276n
Freud, Sigmund, 16
Futurism, 124–7, 156, 208

Gabler, Hans Walter (ed. *Ulysses: a Critical and Synoptic Edition*), 6, 55, 62, 81, 96, 99, 104, 126–7, 155, 161, 163, 211, 217, 237, 243, 267
Gifford, Don and Seidman, Robert J., 52, 57n, 87, 91, 101n–102n, 136n, 152n, 177, 205n–206n, 223, 228, 230n, 239, 257n, 275n–276n
Gilbert, Stuart, 6n, 9, 21, 36n, 117, 136n
Giraudoux, Jean, 45
Glueck, Grace, 125, 127, 136n, 152n
Goldman, Arnold, 118, 136n, 179, 206n
Gonne, Maude, 221
Gould, Stephen J., 63, 70n
Griffith, Arthur, 52–4, 261
Groden, Michael, 78, 205n

Hallam, Arthur, 39
Hardy, Thomas, 20, 39, 42, 75
   Clym Yewbright (*The Return of the Native*), 39
   Jude the Obscure, 42, 75
   "Near Lanivet", 42
   "The Oxen", 42
Hart, Clive, 158, 205n
Hartman, Geoffry H., 3, 6n
Hathaway, Ann, 32, 143, 208, 267
Hayman, David, 121, 136n, 205n
Hermetic Tradition, 265–7
Hertz, T. H., (ed. *Pentateuch and Haftorehs*), 102n, 206n
Heusel, Barbara, 257n
Hofstadter, Douglas, 3, 6n
Homer, 2, 16, 20, 22–4, 33, 37–9, 40, 44–5, 47–9, 56, 63, 85, 111, 116, 134–5, 172–3, 188, 205n, 213, 248, 262, 264
   Iliad, The, 2, 38–9, 45, 83
   Odyssey, The, 2, 17, 21, 37, 40, 60–1, 135, 153, 173, 205n, 217, 265, 275n (Odysseus, 14–15, 17–19, 23–4, 38, 40, 44–5, 56, 58, 65, 67–8, 83, 92, 96, 106, 110–11, 116, 133, 147, 153, 174, 188, 196,

232–3, 243, 262, 274; Penelope, 45, 106, 145, 188, 213, 217, 258, 260, 264; Telemachus, 18–19, 21–2, 38, 45, 71–2, 83, 147, 243)
Humanistic Formalism, 5
Hunter, Alfred H. (model for Bloom), 209
Hyde, Douglas, 89, 174
Hyde, H. Montgomery, 101n

Icarus, 66, 74, 86
Iser, Wolfgang, 58, 69n, 198–9, 203, 206n

Jakobson, Roman, 126
Joyce, George, 224
Joyce, James, 1–276n *passim*
   Dubliners, 26, 83, 107, 112, 114, 117, 268 ("The Dead", 26, 83, 112, 268)
   Finnegans Wake, 19, 23, 134, 179
   "Ireland, Island of Saints and Sages", 50, 116, 118, 264
   Letters, 12, 35n, 189, 196, 206n, 240, 257n, 258–9, 275n
   Portrait of the Artist as a Young Man, A, 9–11, 33, 35n–36n, 68, 71–9 *passim*, 85, 89–90, 92, 95, 97, 99, 101, 107, 124, 139–40, 150, 209, 215, 228, 247, 268–9 (Theory of genres in, 9–13, 71)
   See Ulysses
   "Shade of Parnell, The", 50, 52, 57, 147
   Stephen Hero, 24–5, 36n, 140
Joyce, Stanislaus, 17, 36n, 52, 57n, 222n
Jung, Carl Gustav, 16

Kenner, Hugh, 6n, 117, 120–1, 136n, 196, 205n–206n, 233, 257n
Kermode, Frank, 102n
Kipling, Rudyard, 261
   "The Absent Minded Beggar", 261

Lamb, Charles, 200

Lamed Vov (Just Men), 40–3, 179, 214, 245
Lawrence, D. H., 16, 20–1, 42, 75, 144–5, 240, 259
The Rainbow, 20
The Man Who Died, 42
Sons and Lovers, 75
Lawrence, Karen, 3, 6n, 59–61, 69n–70n, 117, 135n–36n, 159, 164–5, 167, 178, 189, 195, 200, 205n–206n, 207, 225, 230n, 235, 241, 257n, 259
Layman's Missal, 85, 102n
Leonardo de Vinci, 131
Linati, Carlos, 173
Lippo Lippi, Fra, 209
Litz, Walton A., 174, 205n
Lord, George de F., 102n

Macaulay, Thomas Babbington, 205
Maddox, James H., 109, 112, 136n, 260, 275n
Maeterlinck, Count Maurice, 191
Malory, Sir Thomas, 201
Mann, Thomas, 141
Death in Venice, 141
Marinetti, Filippo Tommaso, 125
Futurist Manifesto, 125
Mazzato, Guiseppe, 65
Melchior, Claus, 6
Mephistopheles, 84
Metempsychosis, 1, 16, 29, 33, 97, 198, 265
Michaelangelo, 131
Milton, 2, 63, 91–2, 105–6, 162
Lycidas, 90–1, 105–6 (Edward King, 91)
Samson Agonises, 157
Miro, Joan, 149, 152n
Mosenthal, Salomon Hermann, 163
Deborah, 163
Mozart, Wolfgang
Don Giovanni, 156
Muybridge, Eadweard, 128

Nelson, Lord Horatio, 121–3, 160, 264
New Criticism, 5, 137n
Nietzsche, Friedrich, 14, 16

Noon, Father William, 94, 102n

O'Brien, Darcy, 77, 102n
Odyssean Reader (of *Ulysses*), 27–8, 32, 34, 40, 42–3, 45, 49, 61–9, 79–80, 82, 90, 92–8, 122–3, 133, 154–5, 158, 160–1, 164, 183, 199, 204, 224, 228, 237, 258–9, 268
O'Grady, Standish, 177
Old Woman of Ireland, The, 79–80, 92, 104–5, 122–3, 140, 220, 263–4
O'Leary, John, 115
Orpheus, 157, 269

Parallax, 17, 29, 32, 58, 97, 105, 125, 161, 237
Parnell, Charles Stewart, 1, 43, 50–6, 87, 92–3, 101, 115, 123, 147, 159, 173, 179, 184, 219, 248, 275
Affair with Katherine O'Shea, 50
As Christ, 52–3
As Moses, 52
Parnell, John Howard, 51, 53, 159
Pater, Walter, 140, 165
Peake, C. H., 6n, 39, 56n, 167, 199, 205n–206n
Phoenix Park Murders, 55, 183, 240
Phydias, 131
Picasso, Pablo, 152n
Plato (Platonic and Platonism), 77, 94, 98, 110–12, 139–42, 155, 169, 182, 186, 195, 209, 218, 220, 223, 233–4, 238, 268
Neo-Platonism, 27, 78, 210
Pound, Ezra, 124
Proust, Marcel, 271
Pynchon, Thomas, 18

Rader, Ralph, 8, 25n, 275n
Raleigh, John Henry, 51, 57n, 134, 137n
Reynolds, Mary, 47–8, 56n–57n, 70n
Rich, Penelope, 213, 217
Richardson, John, 152n
Rye, Jane, 125, 136n

Sabellius, 94
Sallust, 127
Schwarz, Daniel, R., 5, 36n, 101n,
    137n, 152n, 257n
Schwarz-Bart, Andre, 41, 56n
    The Last of the Just, 41, 56n
Shakespeare, William, 2, 12, 15,
    17–20, 22–4, 32–3, 35, 37–8, 41,
    45, 49, 56, 63, 65, 72, 75, 84–5,
    90–1, 93, 98–9, 103, 105, 130,
    135, 138–52n *passim*, 158, 163,
    172, 195, 202, 208, 214–19,
    225–7, 230, 232, 237, 239,
    243–6, 249, 251, 255–6, 259,
    265–7, 270, 273–5
    Cymbeline, 142
    Hamlet, 18, 37–8, 45, 72, 75, 103,
        130, 139, 142, 146–7, 150,
        202, 214–15, 217–19, 259
    Henry IV, Pt. I, 84, 234
    Othello, 22, 218
    Tempest, The, 91
Shelley, Percy Bysshe, 12, 145, 173,
    240
Sinn Fein, 30, 52, 123, 223, 261
    Sinn Fein (newspaper), 52, 59
Socrates (Socratic), 141, 175, 191
Souriau, Paul, 125
Stanford, W. B., 45–6, 57n
Steepe, Wolfhard, 6
Steinberg, Leo, 56n, 261
    *The Sexuality of Christ in Renaissance
        Art and Modern Oblivion*, 56n
Stevens, Wallace, 30, 271
    "The Idea of Order at Key
        West", 30
Suprematism, 156
Swift, Jonathan, 2, 22, 44, 63, 173,
    202, 244
    Gulliver's Travels, 44, 173, 202, 244
Swinburne, Algernon Charles, 81,
    140
    "Hymn to Prosperpine", 140

Tennyson, Alfred Lord, 2, 38–9, 219
    Ulysses, 38
Thackeray, William Makepeace, 61
    Dobbin (*Vanity Fair*), 39
Thornton, Weldon, 205

Todorov, Tzvetan, 232, 257n
Tone, Theobald Wolfe, 50, 177

Ulysses

Episodes

I. "Telemachus", 47, 64, 71,
    73–4, 76, 78–87
    passim, 89–93, 103,
    105–6, 109, 140, 195,
    211–12, 219–20, 224,
    229, 233, 240, 263–4,
    277
    See Mulligan (Characters)
II. "Nestor", 21–2, 51,
    64–5, 75, 77, 79, 83–4,
    88, 90–2, 97, 104–5,
    121, 157–9, 187, 204,
    215, 219, 226, 235, 248,
    256, 270, 272, 277
    See Daisy (Characters)
    Stephen's Riddle in
    64–5, 91–2, 97
III. "Proteus", 40, 47, 67–8,
    76, 89–91, 93, 97–101,
    103–5, 108, 111, 120,
    147, 174, 193, 211,
    229–30, 235, 246, 256,
    263, 265, 267, 277
IV. "Calypso", 40, 62, 81, 88,
    92, 103–8, 113, 128,
    132–3, 157, 165,
    168–9, 209, 220,
    233–4, 246, 263, 270,
    274, 277
V. "Lotus-Eaters", 60, 104,
    107–10, 116, 122–3,
    128, 155–6, 163–4,
    210, 214, 218, 228, 234,
    278
    See Martha Clifford
    (Characters)
VI. "Hades", 25, 32, 51, 56,
    62, 104, 106–8,
    111–16, 124, 132–3,
    167, 169, 200, 211–12,

218–20, 228, 236, 240,
278
Death as antagonist of,
111–16
VII. "Aeolus", 23, 27, 29, 32,
43, 47–9, 52, 54, 60–1,
64–5, 69n, 89–90, 105,
107, 115–27 *passim*,
131, 136n–7n, 146–7,
162–3, 170–1, 175–6,
178, 209, 212–13, 217,
263–4, 278
See Futurism
Parable of the Plums, 43,
48, 52, 64–5, 79,
118, 121, 263
VIII. "Lestrygonians", 23, 25,
31, 53, 64, 110–11,
120, 127–35,
136n–37n, 146, 156,
161, 164, 187, 210, 214,
217, 239, 273, 278
See Reverend Dowie
(Characters)
IX. 'Scylla and Charybdis",
12, 15, 18, 20, 23,
31–4, 62, 65, 74, 77,
87, 89, 92–3, 95–6,
98–9, 105, 109, 115,
126, 130, 138–152n
passim 154, 157–8, 163,
169–70, 172, 175, 182,
186, 191, 195, 208,
214–18, 225–6,
237–8, 245, 247–8,
251, 259, 261–4, 267,
270, 279
Stephen's theory of art,
138–152n
X. "Wandering Rocks", 31,
60–1, 66, 88, 105,
123–4, 144, 153, 164,
168–9, 187, 198–9,
208, 210, 234, 260, 279
Father Commee
representing Romantic
Catholic church and
William Humble
representing state,

153–64 *passim*
XI. "Sirens", 2, 48, 60, 66,
69n, 126, 129, 150,
164–73, 176, 178,
186–7, 193–5, 259,
279
"Croppy Boy, The",
172–3
XII. "Cyclops", 11, 27–8, 30,
40–1, 43–4, 52, 54–9,
60, 64, 66, 74, 115–16,
124, 131, 143, 170–89,
193–5, 221, 223–4,
228, 235, 239, 241, 244,
279
Bloom as Elijah, 181–8
See The Citizen and
Garryowen
(Characters)
XIII. "Nausicaa", 11, 28, 35,
43, 64, 90, 123, 158,
170, 173, 176, 178,
180–1, 188–95, 209,
265, 268, 279
Joyce's comments on,
196, 206n
See Gerty MacDowell
(Characters)
XIV. "Oxen of the Sun", 2, 15,
27–8, 42, 53, 66, 170,
176, 178, 195–206n,
221–2, 227, 229, 255,
259, 266–7, 279
Joyce's comments on,
146, 206n
XV. "Circe", 10, 27–8, 30,
32, 34–5, 40, 42–4, 51,
53, 77, 89–91, 99, 124,
126, 142, 150–1, 153,
161, 169, 174–5, 192,
194, 200, 207–32n,
238, 246, 255–6, 261,
264–5, 272, 279
Joyce's metaphorical
bestiary, 211–15
XVI. "Eumaeus", 28, 31, 35,
54–6, 67, 106, 127,
150, 161, 180, 200, 204,
221, 231–50, 257n,

263, 280
See D. B. Murphy
(Characters)
XVII. "Ithaca", 28–9, 35, 42,
48, 66, 101, 126, 144,
150–1, 158, 161, 172,
181, 194, 203, 205, 225,
231–57n, 258, 262–3,
270, 280
Joyce's comments on,
240, 247n
XVIII. "Penelope", 10, 49, 52,
76, 126, 133, 189, 205,
234, 254, 258–76n
Joyce's comments on, 12,
35n, 289–95n

Characters

Blazes, Boylan, 48, 68, 107, 123,
132–3, 157, 160, 164–6, 168,
171–2, 205, 218, 260–1, 267,
269, 271–3
Bloom, Leopold, 1–276n *passim*
"Agendeth Netaim", 95, 104,
120, 131–2, 148, 168, 193,
200, 263, 265
As Aristotelean, 112
As Elijah, 153, 214–19
As Henry Flower, 109, 271
As Jew, 1, 4, 30, 82, 96, 109,
127, 154, 174, 179–81, 214,
218, 223, 228, 246–8, 258,
265
As Mason, 109, 179, 222–3, 229
As Moses, 119
As Platonist, 209
Relationship with Stephen,
221–57n
As Shakespeare, 151, 215–19
Bloom, Milly, 104, 106–8, 111,
191
Bloom, Molly, 1, 2, 11, 13, 18, 28,
35, 38, 48–50, 52, 62, 76,
79–80, 93, 100–1, 104–10,
113–14, 122–3, 126, 129–35,
141–2, 153, 161–2, 164–73,
179, 182, 188–9, 192–4, 196,
204, 208–9, 213, 218, 241,

245, 247, 249–51, 254–5,
258–76n
Bloom, Rudy, 27, 49, 108, 113,
169, 172, 183–4, 197, 211,
224–9
Citizen, The, 11, 28, 44, 54, 74,
111, 143, 173–5, 178–83, 221
Clifford, Martha, 32, 35, 104, 109,
156, 158, 167–9, 138, 192,
209, 264
Cohen, Bella, 35, 188, 265, 268
Cunningham, Martin, 32, 218–19
Deasy, 21–2, 51, 75, 79, 83, 88,
90, 129, 173, 211, 248, 256,
272
Dedalus, Simon, 33, 79, 95, 112,
118, 146, 162, 167, 169, 171,
172–3, 201, 236, 272
Dedalus, Stephen, 1–276 *passim*
"Agenbite of Inwit", 95, 104,
148, 162, 176
As Aristotelean, 142
As Platonist, 110–12, 139–41,
155, 182
Relationship with Bloom,
221–57n
As Shakespeare (shared vision
with Bloom), 215–19
Dignam, Paddy (and family), 38,
62, 68, 103, 111, 162–3, 184,
187, 190, 194, 213–15, 223,
240, 247, 249
Dowie, Reverend, 31, 41, 44, 51,
123, 127, 210
Fitzharris, Skin the Goat, 55, 240
Garryowen, 174–5, 183, 213
MacDowell, Gerty, 28, 35, 90,
178, 188–94, 209, 264, 268
Menton, John Henry, 56, 113
Mulligan, Malachi, 31, 44, 46,
71–2, 73–93 *passim*, 103, 106,
109, 130, 139–41, 153–4,
162–3, 195, 210–12, 218–9,
234, 236, 238, 252, 264, 268,
272
Mulvey, 192, 272–3
Murphy, D. B., 31, 127, 161, 235,
256
Purefoys, 38, 44, 68, 187, 191,

196–7, 200, 203, 210, 223, 249, 261

Vico, 3, 23, 37, 198, 219
 Scienza Nuova, 23
Virgil, 45, 47, 65
Vorticism, 124

Wagner, Richard, 165, 220, 272
Wilde, Oscar, 2, 10, 27, 31, 63, 76–7, 84, 109, 139–41, 195, 219, 229–30, 238, 252
 Critic as Artist, The, 141
 Decay of Lying, The, 77, 141
  Preface to, 77
 Importance of Being Earnest, The, 109
 Picture of Dorian Gray, The, 76, 230
 Portrait of Mr. W. H., The, 139–40

Woolf, Virginia, 18, 20
Wordsworth, William, 221
Yeats, William Butler, 2, 16, 20, 26, 37, 42, 54, 63, 76–9, 115, 127, 153–4, 177, 224–5, 227, 229, 238, 265

Poems and Plays

Countess Cathleen, The, 224, 229
"Magi, The", 42
"Sailing to Byzantium", 27
"September, 1913", 54, 115
"Song of Wandering Aengus, The", 153–4
"Stolen Child, The", 225
"Who Goes with Fergus", 78, 81, 224–5